The Origins of Criminology
A Reader

The Origins of Criminology: A Reader is a collection of nineteenth-century texts from the key originators of the practice of criminology – selected, introduced, and with commentaries by the leading scholar in this area, Nicole Rafter.

This book presents criminology as a unique field of study that took root in a context in which urbanization, immigration, and industrialization changed the class structure of Western nations. As relatively homogenous communities became more sharply divided and aware of a bottom-most group, the "dangerous classes", a new segment of the middle class emerged: professionals involved in the work of social control. Tracing the intellectual origins of criminology to physiognomy, phrenology, and evolutionary theories, this book demonstrates criminology's background in new attitudes toward science and the development of scientific methodologies applicable to social and mental phenomena. Through an expert selection of original texts, it traces the emergence of "criminology" as a new field purporting to produce scientific knowledge about crime and criminals.

Nicole Rafter is Professor and Senior Research Fellow at the College of Criminal Justice, Northeastern University, and an Affiliated Faculty Member of Northeastern's Law, Policy and Society Program. She has been writing about the history of criminology for thirty years, having published numerous articles and several books in this area, including new, annotated translations of the pivotal work of Cesare Lombroso, the first investigator to claim status as a scientific criminologist.

The Origins of Criminology

A Reader

Edited by
Nicole Rafter

Routledge
Taylor & Francis Group
a GlassHouse book

First published 2009
by Routledge
2 Park Square, Milton Park, Abingdon, Oxon OX14 4RN

Simultaneously published in the USA and Canada
by Routledge
270 Madison Ave, New York, NY 10016

A GlassHouse Book

*Routledge is an imprint of the Taylor & Francis Group, an
informa business*

© 2009 Nicole Rafter (ed.)

Typeset in Garamond by
RefineCatch Limited, Bungay, Suffolk
Printed and bound in Great Britain by
CPI Antony Rowe, Chippenham, Wiltshire

British Library Cataloging in Publication Data
A catalog record for this book is available
from the British Library

Library of Congress Cataloging in Publication Data
Rafter, Nicole Hahn, 1939–
    The origins of criminology : a reader / edited by Nicole Rafter.
       p. cm.
    'A GlassHouse book.'
Criminology – History – 19th century.   2. Criminology – History –
19th century – Sources.   I. Title.
    HV6021.R34 2009
    364.09'034 – dc22

                                                    2008043446

ISBN 10: 0–415–45111–6 (hbk)
ISBN 13: 978–0–415–45111–6 (hbk)

ISBN 10: 0–415–45112–4 (pbk)
ISBN 13: 978–0–415–45112–3 (pbk)

ISBN 10: 020–3–86994–X (ebk)
ISBN 13: 978–020–3–86994–9 (ebk)

Contents

Acknowledgements

The idea for this book came from Colin Perrin, who became my editor at Routledge and has been a great help along the way. For reviews of my proposal Colin lined up an excellent set of anonymous readers whose comments widened and deepened the scope of the project. As I worked, I received help from many directions, in particular from Piers Beirne, Neil Davie, Neil Furman of the Argosy Book Store in New York City, Mary Gibson, Frances Heidensohn, John Laub, Al Pisciotta, Marc Renneville, Paul Rock, Richard Wetzell, Judith Yarnall, and Per Ystehede. Northeastern University's Interlibrary Loan Office accessed documents I would not have been able to use otherwise, while Danielle Rousseau, graduate student *par excellence*, again offered expert and efficient help with illustrations. I also appreciate Duke University Press's permission to use illustrations from Mary Gibson's and my translations of Cesare Lombroso's *Criminal Man* and *Criminal Woman*. Robert Hahn edited the introduction and as always provided nurture and diversion. Looking over this list, I see that it includes the usual suspects – those whom I have thanked at the start of more than one book, steadfast friends and colleagues through the years.

Introduction

Criminology began as a series of cottage industries. Small centers of production, makeshift in the sense that criminological work was often peripheral to the researcher's central endeavor, were scattered thinly around Europe and the eastern United States. One could be found in Turin, Italy, another in Perth, Scotland, and still others in London, Lyon, New York, Paris, and Vienna. But what did researchers in these small centers, which sometimes consisted of little more than a desk and a sheaf of notes on criminal cases, aim at accomplishing? How did they conceive of their work? How did they eventually connect with one another to establish professional journals, organize international conferences, and lay the foundations for a new field of knowledge? Did they agree with one another about methodologies and the directions that the new field should take?

Some histories offer accounts of what went on in specific centers of production – an Italian army doctor using his early morning hours to dissect the brain of a Calabrian brigand; a New York City businessman collecting criminals' genealogies in his spare time; Quaker siblings arguing that English absentee landlords should relinquish the brutalizing practices that pushed Irish peasants into crime; Parisian anthropologists readying for battle against the absurdities of Italian criminal anthropology. But few histories attempt synthetic overviews of nineteenth-century criminology that can account for what was going on simultaneously in areas where single scholars, or small groups of them, were starting to contribute to a project they would not have recognized: creation of the field of criminology. Indeed, some of them might have been aghast to learn where their work was leading.

Obstacles to criminology's development

It took close to a century for the work of these scholars to become "criminology." During the nineteenth century, researchers involved in the production of what we now call criminology may have been in contact with only two or three other specialists conducting similar work. (For ease of reference, I will call these researchers "criminologists," even though they would not have understood or accepted the label.) They might have established such contacts through personal correspondence and journal subscriptions (for example, professional journals in the related and more established field of psychiatry often had a "developments abroad" section to keep members up to date). Some maintained a standing order with foreign booksellers for works on a particular subject such as criminal insanity. In addition, later in the century criminologists built networks by attending conferences such as the international congresses of criminal anthropology held between 1886 and 1914.[1] Nonetheless, those who studied crime and criminals were separated by obstacles of which two, over and above geographical distance, were especially significant: language barriers and the fact that criminology had not yet been conceptualized as an independent field of study.

That some criminologists could not read publications in more than one language or converse with foreign colleagues impeded coalescence of the field. French tended to be the lingua franca for nineteenth-century investigators: the French produced much of the period's criminological theory, and French translations of texts written in other languages gave well-educated Italians, Germans, and Britons access to work generated elsewhere. (For example, Cesare Lombroso's *L'uomo delinquente* or *Criminal Man*, arguably the most significant single text in nineteenth-century criminology, was translated into French about a decade after its first, 1876, Italian publication, but not even partially into English until 1911, and not completely into English until 2006.[2]) However, many Americans knew no language other than English, a disadvantage that not only kept them from communicating with Europeans in the developing field, but also doomed them to lack of sophistication.

A prime example can be found in the work of Richard Dugdale, a New York City businessman who pioneered in the study of heredity and crime. While absence of biographical information makes it difficult to tell whether Dugdale was monoglot or simply undereducated (or both),[3] he evidently knew nothing of contemporary French degeneration theory, which in that day constituted the most important criminological concept in Europe. Remarkably, he all but reinvented degeneration theory in his classic study *The "Jukes": A Study in Crime, Pauperism, Disease, and Heredity* (Chapter 20[4]); but with a stronger background Dugdale could have related his findings to the theory French writers had been elaborating for two decades; his diagrams might have been less confusing and his conclusions less subject to misinterpretation.

At the opposite end of the spectrum from Dugdale were criminologists who could read several languages. These included Richard von Krafft-Ebing, the German psychiatrist, and Cesare Lombroso, the Italian psychiatrist whose criminological investigations began with the early-morning dismemberment of a brigand from Calabria. For his pioneering study *Psychopathia Sexualis*, Krafft-Ebing (Chapter 12) gathered examples both from his own patients and works by others; he could hardly have produced so comprehensive a survey of sexual deviations without access to literatures produced in several languages. Lombroso could read English, French, and German and had correspondents in (at least) Argentina, Scandinavia, and Russia; he knew of the latest developments in American theory and practice in a matter of months. As his method, like Krafft-Ebing's, was one of amassing examples to build up proofs, he too benefited immeasurably from being multilingual. But few contemporaries had his linguistic skills or were such omnivorous consumers of research produced elsewhere.

An even greater obstacle lay with the fact that criminology had not yet been conceptualized as a field of study. If the first researchers tended to resemble workers in cottage industries, laboring in separate intellectual structures to produce not piecework contributions but their own theories of crime, that was partly because criminology's territory had not yet been named. Most of it belonged to other intellectual territory – anthropology, evolutionary science, jurisprudence, phrenology, physiology, and (especially) psychiatry. Nor is there evidence that any of the early researchers, with the exception of Lombroso, were anxious to adopt new professional identities. But then, there was as yet no such thing as a criminologist and no such thing as "criminology," a marketplace where they might display their wares, barter in ideas, and try to gain an intellectual monopoly for their favorite theory.

The field formed in two phases. First, in 1876, in *L'uomo delinquente*, Lombroso demonstrated that criminology could become a science.[5] The new field was born, and if at first its relations to anthropology, psychology, and psychiatry remained unclear, those who were studying aspects of crime and criminals at least could think of themselves as laboring on the same scientific project. A core of knowledge began to form, although much of it was hotly contested. Second, in the 1890s the term "criminology" became the name for the new field. Britons became familiar with it when Havelock Ellis published *The Criminal* (Chapter 32), his compendium of criminal anthropology.[6] Americans learned of it when Arthur MacDonald published *Criminology* (Chapter 33), another compendium of criminal anthropology, this one an intellectual hash, but nonetheless the first book to bear that title. While there had been criminology (scientific research on crime and criminals) in earlier decades, now there was "criminology," a way of thinking about that research as a unified field. However, this development should not be viewed as a teleological enterprise carrying us to the promised shore of present-day criminology. As historian David Garland explains, we should not regard eighteenth- and nineteenth-century writings "as proto-criminologies struggling to achieve a form which we have since perfected"; rather, "it seems more appropriate to accept that there are a variety of ways in which crime can be problematized and put into discourse, and that 'criminology' is only one verison among others."[7]

For the same reasons of language and nomenclature, histories of criminology's early development have been slow to materialize. Again the fact that early researchers wrote in a variety of languages has been a major obstacle. To produce a synthetic history of nineteenth-century criminology, with its rich multiplicity of theories and empirical studies, one would need to read English, French, German, and Italian, for starters (Spanish would probably be a good idea too, to take Spain and South America into account).[8] This difficulty is slowly being overcome as the key documents are translated into English, which has replaced French as the lingua franca of scholarly research, and as Google's book program speeds up access to key documents.[9] In addition, an international conference on the history of criminology held in Florence, Italy, in the 1990s, encouraged cross-fertilization among scholars working in English, French, German, and Italian[10] and helped to overcome the field's "collective amnesia" about its roots.[11]

Still, it is not easy to write a history of something that lacks a name. Historians (insofar as they have examined criminology at all) have tended to focus on the period *since* the 1890s, when criminology was so christened.[12] And even then, their studies have often concentrated on a particular country or figure – a perfectly valid and useful procedure, but one that needs supplementation. We also need to know the nineteenth-century history of the field, when it was in the process of formation, and we need cross-national comparisons.[13]

History is vital to the healthy development of a discipline. If criminology is to mature fully as a field of study, it needs to develop a strong sense of its own background, even if that background is full of contradictions, false starts, ludicrous byways, and lamentable thoroughfares. Today, after more than a century of evolution, criminology is close to emerging as a discipline in its own right, with its own set of research questions, methods, traditions, trajectories, journals, conferences, and leaders. However, the process of maturing, as C. Loring Brace has observed with reference to anthropology, involves rediscovering the past:

> It is perfectly true that in a rapidly developing field, research methods and results are often superseded in very short order. However, there is more than a little reason to suspect the maturity of any scholarly realm that is ignorant of the work of the previous generation, or even that of more distant predecessors. Current research cannot be pursued effectively, and future efforts cannot be planned, until our present status is clear. And we cannot really know where we are unless we have some understanding of our past.[14]

Garland has made the same point with specific reference to criminology:

> If we are to understand the central topics which criminology has marked out as its own, if we are to understand the discipline's relation to

institutional practices and concerns, if we are to understand some of the key terms and conceptions which structure the discourse, then we will have to ask genealogical questions about the constitution of this science and examine the historical processes which led to the emergence of an accredited disciplinary specialism.[15]

This book aims at encouraging such genealogical questions and suggesting resources with which they might be answered.

Central concerns in nineteenth-century criminology

Among the major interests or preoccupations of nineteenth-century criminologists, three were overriding and very nearly ubiquitous: those of moral insanity (what we today would call psychopathy); the implications of evolution; and the desire to study crime as a social phenomenon. Although these concerns did not surface in every criminological tract of the period, they constituted major themes or undercurrents that coursed through a wide range of theoretical writings.

Moral insanity

Throughout the century, psychiatrists with an interest in crime tried to explain why some offenders seemed undeterrable and particularly vicious. Time and again, these psychiatrists returned to the puzzle of people who committed crimes repeatedly, sometimes obsessively, no matter how much punishment or treatment they received. Such people, they found, tend to commit crimes that are gruesome and pitiless, thus demonstrating an inability to identify with their victims. Criminology began with efforts scientifically to understand this sort of offender (Chapters 8, 9, and 10).

Theorists used different terms to identify the condition: moral derangement, moral insanity (the most popular label), mania without delirium, degeneration, moral imbecility, incorrigibility, inborn criminality, hereditary unfitness. But although the labels differed, the goal was the same: to explain the actions of morally insane offenders. Theorists concluded that moral insanity was a state, not a set of behaviors. This was a significant innovation, for previously crime had been understood as behavior and punished as such. Cesare Beccaria and other members of the eighteenth-century Classical school of criminology (Chapter 2) had been concerned only with criminal acts, not with criminality. But nineteenth-century theorists who grappled with repeat, remorseless behavior conceived its cause as an innate condition, that of being morally insane (or degenerate, or incorrigible, and so on, depending on terminology). Those in this state (they reasoned) must lack the moral sense, a faculty or ability present in law-abiding people; or at least their moral sense must be in a state of decay, causing them to devolve or go backward down the evolutionary ladder. It seemed clear that the problem lay in offenders' brains; moral insanity was a biological condition, not a social problem.

The theme of moral insanity shaped another preoccupation of nineteenth-century criminology: the habitual offender (Part VII). Repeat offenders had certainly been recognized in earlier periods (see Chapter 1, in which Arthur, an American slave, is executed, apparently for a series of crime sprees), but they were regarded more as annoyances than a special type of offender, and certainly not as a special breed with suspect biology, as habitual offenders became in the work of some nineteenth-century commentators. Ideas about moral insanity flowed into explanations of habitual offenders as incorrigibles, even born criminals. Criminal-justice officials, frustrated by their inability to detect habitual offenders when they changed names or locales, were keenly interested in better methods of identification. These they found, first in Alphonse Bertillon's method of measuring and photographing offenders (Chapter 40), later in fingerprinting (Chapter 41).

Suspicion that some of the worst offenders might actually be morally insane, and thus not criminally responsible, ignited an acrimonious debate over the nature of insanity and use of the insanity defense. On one side were the psychiatrists who argued that moral insanity, even though it did not involve hallucinations and complete loss of contact with reality, was really a mental illness and that its victims should thus be spared the most severe punishments. Opposing them were other psychiatrists and legal theorists who argued that those who were putatively morally insane seemed normal in all respects but one – their criminal tendencies – and thus were not insane at all. Those on the first side tended to argue for scientific determinism, their foes for free will. And the proponents of moral insanity endorsed the idea, increasingly important as the century wore on, of crime as an illness. In their view, the criminal is not corrupt, but sick.

The implications of evolution

Criminology was inevitably shaped by the most disturbing idea of the nineteenth century: that of evolution, the theory that organisms change biologically through the generations. Evolution was not a concept that Darwin pulled out of a hat in 1859, when he published *The Origin of Species*. Decades before that, educated people had become aware that dinosaur bones and geological strata contradicted the Biblical story of God creating every-thing, unchangeably, in a single moment, and they had started to come to terms with evolution's implications. The criminological result was the the-ory of degeneration, according to which some people evolve while others devolve or go backward toward a condition of lesser complexity and savagery.[16]

Degeneration theory, built on the assumption that acquired characteristics such as a tendency toward alcoholism or thievishness could become ingrained and inherited, grouped criminals with paupers, the insane, idiots, and other degenerates. At first, proponents believed degeneration to be a reversible and perhaps even curable condition: by avoiding alcohol, working assiduously, and generally living upright lives, criminals could acquire new and better characteristics and eradicate the old; and although the process of acquiring new traits might take several generations, at least their descendants would not grow up to face the gallows. But as the century wore on and crime and pauperism proved to be intractable problems, theorists became more pessimistic; they replaced their original "soft" determinism with a "harder" hereditarianism, according to which criminality and other social problems were fixed in degenerates' germ plasm.

Pivotal was Richard Dugdale's *"Jukes"* study (Chapter 20). Himself a "soft" hereditarian (at least most of the time), Dugdale proposed environmental changes such as better education to improve the family lines of criminals and paupers. However, his readers took *"The Jukes,"* with its immense genealogical charts showing the flow of degeneration through the generations, as proof positive of the "hard" hereditarian position. Obviously, they concluded, it is foolish to attempt to rescue such an unfit family, and much better to stop its members from reproducing. Dugdale's study inspired the first American eugenics program (Chapter 44).

Like other members of the educated classes, most nineteenth-century criminologists accepted the tenets of so-called scientific racism, according to which whites are the best evolved of all the races. Scientific racism often became part of the explanation of criminal behavior: the worst offenders are like savages, closer to Hottentots and other black-skinned primitives than to normal white people, with their well-evolved moral sense. In this case as in that of degeneration theory, explanations based on ideas about evolution pointed to a biological problem: criminals' brains must be more primitive than those of well-evolved whites.

Crime as a social phenomenon

While some criminologists endorsed a racist eugenics, vilifying the criminal's body (Chapters 46 and 47), others concentrated on studying crime as a social phenomenon. A central task was identifying key variables. Among the first variables to be examined were age (Chapters 49 and 52) and sex (Chapters 49, 52, 54, and 56). Another, perhaps oddly, was weather, a variable whose relationship to crime fascinated nineteenth-century criminologists (Chapter 49). Rapid population growth and industrialization had distended cities with vast numbers of the poor, living in conditions of appalling squalor. The journalist Henry Mayhew was one of the first to investigate the dimensions of the social-class variable. "In the first portion of *London Labour and the London*

Poor," read an advertisement for Mayhew's monumental mid-century investigation,

> the respectable portion of the world were for the first time made acquainted with the habits and pursuits of many thousands of their fellow-creatures, who daily earn an honest livelihood in the midst of destitution, and exhibit a firmness and heroism in pursuing 'their daily round and common task' worthy of the highest commendation. Yet these had long been regarded as the dangerous classes, as men and women who were little higher than Hottentots in the scale of civilization! The publication of Mr. Mayhew's investigations, illustrated by the recitals of the people themselves, for the first time led to a knowledge of the poorer world of London, of which the upper classes knew comparatively nothing.[17]

In his follow-up volume *The Prisons of London* – the work extracted here (Chapters 24, 37, and 56) – Mayhew turned his attention to those who "are in reality the dangerous classes, the idle, the profligate, and the criminal," exposing their social relationships with the great city that bred them.[18] At the same time, urbanization became an important variable. Some investigators visited the city, as Edward Crapsey did the nether side of New York (Chapter 25); others lived in it, as Friedrich Engels did in Manchester (Chapters 23 and 55); but they were all interested in understanding the interrelated effects of social class and urbanization.

The century ended with a rich burst of sociological theorizing. Gabriel Tarde (Chapter 57), a distinguished French jurist and sociologist dissatisfied with criminal anthropology, sought to discover the "laws of crime . . . in a special application of the general laws which appear to us to govern social science."[19] The general law from which he derived his criminology was that of imitation, the human tendency to copy the behavior of others. (To identify which others were most imitated and to explain why were among the tasks Tarde assigned himself.) Although Tarde's specific theory has not stood up, his more general repudiation of biological explanations was tremendously significant, as was his insistence that crime is part of social life. Émile Durkheim, another French sociologist, took this reasoning a step further, boldly concluding that crime is not something we should hope to eradicate, but rather "normal because a society lacking it would be completely impossible." Indeed, crime "is a factor in public health, an integral part of all healthy societies."[20] In the 1890s Edward Alsworth Ross, the well-regarded American sociologist, introduced the concept of social control (Chapter 58); his analysis of the containment of deviance, while not particularly successful in its own right, provided a conceptual tool useful to later sociologists, who conceived of deviance and control as two sides of one coin – and to historians of social control systems. Also at the century's end, the American sociologist W. E. B.

DuBois showed the world how to analyze race sociologically (Chapters 26 and 61).

As criminologists worked to understand the social nature of crime, they developed statistical tools, the first of which was ongoing, national censuses of criminals. They had to decide what to count, how to count it, and how often to count it. They also had to decide what to do with census information. France was the first nation to organize such a census and address these issues, as it did under the direction of Andre-Michel Guerry, a lawyer turned statistician (Chapter 48). Guerry's work was almost immediately seconded by that of Adolphe Quetelet, who argued that since crime statistics fluctuate only slightly from year to year, crime must exist apart from the individual offender and be in some sense embodied in society itself (Chapter 49). The implications of the collection of crime statistics were profound and complex, affecting not only criminological theory, but also politics and jurisprudence, as Tarde observed in his book *La criminalité comparée* (*Comparative Criminology*):

> Everywhere, in France and abroad, notably in Italy, matters of crime and punishment are all the rage. An unarguable need for reforms is felt here, provoked not only by the outburst of crime but by increasingly clear awareness of the nature and causes of this evil thanks to progress in statistics. This entirely new source of information, which habituates the contemporary public to seeing social facts in huge bulk, no longer confused and dubious like earlier generalizations about crime but precise and exact in every detail, leads to the view that all social questions are matters of governance. . . . The criminologist [*criminaliste*] can no longer be simply a jurist, exclusively concerned with the sacred rights of the individual . . .; it is necessary to be a statistical philosopher, concerned above all with the general interest.[21]

With the advent of crime statistics, neither the individual judge nor the statesman nor the general public could avoid viewing crime as a social matter.

Overview of this book

This book is concerned with criminology, not criminal justice; thus readers will not find extracts from their favorite book on, say, nineteenth-century policing, although I have included two extracts (Chapters 40 and 41) that deal with criminal identification, a criminal-justice topic that fed into criminology. The book's sixty-one extracts are organized into ten parts, and within each part they are, for the most part, arranged chronologically. The first and most eclectic part, on eighteenth-century predecessors, is designed merely to give a swift impression of the highly diverse kinds of discourse on crime that could be found in the period leading up to the one covered here.

Some of the other parts deal with a specific theory (phrenology, moral insanity, degeneration, criminal anthropology, eugenic criminology); some are organized around major themes (the underclass and the underworld; habitual criminals); and some cover methodological and theoretical developments (the rise of criminal statistics; the emergence of sociological approaches to crime). Each part has its own introduction, as does each extract.

The extracts were chosen to contribute to their part topics, of course, but I used other selection criteria as well. One had to do with the boundaries of my time period, the nineteenth century, which I violated in only two cases: first, by using Benjamin Rush's 1786 oration on moral derangement, for which I made an exception because it was first in a line of essays on moral insanity and I want to show the development of the idea, from its inception through the entire century; second by using Edward Alsworth Ross's *Social Control*, issued as a book in 1901, but published in a series of articles written over the previous decade. Another selection criterion was the nationality of the authors, for I wanted to give an international overview. If, using the table of contents, one counts first authors (only) and counts every time one of them authored an extract, the breakdown is as follows: British, 18; American, 16; French, 10; Italian, 8; German or Austrian, 6; Hungarian, 1; Russian, 1; and Swiss, 1.[22] Again in order to represent a variety of voices, I went out of my way to include authors who were female or black, although the majority of my authors are white males – an unavoidable circumstance due to the nature of the pool from which I was drawing.

It was impossible to include all of the authors who strongly influenced the development of nineteenth-century criminology. The parts aim at, not full coverage, but illustration. For instance, for Part I, on eighteenth-century background, I limited myself to just three extracts, omitting such major figures as Jeremy Bentham and Henry Fielding. But I needed to reserve space for fuller coverage of the nineteenth-century developments which are, after all, the book's subject.

I tried to achieve continuity through the parts by using the same author for several extracts. For example, I used two passages by Johann Gaspar Spurzheim, the first (Chapter 4) to illustrate a criminological aspect of phrenology, the science he co-founded, and the second (Chapter 42) to illustrate his advocacy of human breeding and make the point that eugenic ideas, far from being born all at once in 1883 from the head of Francis Galton, suffused criminological discourses from the early years of the century. Lombroso provides another example: because he was the period's preeminent criminologist, I wanted to represent various aspects of his work and to draw from his *Criminal Woman* as well as *Criminal Man*. Thus, I included six extracts from his work, and within some of the extracts, I use examples from various editions of *Criminal Man*. Darwin (yet another example) is represented twice (Chapters 18 and 43), not because he was a criminologist, but because these selections indicate how closely some criminological work paralleled his thinking. Other repeats come with work by Francis Galton, J. Bruce Thomson, Henry Mayhew and John Binny, Friedrich Engels, Enrico Ferri, and W. E. B. DuBois. These repeats give readers more than a single taste of some of the great thinkers in nineteenth-century criminology. They also show that one really cannot cordon the part topics off from one another, for often they are closely interrelated.

I omit all of the authors' textual citations and footnotes with one exception: the footnote in which Galton invented the term *eugenics*. That was a historic moment in the evolution of criminology. Otherwise, however, I have cut citations; their absence indicates not a lack of documentation in the original, but rather my need to make difficult decisions about length and coverage. The result, I think, is texts that are easier to read than they would have been with their notes, for often the footnotes have little meaning out of context. They can, of course, be found in the originals, to which I give full citations. As for textual emphases (italics), I have kept them as in the original texts.

The book aims at introducing students and scholars to key documents in nineteenth-century criminology through extracts that show how the field developed and that reveal contradictions, expose national differences, and illustrate international concerns. Many (perhaps most) criminology textbooks give the impression that nineteenth-century criminology began and ended with Lombroso, who was only a silly Italian (the textbooks suggest) who believed that criminals have crossed eyes and the gait of a gorilla. I hope to counter this view by showing how rich, varied, and vigorous nineteenth-century criminology actually was, how it was international in its dimensions, and how it related to other sciences of its day. I would also like to stimulate new research: clearly we need more English translations of (for example) the work of Bénédict Auguste Morel and Pauline Tarnowsky. We need a history of criminological statistics; we need a biography of Tarnowsky, the first female criminologist and one on whom Lombroso relied for data on female crime. We need studies of reactions to criminal anthropology and research on the development of ideas about habitual offenders. Most of all, perhaps, we need an international overview of the sort mentioned earlier, one that would help us overcome our forgetfullness about criminology's past, especially about the pre-1900 period of which we are particularly ignorant. Otherwise, criminologists will be like children growing up with no memory of their past, with no knowledge of who their parents and grandparents were, or of where and how they were raised. History can help criminology overcome its rootlessness and reconnect it with some of the most vital and enduring ideas in its field. In any case, it is unavoidable; in the words of my Northeastern University colleague Ekaterina Botchkovar, "There is no science without a history of science."

Notes

1 Martine Kaluszynski, "The international congresses of criminal anthropology: Shaping the French and international criminological movement, 1886–1914," Ch. 13 in Peter Becker and Richard F. Wetzell, eds., *Criminals and their Scientists: The history of criminology in international perspective* (Cambridge: Cambridge University Press, 2006).
2 Lombroso's *L'uomo delinquente* was partially translated twice in 1911, first in a summary issued (and in part written) by his daughter, Gina Lombroso-Ferrero: *Criminal Man According to the Classification of Cesare Lombroso* (repr. Montclair, NJ: Patterson, Smith, 1968); second as an extract from one edition of *L'uomo delinquente* titled *Crime: Its Causes and Remedies* (repr. Montclair, NJ: Patterson Smith, 1968). The new translation, complete in the sense that it translates the significant sections from all five editions, is Cesare Lombroso, *Criminal Man*, A new translation with introduction and notes by Mary Gibson and Nicole Rafter (Durham, NC: Duke University Press, 2006).
3 Dugdale was actually born in Paris, where his father was engaged in business, but both parents were English and he moved to London when he was seven (slightly later to the United States). Due to ill health, his education was spotty. The only biography seems to be Edward Morse Shepard, "The work of a social teacher. Being a memorial of Richard L. Dugdale," *Economic Tracts* XII (1884): 1–14. For more on Dugdale's unfamiliarity with sources which might have boosted his sophistication, see Nicole Rafter, *The Criminal Brain* (New York: New York University Press, 2008).
4 Full references to excerpted works, because they can be found in their individual introductions, are omitted here in this general introduction.
5 Cesare Lombroso, *L'uomo delinquente studiato in rapporto alla antropologia, alla medicina legale ed alle discipline carcerarie* (Milan: Hoepli, 1876).
6 David Garland, "British criminology before 1935," *The British Journal of Criminology* 28 (2) (1985): 1–17.
7 David Garland, "Of crimes and criminals: The development of criminology in Britain," Ch. 1 (pp. 17–68) in Mike Maguire, Rod Morgan, and Robert Reiner, eds., *The Oxford Handbook of Criminology* (Oxford: The Clarendon Press, 1994), p. 17.
8 Some of the groundwork has already been laid; see, for example, Neil Davie, *Tracing the Criminal: The rise of scientific criminology in Britain, 1860–1918* (Oxford: Bardwell Press, 2005); Delia Frigessi, *Cesare Lombroso* (Turin: Einaudi Editore, 2003); Garland, "British criminology before 1935," op. cit. and "Of crimes and criminals," op. cit; Mary Gibson, "Biology or environment? Race and southern 'deviancy' in the writings of Italian criminologists," pp. 99–115 in Jane Schneider, ed., *Italy's "Southern Question": Orientalism in one country* (New York: Berg, 1998); Mary Gibson, *Born to Crime: Cesare Lombroso and the origins of biological criminology* (Westport, CT: Praeger, 2002); Mary Gibson, "Cesare Lombroso and Italian criminology: Theory and politics," Ch. 6 (pp.137–58) in Becker and Wetzell, eds., *Criminals and their Scientists*, op. cit.; Laurent Mucchielli, 2006 "Criminology, hygienism, and eugenics in France, 1870–1914: The medical debates on the elimination of 'incorrigible' criminals," Ch. 9 (pp. 207–30) in Becker and Wetzell, eds., *Criminals and their Scientists*, op. cit.; Nicole Hahn Rafter, *Creating Born Criminals* (Urbana: University of Illinois Press, 1997); Nicole Rafter, *The Criminal Brain*, op. cit.; Richard F. Wetzell, *Inventing the Criminal: A history of German criminology 1800–1945* (Chapel Hill: University of North Carolina Press, 2000). This list is not meant as a full bibliography, but as an indication of the sorts of sources available.

9 The search engine Google plans to put large numbers of books online, and it has already digitalized many nineteenth-century books relevant to criminology. Go to Google.com, ask for "Google books," and then type in the name and author of the volume you seek. Google's famous search engine actually does not work very well in locating its own titles, but by working at it (e.g., type author's name first, or author's name only, or first author's name only) you can get what you want, if indeed it has been digitalized.

10 The conference's proceedings were published in Becker and Wetzell, eds., *Criminals and their Scientists*, op. cit.

11 The phrase comes from John H. Laub, "The life course of criminology in the United States," *Criminology* 42 (1) (2004): 1–26, p. 2.

12 See, for example, Piers Beirne, 1988 "Heredity versus environment: A reconsideration of Charles Goring's *The English Convict* (1913)," *British Journal of Criminology* 28 (3): 315–39; John H. Laub, *Criminology in the Making: An oral history* (Boston: Northeastern University Press, 1983).

13 For cross-national work see, in addition to sources already cited, Peter d'Agostino, "Craniums, criminals, and the 'cursed race': Italian anthropology in American racial thought, 1861–1924," *Comparative Studies in Society and History* 44 (2) (2002): 310–43; Peter Becker, "The Criminologists' gaze at the underworld: Toward an archeology of criminological writings," Ch. 5 (pp. 105–33) in Becker and Wetzell, eds., *Criminals and their Scientists*, op. cit.; Piers Beirne, *Inventing Criminology: Essays on the rise of "Homo Criminalis"* (Albany: State University of New York Press, 1993); Piers Beirne, ed., *The Origins and Growth of Criminology: Essays on intellectual history, 1760–1945* (Aldershot: Dartmouth, 1994); Mariacarla Gadebusch Bondio, "From the 'atavistic' to the 'inferior' criminal type: The impact of the Lombrosian theory of the born criminal on German psychiatry," Ch. 8 (pp. 183–206) in Becker and Wetzell, eds., *Criminals and their Scientists*, op. cit.; Michel Foucault, *Discipline and Punish* (New York: Pantheon, 1977); Stephen Jay Gould, *The Mismeasure of Man* (New York: W. W. Norton, 1981); Marie-Christine Leps, *Apprehending the Criminal: The production of deviance in nineteenth-century discourse* (Durham, NC: Duke University Press, 1992); Hermann Mannheim, ed., *Pioneers in Criminology* (2d ed. enlrg. Montclair, NJ: Patterson Smith, 1972); Robert A. Nye, "Heredity or milieu: The foundations of modern European criminological theory," *Isis* 47 (238) (1976): 335–55; Guiliano Pancaldi, *Darwin in Italy: Science across cultural frontiers* (Bloomington: Indiana University Press, 1991); Daniel Pick, *Faces of Degeneration: A European disorder, c. 1848–c. 1919* (Cambridge: Cambridge University Press, 1989); Susanne Regener, "Criminological museums and the visualization of evil," *Crime, History, and Societies* 7 (1) (2003): 43–56; Paul E. Rock, ed., *History of Criminology* (Aldershot, England: Dartmouth Publishing Co., 1994). Again, this list is not intended as a full and definitive bibiography.

14 C. Loring Brace, "The roots of the race concept in American physical anthropology," Ch. 1 (pp. 11–29) in Frank Spencer, ed., *A History of American Physical Anthropology 1930–1980* (New York: Academic Press, 1982), p. 11.

15 David Garland, "Of crimes and criminals," op. cit., p. 19.

16 See, especially, Pick, *Faces of Degeneration*, op. cit.

17 "Advertisement" in Henry Mayhew and John Binny, *The Criminal Prisons of London* (London: Griffin, Bohn, and Comany, 1862), p. iii.

18 Ibid.

19 Gabriel Tarde, *Penal Philosophy* (orig. transl. 1912; repr. Montclair, NJ: Patterson Smith, 1968), p. 321.

20 Émile Durkheim, *Les règles de la méthode sociologique* (orig. 1895; repr. Paris: Presses Universitaires de France, 1960), p. 66.
21 Gabriel Tarde, *La Criminalité comparée* (Paris: Ballière et Félix Alcan, 1890), pp. v–vi.
22 Little research has been published on the early development of criminology in South America; for a taste of later developments, see Ricardo D. Salvatore, "Positivist criminology and state formation in modern Argentina, 1890–1940," Ch. 11 in Peter Becker and Richard F. Wetzell, eds., *Criminals and Their Scientists*, op. cit.

Part I

Eighteenth-century predecessors

Eighteenth-century predecessors

Introduction to Part I

Every science has its predecessors. Although this is a book about the nineteenth-century origins of scientific criminology, those origins grew in soil of their own, the rich loam of late eighteenth-century speculations about the nature of criminality on the one hand, and the nature of science on the other. The three extracts in this section represent three facets of that speculative background: popular narratives about criminals; legal debates about crime prevention; and efforts to create a science of man.

On both sides of the Atlantic, popular criminology in the late eighteenth century consisted of ballads, sermons, news accounts, and gallows narratives such as *The Life, and Dying Speech of Arthur, a Negro Man, Executed for a Rape* (1768) (Chapter 1). These popular discourses on crime – narratives produced for and consumed by the general public – were that period's equivalents of today's crime films, police television series, Internet crime news stories, and crime novels; they made no claims for scientific status, but rather fed a public hunger for commonsense explanations of actual and fictional crimes.

Legal debates about crime repression and prevention were commonplace in the late eighteenth century as social planners worked to create rational and fair bases for democratic criminal-justice systems to replace those of fallen or falling monarchies. Of all the results of these debates, the most famous was *On Crimes and Punishments* (1764), Cesare Beccaria's argument for preventing crimes through deterrence. Even though Beccaria focused on punishment rather than theories about the causes of crime, a criminological theory, based on the philosophy of utilitarianism, lies at the heart of his work, which assumes that man – a rational being – will choose whatever is in his best interest, be it illegal gain or the avoidance of punishment. If punishment is swift, certain, and fair (proportional to the offense), criminals will be deterred and crime will diminish.

The late eighteenth century also saw the beginning of efforts to apply scientific methods to the study of human behavior – efforts that eventually led to the development of anthropology, psychology, sociology, and (a little later) criminology. Some of the first steps toward a science of man were taken by the Swiss physiognomist Johann Kaspar Lavater (Chapter 3), who tried to work out a science of human behavior (including law-breaking) based on facial expressions.

These late eighteenth-century discourses on the meaning and nature of criminality helped to create the background against which scientific criminology emerged in the following century.

Chapter 1

The life, and dying speech of Arthur, a Negro man, executed for a rape, 1768

The Life, and Dying Speech of Arthur, a one-page broadside issued in Boston following a 1768 hanging in Worcester, Mass., offers a sensational and moralistic tale of a criminal career, referring only incidentally and formulaically to the causes of crime. It conforms to the pattern of other American crime narratives of its day, especially those featuring a black culprit, in which a servant or slave violates the trust of a benevolent master.[1] In this particular case, the slave Arthur (1747–68) goes on crime sprees of epic proportions which come to include the rape of a white woman. Mrs. Metcalfe, reluctant to see Arthur hanged, settles for financial compensation, freeing Arthur to commit a host of additional offenses for which the authorities eventually sentence him to death. However, in keeping with a late eighteenth-century trend to sensationalize crime and, in the case of black men, to elaborate the figure of the black rapist, the broadside's title misrepresents Arthur's conviction offense as rape alone. Like other confessional narratives of the time, this one concludes with repentance and recognition of the justice of the law.

Arthur's tale, recorded and shaped by the officiating minister, identifies three causes of crime: drinking, fornicating, and rebellion against the white master. Indirectly, it hints that colonial constables, like today's police officials, occasionally cleared their books by attributing a host of unsolved crimes to a single malefactor: Arthur seems to confess to more crimes than he could possibly have committed in his brief lifetime, but his enumerations enable the authorities to "solve" and shut the books on these offenses.

The full text, titled *The Life, and Dying Speech of Arthur, a Negro Man; Who was Executed at Worcester, October 20, 1768. For a Rape committed on the Body of one Deborah Metcalfe*, is available at http://docsouth.unc.edu/neh/arthur/arthur.html

THE LIFE, AND DYING SPEECH OF ARTHUR, A NEGRO MAN, EXECUTED FOR A RAPE

I was born at *Taunton*, January 15, 1747, in the house of *Richard Godfrey*, Esq., my Mother being his Slave, where I lived fourteen Years; was learned to read and write, and was treated very kindly by my Master; but was so unhappy as often to incur the Displeasure of my Mistress, which caused me then to run away: And this was the beginning of my many notorious Crimes, of which I have been guilty. I went first to *Sandwich*, where I lived two Months in a very dissolute Manner, frequently being guilty of Drunkenness and Fornication; for which crimes I have been since famous, and by which I am now brought to this untimely Death.

At *Sandwich*, I stole a Shirt, was detected, and settled the Affair, by paying twenty Shillings. My Character being now known, I thought proper to leave the Place; and accordingly shipped myself on board a Whaling Sloop, with Capt. *Coffin*, of *Nantucket*: We were out eight Months, and then returned to *Nantucket*, from whence we sailed, where I tarried six Weeks. In which Time I broke a Store of Mr. *Roach's*, from which I stole a Quantity of Rum, a pair of Trowsers, a Jacket, and some Callicoe – The next Day I got drunk, and by wearing the Jacket, was detected, for which Offence I was whip'd with fifteen Stripes, and committed to Goal [jail – N.R.], for the Payment of Cost, &c. from whence I escaped in half an Hour, by breaking the Lock. Being now hardened in my Wickedness, I the next Night broke another Store in the same Place, from which I took several Articles, and then shipped my self on board a Vessel bound to *Swanzey*, where I was discovered, taken on Shoar, and whip'd sixteen Stripes; being then set at Liberty, I returned to *Taunton*, after one Year's absence, where my Master received me kindly, whom I served three Years. . . .

In the mean Time, my Master being sent for, once more took me home, where I had not three Weeks, before another Negro of my Master's told me that the young Squaw, so often mentioned, was desirous of seeing me. I one Night, after having stole some Rum from my Master, got pretty handsomely drunk, took one of his Horses, and made the best of my way to her usual Place of Abode; but she not being at home, the Devil put it into my Head to pay a Visit to the Widow *Deborah Metcalfe*, whom I, in a most inhumane manner, ravished: The Particulars of which are so notorious, that it is needless for me here to relate them. The next Morning the unhappy Woman came and acquainted my Master of it, who immediately tyed me, to prevent me running away, and told her (if she was desirous of prosecuting me) to get a Warrant as soon as possible; but she being unwilling to have me hanged, proposed making the Matter up for a Proper Consideration, provided my Master would send me out of the Country; to which he agreed, and accordingly set off with me for *Albany*. . . .

At *Weston* we stole some Butter from off a Horse. At *Waltham* we broke into a House belonging to one Mr. *Fisk*, from whom we took a small Sum of Money, some Chocolate and Rum. At *Watertown* we stole a Brass Kettle from one Mrs. *White* of that Place. My Companions now left me; upon which I went to Mr. *Fisk's* in *Waltham*, who knew me: And having heard of my Escape from *Worcester* Goal, immediately secured me, and with the Assistance of another Man, brought me back again, where on the 17th of September following, I was tryed and found guilty. Upon which, by the Advice of my Counsel, I prayed for the Benefit of the Clergy; which after a Year's Consideration, the Court denied me: And accordingly I was, on the 24th of Sept. last, sentenced to be hanged, which I must confess is but too just a Reward for many notorious Crimes. . . .

I earnestly desire that this Recital of my Crimes, and the ignominious Death to which my notorious Wickedness has bro't me, may prove a Warning to all Persons who shall become acquainted therewith. But in a particular Manner, I would solemnly warn those of my Colour, as they regard their own souls, to avoid Desertion from their Masters, Drunkenness and Lewdness; which three Crimes was the Source from which have flowed the many Evils and Miseries of my short Life. Short indeed! For I am now at the Age of 21 Years only, just going to launch into a neverending Eternity. . . .

Worcester Goal Oct. 18, 1768

Note

1   Richard Slotkin, "Narratives of Negro crime in New England, 1675–1800," *American Quarterly* 25 (1) (March 1973): 3–31.

Chapter 2

Cesare Beccaria: Of the means of preventing crimes, 1764

The small volume *On Crimes and Punishments* by the Italian nobleman Cesare Beccaria (1738–94) proved to be one of the three or four most influential texts in the history of criminology. From one point of view, this is not a criminological text at all, but rather a treatise on the nature of law – on the legal changes that autocratic governments should make to reduce crimes. Nor does it attempt to analyze crime scientifically, as later theorists tried to. But implicit in Beccaria's legal recommendations and in his philosophy of punishment is a theory about the nature of man and the causes of crime.

In Beccaria's view, man is a rational being, capable of making self-interested choices. If the laws are clear, administered fairly, and punitive in proportion to crimes, no sensible person will break the law. Free men curb their selfish passions if they know the result will be punishment. Education, too, is crucial, for knowledgeable citizens will realize the benefits of conforming to law; and a wise ruler will reward virtue – another means of preventing crime. But above all, it is rationality in the criminal law, education, and giving men the opportunity to choose the right course that will reduce the number of offenses.

Appearing shortly before the French and American revolutions, Beccaria's short tract fundamentally shaped concepts of crime and justice in the new republics. The following text is excerpted from Chapters 41, 42, 44, and 45 of the first American edition: Cesare Beccaria, *On Crimes and Punishments* (Philadelphia: R. Bell, 1778).

CESARE BECCARIA: OF THE MEANS OF PREVENTING CRIMES

Would you prevent crimes? Let the laws be clear and simple, let the entire force of the nation be united in their defence, let them be intended rather to favour every individual than any particular classes of men, let the laws be feared, and the laws only. The fear of the laws is salutary, but the fear of men is a fruitful and fatal source of crimes. Men enslaved are more voluptuous, more debauched, and more cruel than those who are in a state of freedom. These study the sciences, the interest of nations, have great objects before their eyes, and imitate them; but those, whose views are confined to the present moment, endeavour, amidst the distraction of riot and debauchery, to forget their situation; accustomed to the uncertainty of all events, for the laws determine none, the consequences of their crimes come problematical, which gives an additional force to the strength of their passions. . . .

Would you prevent crimes? Let liberty be attended with knowledge. As knowledge extends, the disadvantages which attend it diminish and the advantages increase. A daring impostor, who is always a man of some genius, is adored by the ignorant populace, and despised by men of understanding. Knowledge facilitates the comparison of objects, by showing them in different points of view. When the clouds of ignorance are dispelled by the radiance of knowledge, authority trembles, but the force of the laws remains movable. Men of enlightened understanding must necessarily approve those useful conventions which are the foundation of public safety; they compare with the highest satisfaction, the inconsiderable portion of liberty of which they are deprived with the sum total sacrificed by others for their security; observing that they have only given up the pernicious liberty of injuring their fellow-creatures, they bless the throne, and the laws upon which it is established. . . .

Yet another method of preventing crimes is, to reward virtue. . . .

Finally, the most certain method of preventing crimes is, to perfect the system of education. . . . This chiefly consists in . . . leading the pupil to virtue by the easy road of sentiment, and in withholding him from evil by the infallible power of necessary inconveniences, rather than by command, which only obtains a counterfeit and momentary obedience.

Chapter 3

Johann Kaspar Lavater: On physiognomy, 1789

The science of physiognomy aimed at reading character and other psychological traits from outer physical signs, especially those of the face. Although it had ancient roots, physiognomy was not codified and systematized until the late eighteenth century, when the Swiss poet and cleric Johann Kaspar Lavater published his *Essays on Physiognomy*. Lavater (1741–1801) did not focus specifically on criminality, but his analysis of facial features associated aspects of appearance with crime and other forms of negative behavior. He was thus one of the first scholars to attempt to apply science to the understanding of deviant behavior.

This excerpt comes from Lavater's *Essays on Physiognomy* (London: Printed for G. G. J. and J. Robinson, 1789), pp. 14–19, 67–80, 204–5, and 229.

JOHANN KASPAR LAVATER: ON PHYSIOGNOMY

Although the physiological, intellectual, and moral life of man, with all their subordinate powers, and their constituent parts, so eminently unite in one being; although these three kinds of life do not, like three distinct families, reside in separate parts, or stories of the body; but coexist in one point, and, by their combination, form one whole; yet is it plain that each of these powers of life has its peculiar station, where it more especially unfolds itself, and acts.

It is beyond contradiction evident that, though physiological or animal life displays itself through all the body, and especially through all the animal parts, yet does it act most conspicuously in the arm, from the shoulder to the ends of the fingers.

It is equally clear that intellectual life, or the powers of the understanding and the mind, make themselves most apparent in the circumference and form of the solid parts of the head; especially the forehead, though they will discover themselves, to an attentive and accurate eye, in every part and point of the human body, by the congeniality and harmony of the various parts, as will be frequently noticed in the course of this work. Is there any occasion to prove

Figure 3.1 The Science of Physiognomy. J. K. Lavater aimed at codifying the signs of facial expressions. From Johann Kaspar Lavater, *Essays on Physiognomy*, translated by Thomas Holcroft (19th ed., London: Ward, Lock & Bowden, n.d., ca. 1890), Plate IV. Courtesy of Neil Furman, Argosy Book Store, New York City.

that the power of thinking resides neither in the foot, in the hand, nor in the back; but in the head, and its internal parts?

The moral life of man, particularly, reveals itself in the lines, marks, and transitions of the countenance. His moral powers and desires, his irritability, sympathy, and antipathy; his facility of attracting or repelling the objects that surround him; these are all summed up in, and painted upon, his countenance, when at rest. When any passion is called into action, such passion is depicted by the motion of the muscles, and these motions are accompanied by a strong palpitation of the heart. If the countenance be tranquil, it always denotes tranquillity in the region of the heart and breast.

This threefold life of man, so intimately interwoven through his frame, is still capable of being studied in its different appropriate parts; and did we live in a less depraved world we should find sufficient data for the science of physiognomy.

The animal life, the lowest and most earthly, would discover itself from the rim of the belly to the organs of generation, which would become its central or focal point. The middle or moral life would be seated in the breast, and the heart would be its central point. The intellectual life, which of the three is supreme, would reside in the head, and have the eye for its centre. If we take the countenance as the representative and epitome of the three divisions, then will the forehead, to the eyebrows, be the mirror, or image, of the understanding; the nose and cheeks the image of the moral and sensitive life; and the mouth and chin the image of the animal life; while the eye will be to the whole as its summary and center. I may also add that the closed mouth at the moment of most perfect tranquillity is the central point of the radii of the countenance. It cannot however too often be repeated that these three lives, by their intimate connection with each other, are all, and each, expressed in every part of the body. . . .

We have already informed our readers they are to expect only fragments on physiognomy from us, and not a perfect system. However, what has been said may serve as a sketch for such a system. To acquire this perfection it is necessary separately to consider the physiological part, or the exterior characters of the physical and animal powers of man; the intellectual part, or the expression of the powers of the understanding; and the moral part, or the expression of the feeling and sensitive powers of man, and his irritability. . . .

Taking it in its most extensive sense, I use the word physiognomy to signify the exterior, or superficies, of man, in motion or at rest, whether viewed in the original or by portrait.

Physiognomony, or, as more shortly written, Physiognomy is the science or knowledge of the correspondence between the external and internal man, the visible superficies and the invisible contents.

Physiognomy may be divided into the various parts, or views under which man may be considered; that is to say, into the animal, the moral, and the intellectual. . . .

Physiognomy a science

Though there may be some truth in it, "still, physiognomy never can be a science." Such are the assertions of thousands of our readers, and, perhaps, these assertions will be repeated, how clearly soever their objections may be answered, and however little they may have to reply.

To such objectors we will say, physiognomy is as capable of becoming a science as any one of the sciences, mathematics excepted. As capable as experimental philosophy, for it is experimental philosophy; as capable as physic, for it is a part of the physical art; as capable as theology, for it is theology; as capable as the belles lettres, for it appertains to the belles lettres. Like all these, it may, to a certain extent, be reduced to rule and acquire an appropriate character, by which it may be taught. As in every other science, so, in this, much must be left to sensibility and genius. At present it is deficient in determinate signs and rules. . . .

Whenever truth or knowledge is explained by fixed principles, it becomes scientific, so far as it can be imparted by words, lines, rules, and definitions. The question will be reduced to whether it be possible to explain the undeniable striking differences, which exist between human faces and forms, not by obscure, confused conceptions, but by certain characters, signs, and expressions; whether these signs can communicate the strength and weakness, health and sickness, of the body; the folly and wisdom, the magnanimity and meanness, the virtue and the vice of the mind. This is the only thing to be decided; and he, who, instead of investigating this question, should continue to declaim against it, must either be deficient in logical reasoning or in the love of truth. . . .

Physiognomonical truth may, to a certain degree, be defined, communicated by signs, and words, as a science. We may affirm, this is sublime understanding. Such a trait accompanies gentleness, such another wild passion. This is the look of contempt, this of innocence. Where such signs are, such and such properties reside. By rule may we prescribe – "In this manner must thou study. This is the route thou must pursue. Then wilt thou arrive at that knowledge which I, thy teacher, have acquired." . . .

Physiognomy is the terror of vice. No sooner should physiognomonical sensation be awakéned into action, than consistorial chambers, cloisters, and churches, must become branded with excess of hypocritical tyranny, avarice, gluttony, and debauchery; which, under the mask, and to the shame, of religion, have poisoned the welfare of mankind. The esteem, reverence, and love, which have hitherto been paid them, by the deluded people, would perish like autumnal leaves. The world would be taught that to consider such degraded, such pitiable, forms, as Saints, pillars of the church and state, friends of men, and teachers of religion, were blasphemy. . . .

[The following examples refer to illustrations in Lavater's original, only one of which is reproduced here.].

Figure 3.2 A Countenance by Vice Rendered Fiend-like. Johann Kaspar Lavater, *Essays on Physiognomy*, translated by Thomas Holcroft (19th ed., London: Ward, Lock & Bowden, n.d., ca. 1890), Plate X, between pages 110 and 111. Courtesy of Neil Furman, Argosy Book Store, New York City.

- NATURE forms no such countenance; at least, no such mouth. Vice only can thus disfigure. Rooted unbounded avarice. Thus does brutal insensibility deform God's own image. Enormous depravity has destroyed all the beauty, all the resemblance. Can any benevolent, wise, or virtuous, man, look, or walk, thus? Where is the man, however inobservant, daring enough to maintain the affirmative?
- A DEGREE still more debased [See illustration 3.2.] – A countenance by vice rendered fiend-like, abhorrent to nature, in which salaciousness is sunken almost below brutality. Every spark of sensibility, humanity, nature, is extinguished. Distortion, deformity in excess – and, though sensuality should not appear with this particular kind of ugliness, yet, may it not incur ugliness still more dreadful? Whoever has frequently viewed the human countenance in houses of correction and jails will often scarcely believe his eyes, will shudder at the stigmas with which vice brands her slaves.
- HERE are traits of drunkenness combined with thoughtless stupidity. Who can look without disgust? Would these wretches have been what they are had they not, by vice, erased nature's marks? Can perversion be more apparent than in the middle profile?
- THE last stage of brutal corruption, apparent most in the under part of the male profile, and in the forehead, and nose, of the female (the ears not included). Can any supposition be more absurd than that such a countenance should be the abode of a wife, a virtuous, or an exalted mind?

  We turn with horror from nature thus debased, and rejoice that millions of people afford not any countenance so abominable. . . .
- THE infamous Knipperdolling – Villany and deceit in the mouth; in the forehead and eye courage. How much had virtue and man to expect from the power and determination of such a countenance! What acts of wisdom and heroism! At present all is inflexibility, coldness, and cruelty; an eye without love, a mouth without pity. In the mouth (a) drawn by the side of this head, is the reverse of arrogance and obstinacy. It is contempt without ability.

Part II

Phrenology

Phrenology
Introduction to Part II

The field or science of phrenology, the first systematic explanation of human behavior, was founded by Franz Josef Gall in the late eighteenth century and popularized by his student-colleague Johann Gaspar Spurzheim. Phrenologists believed that the brain is divided into various mental "faculties" or organs such as Combativeness and Destructiveness, each with its own function. The more active a faculty, they taught, the larger its size; and the size of a faculty can be gauged by inspecting the contours of the skull. Gall and Spurzheim had a falling out, in part over Spurzheim's optimistic conviction that the size of the mental faculties can be changed through exercise and self-control, and Spurzheim went on to introduce the new science to the English-speaking world. His science also attracted passionate followers in Belgium, France, and Italy, among other countries.

Even though phrenology has been dismissed as a pseudo-science and "bumpology," it in fact constituted an important early science of the mind. The theories that phrenologists generated in the fields today called criminology, criminal jurisprudence, and penology influenced those fields long after the phrenological map of the brain had been forgotten.[1]

Note

1 See Nicole Rafter, "The murderous Dutch fiddler: Criminology, history, and the problem of phrenology," *Theoretical Criminology* 9 (1) (2005): 65–96.

Chapter 4

Johann Gaspar Spurzheim: On justice, 1834

When Johann Gaspar Spurzheim (1776–1832) moved from his home in Germany to Vienna to study medicine, he met Franz Joseph Gall, the founder of the new (and at the time, totally obscure) science of phrenology. Their friendship and collaboration determined the course of both men's lives. Gall's phrenological system of explaining behavior in terms of sentiments or faculties localized in parts of the brain – and knowable from the contours of the skull – would never have been popularized had Spurzheim not carried it forward, explaining it in books accessible to ordinary readers and adding his own optimistic belief that people can themselves change the size of their faculties.

Eventually the two men parted company over their different approaches to phrenology, although both were serious scientists who tried to explain the causes of human behavior in biological terms. Spurzheim's version, with its appeal to self-improvement, became the basis for a theory of criminal behavior and, following from that, a theory of punishment and reformation. It inspired early nineteenth-century campaigns against the death penalty and in favor of building prisons in which convicts could be induced to strengthen their higher faculties.

In this passage Spurzheim explains why humans so frequently fail to achieve justice, even though the concept is inborn and universal. The sense of justice is part of Conscientiousness, a moral sentiment or faculty that, like the other moral sentiments (Hope, Spirituality, Veneration, and Benevolence), is located at the top of the head and toward the front. Most people allow their lower faculties (those that can also be found in animals, and that are located lower on the skull) to dominate their behavior. This is why there are so few democratic societies, run in accordance with the principles of justice, and why we need so many laws threatening punishment for crime.

This passage comes from Johann Gaspar Spurzheim, *Phrenology, in Connexion with the Study of Physiognomy* (Boston: Marsh, Capen & Lyon, 1834), pp. 225–6.

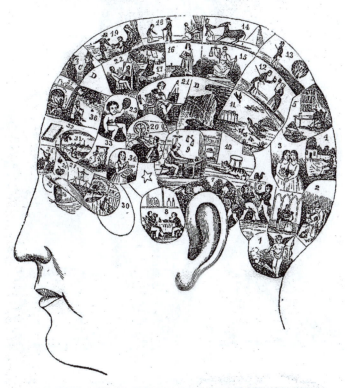

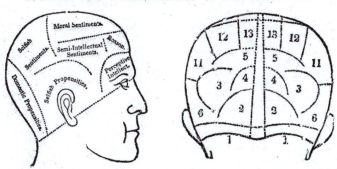

Figure 4.1 Symbolic Heads. Spurzheim used these images to teach the location of the various faculties and propensities. From Johann Gaspar Spurzheim, *Education: Its elementary principles, founded on the nature of man* (New York: Samuel R. Wells, 1872), p. 322.

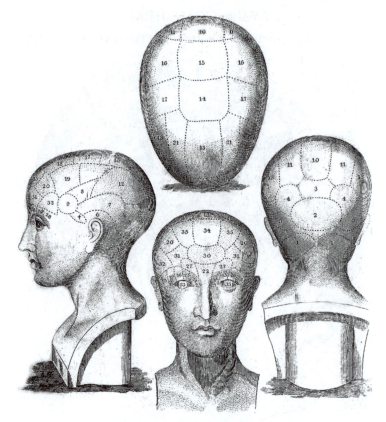

NAMES OF THE PHRENOLOGICAL ORGANS

REFERRING TO THE FIGURES INDICATING THEIR RELATIVE POSITIONS.

	AFFECTIVE		INTELLECTUAL	
I. PROPENSITIES	*II. SENTIMENTS*	*I. PERCEPTIVE*	*II. REFLECTIVE*
1 Amativeness	*10 Self-esteem*	*22 Individuality*	*34 Comparison*
2 Philoprogenitiveness	*11 Love of approbation*	*23 Form*	*35 Causality*
3 Concentrativeness	*12 Cautiousness*	*24 Size*	
4 Adhesiveness	*13 Benevolence*	*25 Weight*	
5 Combativeness	*14 Veneration*	*26 Colouring*	
6 Destructiveness	*15 Firmness*	*27 Locality*	
† Alimentiveness	*16 Conscientiousness*	*28 Number*	
7 Secretiveness	*17 Hope*	*29 Order*	
8 Acquisitiveness	*18 Wonder*	*30 Eventuality*	
9 Constructiveness	*19 Ideality*	*31 Time*	
	Unascertained	*32 Tune*	
	20 Wit or Mirthfulness	*33 Language*	
	21 Imitation		

Published by Marsh, Capen and Lyon, Boston, 1835.

Figure 4.2 Names of the Phrenological Organs. Phrenologists used busts like the one illustrated here to teach the location of the various organs. From George Combe, *Elements of Phrenology* (4th ed., Boston: Marsh, Capen & Lyon, 1835), frontispiece.

JOHANN GASPAR SPURZHEIM: ON JUSTICE

The moral sentiments, particularly that of justice, exert a very secondary influence over the greater number of persons; the faculties common to man and animals determine the actions of the majority of mankind. This lamentable truth is generally admitted, and whilst various reasons have been assumed as accounting for it, all kinds of means have been thought of, and employed, in the view of strengthening the moral part of man: hitherto, however, the success attending these attempts has not been commensurate with the pains that have been taken. Deficiency in the superior sentiments, particularly in justice, is the cause why no large society has hitherto been able to maintain a republican form of government; why kings must be declared inviolable, and their ministers made responsible; why all religious systems admit future rewards and punishments; why so few persons can be left to themselves, and positive laws are indispensable; finally, why fear prevents more mischief, than *love* effects good.

On the other hand, again, though their actions be not in conformity with its dictates, justice is felt and admired by the great bulk of mankind. Phrenology alone affords an explanation of this state of things. The sentiment of justice exists in a greater or less degree in every individual; it is at least felt and necessarily approved of by almost every one's intelligence. The great mass of mankind, therefore, claim justice and assent to its being done, so long as their inferior or animal feelings, as amativeness, philoprogenitiveness, individual attachment, self-esteem, love of approbation, acquisitiveness, or selfishness in general, are not in opposition; but justice is commonly overwhelmed as soon as it is assailed by the animal propensities: the combat then becomes unequal, for very few possess justice strong enough to triumph over and keep the lower feelings in subordination.

Chapter 5

Nahum Capen: The visit of Gall and Spurzheim to Spandau prison, 1834

In 1802, Gall was told by the Austrian government that he could no longer lecture on phrenology because his doctrines posed a threat to religion. Thus, he and his disciple Spurzheim left Vienna for Berlin, where their teachings met a warmer reception. In this excerpt, Nahum Capen, an American writer, publisher, and advocate of phrenology, describes one of Gall's near-miraculous demonstrations of phrenology; it must have taken place some time before 1812, the year in which Gall and Spurzheim had their falling out.

This passage comes from Capen's "Biography," printed in Johann Gaspar Spurzheim's *Phrenology, in Connexion with the Study of Physiognomy* (Boston: Marsh, Capen & Lyon, 1834), pp. 25–7.

NAHUM CAPEN: THE VISIT OF GALL AND SPURZHEIM TO SPANDAU PRISON

"A feature of these memorable travels," in the words of Chenevix, "was their visit to the prison of Berlin, and the fortress of Spandau. On the 17th of April, 1805, in the presence of the chiefs of the establishment, of the inquisitors of the criminal department, of various counsellors, and of many other witnesses, they were conducted to the prison at Berlin, where upwards of two hundred culprits, of whom he had never heard till that moment, to whose crimes and dispositions they were total strangers, were submitted to their inspection. Dr. Gall lays much weight upon this visit, as a very great practical test of the truth of his system; and the result is official, being witnessed by persons in the employment of the Prussian government, and proposed for that purpose.

Dr. Gall immediately pointed out, as a general feature in one of the wards, an extraordinary development in the region of the head where the organ of theft is situated, and in fact every prisoner there was a thief. Some children, also detained for theft, were then shown to him; and in them, too, the same organ was very prominent. In two of them, particularly, it was excessively large; and the prison-registers confirmed his opinion that these two were most incorrigible. In another room, where the women were kept apart, he distinguished one dressed exactly like the others, occupied like them, and differing in no one thing but in the form of her head. "For what reason is this woman here," asked Gall, "for her head announces no propensity to theft?" The answer was, "She is the inspectress of this room." One prisoner had the organs of benevolence and of religion as strongly developed as those of theft and cunning; and his boast was, that he never had committed an act of violence, and that it was repugnant to his feelings to rob a church. In a man named Fritze, detained for the murder of his wife, though his crime was not proved, the organs of cunning and firmness were fully developed; and it was by these that he eluded conviction. In Maschke, he found the organ of mechanical arts, together with the head very well organized in many respects; and

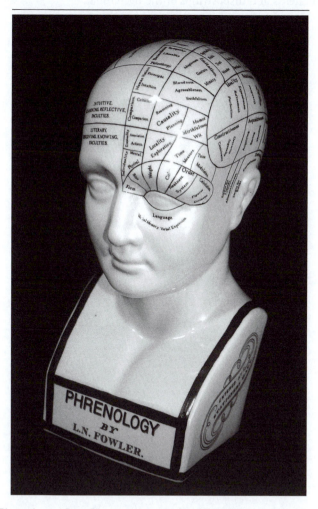

Figure 5.1 Phrenological Bust. Photograph courtesy of Danielle Rousseau.

his crime was coining. In Troppe he saw the same organ. This man was a shoemaker, who, without instruction, made clocks and watches, to gain a livelihood in his confinement. On a nearer inspection, the organ of imitation was found to be large. "If this man had ever been near a theatre," said Gall, "he would, in all probability, have turned actor." Troppe, astonished at the accuracy of this sentence, confessed that he had joined a company of strolling players for six months. His crime, too, was having personated a police officer to extort money. The organs of circumspection, prudence, foresight, were sadly deficient in Heisig, who, in a drunken fit, had stabbed his best friend. In some prisoners he found the organ of language, in others of color, in others of mathematics; and his opinion, in no single instance, failed to be confirmed by the known talents and dispositions of the individual.

Chapter 6

Marmaduke B. Sampson: Criminal jurisprudence and cerebral organization, 1846

While few phrenologists focused exclusively on crime, the English journalist Marmaduke B. Sampson produced an entire treatise explaining phrenology's implications for criminal jurisprudence and the reformation of convicts. It is excerpted here from Marmaduke B. Sampson and Eliza W. Farnham, *Rationale of Crime and Its Appropriate Treatment* (New York: D. Appleton and Co., 1846), pp. 2–6 and 41–50. Farnham's editorial notes are omitted here, but reproduced in the next excerpt.

MARMADUKE B. SAMPSON: CRIMINAL JURISPRUDENCE AND CEREBRAL ORGANIZATION

It is now acknowledged as an unquestionable truth, that all the manifestations of the mind, including the feelings and the passions, are dependent upon the conformation and state of health of its material instrument, the brain; and that all derangements of this organ arise from causes analogous to those which produce derangement of any other organ of our physical frame. The question then arises, Why do we not treat irregularities of the mind in the same way as we treat all other physical disorders, viz., by confining ourselves solely to an attempt to cure the patient? and why do we talk of punishment when we are considering a case of morbid action of the brain, any more than when we are considering a case of morbid action of the heart, the lungs, or any other organ?

The difference has arisen from the confused notions which have been universally entertained regarding the social responsibility of man, all tending to the belief that there exists a middle ground, not to be doubted, yet never to be defined, where responsibility ends and irresponsibility begins.

It will be admitted, that if a man could be found in whom *all* the qualities of mind and body were healthfully constituted and harmoniously developed, we should then behold a being who would realize, humanly speaking, our ideas of perfection. That all men fall far short of this standard, is a truth which religion and experience alike confirm; but, some approach more nearly to it than others; and the question that we have to consider, in estimating the qualities of our fellow-men, is not, whether any one exists whose mind and body are thus perfectly sane, but, What is the relative degree of his divergence from the perfect type which we have supposed? The tendency to evil, which, more or less, is the characteristic of all men, indicates in each the amount of this divergence from that harmonious balance of the mental powers in which alone true soundness of mind can consist. False impressions, ungovernable desires, deficiencies of intellect or feeling – in short, all that makes up the sum of human errors – arise from an unbalanced action of the various faculties of the mind; and to the extent, therefore, that any one faculty is deficient in its comparative relation to the others in any individual, such is the extent of his departure from true soundness of mind in regard to those objects to which that faculty may relate. . . .

To the extent, then, that any one power of the mind assumes an irregularity of development, such is the extent of the departure from mental sanity, and the consequent tendency to a disobedience of the moral or physical law over which the defective faculty was intended to preside; and, as there exists not an individual in whom a perfect balance of all the faculties can be found, so it has been well said, that, "If we speak with rigorous exactness, there is no human mind in its right state." . . .

Irregularities of disposition arise from two causes, – viz., the transmission of an irregular cerebral organization from parent to child; and, subsequently, the effect of accidental circumstances, as bad example, ill-conducted education, injuries of the head, &c. It is precisely from analogous causes that irregular conditions are occasioned in other organs of the body. They are more or less, in all cases, transmitted in an imperfect and unhealthy state; and the subsequent effect of defective physical education and accidents aggravates the predisposition to morbid action which was thus originally established. If a child be born with an irregular organization of brain (and to say that every child is born thus, is merely to aver that none are born perfect), he comes into the world to the extent of that irregularity insane; and as, by subsequent education, that irregularity may be reduced or increased, so will this insanity be aggravated or relieved. . . .

All affections or diseases of the body may be traced to causes analogous to those which produce affections or diseases of the brain, viz., original malformation, sympathy with other diseased parts of the system, ill-directed exercise, contagious association, accidental lesion, &c. &c.; but when we speak of persons being in ill health, in cases where any other organ of the body than *the brain* is affected, we never think of expressing a desire to *punish* them for their misfortune, because we consider that the pain they must necessarily suffer, and the restraint and confinement to which they must submit, in order to promote recovery, are circumstances that should awaken our pity rather than our anger, and we urge them to seek the aid of a competent physician.

Yet the moment the brain is discovered to be the organ that is in an unsound state, our view of the matter immediately changes. We then talk of "responsibility," and of the necessity of "punishment" (without questioning as to whether these terms must necessarily be united); although it would be quite as rational to flog a man at the cart's tail for having become infected with the scarlet fever, owing to a predisposition and exposure to the disease, as to pursue the same course to one who, falling into temptation, had given way to a predisposition for taking possession of whatever he could lay his hands upon. To be sure, it might be said, that the flogging could not operate so as to deter the man from catching another fever, while it might deter the thief from repeating his offence; but this distinction will not hold good, because, in the first instance, dread of the punishment might possibly induce the patient to attend in future so closely to the laws of health as to keep him safe from infection, and it could do no more in the latter case with regard to the laws of morality. . . .

With regard to Responsibility:

Although upon this great question legislators, lawyers, physicians, and moralists have differed and doubted from all time, almost all of them have been unanimous in what appears to me to be the one great error – of allowing that there exists "somewhere" a line of demarkation where responsibility ceases, and irresponsibility, by reason of insanity, is to be allowed; the former being subject, in cases of murder, &c., to the punishment of death, the latter entitling the culprit to immunity. The application of these views depends entirely, of course, upon the peculiar metaphysical opinions which may dwell in the minds of the jury before whom a criminal is tried; and, as no fixed ideas exist, a person may be executed as "responsible" under the verdict of one jury, for the very same offence which, committed under like circumstances, might, in the eyes of another jury, entitle him to the plea of insanity. In illustration of this fact, I cite from a numerous collection, the following remarkable case: –

Catharine Ziegler was tried at Vienna for the murder of her bastard child. She confessed the act, and said she could not possibly help it; she was forced to do it; she could not any how resist the desire she felt to commit the murder. The frankness of this her confession, connected with favourable circumstances, her good character, &c., induced the tribunal to pass a merciful sentence; and, on the ground of insanity (which she did not herself plead), she was acquitted, and at length let out of prison. But she told the court, that, if they let her escape, they would be responsible for the next murder she committed, for that if she ever had a child again she should certainly kill it. And so in fact she did. About ten months after her release from prison, she was delivered of a child, which she soon murdered. Brought again to her trial, she repeated her old story; and added, that she became pregnant merely for the sake of having a child to kill. It does not appear whether she was brought before the same judges as before; most likely not; she was *executed* for this second murder.

Cases have also been known where a criminal has been executed under the verdict of a jury, although the well-in-formed and more experienced judges of the court before whom the trial was had, entertained no doubt of his insanity. The following case occurred in one of the New England States: – On the morning of the 23d June, 1833, Abraham Prescott went into a field with Mrs. Cochran, his foster-mother, to pick strawberries. They had been gone but a short time, when Prescott returned nearly to the house, and was heard crying, or whining, so as to attract the attention of Mr. Cochran, who was left in the house reading. Upon inquiry of Prescott why he cried, he replied, that "he had killed Sally" in the pasture; which, upon examination, proved true: near to her was a billet of wood that had been a stake in the fence, with which he had struck her on the head. On his trial, it was proved that Prescott had, in the month of January preceding, risen in the night, about ten or eleven o'clock, and built a fire in the kitchen, preparatory to butchering swine, which was to have been done the next day; that Mr. and Mrs. Cochran slept in an adjoining room; that Prescott, without waking them, took an axe, and entered their room, and there inflicted on the head of each a severe blow, which left them entirely senseless. This extraordinary transaction was supposed at the time, both by the physician and the wounded friends of Prescott, to have been done in a fit of somnambulism. He disclaimed any knowledge of the affair, and was diligent and active in procuring relief. He had lived with Mr. Cochran some six or eight years, and had always been respectful and affectionate, particularly to Mrs. Cochran. Upon inquiry of him how he came to do so diabolical a deed, he stated that he had a violent toothache come on while in the strawberry-field, and sat down upon a stump; after which he disclaimed any knowledge of what had happened till he found Mrs. Cochran dead before him. After his arrest, he made various confessions in the gaol, so discordant, that the Chief Justice, in his charge to the jury, declared them worthy of no consideration whatever. The plea of insanity was made on his trial; but the jury gave a verdict of wilful murder, and he was sentenced to be executed.

A second trial was had, in consequence of some irregularity in the proceedings of the first jury. At this trial there was little or nothing proved differing from the first; and, although the court evidently felt favourably disposed towards the prisoner, he was condemned to death, and was executed.

After the second trial and verdict, the Judges of the court before whom the trial was had, united in a petition to the Executive, that execution of the sentence might be postponed till the legislature should be convened, that an opportunity might be afforded for a commutation of punishment to perpetual confinement. This petition, signed by all the Judges of the highest court in the State, contained the following language: – "The defence set up by the counsel assigned him (Prescott) was insanity; and the very strange circumstances which attended and preceded the act, go far, in our opinion, to raise reasonable doubts whether he was at the time of sound mind." Speaking of the jurors who tried him, they say — "But the circumstances tending, in our opinion, to excite doubts of the prisoner's sanity, do not appear to have operated with the same force upon their minds as upon ours."

The extraordinary degree of confusion which prevails regarding the question of moral responsibility, and the necessity that exists for a more perfect definition of insanity, was well exemplified in the trial of the imbecile Edward Oxford.

In this case, it was asserted that the grandfather of the culprit had been insane: it was fully proved that the father had always been subject to destructive and suicidal mania; that the mother was affected by nervous delusions; that one of her children had been born an idiot; and that, during the time when she was pregnant with the subject of the inquiry, she was exposed to great distress, from frequently receiving from her husband blows on the head which rendered her insensible; and that on one occasion she was subjected to the greatest terror by his presenting a loaded gun at her person. These things were coupled with proofs of habitual conduct on the part of the prisoner chiefly of a similar character to the following: — "When he was out, he would get stinging-nettles, and beat children with them on their arms until their [arms] were quite blistered. He was sometimes given to laugh and cry violently at the same time, without any cause. When any one boxed his ears for doing any thing wrong, he would laugh in a very peculiar manner; and he was often in the habit of breaking, or throwing out of windows, different articles that came in his way." With all these facts before them, coupled with the absurdity of his plans, and the subsequent indifference of the prisoner; with the knowledge that by far the largest class of insane cases can be traced to hereditary causes; that the impressions produced upon the mind of the mother during the period of gestation are usually the source of peculiar dispositions on the part of the child; that the want of power to repress ordinary emotions is one of the most frequent symptoms of insanity; and that this disease, when it arises from transmission, usually assumes its most violent appearance at about the age at which the prisoner had arrived; — we see the counsel for the prosecution, among the highest legal authorities of the realm, gravely attempting to assert the sanity of the individual, with the view of subjecting him to a verdict that shall involve the penalty of a public death; and while, in common with the medical witnesses, they stated their utter inability to draw the line where responsibility ends and irresponsibility begins, perfectly willing to condemn in ignorance, and to leave the definition upon this point to future inquirers.

In the evidence upon this trial, Dr. Chowne stated: "I have patients often come to consult me who are impelled to commit suicide without any motive for so doing. They tell me they are happy and comfortable in other respects, but that they have a strong desire to commit suicide." This showed that persons may be insane, and yet possess a perfect knowledge of what they are about. The jury listened to this evidence from a high authority; and, half an hour afterwards, they were informed by one of the legal advisers of the crown, that "if the prisoner was of unsound mind, unless he was so mad, so unconscious, that he did not know what he was doing, or what would be the effect of his pulling the trigger, the plea of insanity would not avail!" Fortunately, the jury determined otherwise. Yet it is evident that, amidst all the conflicting arguments by which they were perplexed, the fate of the prisoner completely hung upon the result of their theoretical opinions, instead of upon the operation of any well-defined and rational law.

Thus we see that the line of demarkation between responsibility and irresponsibility shifts place according to the imaginations of different individuals; and that, although in all other respects the laws of the country are so narrowly defined that the Executive is not suffered to swerve a hair's-breadth in the administration of them, the law of responsibility is perfectly enveloped in doubt, and its administration, upon which in reality depends the fate of the criminal, is left to the casual decision of, in many cases, uneducated jurors, whose metaphysical notions may be reasonably presumed to be somewhat capricious and indefinite.

The doctrine of responsibility, which appears to me to be alone consistent with reason, religion, and morality, is simply this: that, so far from the Creator having sent into the world some beings who are responsible, and others who are exempt from responsibility, there is, in fact, no exception whatever; and that every human being is alike responsible, – responsible (according to the degree of his departure, either in mind or body, from that degree of sanity necessary to the proper discharge of his social duties,) to undergo the painful but benevolent treatment which is requisite for his cure. . . .

Chapter 7

Eliza W. Farnham: Phrenology and crime, 1846

Several years after Marmaduke B. Sampson first published his *Treatise*, an American phrenologist and reformer, Eliza W. Farnham, reprinted it, adding her own extensive notes and an appendix of illustrations. (The illustrations were woodcut renditions of prisoner photographs made for Farnham by the pioneering photographer Mathew Brady.) Farnham (1815–64) briefly headed the Mt. Pleasant State Prison for Women at Sing Sing, New York, where she actually applied phrenological principles in efforts to reform her convicts; thus hers is one of the most immediate and persuasive of all phrenological commentaries on crime.[1] The passages excerpted here come from Marmaduke B. Sampson and Eliza W. Farnham, *Rationale of Crime and Its Appropriate Treatment* (New York: D. Appleton and Company, 1846), pp. 8–10, 18–19, 66–7, and 76.

ELIZA W. FARNHAM: PHRENOLOGY AND CRIME

No. 1 [p. 34] is the head of a very depraved person. The drawing indicates great firmness, with a very large development of the inferior propensities. He has always been coarse and brutal in his conduct, an object of terror to children, and the dread of peaceable citizens. His whole person is characterized by the rudeness and coarseness of his mind. His temperament is a combination of the sanguine and lymphatic, and the texture and contour of his frame are loose, harsh, and offensive. He is 24 years old, and is under a sentence of ten years for arson in the third degree. The circumstances of his crime are strongly indicative of his character. He had made a bet of five dollars that at the next fire a certain engine company would be the first at the scene of action. The next night he fired the building contiguous to their house in order to secure his bet!

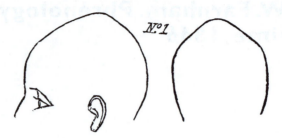

No. 2, an Englishman, 23 years of age, of a nervous sanguine temperament, and much addicted to intemperance. He is under a sentence of six years for grand larceny. He is a professed thief and burglar. Some of the most daring burglaries ever committed in New-York were planned and executed by him.

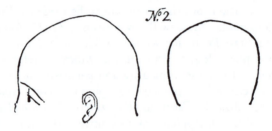

Whenever he is arrested, he suddenly becomes, in appearance, very pious, professing the strongest intentions to abandon his wicked ways; he will even write out and adopt in form resolutions indicative of great integrity of purpose, to be executed when restored to liberty. He is therefore detested among his associates as a hypocrite; and has that other mark of a coward, brutal cruelty. The organ of destructiveness is largely developed in his head, and must, from his peculiarly irritable temperament, receive great stimulus from the use of intoxicating drinks. He boasts of acts of cruelty which would make the most degraded men shudder. The drawing indicates an exceedingly imperfect development of the superior sentiments. He has no education beyond reading and writing.

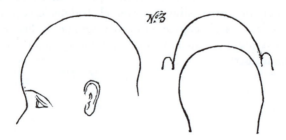

This is the head of a coloured female, 26 years of age, under her third sentence to the Mt. Pleasant State prison for larceny. Her organization is strongly marked by a predominance of acquisitiveness, secretiveness, and destructiveness. The social characteristics of her race are likewise largely developed; so that she presents, under different circumstances, two distinct phases of character. In one, the predominant influences are benevolence, philoprogenitiveness, and adhesiveness; in the other selfishness, cunning and cruelty. The disguises which she assumes are so complete as to elude almost any observation, and the quietness of her manner such that, without acquaintance with her cerebral constitution, it would be impossible to believe her the author of the mischief which appears to come from sources so remote from her. She will doubtless spend her life in prison, for she is constitutionally a criminal. . .

The popular idea of responsibility is, that society has a right to punish an offender for his crime. The punishment is to be inflicted purely as such. Respecting the individual, the prominent object is, to compel him to endure an amount of suffering which shall be esteemed an adequate retribution for his crime; the second and indirect object is to deter him from a repetition of the offence, and others from following his example. But the spirit both of the law and its executors, awakens in those of his class who witness or contemplate his sufferings, a love of endurance and of daring provocation, which is in itself a very dangerous exercise of the propensities. No single feeling which might have a tendency to make him relent in his course of crime, is appealed to by these penalties, save the fear of suffering; and this, in most criminals, is feeble compared with the combined action of all those propensities, whose diseased and tremendous demands indulgence alone can satisfy. Nothing is more clearly established, than that severity of punishment does not elevate the character, or stimulate the moral sentiments, whose action must not only regulate a pure conduct, but constitute the very essence and body of moral life.

Yet responsibility, in the popular sense, is fearfully increased by detection and punishment. Every penalty, it is conceived, should prevent the future indulgence of criminal desires; and, though both in its character and mode of infliction, it may have outraged or destroyed the natural restraints upon propensity, yet on the next detection the offender is judged all the more harshly, as he is supposed to have violated more numerous obligations, and set at naught the experience of former suffering. This truth was well presented not long since, in the case of a woman, who had paid her penalty of two years for a larceny, and during the whole of that time had been exposed to the worst influences, having her resentful and aggressive faculties provoked to their highest action, and indeed all her propensities daily trained in the most effective manner. After her release, the fruits of this punishment appeared in a most abandoned life, and a second felony, for which she was adjudged to a penalty exceeding double the term of her first imprisonment; the event, doubtless, considering that her previous incarceration ought to have prepared her to become a safe and honest citizen! The first year of her second term was spent under influences similar to those which had presided over her former experience. She grew daily more abandoned and desperate, until a change in the government of the prison produced one in the influences by which she was addressed. As was to have been expected, these, at first, were violently resisted. When, however, the violence had been subdued by firm and quiet measures, then came the time for awakening self-restraint, and whatever of moral sensibility there yet remained. This was a work demanding great patience, kindness, and industry. The inflamed propensities were often stimulated by uncontrollable causes, and as often seemed on the point of asserting their superiority. But this was prevented by watchfulness and kind interposition between her and the temptation. These, together with the instruction given her upon the peculiarities of her mental constitution, and the sources and character of her temptation, have enabled her thus far to adhere so faithfully to the dictates of her better powers, that she has long afforded an example of restraint and good conduct, to which all may be pointed. She has been restored to liberty, and in all her demeanour thus far, has given most satisfactory evidence that her improved conduct is the offspring of genuine and sound internal motives. . .

I have found nothing more encouraging in the treatment of criminals, than the excellent effect which flows from imparting to them a knowledge of the peculiar constitution of their own minds. As soon as the source of their evil desires is brought clearly within their comprehension, all mystery, doubt and uncertainty are cleared away. Show them that the strength of these desires is governed by physical laws, in the same manner as the strength of a limb or other organs of the body; that by indulgence this power will continually increase; and that it is in the restraints which their own moral sentiments and intellect impose upon propensity, that sound and healthy advancement can be made in the path of moral reformation, and they have then some well-defined idea of what their duty is, and of the means of discharging it. Add to this some knowledge of the adaptation of their own constitution to that of external nature, of the conditions of human happiness, and the invariableness of the laws on which it depends, and of the relation subsisting between themselves and their Maker, and if there be sufficient intellectual energy to comprehend something of the force and value of these truths, they will rarely fail to produce the highest efforts of which the mind is capable. This sort of instruction, while it offers every incentive to the moral powers, furnishes also to the judgment a sufficient reason for every requirement made by it. So great in my estimation is the value of this knowledge, that, next to the Scriptures, I would require our prisons to be furnished with books designed to impart it. At the head of this kind of works stands Combe on the Constitution of Man. I have adopted this in my instructions in this prison. Of the little time that is afforded for this purpose, I am now and for the last four months have been spending a great part in reading, illustrating and enforcing the truths taught in this admirable work. Among the better class of minds thus taught, are many who receive and understand the laws therein expounded, and there is not one, even the most stupid, who has not been made better by its clear and forcible expositions of duty and of the sources and conditions of happiness. I am persuaded that the improvement in this prison is due as much to this as to any other efforts which have been made in it. In addition to this public reading, I have placed this and kindred works in the hands of our most intelligent convicts for private study. One colored woman, who has been especially instructed in this kind of knowledge, expresses herself thus on the origin and character of moral evil.

"Who and what is the devil is a subject that has often occurred to my mind. As far back as I can remember I have heard of the devil, and from the way I have heard some people talk and preach of him, I have until lately believed him (if it is a he) to be an external being that had great power, who having nothing good in himself nor could ever be good, tried to make others as bad on the earth as himself, and also to preserve dominion over those that had been his subjects, having an endless burning lake."

"I come to the following conclusion according to my own judgment, and it seems as probable to me as the above. According to phrenology, I understand we have two distinct sets of qualities, one called the moral sentiments, and the other animal propensities. I see that if these last were large, or even one organ large, for instance destructiveness, and I, following the dictates of that organ, were to knock a man down and kill him, some one would say the devil was in me, or that he had such possession of me as made me go and kill a man. Now I do not see how any devil external made me kill, and if he was in me he must have been born in me, and if I had not had destructiveness or combativeness, I would not have struck or killed, without the devil had taken me up, bodily, and used me as an instrument." . . .

The treatment best adapted to the cure of excessive propensities, must be that which at once restrains these faculties and stimulates those of a higher character. No treatment, save that which inflicts physical torture, could be more severe than this to the individual who has been accustomed to live in the constant and unrestrained indulgence of his appetites and desires. . . .

M. B. [figure 7.1] is a negro man, under confinement for petit larceny, born in slavery; freed himself, and has lived at the north several years. He is a man of great determination and fixedness of mind and character; can scarcely be thrown off his guard, or induced to do any thing which his own mind does not deliberately consent to. He possesses great strength of purpose, strong powers of reason, and much capacity to plan, as well as energy to execute. He is esteemed by his officers an obliging, good man.

M. B.

Figure 7.1   M.B., a Negro Man. Farnham, an ardent phrenologist, used prisoners' portraits to analyze their head configurations and hence their character. Reproduced from a photograph by Mathew Brady for Eliza Farnham's "Appendix" to Marmaduke B. Sampson and Eliza W. Farnham, *Rationale of Crime* (orig. 1846; repr. Montclair, NJ: Patterson Smith, 1973), p. 156.

D. M.

Figure 7.2   D.M., an Abandoned and Profligate Woman. Reproduced from a photograph by Mathew Brady for Eliza Farnham's "Appendix" to Marmaduke B. Sampson and Eliza W. Farnham, *Rationale of Crime* (orig. 1846; repr. Montclair, NJ: Patterson Smith, 1973), p. 159.

The head indicates very strongly all these characteristics. With a very powerful temperament, are combined a large brain, well developed in the intellectual region, particularly the superior faculties, large self-esteem, firmness, caution, and secretiveness. He has the capacity to be made a very useful or a very desperate and dangerous man.

D. M. [figure 7.2] has been an inmate of the county prisons of New-York, a greater part of the last seven or eight years. She is notoriously abandoned and profligate; and for the last few years has added intemperance to her other vices. She seems utterly lost to all sense of decency and to every moral tie of humanity. With all this degradation she possesses a good mind, with much shrewdness and quickness of perception.

The drawing indicates a large development of propensity with fair intellect, but a total destitution of moral endowment. The scanty development of the coronal region of her head is very striking.

Note

1   For information on Farnham's innovative tenure as Sing Sing's matron, see Nicole Hahn Rafter, *Partial Justice: Women, prisons, and social control* (2d ed., New Brunswick, NJ: Transaction Publishers, 1990).

Part III

Moral and mental insanity

Moral and mental insanity
Introduction to Part III

Nearly all of the first scientific explanations of crime came from alienists – physicians who dealt with alienated minds (today's psychiatrists). Many of these men superintended lunatic asylums, where they gained firsthand experience with the criminally insane, and many of them objected to execution of the insane. The M'Naughten Rule of 1843, formulated in England but also applied in United States, stressed cognitive, not affective, factors in determinations of legal insanity, so that to avoid conviction, criminal defendants had to show that they had not known what they were doing, or, if they had known, had not understood that it was wrong. This very strict standard led courts to find that defendants suffering from severe mental illnesses were criminally responsible; so long as they were not raving lunatics, off they went to the gallows. The injustice of such executions encouraged psychiatrists to study the relationship between crime and mental disease.

In particular, psychiatrists were fascinated by cases of *moral insanity*, instances in which criminals offended repeatedly and without remorse, apparently unable to control their behavior. (Today this condition is known as *psychopathy*.) Although the term has lost its meaning, moral insanity constituted a major theme in nineteenth-century discussions of crime and mental disease; once identified, the phenomenon became a focal point for scientific curiosity. The process through which moral insanity was identified and defined began even before the nineteenth century, in the late eighteenth-century writings of Benjamin Rush, the towering figure of early American psychiatry (Chapter 8). Anticipating the faculty psychology of phrenologists, Rush defined the phenomenon, which he termed *moral derangement*, in terms of a missing or underdeveloped moral faculty. His efforts to explain moral derangement constituted the first criminological theory in the United States; notably, it was a biological theory.

The idea of moral insanity was next developed by Philippe Pinel, the internationally respected French alienist, who termed it *mania without delirium* (Chapter 9), and later still by the English asylum physician James Cowles Prichard, who gave it the simpler (and enduring) name of *moral insanity* (Chapter 10). Usage of the term broadened and shifted over the course of the nineteenth century, but moral insanity itself became accepted as a form of mental illness (Chapter 11).

Meanwhile, other psychiatrists continued to explore relationships between more familiar types of mental illness and crime. Richard Krafft-Ebing, renowned for his pioneering research on sexual pathologies, investigated the relationships of various sex crimes to insanity, trying to determine the line between criminal responsibility and insanity (Chapter 12). Cesare Lombroso, the Italian criminal anthropologist, was also drawn to mental-illness explanations of criminality, partly due to his experiences as a physician in institutions for the criminally insane. As Lombroso elaborated his theory of the born criminal, the concept of moral insanity played an ever larger part in his thinking, to the point that he declared that childhood is characterized by moral insanity: children are born without morality, and it is the job of their parents and teachers to eradicate their innate tendencies to commit crime (Chapter 13). Eventually epilepsy, too, became part of Lombroso's mental-illness explanation of criminality (Chapter 14).

Toward the century's end, the French alienist Prosper Despine, in his *Psychologie Naturelle*, seemed to prove definitively that criminals are morally insane and hence not criminally responsible (Chapter 15). Despine's work firmly soldered the link between mental illness and criminality, and while psychiatrists continued to debate the degree to which minor offenders were mentally abnormal, the medical model of crime, according to which the criminal is sick, was accepted throughout the Western world.

Chapter 8

Benjamin Rush: The influence of physical causes upon the moral faculty, 1786

Benjamin Rush (1745–1813), one of the most famous Americans in the early days of the new republic, fought in the Revolutionary War, signed the Declaration of Independence, and helped found the field known today as psychiatry. Rush, who was particularly interested in mind-body relationships, wrote several essays – including the one excerpted here – that stand among the first investigations of biology and crime, or, as he put it, of the influence of physical causes on the "moral faculty" or ethical capacity. In the course of his work, Rush discovered a few cases of people who seemed to lack the moral faculty entirely – early instances of those today called psychopaths.

Rush taught medicine at the University of Pennsylvania, but also found time to write on a range of subjects, including public health, slavery (which he vehemently opposed), education, sore legs, the sugar maple tree, and the evils of capital punishment.

An Inquiry into the Influence of Physical Causes upon the Moral Faculty, from which this extract is taken, was delivered as an oration before the American Philosophical Society in Philadelphia on February 27, 1786. A complete version can be found in Benjamin Rush, *Medical Inquiries and Observations* (4th ed., Vol. 1, Philadelphia: M. Corey, 1815), pp. 93–124; a slightly abbreviated version appears in Dagobert D. Runes, ed., *The Selected Writings of Benjamin Rush* (New York: Philosophical Library, 1947). I have extracted from the latter, pp. 181–211.

BENJAMIN RUSH: THE INFLUENCE OF PHYSICAL CAUSES UPON THE MORAL FACULTY

By the moral faculty I mean a capacity in the human mind of distinguishing and choosing good and evil, or, in other words, virtue and vice. It is a native principle, and though it be capable of improvement by experience and reflection, it is not derived from either of them. St. Paul and Cicero give us the most perfect account of it that is to be found in modern or ancient authors. "For when the Gentiles (says St. Paul,) which have not the law, do by nature the things contained in the law, *these*, having not the law, are a *law* unto themselves; which show the works of the law written in their hearts, their consciences also, bearing witness, and their thoughts the mean while accusing, or else excusing, another." . . .

This faculty is often confounded with conscience, which is a distinct and independent capacity of the mind. This is evident from the passage quoted from the writings of St. Paul, in which conscience is said to be the witness that accuses or excuses us, of a breach of the law written in our hearts. The moral faculty is what the schoolmen call the "regula regulans;" the conscience is their "regula regulata;" or, to speak in more modern terms, the moral faculty performs the office of a lawgiver, while the business of conscience is to perform the duty of a judge . . .

The celebrated Servin, whose character is drawn by the Duke of Sully, in his Memoirs, appears to be an instance of the total absence of the moral faculty, while the chasm produced by this defect, seems to have been filled up by a more than common extension of every other power of his mind. I beg leave to repeat the history of this prodigy of vice and knowledge. "Let the reader represent to himself a man of a genius so lively, and of an understanding so extensive, as rendered him scarce ignorant of any thing that could be known; of so vast and ready a comprehension, that he immediately made himself master of whatever he attempted; and of so prodigious a memory, that he never forgot what he once learned. He possessed all parts of philosophy, and the mathematics, particularly fortification and drawing. Even in theology he was so well skilled, that he was an excellent preacher, whenever he had a mind to exert that talent, and an able disputant for and against the reformed religion, indifferently. He not only understood Greek, Hebrew, and all the languages which we call learned, but also all the different jargons, or modern dialects. He accented and pronounced them so naturally, and so perfectly imitated the gestures and manners both of the several nations of Europe, and the particular provinces of France, that he might have been taken for a native of all, or any, of these countries: and this quality he applied to counterfeit all sorts of persons, wherein he succeeded wonderfully. He was, moreover, the best comedian, and the greatest droll that perhaps ever appeared. He had a genius for poetry, and had wrote many verses. He played upon almost all instruments, was a perfect master of music, and sang most agreeably and justly. He likewise could say mass, for he was of a disposition to do, as well as to know, all things. His body was perfectly well suited to his mind. He was light, nimble, and dexterous, and fit for all exercises. He could ride well, and in dancing, wrestling, and leaping, he was admired. There are not any recreative games that he did not know, and he was skilled in almost all mechanic arts. But now for the reverse of the medal. Here it appeared, that he was treacherous, cruel, cowardly, deceitful, a liar, a cheat, a drunkard, and a glutton, a sharper in play, immersed in every species of vice, a blasphemer, an atheist. In a word, in him might be found all the vices that are contrary to nature, honour, religion, and society, the truth of which he himself evinced with his latest breath; for he died in the flower of his age, in a common brothel, perfectly corrupted by his debaucheries, and expired with the glass in his hand, cursing and denying God." . . .

There are persons who are moral in the highest degree as to certain duties, who nevertheless live under the influence of some one vice. I knew an instance of a woman, who was exemplary in her obedience to every command of the moral law, except one. She could not refrain from stealing. What made this vice the more remarkable was, that she was in easy circumstances, and not addicted to extravagance in any thing. Such was her propensity to this vice, that when she could lay her hands upon nothing more valuable, she would often, at the table of a friend, fill her pockets secretly with bread. As a proof that her judgment was not affected by this defect in her moral faculty, she would both confess and lament her crime, when detected in it . . . .

It is perhaps only because the diseases of the moral faculty have not been traced to a connection with physical causes, that medical writers have neglected to give them a place in their systems of nosology, and that so few attempts have been hitherto made to lessen or remove them, by physical as well as rational and moral remedies . . . .

1. The effects of CLIMATE upon the moral faculty claim our first attention. Not only individuals, but nations, derive a considerable part of their moral, as well as intellectual character, from the different portions they enjoy of the rays of the sun. Irascibility, levity, timidity, and indolence, tempered with occasional emotions of benevolence, are the moral qualities of the inhabitants of warm climates, while selfishness, tempered with sincerity and integrity, form the moral character of the inhabitants of cold countries. The state of the weather, and the seasons of the year also, have a visible effect upon moral sensibility. The month of November, in Great Britain, rendered gloomy by constant fogs and rains, has been thought to favour the perpetration of the worst species of murder, while the vernal sun, in middle latitudes, has been as generally remarked for producing gentleness and benevolence.

2. The effects of DIET upon the moral faculty are more certain, though less attended to, than the effects of climate. "Fullness of bread," we are told, was one of the predisposing causes of the vices of the Cities of the Plain. The fasts so often inculcated among the Jews were intended to lessen the incentives to vice; for pride, cruelty, and sensuality, are as much the natural consequences of luxury, as apoplexies and palsies. But the *quality* as well as the quantity of aliment has an influence upon morals; hence we find the moral diseases that have been mentioned are most frequently the offspring of animal food. . . .

3. The effects of CERTAIN DRINKS upon the moral faculty are not less observable, than upon the intellectual powers of the mind. Fermented liquors, of a good quality, and taken in a moderate quantity, are favourable to the virtues of candour, benevolence, and generosity; but when they are taken

in excess, or when they are of a bad quality, and taken even in a moderate quantity, they seldom fail of rousing every latent spark of vice into action. . . .

4. EXTREME HUNGER produces the most unfriendly effects upon moral sensibility. It is immaterial, whether it act by inducing a relaxation of the solids, or an acrimony of the fluids, or by the combined operations of both those physical causes. The Indians in this country whet their appetites for that savage species of war, which is peculiar to them, by the stimulus of hunger; hence, we are told, they always return meagre and emaciated from their military excursions. . . .

5. I hinted formerly, in proving the analogy between the effects of DISEASES upon the intellects, and upon the moral faculty, that the latter was frequently impaired by fevers and madness. I beg leave to add further upon this head, that not only madness, but the hysteria and hypochondriasis, as well as all those states of the body, whether idiopathic or symptomatic, which are accompanied with preternatural irritability – sensibility – torpor – stupor or mobility of the nervous system, dispose to vice, either of the body or of the mind. It is in vain to attack these vices with lectures upon morality. They are only to be cured by medicine, – particularly by exercise, – the cold bath, – and by a cold or warm atmosphere. . . .

6. Idleness is the parent of every vice. It is mentioned in the Old Testament as another of the predisposing causes of the vices of the Cities of the Plain. Labor of all kinds favors and facilitates the practice of virtue. The country life is happy, chiefly because its laborious employments are favourable to virtue, and unfriendly to vice. It is a common practice, I have been told, for the planters in the southern states, to consign a house slave, who has become vicious from idleness, to the drudgery of the field, in order to reform him. The bridewells and workhouses of all civilized countries prove that LABOR is not only a very severe, but the most benevolent of all punishments, in as much as it is one of the most suitable means of reformation. . . .

7. The effects of EXCESSIVE SLEEP are intimately connected with the effects of idleness upon the moral faculty; hence we find that moderate, and even scanty portions of sleep, in every part of the world, have been found to be friendly, not only to health and long life, but in many instances to morality. . . .

8. The effects of BODILY PAIN upon the moral, are not less remarkable than upon the intellectual powers of the mind. . . . Bodily pain, we find, was one of the remedies employed in the Old Testament, for extirpating vice and promoting virtue: and Mr. Howard tells us, that he saw it employed successfully as a means of reformation, in one of the prisons which he visited. If pain has a physical tendency to cure vice, I submit it to the consideration of parents and legislators, whether moderate degrees of corporal punishments, inflicted for a great length of time, would not be more medicinal in their effects, than the violent degrees of them, which are of short duration.

9. Too much cannot be said in favour of CLEANLINESS, as a physical means of promoting virtue. . . .

10. I hope I shall be excused in placing SOLITUDE among the physical causes which influence the moral faculty, when I add, that I confine its effects to persons who are irreclaimable by rational or moral remedies. Mr. Howard informs us, that the chaplain of the prison at Liege in Germany assured him "that the most refractory and turbulent spirits, became tractable and submissive, by being closely confined for four or five days." In bodies that are predisposed to vice, the stimulus of cheerful, but much more of profane society and conversation, upon the animal spirits, becomes an exciting cause, and like the stroke of the flint upon the steel, renders the sparks of vice both active and visible. By removing men out of the reach of this exciting cause, they are often reformed, especially if they are confined long enough to produce a sufficient chasm in their habits of vice. . . .

Hitherto the cultivation of the moral faculty has been the business of parents, schoolmasters and divines. But if the principles, we have laid down, be just, the improvement and extension of this principle should be equally the business of the legislator – the natural philosopher – and the physician; and a physical regimen should as necessarily accompany a moral precept, as directions with respect to the air – exercise – and diet, generally accompany prescriptions for the consumption and the gout. To encourage us to undertake experiments for the improvement of morals, let us recollect the success of philosophy in lessening the number, and mitigating the violence of incurable diseases. The intermitting fever, which proved fatal to two of the monarchs of Britain, is now under absolute subjection to medicine. Continual fevers are much less fatal than formerly. The small-pox is disarmed of its mortality by inoculation, and even the tetanus and the cancer have lately received a check in their ravages upon mankind. . . .

Should the same industry and ingenuity, which have produced these triumphs of medicine over diseases and death, be applied to the moral science, it is highly probable, that most of those baneful vices, which deform the human breast, and convulse the nations of the earth, might be banished from the world. I am not so sanguine as to suppose, that it is possible for man to acquire so much perfection from science, religion, liberty and good government, as to cease to be mortal; but I am fully persuaded, that from the combined action of causes, which operate at once upon the reason, the moral faculty, the passions, the senses, the brain, the nerves, the blood and the heart, it is possible to produce such a change in his moral character, as shall raise him to a resemblance of angels – nay more, to the likeness of GOD himself.

Chapter 9

Philippe Pinel: Mania without delirium, 1806

Philippe Pinel (1745–1826) superintended Parisian mental hospitals at the time of the French Revolution and wrote a book that proved to be a milestone in the history of psychiatry and psychology: *A Treatise on Insanity* (originally 1801; revised second edition, 1806). The French Revolution initiated not only a new political order, but also a revolution in attitudes toward mental derangement, which previously had been seen as a sign of demonic possession. Pinel and others reinterpreted mental derangement as a form of illness, a disease of the mind. He insisted on humane treatment of the mentally ill (a famous painting shows Pinel unlocking their chains), and he classified mental diseases, distinguishing among their major types. In some ways he was the French counterpart to the American Benjamin Rush; but while both men were among the founders of the field of psychiatry, Pinel approached the study of mental diseases more scientifically, relying more on direct observation and less on biblical and literary examples.

Pinel's concern lay with insanity, not criminality, but the two disorders intersected in violent and aberrant behaviors. Like Rush, Pinel identified cases of people who seemed to be insane, but were still in command of many of their faculties. Instead of acting totally deranged, such people could reason well, and their intellectual capacities remained intact. Otherwise, however, they were violent and dangerous. Pinel named this disorder *mania without delirium*. His writings on it, and on insanity in general, influenced later interpretations of crime as a form or result of mental disease.

This extract is taken from the first English edition of the *Treatise*: Philippe Pinel, *A Treatise on Insanity* (Sheffield, England: Printed by W. Todd, 1806), pp. 150–6.

PHILIPPE PINEL: MANIA WITHOUT DELIRIUM

An instance of maniacal fury without delirium

The following relation will place in a conspicuous point of view, the influence of a neglected or ill directed education, in inducing upon a mind naturally perverse and unruly, the first symptoms of this species of mania. An only son of a weak and indulgent mother, was encouraged in the gratification of every caprice and passion, of which an untutored and violent temper was susceptible. The impetuosity of his disposition increased with his years. The money with which he was lavishly supplied, removed every obstacle to his wild desires. Every instance of opposition or resistance, roused him to acts of fury. He assaulted his adversary with the audacity of a savage; sought to reign by force, and was perpetually embroiled in disputes and quarrels. If a dog, a horse, or any other animal offended him, he instantly put it to death. If ever he went to a fête or any other public meeting, he was sure to excite such tumults and quarrels, as terminated in actual pugilistic rencounters, and he generally left the scene with a bloody nose. This wayward youth, however, when unmoved by passions, possessed a perfectly sound judgement. When he came of age, he succeeded to the possession of an extensive domain. He proved himself fully competent to the management of his estate, as well as to the discharge of his relative duties; and he even distinguished himself by acts of beneficence and compassion. Wounds, law-suits, and pecuniary compensations, were generally the consequences of his unhappy propensity to quarrel. But an act of notoriety put an end to his carreer of violence. Enraged at a woman, who had used offensive language to him, he precipitated her into a well. Prosecution was commenced against him, and on the deposition of a great many witnesses, who gave evidence to his furious deportment, he was condemned to perpetual confinement at Bicetre {a Parisian mental hospital – N. R.}.

Madness without delirium, confirmed by a well established fact

A fully developed case of this species of mental derangement will clearly establish its claims to nosological attention.

A mechanic, confined at Bicetre, was subject, at irregular intervals, to paroxysms of maniacal fury, unaccompanied by any lesion of the intellect. The first symptom which manifested itself was a burning heat in the abdominal region; which was accompanied by great thirst and costiveness. It extended itself, by degrees, to the chest, neck, and face, of which it heightened the complexion. When it reached the temples, it became still more intense, and produced violent and accelerated pulsations of the arteries of those parts. At length, the brain itself was affected, when the maniac was seized by an irresistible propensity to sanguinary deeds: and could he have possessed himself of an instrument of offence, he would have sacrificed to his fury the first person that came in his way. In other respects, however, he enjoyed the free use of his reason, even during his paroxysms. He answered without hesitation the questions that were proposed to him, and evinced no incoherence in his ideas, nor any other symptom of delirium. He was deeply conscious of the horror of his situation, and was stung with remorse, as if he had been really accountable for his furious propensities. Before his confinement at Bicetre, he was one day seized by a furious paroxysm at his own house. He instantly gave warning of it to his wife, to whom he was tenderly attached, and advised her by an immediate flight to avoid certain death. At Bicetre he experienced similar accessions of periodical fury, and his propensity to acts of atrocity was sometimes directed even against the governor, to whose compassionate attention and kindness he never appeared insensible. These internal conflicts, in which he shewed himself to be possessed of sound reason, and at the same time, to be actuated by sanguinary cruelty, occasionally overwhelmed him with despair, and he often sought to terminate by death the dreadful struggle. He one day seized the cutting knife of the hospital shoemaker, and wounded himself deeply in the right breast and arm. The consequence was a violent hæmorrhage. Close confinement, and the strait-waistcoat were employed to prevent the execution of his bloody project.

Another instance of mania without delirium

At a period of the revolution, which it is to be wished could be effaced from the annals of our history, a case of mania without delirium, gave rise to an extraordinary scene at the Asylum de Bicetre. The Brigands, after the massacre of the prisons, broke like madmen into the above hospital under pretence of emancipating certain victims of the old tyranny, whom it had endeavoured to confound with the maniacal residents at that house. They proceeded in arms from cell to cell, interrogating the prisoners, and passing such of them as were manifestly insane. A maniac, bound in chains, arrested their attention by the most bitter complaints which he preferred with apparent justice and rationality. "Is it not shameful," said he, "that I should be bound in chains and confounded with madmen?" He defied them to accuse him of any act of impropriety or extravagance. "It is an instance of the most flagrant injustice." He conjured the strangers to put an end to such oppression, and to become his liberators. His complaints excited, amongst the armed mob, loud murmurs and imprecations against the governor of the hospital. They immediately sent for that gentleman, and, with their sabres at his breast, demanded an explanation of his conduct. When he attempted to justify himself, they imposed silence upon him. To no purpose did he adduce, from his own experience, similar instances of maniacs, who were free from delirium, but at the same time, extremely dangerous from their outrageous passions. They answered him only with abuse; and had it not been for the courage of his wife, who protected him with her own person, he would have been sacrificed to their fury. They commanded him to release the maniac, whom they led in triumph, with reiterated shouts of Vive la République. The sight of so many armed men, their loud and confused shouts, and their faces flushed with wine, roused the madman's fury. He seized, with a vigorous grasp, the sabre of his next neighbour, brandished it about with great violence, and wounded several of his liberators. Had he not been promptly mastered, he would have soon avenged the cause of outraged humanity. The savage mob then thought proper to lead him back to his cell, and, with shame and reluctance, yielded to the voice of justice and experience.

Specific character of mania without delirium

It may be either continued or intermittent. No sensible change in the functions of the understanding; but perversion of the active faculties, marked by abstract and sanguinary fury, with a blind propensity to acts of violence.

Chapter 10

James Cowles Prichard: Moral insanity, 1835

James Cowles Prichard (1786–1848), the English anthropologist, linguist, physician, and psychiatrist, drew worldwide attention to the phenomenon he named *moral insanity* and defined as a mental disease or group of diseases underlying compulsive criminal behavior. Prichard's first influential book, *Researches into the Physical History of Man* (1813), dealt with not mental disease, but anthropology, arguing for the essential unity of the human races. At a time when other anthropologists maintained that the races were separate in origin and innately different in quality, Prichard, using a wealth of ethnological and linguistic data, advanced the opinion that the original race was black, with the others evolving from it.

Prichard's 1835 *Treatise on Insanity* popularized the term *moral insanity* for the affliction that Rush had termed a disease of the moral faculty or *moral derangement* and Pinel *mania without delirium*. Thereafter, Prichard's more succinct and clearly defined term was used by U.S. and European psychiatrists and criminologists to denote afflictions in which the feelings or emotions (the "moral" dispositions) alone are disordered, with no corresponding change in intellectual capacity. While Prichard's term covered not only criminal behavior but also other disorders in which a person became severely eccentric or compulsive, the condition he described clearly encompassed the set of syndromes that today is termed *psychopathy*. Prichard's focus on moral insanity was controversial at a time when most medical and legal experts defined insanity as a defect in intellection and reasoning, usually accompanied by delusions and hallucinations.

The following material is drawn from Prichard's *Treatise on Insanity* (London: Sherwood, Gilbert, and Piper, 1835), pp. 12–25 and 380–99.

JAMES COWLES PRICHARD: MORAL INSANITY

This form of mental derangement has been described as consisting in a morbid perversion of the feelings, affections, and active powers, without any illusion or erroneous conviction impressed upon the understanding: it sometimes co-exists with an apparently unimpaired state of the intellectual faculties.

There are many individuals living at large, and not entirely separated from society, who are affected in a certain degree with this modification of insanity. They are reputed persons of a singular, wayward, and eccentric character. An attentive observer will often recognize something remarkable in their manners and habits, which may lead him to entertain doubts as to their entire sanity; and circumstances are sometimes discovered, on inquiry, which add strength to his suspicion. In many instances it has been found that an hereditary tendency to madness has existed in the family, or that several relatives of the person affected have laboured under other diseases of the brain. The individual himself has been discovered to have suffered, in a former period of life, an attack of madness of a decided character. His temper and dispositions are found to have undergone a change; to be not what they were previously to a certain time: he has become an altered man, and the difference has, perhaps, been noted from the period when he sustained some reverse of fortune, which deeply affected him, or the loss of some beloved relative. In other instances, an alteration in the character of the individual has ensued immediately on some severe shock which his bodily constitution has undergone. This has been either a disorder affecting the head, a slight attack of paralysis, a fit of epilepsy, or some febrile or inflammatory disorder, which has produced a perceptible change in the habitual state of the constitution. In some cases the alteration in temper and habits has been gradual and imperceptible, and it seems only to have consisted in an exaltation and increase of peculiarities, which were always more or less natural and habitual. . . .

Besides the more usual aspects of moral insanity which refer themselves to morbid depression and excitement, particular cases are marked by the prevalence of certain passions and mental habits when displayed under modifications of which the human mind in a sane state appears scarcely to be susceptible.

One of the most striking of these forms is distinguished by an unusual prevalence of angry and malicious feelings, which arise without provocation or any of the ordinary incitements. All the examples of madness without delirium reported by Pinel belong to this class of disorders. On this account the cases described by Pinel failed for a long time to produce conviction on my mind, as to the existence of what he terms *manie sans délire*, or *folie raisonnante*. I am now persuaded that he was correct in his opinion, and I have even been led to generalise his statement. . . . There are instances of insanity in which the whole disease, or at least the whole of its manifestations, has consisted in a liability to violent fits of anger breaking out without cause, and leading to the danger or actual commission of serious injury to surrounding persons. The characteristic feature of this malady is extreme irascibility depending on a physical morbid cause. There are other instances in which malignity has a deeper die. The individual, as if actually possessed by the demon of evil, is continually indulging enmity and plotting mischief, and even murder, against some unfortunate object of his malice. When this is connected with the false belief of some personal injury actually sustained, the case does not fall under the head of moral insanity. It involves hallucination or erroneous conviction of the understanding; but when the morbid phenomena include merely the expressions of intense malevolence, without ground or provocation actual or supposed, the case is strictly one of the nature above described. . . .

A propensity to theft is often a feature of moral insanity, and sometimes it is its leading if not the sole characteristic. I have lately seen a lunatic, confined in an asylum, who would only eat when he had stolen food, and his keeper made it a constant practice to put into some corner within his reach various articles destined for his sustenance, in order that he might discover and take them furtively. Many instances are upon record of individuals noted for a propensity to steal, without the desire of subsequent possession, though in other respects of sound mind, or at least not generally looked upon as deranged. Probably some of these would afford, if accurately scrutinized, examples of moral insanity, while others might be found referable to eccentricity of character. The discrimination – if indeed the two things are essentially different – could only be made in particular instances by taking into the account a variety of circumstances, such as the hereditary history of the individual and his consanguinity with persons decidedly insane, his former character and habits, and the inquiry whether he has undergone a change in these respects at some particular period of his life. . . .

A variety of instances are mentioned by systematical writers in which the unusual intensity of particular passions or emotions has been thought to constitute mental disease, and a series of compound epithets has been invented for the purpose of affording names to such states of the mind and its affections. Nostalgia and erotomania have been considered as disorders of sentiment; satyriasis and nymphomania of the physical feelings. The excessive intensity of any passion is disorder in a moral sense; it may depend physically on certain states of the constitution; but this does not so clearly constitute madness as the irregular and perverted manifestation of desires and aversions. There is reason to believe that this species of insanity has been the real source of moral phenomena of an anomalous and unusual kind, and of certain perversions of natural inclination which excite the greatest disgust and abhorrence [probably a reference to homosexuality – N.R.] . . . .

The prognosis in cases of moral insanity is often more unfavourable than in other forms of mental derangement. When the disorder is connected with a strong natural predisposition, it can scarcely be expected to terminate in recovery. . . .

Of moral insanity, in its relation to criminal and civil law . . .

In the preceding pages of this work I have described a form of mental derangement, under the title of moral insanity, consisting in disorder of the moral affections and propensities, without any symptom of illusion or error impressed on the understanding. The question whether such an affection really exists or not is very important in connexion with medical jurisprudence, and I think it indispensable to make some remarks on this subject on the present occasion.

I must first observe that no such disorder has been recognized in the English courts of judicature, or even admitted by medical writers in England. In general, it has been laid down that insanity consists in, and is co-extensive with, mental illusion. . . .

The principal consideration in which the subject of moral insanity is important in criminal jurisprudence, is that of insane propension to such acts of violence. Homicide, infanticide, suicide have been committed in numerous cases under circumstances which gave room for suspicion as to the sanity of the agent. This plea has been set up in many trials, and has often been rejected by juries, while it has been the opinion of medical persons that there were ample grounds for maintaining it. The questions connected with homicidal insanity require all the elucidation that can be afforded to them, and I shall devote the next section to this subject.

General observations on homicidal madness

Homicidal madness is of two very different kinds. Cases are well known to take place in which lunatics, under hallucinations, without any malignant or destructive propensity manifested in their temper or dispositions, have attempted to put men to death for the sake of conferring on them some great fancied benefit, or under an impression that they are fulfilling the commands of an angel or of the Deity. . . . But there have been many cases of a different kind in which no lesion of intellect has been discovered: the individual affected has experienced no other mental change than a powerful impulse to commit an act destructive of life on some particular individual, against whom, even at the time of commission, it has sometimes appeared that he has entertained no malicious feeling. The fact seems improbable, but it is established by ample and unquestionable evidence. I shall cite some strong examples.

The following instances were published by M. Marc, and have already been alluded to by several writers. The facts display, as the author observes, a contest in the mind of the individual between the instinctive desire which constitutes the whole manifestation of disease, and the judgement of the understanding still unaffected and struggling against it.

"In a respectable house in Germany, the mother of the family returning home one day, met a servant, against whom she had no cause of complaint, in the greatest agitation; she begged to speak with her mistress alone, threw herself upon her knees, and entreated that she might be sent out of the house. Her mistress, astonished, inquired the reason, and learned that whenever this unhappy servant undressed the little child which she nursed, she was struck with the whiteness of its skin, and experienced the most irresistible desire to tear it in pieces. She felt afraid that she could not resist the desire, and preferred to leave the house." "This circumstance occurred about twenty years ago in the family of M. le Baron de Humboldt, and this illustrious person permitted me to add his testimony."

"A young lady," continues M. Marc, "whom I examined in one of the asylums of the capital, experienced a violent inclination to commit homicide, for which she could not assign any motive. She was rational on every subject, and whenever she felt the approach of this dreadful propensity, she entreated to have the strait-waistcoat put on, and to be carefully watched until the paroxysm, which sometimes lasted several days, had passed."

"M. R——, a distinguished chymist and a poet, of a disposition naturally mild and sociable, committed himself a prisoner in one of the asylums of the Fauxbourg St. Antoine." "Tormented by the desire of killing, he often prostrated himself at the foot of the altar, and implored the divine assistance to deliver him from such an atrocious propensity, and of the origin of which he could never render an account. When the patient felt that his will was likely to yield to the violence of this inclination, he hastened to the head of the establishment, and requested to have his thumbs tied together with a riband. This slight ligature was sufficient to calm the unhappy R., who, however, finished by endeavouring to commit homicide upon one of his friends, and perished in a violent fit of maniacal fury."

"A servant-maid, twenty-six or twenty-eight years of age, whose bodily functions were perfectly natural, nevertheless experienced at each period of the catamenia [menstruation – N.R.] a sort of excitement which did not apparently affect her judgment, but which rendered her extremely dangerous, since, without provocation, she menaced every person with her knife; and one day having realized her menaces, she was sent to a lunatic hospital."

The following instances of propensity to infanticide are given by Dr. Michu. In both cases the individuals were afflicted by the consciousness of their state, confessed it, and recovered without any sinister event.

"A countrywoman, twenty-four years of age, of a bilious sanguine temperament, of simple and regular habits, but reserved and sullen manners, had been ten days confined with her first child, when suddenly, having her eyes fixed upon it, she was seized with the desire of strangling it. This idea made her shudder; she carried the infant to its cradle, and went out in order to get rid of so horrid a thought. The cries of the little being, who required nourishment, recalled her to the house: she experienced still more strongly the impulse to destroy it. She hastened away again, haunted by the dread of committing a crime of which she had such horror; she raised her eyes to heaven, and went into a church to pray.

"This unhappy mother passed the whole day in a constant struggle between the desire of taking away the life of her infant, and the dread of yielding to the impulse. She concealed, until the evening, her agitations from her confessor, a respectable old man, the first who received her confidence, who, having talked to her in a soothing manner, advised her to have recourse to medical assistance.

"When we arrived at the patient's house, she appeared gloomy and low, and felt ashamed of her situation. Being reminded of the tenderness due from a mother to her child, she replied, 'I know how much a mother ought to love her child; but if I do not love mine, it does not depend upon me.' " . . .

On the whole it seems fully manifest that there is a form of insanity, existing independently of any lesion of the intellectual powers, in which, connected in some instances with evident constitutional disorder, in others with affections of the nervous system excited according to well-known laws of the animal economy, a sudden and often irresistible impulse is experienced to commit acts which under a sane condition of mind would be accounted atrocious crimes. . . .

It must be allowed that instances may and do occur in which the discrimination would be difficult between manifestations of insanity and acts of a criminal nature, and that this difficulty would be increased by the admission of a form of insanity free from hallucination or illusion. . . .

The difficulties with which administrators of justice have to contend in distinguishing crimes from the result of insane impulse will never be entirely removed, but they will be rendered much less important when the good sense of the community shall have produced the effect of abolishing all capital punishments. That this will sooner or later happen I entertain no doubt. Many persons have begun already to hesitate as to the moral rectitude of putting men to death in cases in which the powerful motive of self-defence cannot be pleaded, and when it is easy to keep the offending individual out of the way of committing further mischief. A single private individual would scarcely think himself justified in taking upon himself the office of the Almighty, and inflicting mortal punishment on a person whom he knew to have perpetrated a crime. If such an act would be, not meritorious, but culpable, when executed by one individual, it does not seem clear how it becomes more righteous when that person has any given number of accomplices, or in other words, what invests any number of individuals, say twelve men, over whom presides a thirteenth, with the right to put to death a fellow-creature who has incurred guilt. The community is but an aggregate of individuals. How comes such an aggregate of individuals to be possessed, morally, of the right to take away life, the plea of self-defence being precluded by the circumstances of the case?

Chapter 11

Daniel Hack Tuke: Case of moral insanity or congenital moral defect, 1885

Daniel Hack Tuke (1827–95) came from a long line of physicians associated with the York Retreat, an asylum for the mentally ill in northern England that was famous for its progressive approaches to treatment. After earning his medical degree, Daniel Hack Tuke began writing about the causes of insanity, treatment of the insane, and lunacy laws. Eventually he became superintendent of London's Bethlem Hospital and a co-editor of the *Journal of Mental Science*, England's chief journal on mental illnesses. His travels included a visit to North America that resulted in the article reproduced here and in a book, *The Insane in the United States and Canada* (1885).

This extract reprints nearly all of Daniel Hack Tuke, "Case of moral insanity or congenital moral defect, with commentary," originally published in the *Journal of Mental Science* 31 (October 1885): 360–6.

DANIEL HACK TUKE: CASE OF MORAL INSANITY OR CONGENITAL MORAL DEFECT

When I was at the Kingston Asylum, Ontario, last August, a male patient had just escaped from the institution, and made a criminal assault upon a little girl in the neighbourhood. From the inquiries I made, I found that the case was one of much interest in its bearing on moral insanity (or imbecility), and I was allowed to read the notes in the well-kept case-book of the asylum. Dr. Metcalf, the medical superintendent, has very kindly permitted me to make use of them, and the further particulars of this patient's history and acts, which he has given me. . . .

> W. B. was born at Swansea, Wales, on 26th June, 1843. In his tenth year he emigrated to Canada with his father, stepmother, and brothers. He was not known to his stepmother until about a fortnight before leaving for Canada, as he had been away at school. His stepmother states that he has been of a sullen disposition ever since she has known him; uncommunicative, idle, sly, and treacherous; that at an early age he evinced a

disposition to torture domestic animals, and to cruelly treat the younger members of the family.

On one occasion he took with him his young brother, a lad five or six years of age, ostensibly to pick berries, which grew wild, not far away. On arriving at a secluded spot, he removed the clothes from the child, and proceeded to whip him with long lithe willows, and, not satisfied with this, he bit and scratched the lad terribly about the arms and upper part of the body, threatening that if he made an out-cry he would kill him with a table-knife, which he had secretly brought with him. The cries of the boy attracted the attention of a labourer, who promptly came to the rescue, and in all probability saved the little fellow's life. Shortly after this act of cruelty to his brother, B. was apprehended for cutting the throat of a valuable horse belonging to a neighbour. For some little time prior to this act, considerable anxiety had been felt by people in the neighbourhood where B. lived, for their live-stock. Horses were unsafe at night in the pastures, as several had been found in the mornings with wounded throats. In the stables they were equally unsafe, as a valuable beast was killed in its stall in broad daylight. About this time, also, people in the neighbourhood observed an unaccountable decrease in the number of their fowls. When B. was apprehended for cutting the horse's throat, he confessed that he not only did this vile act, but also that he had maimed the other animals to which reference has been made, and that he had killed the fowls, twisted their necks, and then concealed them in wood piles, &c. For these offences he was sentenced to twelve months in gaol. When he returned home after serving out his sentence, his family were more suspicious of him, owing to past experience, and he was more carefully looked after. He was watched during the day, and locked in a separate room at night. These measures were necessary to protect the family, as he had made an effort to strangle a younger brother while occupying a dormitory with him.

One day, soon after his discharge from gaol, B.'s stepmother left a little child asleep upstairs while she proceeded with her household duties, not knowing that B. was in the house. In a short time afterwards she was informed by one of the other children that the baby was crying, and on going to the room where she had left the sleeping baby, she discovered that it had disappeared. B. had taken the little child to his own room, put it in his bed, and then piled a quantity of clothing, &c., on top of it. When rescued, the child was nearly suffocated, and was revived with difficulty. Immediately after this attempt to suffocate his baby sister, B. abstracted a considerable sum of money from his father's desk, and attempted to escape with it; he was re-captured, however, and the money taken from him. For this offence he was tried, found guilty, and sentenced to serve seven years in the Penitentiary. While serving out this sentence he was transferred to the criminal asylum connected with the prison, but on the expiration of his sentence he was discharged. On being released he crossed over to the United States, and enlisted in a cavalry regiment. In consequence of the horse assigned to him not being a good one, he was obliged to fall behind on a march, and, taking advantage of this, a favourable opportunity offering, he drove this animal into a deep morass, and belaboured the poor beast until it was fast in the mire, there he left it to its fate, and it was found dead the next morning. B. now deserted, and after undergoing some hardships, again returned home, where he was, as before, carefully watched.

His next escapade was the result of an accident. B. and his father were at a neighbour's one evening, and while paring apples, the old man accidentally cut his hand so severely as to cause the blood to flow profusely. B. was observed to become restless, nervous, pale, and to have undergone a peculiar change in demeanour. Taking advantage of the distraction produced by the accident, B. escaped from the house and proceeded to a neighbouring farm-yard, where he cut the throat of a horse, killing it.

Recognizing the gravity of his offence, he escaped to the woods, where he remained in concealment until circumstances enabled him to commit another and still graver crime. Observing a young girl approaching the wood, he waited until she came near to his hiding-place, when he rushed out, seized her, and committed a criminal assault on her; for this last crime he was condemned to be hanged, but the sentence was commuted to imprisonment for life. While serving sentence he was again transferred to the prison-asylum. After serving about ten years of his sentence he was pardoned; *why* he was pardoned remains a mystery. On his way home from prison, and when within a short distance of his father's house, he went into a pasture, caught a horse, tied it to a telegraph pole, and mutilated it in a shocking manner, cutting a terrible gash in its neck, another in its abdomen, and a piece off the end of its tongue. For this act of atrocity he was tried, and though there was no doubt of his guilt, he was acquitted on the ground of insanity, and by warrant of the Lieutenant-Governor transferred to the Kingston Asylum. He was received at the asylum on the 29th Sept., 1879, and placed under careful supervision.

On the 19th August, 1884, he made his escape while attending a patients' pic-nic. He had only been absent from the asylum about an hour, and while almost in sight of pursuing attendants, overtook a young girl whom he attempted to outrage. Her cries, however, brought help, and his designs were frustrated. For this offence he was handed over to the civil authorities, tried, convicted, and sentenced to six months in gaol. He is now serving out this sentence, and on its expiration will, no doubt, be released – to commit it is to be feared, more crimes. . . .

His grave offences have been enumerated in the preceding statement, but besides these, B. was guilty of very many minor offences, both while at home and while in the prison and asylum. While in the Criminal Asylum he attempted to castrate a poor imbecile inmate with an old shoe knife, which he had obtained in some unknown way. Another helpless imbecile he punctured in the abdomen with a tablefork until the omentum protruded; not satisfied with this, he bit the poor fellow, who had not even sense enough to cry out, in many places over the abdomen and chest.

He killed many small animals and birds, such as dogs, cats, doves, fowls, &c. He taught many innocent patients to masturbate, and introduced even more vicious habits. . . .

If so situated that he could not indulge his evil propensities, he was a quiet and useful man, but he could never be trusted. He had a fair education, and enjoyed reading newspapers, letters, etc., sent to him.

It is very doubtful if he entertained much affection for anyone. He seemed to like his stepmother better than anyone else, but even she, who had been a mother to him since early boyhood, he, according to his own confession, planned to outrage.

Commentary. – I would point out the great interest of this case over and above the moral insanity or congenital defect of the moral sense under which this man labours, in regard to the influence of blood upon him. There can be no doubt that with some individuals it constitutes a fascination. If it be allowable to add to our psychological terms, we might speak of a *mania sanguinis.* Dr. Savage admitted a man from France into Bethlem Hospital some time ago, in a state of acute mania, one of whose earliest symptoms of insanity was the thirst for blood, which he endeavoured to satisfy by going to an abattoir in Paris. The man whose case I have brought forward had the same passion for gloating over blood, but had no attack of acute mania. The sight of blood when he cut the horse's throat was distinctly a delight to him, and at any time blood aroused in him the worst elements of his nature. Instances will easily be recalled in which murderers, undoubtedly insane, have described the intense pleasure they experienced in the warm blood of children. Is it not a more scientific proceeding to recognise and study this taste for blood than to deny its existence as a moral insanity?

In reference to moral imbeciles, I would cite the opinion of Dr. Kerlin, because his views as to educating them are very striking and important, coming as they do from the head of an institution for idiots. He says, in his last Annual Report: – "It is a mournful conclusion that has been reached after twenty-five years of experience, that in every institution of this kind, and probably to a far greater extent in our refuges and charity schools, there exists a class of children to whom the offices of a school-room should not be applied; these are the so-called moral idiots, or juvenile insane, who are often precocious in their ability to receive instruction, but whose moral infirmity is radical and incurable. The early detection of these cases is not difficult; they should be subjects for life-long detention; their existence can be made happy and useful, and they will train into comparative docility and harmlessness if kept under a uniform, temperate, and positive restriction. The school-room fosters the ill we would cure; in teaching them to write we give them an illimitable power of mischief – in educating them at all, except to physical work, we are adding to their armament of deception and misdemeanour." . . .

The practical question which presents itself is that of punishment. If we could but free ourselves for a moment from the legal questions connected with such a case as that I have narrated, we should surely be more able to study it from a purely pathological standpoint. We are still, it seems to me, if I might use a theological term, under the curse of the law. Is it not, then, true that men are born with organizations which prompt them to the commission of acts like those committed by this unfortunate man, and that the lower instincts are in abnormal force, or the controlling power is weak? Such a man as this is a reversion to an old savage type, and is born by accident in the wrong century. He would have had sufficient scope for his bloodthirsty propensities, and been in harmony with his environment, in a barbaric age, or at the present day in certain parts of Africa, but he cannot be tolerated now as a member of civilized society. But what is to be done with the man who, from no fault of his own, is born in the nineteenth instead of a long-past century? Are we to punish him for his involuntary anachronism? It is scarcely possible to conceive a more delicate question for medical or legal adjudication than whether the man who commits a crime is an example of vice, or whether he has so far passed beyond the influence of deterrent motives that he is morally irresponsible for the act.

Chapter 12

Richard von Krafft-Ebing: Pathological sexuality, 1892

Richard von Krafft-Ebing (1840–1902), the Austro-German psychiatrist and teacher, wrote *Psychopathia Sexualis*, one of the first scientific studies of sexual deviation. Although Krafft-Ebing was not directly concerned with criminality, his subject matter – encompassing rape, homosexuality (at the time a criminal offense), and bestiality, among other offenses – naturally touched on the causes of crime and criminal responsibility. Thus, *Psychopathia Sexualis* can be considered the first text to systematically explore sexual offenses, even though that was not Krafft-Ebing's primary aim. He took the book through twelve editions, and it was widely translated, becoming perhaps the most widely read work on sexuality before Freud.

Krafft-Ebing collected cases in the course of his psychiatric practice and from books such as those written by the Italian psychiatrist and criminologist Cesare Lombroso. Although he is at times moralistic, he tries to discuss his examples dispassionately and objectively.

Krafft-Ebing believed that sexual abnormalities were on the increase due to "degeneration," a hereditary tendency to develop constitutional abnormalities that was much discussed in the late nineteenth century (see Part IV). Problems with the central nervous system, he explains, naturally lead to problems with other parts of the body, including the sexual organs. Degeneration, in turn, is brought on in part by urbanization, with big-city life causing sexual overstimulation and leading as well to self-indulgence and dissipation.

The following passages were chosen to give readers a sense of the richness of *Psychopathia Sexualis* and its multidimensionality. In the first passage, Krafft-Ebing generally explains the origins of sexual abnormality and reasons for its recent increase. Next he discusses sadism (the conjunction of lust with cruelty), explaining its origins and relating it to more ordinary behavior. The following extract, illustrating his approach to classification, analyzes cases of lust-murder, including several involving anthropophagy or the eating of the victim after lust-murder. Another excerpt illustrates Krafft-Ebing's approach to the legal implications of pathological sexuality. He calls for close cooperation between judges and psychiatrists in determinations of criminal responsibility in sex-crime cases. Then, to exemplify his approach to specific legal matters, I excerpt material pertaining to Austrian law against rape and lust-murder, child sexual abuse, and bestiality.

The extracts come from an 1892 English translation of the seventh German edition of *Psychopathia Sexualis* (Philadelphia and London: The F. A. David Co.), pp. 34, 49, 57–64, 378–9, 397, and 402–5. When Krafft-Ebing describes a case, he uses smaller type and block quotations; I reproduce this method by putting his cases (some numbered, some not) into block quotations.

RICHARD VON KRAFFT-EBING: PATHOLOGICAL SEXUALITY

Abnormality of the sexual functions proves to be especially frequent in civilized races. This fact is explained in part by the frequent abuse of the sexual organs, and in part by the circumstance that such functional anomalies are often the signs of an abnormal constitution of the central nervous system, which is, for the most part, hereditary ("functional signs of degeneration").

Since the generative organs stand in important functional connection with the entire nervous system, and especially with its psychical and somatic functions, it is easy to understand the frequency of general neuroses and psychoses arising in sexual (functional or organic) disturbances. . . .

Those living in large cities, who are constantly reminded of sexual things and incited to sexual enjoyment, certainly have more sexual desire than those living in the country. A dissipated, luxurious, sedentary manner of life, preponderance of animal food, and the consumption of spirits, spices, etc., have a stimulating influence on the sexual life. In woman the sexual inclination is post-menstrually increased. At this time, in neuropathic women, the excitement may reach a pathological degree. . . .

Association of active cruelty and violence with lust – sadism

That lust and cruelty frequently occur together is a fact that has long been recognized and not infrequently observed. Writers of all kinds have called attention to this phenomenon. . . .

In an attempt to explain the association of lust and cruelty, it is necessary to return to a consideration of the quasi-physiological cases, in which, at the moment of most intense lust, very excitable individuals, who are otherwise normal, commit such acts as biting and scratching, which are usually the result of anger. It must further be remembered that love and anger are not only the most intense emotions, but also the only two forms of active (sthenic) emotion. Both seek their object, try to possess themselves of it, and naturally exhaust themselves in a physical effect on it; both throw the psycho-motor sphere into the most intense excitement, and thus, by means of this excitation, reach their normal expression.

From this stand-point it is clear how lust impels to acts that otherwise are expressive of anger. The one, like the other, is a state of exaltation, an intense excitation of the whole psycho-motor sphere. Thus there arises an impulse to react on the object that induces the stimulus, in every possible way, and with the greatest intensity. . . .

Through such cases of infliction of pain, during the most intense emotion of lust, we approach the cases in which a real injury, wound, or death, is inflicted on the victim. In these cases, the impulse to cruelty, which may accompany the emotion of lust, becomes unbounded in a psychopathic individual; and, at the same time, owing to defect of moral feeling, all normal inhibitory ideas are absent or weakened. Such monstrous, sadistic acts have, however, in men, in whom they are much more frequent than in women, another source in physiological conditions. In the intercourse of the sexes, the active or aggressive *rôle* belongs to man; woman remains passive, defensive. It affords a man great pleasure to win a woman, to conquer her; and in the *ars amandi*, the modesty of a woman who keeps herself on the defensive until the moment of surrender, is an element of great psychological significance and importance. Under normal conditions a man meets obstacles which it is his part to overcome, and for which nature has given him an aggressive character. This aggressive character, however, under pathological conditions, may likewise be excessively developed, and express itself in an impulse to subdue absolutely the object of desire, even to destroy or kill it. . . .

Sadism is thus nothing else than an excessive and monstrous pathological intensification of phenomena, – possible, too, in normal conditions in rudimental forms, – which accompany the psychical vita sexualis, particularly in males. . . .

Lust-murder (lust potentiated as cruelty, murderous lust extending to anthropophagy)

The most horrible example, and one which most pointedly shows the connection between lust and a desire to kill, is the case of Andreas Bichel. . . .

> With reference to one of his victims, at his examination he expressed himself as follows: "I opened her breast and with a knife cut through the fleshy parts of the body. Then I arranged the body as a butcher does a beef, and hacked it with an axe into pieces of a size to fit the hole which I had prepared up in the mountain for burying it. I may say that while opening the body I was so greedy that I trembled, and could have cut out a piece and eaten it."

> Lombroso, too, mentions cases falling in the same category. A certain Phillipe indulged in choking prostitutes, post-actum, and said: "I am

fond of women, but it is sport for me to choke them after having enjoyed them." . . .

It cannot be doubted, from what has gone before, that a great number of so-called lust-murders depend upon a combination of hyperæsthesia and paræsthesia sexualis. As a result of this perverse coloring of the feelings, further acts of bestiality with the body may result, – e.g., cutting it up and wallowing in the intestines. . . .

> Case 18. Alton, a clerk in England, goes out of town for a walk. He lures a child into a thicket, and returns after a time to his office, where he makes this entry in his note-book: "Killed to-day a young girl; it was fine and hot." The child was missed, searched for, and found cut into pieces. Many parts, and among them the genitals, could not be found. A. did not show the slightest trace of emotion, and gave no explanation of the motive or circumstances of his horrible deed. He was a psychopathic individual, and occasionally subject to states of depression with tædium vitæ. His father had had one attack of acute mania. A near relative suffered from mania with homicidal impulses. A. was executed.

In such cases it may even happen that appetite for the flesh of the murdered victim arises, and, in consequence of this perverse coloring of the idea, parts of the body may be eaten.

> Case 19. Leger, vine-dresser, aged 24. From youth moody, silent, shy of people. He starts out in search of a situation. He wanders about eight days in the forest, there catches a girl twelve years old, violates her, mutilates her genitals, tears out her heart, eats of it, drinks the blood, and buries the remains. Arrested, at first he lied, but finally confessed his crime with cynical cold-bloodedness. He listened to his sentence of death with indifference, and was executed. At the post-mortem examination, Esquirol found morbid adhesions between the cerebral membranes and the brain. . . .

Pathological sexuality in its legal aspects

The laws of all civilized nations punish those who commit perverse sexual acts. Inasmuch as the preservation of chastity and morals is one of the most important reasons for the existence of the commonwealth, the state cannot be too careful, as a protector of morality, in the struggle against sensuality. This contest is unequal; because only a certain number of the sexual crimes can be legally combated, and the infractions of the laws by so powerful a natural instinct can be but little influenced by punishment. It also lies in the nature of the sexual crimes, that but a part of them ever reach the knowledge of the authorities. Public sentiment, in that it looks upon them as disgraceful, lends much aid.

Criminal statistics prove the sad fact that sexual crimes are progressively increasing in our modern civilization. This is particularly the case with immoral acts with children under the age of fourteen. The moralist sees in these sad facts nothing but the decay of general morality, and in some instances comes to the conclusion that the present mildness of the laws punishing sexual crimes, in comparison with their severity in past centuries, is in part responsible for this.

The medical investigator is driven to the conclusion that this manifestation of modern social life stands in relation to the predominating nervousness of later generations, in that it begets defective individuals, excites the sexual instinct, leads to sexual abuse, and, with continuance of lasciviousness associated with diminished sexual power, induces perverse sexual acts.

It will be clearly seen, from what follows, how such an opinion is justified, especially with respect of the increasing number of sexual crimes committed on children. It is at once evident, from what has gone before, that neuropathic, and even psychopathic, states are largely determinate for the commission of sexual crimes. Here nothing less than the responsibility of many of the men who commit such crimes is called in question.

Psychiatry cannot be denied the credit of having recognized and proved the psycho-pathological significance of numerous monstrous, paradoxical sexual acts. Law and Jurisprudence have thus far given but little attention to the facts resulting from investigations in psychopathology. Law is, in this, opposed to Medicine, and is constantly in danger of passing judgment on individuals who, in the light of science, are not responsible for their acts.

Owing to this superficial treatment of acts that deeply concern the interests and welfare of society, it becomes very easy for justice to treat a delinquent, who is as dangerous to society as a murderer or a wild beast, as a criminal, and, after punishment, release him to prey on society again; on the other hand, scientific investigation shows that a man mentally and sexually degenerate *ab origine*, and therefore irresponsible, must be removed from society for life, but not as a punishment.

A judge who considers only the crime, and not its perpetrator, is always in danger of injuring not only important interests of society (general morality and safety), but also those of the individual (honor).

In no domain of criminal law is co-operation of judge and medical expert so much to be desired as in that of sexual delinquencies; and here only anthropological and clinical investigation can afford light and knowledge. The nature of the act can never, in itself, determine a decision as to whether it lies within the limits of mental pathology, or within the bounds of mental physiology. The perverse act does not indicate perversion of instinct. At any rate, the most monstrous and perverse sexual acts have been committed by persons of sound mind. The perversion of feeling must be shown to be pathological. . . .

Rape and lust-murder
(Austrian Statutes, § 125, 127; Austrian Abridgment, § 192;
German Statutes, § 177.)

By the term rape, the jurist understands coitus, outside of the marriage relation, with an adult, enforced by means of threats or violence; or with an adult in a condition of defenselessness or unconsciousness; or with a girl under the age of fourteen years. Immissio penis, or, at least, conjunctio membrorum (Schütze), is necessary to establish the fact. To-day, rape on children is remarkably frequent. Hofmann and Tardieu report horrible cases.

The latter establishes the fact that, from 1851 to 1875 inclusive, 22,017 cases of rape came before the courts in France, and, of these, 17,657 were committed on children.

The crime of rape presumes a temporary, powerful excitation of sexual desire, induced by excess in alcohol, or by some other condition. It is highly improbable that a man morally intact would commit this most brutal crime. Lombroso considers the majority of men who commit rape to be degenerate, particularly when the crime is done on children or old women. He asserts that, in many such men, he has found actual signs of degeneracy.

It is a fact that rape is very often the act of degenerate male imbeciles, where, under some circumstances, the bond of blood is not respected. . . .

Violation of individuals under the age of fourteen
(Austrian Statutes, §128, 132; Austrian Abridgment, § 189, 191;
German Statutes, § 174, 176)

By violation of sexually immature individuals, the jurist understands all the possible immoral acts with persons under fourteen years of age that are not comprehended in the term rape. The term violation, in the legal sense of the word, comprehends the most horrible perversions and acts, which are possible only to a man who is controlled by lust and morally weak, and, as is usually the case, lacking in sexual power.

A common feature of these crimes, committed on persons that are more or less children, is that they are unmanly, childish, and often silly. It is a fact that such acts, with exceptions in pathological cases, like those of imbeciles, paretics, and senile dements, are almost exclusively committed by young men who lack courage or have no faith in their virility; or by roués who have, to some extent, lost their virility. It is psychologically incomprehensible that an adult of full virility, and mentally sound, should indulge in sexual abuses with children.

The imagination of debauchees, in actively or passively picturing the immoral acts, is exceedingly lively; and that the following enumeration of the sexual acts of this kind known to law exhausts all the possibilities is questionable. Most frequently the abuse consists of sexual handling (under some circumstances, flagellation), active manustupration, or seducing children by inducing them to perform onanism, or lustful handling, on the seducer. Less frequent acts are cunnilingus, irrumare on boys or girls, pædicatio puellarum, coitus inter femora, and exhibition. . . .

> Case 186. X., priest, aged 40. He was accused of enticing girls, aged from ten to thirteen, undressing and fondling them lustfully, and finally masturbating. He is tainted, and has been an onanist from childhood; morally imbecile; always very excitable sexually. Head somewhat small. Penis unusually large; indications of hypospadiasis. . . .

Unfortunately it must be admitted that the most revolting of these crimes are done by sane individuals who, by reason of satiety in normal sexual indulgence, lasciviousness, and brutality, and not seldom during intoxication, forget that they are human beings.

A great number of these cases, however, certainly depend upon pathological states. This is particularly true where old men become the seducers of children. . . .

Unnatural abuse – sodomy
(Austrian Statutes, § 129; Abridgment, § 190; German Statutes, § 175.)

Violation of animals – bestiality
Violation of animals, monstrous and revolting as it seems to mankind, is by no means always due to psycho-pathological conditions. Low morality and great sexual desire, with lack of opportunity of natural indulgence, are the principal motives of this unnatural means of sexual satisfaction, which is resorted to by women as well as by men.

> To Polak we owe the knowledge that in Persia bestiality is frequently practiced because of the delusion that it cures gonorrhœa; just as in Europe an idea is still prevalent that intercourse with children heals venereal disease.
>
> Experience teaches that bestiality with cows and horses is none too infrequent. Occasionally the acts may be undertaken with goats, bitches, and, as a case of Tardieu's and one by Schanenstein show, with hens.
>
> The action of Frederick the Great, in the case of a cavalryman who had committed bestiality with a mare, is well known: "The fellow is a beast, and shall be reduced to the infantry."

The intercourse of females with beasts is limited to dogs. A monstrous example of the moral depravity in large cities is related by Maschka, – the case of a Parisian female who showed herself in the sexual act with a trained bull-dog, to a secret circle of *roués*, at 10 franes a head.

There has been, heretofore, but little legal consideration of the mental condition in those given to violation of animals. In several cases known to the writer, the individuals were weak-minded. In Schauenstein's case there was insanity. . . .

Case 190. *Impulsive Sodomy*. – A., aged 16; gardener's boy; born out of wedlock; father, unknown; mother, deeply tainted, hystero-epileptic. A. has a deformed, asymmetrical cranium, and deformity and asymmetry of the bones of the face; the whole skeleton is also deformed, asymmetrical, and small. From childhood he was a masturbator; always morose, apathetic, and fond of solitude; very irritable, and pathological in his emotional reaction. He is imbecile, probably much reduced physically by masturbation, and neurasthenic. Besides, he presents hysteropathic symptoms (limitation of the visual field, dyschromatopsia; diminution of the senses of smell, taste, and hearing on the right side; anæsthesia of the right testicle, clavus, etc.).

A. is convicted of having committed masturbation and sodomy on dogs and rabbits. When twelve years old he saw how boys masturbated a dog. He imitated it, and thereafter he could not keep from abusing dogs, cats, and rabbits in this vile manner. Much more frequently, however, he committed sodomy on female rabbits, – the only animal that had a charm for him. At dusk he was accustomed to repair to his master's rabbit-pen, in order to gratify his vile desire. Rabbits with torn rectums were repeatedly found. The act of bestiality was always done in the same manner. There were actual attacks which came on every eight weeks, always in the evening, and always in the same way. A. would become very uncomfortable, and have a feeling as if some one were pounding his head. He felt as if losing his reason. He struggled against the imperative idea of committing sodomy with the rabbits, and thus had an increasing feeling of fear and intensification of headache, until it became unbearable. At the height of the attack there was sound of bells, cold perspiration, trembling of the knees, and, finally, loss of resistive power, and impulsive performance of the perverse act. As soon as this was done, he lost all anxiety; the nervous cycle was completed, and he was again master of himself, deeply ashamed of the deed, and fearful of the return of an attack. A. states that, in such a condition, if called upon to choose between a woman and a female rabbit, he could make choice only of the latter. In the intervals, of all domestic animals, he is partial only to rabbits. In his exceptional states simple caressing or kissing, etc., of the rabbit suffices, as a rule, to afford him sexual satisfaction; but sometimes he has, when doing this, such furor sexualis that he is forced to wildly perform sodomy on the animal.

The acts of bestiality mentioned are the only acts which afford him sexual satisfaction, and they constitute the only manner in which he is capable of sexual indulgence. A. states that, in the act, he never had a lustful feeling, but satisfaction, inasmuch as he was thus freed from the painful condition into which he was brought by the imperative impulse.

The medical evidence easily proved that this human monster was a psychically degenerate, irresponsible invalid, and not a criminal.

Chapter 13

Cesare Lombroso: Insanity and crime, 1876, 1884, and 1889

Cesare Lombroso (1835–1909), the Italian physician and psychiatrist, is generally recognized as the founder of the field of criminology, for he was the first person to insist that the scientific study of crime and criminals could lead to definitive information on the causes of crime. Lombroso set forth the results of his own and others' scientific research in *L'uomo delinquente* or *Criminal Man* in 1876. Constantly modifying his theories in light of new evidence, he took this classic text through four further editions (1878, 1884, 1889, and 1896–7), works that were widely translated and disseminated around the globe.

At the core of Lombroso's teachings was the notion of the born criminal, a biological throwback to an earlier evolutionary stage, marked by physical and mental anomalies and doomed to constantly break the law. Clearly, evolutionary theory powerfully shaped Lombroso's thinking. However, his thought was also shaped by other major nineteenth-century understandings of deviance, including moral insanity and degeneration. As a psychiatrist specializing in cases of criminal insanity, Lombroso was particularly drawn to mental-disease explanations of crime.

In the following passages from the first, third, and fourth editions of his magnum opus (1876, 1884, and 1889), Lombroso sets forth his ideas about the relationship between crime, mental disease, and moral insanity. The extracts come from a new translation of *Criminal Man* by Mary Gibson and Nicole Hahn Rafter (Durham, NC: Duke University Press, 2006), pp. 81–4, 188–90, 212–18, and 271–3.

CESARE LOMBROSO: INSANITY AND CRIME

From the first edition of *Criminal Man* (1876)

Insanity and Crime

Few would doubt that crime is often caused by cerebral afflictions and, above all, madness. Many well-known criminals, including Verger, Villet, and

Schults, not only had insane relatives but themselves exhibited signs of madness. In a sample of 290 criminals, I found 3 with epilepsy, 2 with imbecility, 4 with partial paralysis, 1 with delirium tremens, 3 with facial convulsions, 4 with continual headaches, and 4 in a full state of insanity. In all, those with severe neuropathic diseases amounted to 7.2 percent of the sample; but the true level would be higher had I included the 11 percent with degeneracy of the temple arteries and the 3 percent with unequal pupil size (often an indication of incipient paralysis). . . .

The same factors create a predisposition to both crime and madness: civilization, celibacy, a hot climate, being male, living in an urban area, and working at certain jobs (shoemaker, cook, domestic servant, and, perhaps, soldier). Many criminals have insane relatives; and in many the tendency to crime or madness is provoked by trauma, anomalies of the head, and liquor. Meteorological conditions, especially heat, influence both murderers and the mad. Thomson [J. B. Thomson; see Chapter 17 – N.R.] has noted that both criminals and the insane tend to succumb to illnesses like meningitis, softening of the brain, and sleepwalking. Moreover, many of the insane present the same physical deformities as criminals: abnormal ears, scanty beards, filmy and wandering eyes, darkened skin, headaches, and arrested physical development. Like the insane, some criminals are completely insensitive to pain; and members of both group exhibit emotional imbalance, manifesting great affection for their friends, children, or a lover, but very little for their family.

But the opposite is also true. Criminals and the mad frequently lack affection entirely, showing neither pity nor benevolence nor remorse. They are capable of eating and dancing near the cadaver of their victim, all the while boasting of their crime. In addition, they manifest little affection for their companions. . . .

There are cases in which madness is simply a criminal tendency, a lack of any sense of morality. The English call this moral insanity. In general, victims of moral insanity are born to mad or neuropathic parents, suffer nervous disease or hallucinations beginning in childhood, and experience emotions in a bizarre way. They hate and sometimes kill their own children or fathers for the slightest reason. Not only do they commit crimes without feeling any remorse, they say so. They are amazed to discover that others have feelings. Nevertheless, even in childhood they are precociously intelligent and unusually active. . . .

Mentally ill criminals sometimes simulate madness at the suggestion of others, but they are seldom convincing since they try to imitate insane rages or complete imbecility. Like true criminals, they feel no remorse; but they confess everything, while true criminals hide it. And while criminals know their behavior is loathsome to the general public, the mentally ill are seldom capable of making that realization . . . .

Instead of trying to hide their misdeeds, mad criminals chat about them with pleasure and describe them in their autobiographies. This is not because they are impudent or filled with false pride, but because they are confident of their innocence, believing themselves to have acted in self-defense and even to have behaved meritoriously.

From the third edition of *Criminal Man* (1884)

Moral insanity and crime among children

. . . Children lack any sense of morality in the first months and even the first year of their lives. Good and evil for them is that which is permitted or prohibited by their parents. On their own, they have no sense of what is bad; only when they have been punished and told what is wrong do they start to develop a sense of justice and property. The first sign of a moral sense comes when they register a certain tone of their parents' voice, understand the meaning of reprimand, and begin to obey out of fear or habit.

Self-interest, strong feeling, the development of the intelligence, and reflection teach the child the difference between good and evil. The most effective means of instruction are kindness, good examples, and inculcation of fear of reprimand. These approaches help mold the child's moral conscience. He will be more or less inclined to develop it according to his own capacity and circumstances.

Moral insanity and born criminality

The cultivated reader will no doubt resist my identification of the morally insane with born criminals. . . . But . . . it is impossible to differentiate between insanity and crime now that researchers are uniting in support of criminal insane asylums and discovering cases, such as those of Verzeni, Guiteau, and Sbro . . . that prove the similarity between the two conditions. In addition, authors like Krafft-Ebing, Holländer, Savage, and Mendel have recently outlined the characteristics of moral insanity. I myself have found that both groups exhibit similar anomalies including insensitivity, analgesia, abnormal reflexes, left-handedness, and atypia of the cranium and brain. . . .

Like criminality, moral insanity appears to be extremely rare among women. However, prostitution constitutes a sort of equivalent to both crime and moral insanity, at the same time serving as a safety valve for both.

Classic cases of moral insanity reveal a cluster of characteristics resembling those of the born criminal.

Skulls. First Morel, then Legrand de Saulle, and now Krafft-Ebing have found among the morally insane skulls that are small and pointed, extremely large, elongated or abnormally round, or that exhibit bony crests. The faces of the morally insane display asymmetry between the two halves, thick lips, large mouths, malformed teeth with premature losses in the worst cases, and flattened, misshapen, or bifurcated roofs of the mouth. The ears of the morally insane are often large and unequal in size. We have already come across these abnormalities, particularly those of the skull, among criminals.

Physiognomy. The physiognomy of morally insane offenders reveals that they have all the characteristics of the criminal man: large jaws, facial asymmetry, unequal ears, scanty beards in men, and virile physiognomy in women. In the photographs from the *Album of German Criminals*, four out of the six morally insane individuals display the true criminal type.

Although the morally insane in general present fewer cranial and facial abnormalities than born criminals, this is because moral insanity is brought on by typhoid and other illnesses and tends to develop later in life. Thus the morally insane acquire their sinister physiognomy more slowly than born criminals. For criminals living in the midst of evil companions from infancy, environment shapes the face and gives them all a similar aspect, especially when communal life continues in reformatories and prisons. Fear of being caught and the anxiety of a life spent outside the law also mold their expression. . . .

Sexuality. Among the morally insane, Krafft-Ebing has observed early signs of sexual perversion and sexual overindulgence followed by impotence, a phenomenon I have seen in criminals. "The sexual impulses of the morally insane," Krafft-Ebing continues, "are often precocious or unnatural and preceded or accompanied by a ferocious bloodlust."

Moral Sense. In the realm of moral character, the analogy between criminals and the morally insane is incontestable. According to my fellow psychiatrist Battanoli (*Relazione statistica di San Servolo*, Venice, 1880), "The morally insane are unhappy about the madness in their blood, something they have had since conception and that was nourished at the maternal breast. They lack sentiments of affection and moral sense. They are born to savor evil and commit it. Always at war with society, they believe they are its victims. Easily influenced and therefore very dangerous, they often figure in political revolutions." He describes two morally insane patients as follows: "Both are bright and comprehending, with ready memories; they are both egoists, lacking feelings of affection. Concerned only with the present, they care nothing for the future." . . .

Heredity. The most solid proof of the similarity between moral insanity and crime lies in the etiology of these disorders. Both born criminals and the morally insane manifest their tendencies from infancy or puberty. Savage, Mendel, and Krafft-Ebing have identified an early form of moral insanity that appears between the ages of five and eleven years in the form of thefts, an eccentric aversion to family life, disinterest in education, cruelty toward animals and fellow students, lying, cunning, cynicism in concealing misdeeds, and sexual precocity, especially masturbation.

Many of the morally insane have mad parents. This is also true of the insane, although the proportions are smaller. In addition, the morally insane have a greater proportion of egotistic, vice-ridden, and criminal relatives than do common madmen.

From the fourth edition of *Criminal Man* (1889)

Biology and psychology of insane criminals

I examined one hundred photographs of insane criminals, who were mad before committing their crimes and not epileptic. These photographs reveal that 44 percent of these insane criminals embody the full criminal type, which is marked by five or six degenerative characteristics, particularly jug ears, enlarged sinuses, large jaws and cheekbones, sullen or crossed eyes, and thin upper lips. This is a higher proportion than for criminals in general.

Etiological and somatic similarities demonstrate that insanity and criminality are so closely linked as to be nearly identical. The same factors predispose individuals to either insanity or criminality: civilization, celibacy, hot climate, being male, urban residence, and membership in certain professions (such as cobbler, cook, domestic, and, perhaps, soldier). Moreover, many criminals have insane relatives. Crime and insanity are both provoked by trauma, cranial malformations, and alcoholism. Among the insane as among murderers, meteorological conditions – especially hot temperatures – bring on abnormal behavior and fits. According to Thomson, both madmen and criminals are prone to such illnesses as meningitis, softening of the brain, and somnambulism. . . .

Certain types of insanity lie at the root of specific subcategories of criminality. For example, the mental aberrations of *pyromania* and *homicidal monomania* lead to the crimes of arson and murder, respectively. Women often steal impulsively due to *kleptomania*, a tendency to appropriate things that are of little use or value and that are usually returned. Degeneration causes these psychological disorders, which are symptoms of defective sentiments and instincts that obstruct the development of a resolute character and weaken the subject's resistance to impulse. . . .

Kleptomania. The legal category of theft corresponds to the psychiatric diagnoses of kleptomania. Although many experts deny the reality of kleptomania, it occurs so frequently that it must exist. Krafft-Ebing writes that "kleptomania, a symptom of mania or a similar state, is often observed in pregnant women, who suffer from so-called needs; the things they desire can be food, precious objects, or anything at all. Kleptomania also occurs frequently in women with nervous illnesses, especially hysteria, which can inspire them to swallow inedible or even repugnant substances such as straw, wood, sand, and human flesh. It is common in individuals who suffer psychological depression linked to fixed ideas. Then again, theft of valuable objects may be rooted in maniacal excitement."

Sexual Inversion. The crimes of rape and pederasty may be caused by sexual inversion (*Conträre Sexualempfindung*, to use Krafft-Ebing's term). When the erotic impulses of an individual do not correspond to his physical constitution, he seeks sexual satisfaction among his own kind. Sexual inversion leads not only to perverted lust (pederasty and lesbianism) but also to a morbid propensity for platonic love and idealization of individuals of the same sex. This strange anomaly often shapes the person's entire psychology.

Chapter 14

Cesare Lombroso and Guglielmo Ferrero: Epileptic criminals and the morally insane, 1893

Cesare Lombroso was not only the first criminologist; he was also the first criminologist to devote extensive attention to the topic of female criminality. From the first edition of *Criminal Man* (1876) onward, Lombroso included data on female as well as male criminals, recognizing women's much lower rates of offending and attempting to account for this difference. When he eventually decided to publish a separate volume on female criminals, he invited a young scholar, Guglielmo Ferrero, to assist him with the project and generously gave Ferrero co-authorship. (Years later, Ferrero married Lombroso's daughter, Gina.) The result was *La donna delinquente, la prostituta e la donna normale*, or *Criminal Woman, the Prostitute, and the Normal Woman* (1893). The work was quickly translated into English as *The Female Offender* (1895), and it remained one of the very few studies of female criminality until the 1970s. It is a complex book and not easily summarized, but if it has one central theme, it is that of female inferiority: women are less criminal than men (and less susceptible to mental diseases) because they have simpler brains.

As in *Criminal Man*, in *Criminal Woman* Lombroso wove togther major strands of European theory about the causes of deviance, including evolutionism, the notion of moral insanity, and degeneration theory (the idea that some people devolve or go backward down the evolutionary scale). In addition, a few years before he began writing *Criminal Woman*, he joined other European psychiatrists in also recognizing epilepsy as a significant cause of crime and, perhaps, the fundamental cause of mental illness and moral insanity as well. (Like other psychiatrists of his day, Lombroso spoke of hidden epilepsy or very small convulsions that only trained doctors could detect.) In the following passages, he first explores the relationship of epilepsy to moral insanity and criminality. He then describes actual cases of morally insane women, most of whom were so-labeled due to sexual deviance.

These extracts come from a new translation of *Criminal Woman* by Nicole Hahn Rafter and Mary Gibson (Durham, NC: Duke University Press, 2004), pp. 231–3.

CESARE LOMBROSO AND GUGLIELMO FERRERO: EPILEPTIC CRIMINALS AND THE MORALLY INSANE

Epileptic criminals

The same relationship that we have found in men between moral insanity and epilepsy also appears among women. The main difference is that epilepsy and moral insanity are much rarer among female than male prisoners. Marro reported that motor epilepsy occurs about one-third less frequently in female than male criminals. Rarer still in women is psychological epilepsy, or epileptic insanity. Epilepsy is relatively infrequent not only among female prisoners but also women who are inmates of insane asylums.

The extraordinary difference between male and female rates of epilepsy can only be explained by women's cerebral cortex. Although their cerebral cortex is as irritable as men's in its motor centers, it is much less so in its psychological centers, precisely because there are fewer of these.

Moral insanity, too, is more prevalent among men than women; and moral insanity is closely linked to both inborn criminality and epilepsy. The relative rarity among women of epileptic insanity and moral insanity helps explain why women are so much more often merely occasional criminals and why, even when they are criminals from passion, they so seldom commit crimes in one of those sudden impulses which are always partially epileptoid. It also helps explain why women who commit ordinary crimes premeditate and gloat in a way incompatible with offenses that spring instantaneously from an epileptic seizure. Further, women's lower rate of epilepsy sheds light on the slow reactions of the female offender; and while it indirectly confirms our theory of the link between congenital criminality and epilepsy, it works as well to explain sexual differences in offense rates.

In the few instances of female born criminals, I have always been able to find signs of epilepsy, as in male born criminals. In the most serious female offenders, motor forms of epilepsy are rarer than in men while the psychological forms predominate. One example is that of Maria Br.: age 47; face of the Mongolian type; cranial capacity 1,426; sense of touch somewhat dull; slight insensibility to pain; vision affected by peripheral scotomata in the internal superior quadrant. From youth she had drunk five or six litres of wine a day, plus eight glasses of liquor. At the age of twenty she stole a thousand lire, which she squandered on fancy clothes and drink. Later, she wounded a lover who had deserted her for another woman. This woman has no idea that she is epileptic, yet many times when working in the kitchen she has cut her hand without realizing it. She has become dizzy for no reason and fallen to the ground; and on three occasions she had psychological fits. On one of these occasions, when ordered by her mistress to carry the night soil to the latrine, she instead headed toward the bureau and attempted to open the drawers, complaining that she was unable to do it. On another occasion, she made a chain of three clean shirts and hung them from the kitchen chimney, not to hide them but only because she had no idea what she was doing. On the third occasion, she tried to light the fire with a fifty-lire note and would have succeeded if her mistress had not snatched it from her hand. She has no direct memory of these fits, just as she had no consciousness of them at the time, and relates the incidents as they were told to her. . . .

Morally insane women

In 1888 in Italian insane asylums there were 148 cases of moral insanity, of which 105 were male and 43 female, or 40.9 women for every 100 men. Noncriminal morally insane women have several traits in common with prostitutes: anger, excessive hatred, obscenity, and a tendency to lesbianism.

A unique case of what might be called "altruistic" obscenity among morally insane women is presented by the example of X. di Legrand, who, under pretext of protecting her son against syphilis and other illnesses, initiated him into carnal love herself, little by little, reasoning that he would not suffer thereby. When she became pregnant, she wanted to abort so she would not spoil her good looks and through that drive her son away; if he left she planned to commit suicide. Moreover, she brooked no criticism, saying "I have been absolved by God, who is infallible."

Catt. di Bonvecchiato, to conceal her lesbianism, pretended to be paralyzed and summoned nymphomaniacs to assist her. She made up a hundred illnesses to avoid working in the asylum, and she turned the hysterics on her ward into a veritable association of false accusers.

I knew a woman of outstanding family who wrote verses and was in fact very well educated but gave herself to everyone, from the grandest dignitary to the lowliest street sweeper. With extraordinary finesse she accused her husband of adultery and of wanting to lock her up to be free for his other loves; she even took this story to the authorities. In the asylum she boasted that she had never passed a day without making love, and she teased the officials for being like her in this respect. Moreover, in the asylum she succeeded, despite advanced age, in initiating intrigues and false accusations. Her only perversion was dumping her feces and urine on her food, which she might do on the same day that she wrote with tremendous lyricism about the purity of platonic love.

Another woman walked around the ward half-dressed in front of the nurses. She described her husband's obscene demands and her own body in intimate detail. Sometimes she touched and ate feces, an act that was often accompanied by obscenity, and she washed her eyes with urine. But in front of doctors and judges she knew how to justify her oddities. For instance, when asked why she washed her eyes with urine, she said that this was a way of healing them, and that everyone used this cure, and so on. She even succeeded in instituting legal proceedings against her husband.

Prosper Despine: The psychological state of criminals, 1868

Few late nineteenth-century criminologists failed to cite Prosper Despine's *Psychologie naturelle* (1868), the full title of which, had it been translated into English, would have been *Natural Psychology: A study of the intellectual and moral faculties in their normal state and in their anomalous manifestations among madmen and criminals*. Despine (1812–92) seemed to have scientifically confirmed the moral insanity (or moral imbecility) of the criminal, and thus his kinship with madmen. Criminals, Despine demonstrated, using news reports of trials, are morally anomalous beings, different from normal men in their lack of free will and the sense of duty. They cannot help choosing the wrong path and are incapable of remorse. Given that they are born without a moral sense, it is futile and even self-defeating to punish them. Rather, they should be given moral treatment designed to replace the faculties they lack. A practicing psychiatrist, Despine helped to establish criminology as a psychological, as well as a sociological and anthropological, science.

I translated this excerpt from Prosper Despine, *Psychologie naturelle: Étude sur les facultés intellectuelles et morales* (Paris: F. Savy, 1868), pp. 541–5.

PROSPER DESPINE: THE PSYCHOLOGICAL STATE OF CRIMINALS

Now comes the most interesting and important part of this work, that which deals with the psychological state of criminals. A long and conscientious study, made from the summaries of criminal trials in the *Gazette des tribunaux* from 1825 to the current day, reveals that serious offenders are deprived of humanity's noblest feelings, especially of the moral sense (the faculty that rules the higher moral reason), the moral conscience, and free will. Deprived of the sense of duty and of free will, the criminal, subjected to the law of self-interest, decides his course of action only in accordance to his strongest desires, desires that are involuntary manifestations of the depraved instincts with which he was born. When, impelled by his depraved lusts, he has to make a choice, he inevitably does the thing which is worst. If the criminal, deprived of the moral sense and free will, inevitably acts in accordance with his strongest desire, it follows that he is not morally responsible for his odious acts. This conclusion may seem brutal. But it is important to show that the criminal really is destitute of the moral sense, and that I have done in my clinical study of a great number of criminals.

Presenting an analysis of the psychological state of several famous malefactors, this study must be considered no more than a guide to criminality. Anyone can pursue its study by reading the daily summaries of trials of the court of assizes, thereby confirming that serious offenders totally lack the moral sense. This psychological anomaly shows up, first, in the absence of moral reprobation before the crime, and second in the absence of remorse afterwards. I have taken pains to show that we should not confuse the egotistical regrets of criminals who are about to be punished, especially by death, with true remorse, in which the moral sense recoils from and condemns an act after it has been committed.

Two psychological traits constantly converge in serious offenders: perversity, which gives birth to the desire to commit a crime, and moral insensibility, that is to say the absence of the moral sense and other elevated moral feelings. These two conditions are necessary to commit a crime. . . .

Given that serious offenders are affected by a grave anomaly, moral treatment rather than punishments are suitable for them. I have critiqued the various punishments to which criminals have been submitted over time – punishments that have no preventive effect and actually aggravate the moral sickness of these morally incomplete beings – and I have established the foundations of moral treatment. I have not torn anything down without reconstructing it on a better basis. All the methods that I have proposed – means that are rational and that follow from natural and scientific psychology – have already been sanctioned by experience. . . . In proposing such treatment, I have been guided at all points by two goals: to spare these unfortunate moral idiots from cruel punishments which only make them worse; and to improve them as much as possible, so they become more capable of living in society and of conducting themselves without troubling others. I aim at safeguarding the interests of society, which have been gravely compromised by the absurd and dangerous treatments to which criminals have been subjected up to this very day.

To hold that criminals are moral madmen and thus irresponsible for their monstrous acts is hardly a new idea; that which is new is to have established . . . that criminals have neither moral reason nor free will, and that they are involuntary slaves to their immoral desires.

Evolution, degeneration, and heredity

Evolution, degeneration, and heredity

Introduction to Part IV

While the concept of degeneration, like that of moral insanity, has today lost most of its original meaning, it too was a major theme of nineteenth-century criminology. In fact, it was far more powerful than moral insanity, for the idea that some people were degenerating – going backward down the evolutionary ladder – shaped thinking about all kinds of social problems, including insanity, imbecility, and pauperism as well as criminality, and it laid the basis for eugenics, the program for eliminating social problems by preventing degenerates from reproducing.

The idea of degeneration affected criminology in four important ways. First, it offered an explanation for offending: criminals, acording to degeneration theorists, break the law not out of free will, but because they are afflicted by degeneration, a process of slow decay that leaves them prey to baser instincts (Chapter 19). Degeneration is a condition, a state that pre-exists criminal behavior and somehow causes it. Degeneration theorists also identified causes of degeneration, which they traced to alcohol abuse, egotism, unhealthy environments, and general immorality (Chapters 16 and 21). Criminality was not only a result of degeneration, but also one of its causes. The two fed one another in an unbroken loop.

Second, the concept of degeneration helped criminologists understand why crime was so often associated with pauperism, insanity, and other social ills. All of these problems flowed from the underlying condition of degeneration; what mattered was the condition itself, not its external manifestations, which were fleeting and interchangeable, so that a pauper family would naturally produce criminals and the occasional idiot, and the children of criminals would almost certainly be either criminals themselves or some other problematic type (Chapters 16 and 20). Policymakers began to think in terms of the "three D's": dependants (the poor), defectives (the insane, feebleminded, deaf and dumb), and delinquents (adult as well as juvenile offenders); what they had in common was the fourth "D" – degeneration.[1]

Third, degeneration meshed well with ideas about evolution. Speculation about evolution was rife even before Darwin published *The Origin of the Species* (1859), and it took a long time for Darwin's theory of natural selection to be accepted. Many criminologists found what seemed a better alternative in degeneration theory, which offered a plausible explanation of why some individuals, families, and nations evolved while others lost out in the struggle for existence. The underlying theory here was that of use-inheritance: sustained use strengthens organs, faculties, and abilities, while neglect and abuse weaken them so that they eventually cease to function. The "fit" evolve, and the degenerate "unfit" devolve. Good people inherit good qualities, bad people a tendency to degenerate. However, many degenerationists agreed with Richard Dugdale (Chapter 20) that it is possible to reform degenerates – to so strengthen their organs, faculties, and abilities that the process of decay is reversed. That is, they were "soft" hereditarians, in contrast to "hard" hereditarian eugenicists, who insisted that devolution is irreversible and that, therefore, degenerates must be sterilized or otherwise prevented from reproducing.

Fourth and finally, degeneration theory was important because it prepared the way for criminal anthropology, the next influential criminological theory. If criminals are degenerates, they must be lower on the evolutionary ladder than law-abiding people, closer to savages than to refined white Europeans. And if they are degenerates, they are probably marked in various ways that indicate their mental and physical inferiority (Chapters 17 and 19). Here in embryonic form was Lombroso's theory of the anthropological born criminal (Part VI).

Note

1   These categories even affected the organization of the US census; see Chapter 52. Also see Charles Richmond Henderson's popular textbook, *An Introduction to the Study of the Dependent, Defective and Delinquent Classes* (Boston: D.C. Heath, 1893).

Chapter 16

Bénédict-August Morel: Degeneration and its causes, 1857

Bénédict-August Morel (1809–73) trained as a physician, but specialized in psychiatry, becoming chief medical officer of the insane asylum at St.-Yon, France. His 1857 book *Traité des dégénérescences physiques, intellectuelles et morales de l'espèce humaine* (*Treatise on the Physical, Intellectual, and Moral Degenerations of the Human Species*) argued that afflictions such as criminality, imbecility, and insanity were symptoms of an underlying condition, *degeneration*, that could manifest itself in any one of a number of forms and be passed down the generations from parent to child. The idea of degeneration spread rapidly in Europe and the United States, partly because it was a natural outgrowth of the belief, long held by phrenologists and others, that overeating, abusing alcohol and tobacco, overusing the sexual organs, and so on could affect the biological makeup of one's brain and hence one's physical, moral, and intellectual qualities.

Morel's theory further appealed because it fit well with a growing pessimism in Europe and the United States about society's ability to cope with social problems. Indeed, problems such as pauperism, criminality and insanity seemed to be spreading and intractable. They also seemed, increasingly, to be hereditary, since one could so often find pauperized or criminal parents with pauperized or criminal children. This pessimism led to the belief that nations as well as individuals were in a state of decline brought on by degeneration.[1] Finally, Morel's theory was popular because it was easy to prove: as he insists in one of the excerpts below, to demonstrate that a form of degeneration is hereditary, one need not find a child with the same affliction as its parent; it is enough to find a child with *some* sort of affliction, *some* sign of degeneration.

Morel anticipated Lombroso and other criminal anthropologists in treating physical anomalies as signs of an underlying condition of decay. And like the criminal anthropologists, he found interconnections between criminality, mental illness, imbecility, and other socially problematic conditions. Morel was also in a sense a precursor of today's genetic psychiatrists who, while eschewing the notion of degeneration, nonetheless argue that alcohol poisoning, drug use, and maternal malnutrition can lead to fetal damage and hence to social difficulties after birth.

Morel frequently uses the word *morbid* to describe what he means by degeneration; for him *morbid* means diseased, wasting away, pathological, and unhealthy to an extent that the very tissue of the body and brain is affected. I have chosen the following passages from his *Traité* (Paris: J. B. Baillière, 1857) to give a general impression of his work on degeneration, starting with his preface (pp. ii–v), including his definition of degeneration (pp. 1, 4–5), and continuing on to materials on the main causes of degeneration (extracts from pp. 47–62, 72). The two final passages cover his associations among mental illness, suicide, and crime (pp. 376–7, 386, 390) and his understanding of heredity (pp. 564–5). The translations are my own.

BÉNÉDICT-AUGUST MOREL: DEGENERATION AND ITS CAUSES

Preface

Mentally ill people who are locked up in our asylums are, in most cases, nothing other than representatives of certain morbid types of the species, improvable in some cases, incapable of change in others. Whatever the other causes of their afflictions may be, all are in a state of degeneration. . . .

Mental illness is found at all points of the globe, always with the same set of intellectual, physical, and moral symptoms that characterize morbid types. One can study the insane in terms of their tendencies and actions, the typical patterns of their illnesses, or their appearance and head conformations – but in all cases it is clear that they represent the same degenerative condition. This condition affects people everywhere, and always in the same manner.

The incessant increase in Europe of not only mental illness but of all those abnormal states relating to physical and moral illnesses is a fact of nature.

Everywhere I have heard physicians complain about the growing number of the insane; about increases in general paralysis and epilepsy; and about the enfeeblement of those mental and physical powers that otherwise might make cures possible. Moreover, neuroses such as hysteria and hypochondria, often accompanied by suicidal tendencies, increasingly attack workers and country people alike, whereas formerly they were mainly found among the rich and bored. Finally, congenital and acquired imbecility, idiocy, and other forms of arrested development of the physical and intellectual faculties are ominous signs that degeneration even affects fetal life.

While we psychiatrists study these phenomena in our particular domain, other men have busied themselves, not only in France but in Europe and the United States as well, with the compilation of statistics on morality and criminality. These unfortunately corroborate our own predictions.

The growing number of suicides and crimes; the terrifyingly young age of youthful criminals; and the bastardization of the national stock which in many places is now unfit to meet the standards for military service – these are irrefutable facts. European governments have justly taken alarm. . . .

This book is intended to demonstrate *the origin and formation of morbid types in the human species*. From now on it will be impossible to separate the study of mental illness from that of the causes of fixed and permanent degenerations, which increasingly threaten the healthy part of the population.

Definition of *degeneration*

. . . Finding himself in new circumstances, primitive man had to deal with them, and his descendants were able to escape neither the influence of heredity nor that of factors that forced them to deviate more and more from the original primitive type.

These deviations led to variations, of which some constituted races capable of transmitting their typical characteristics, while others created in the diverse races those abnormal states that I indicate by the name of *degenerations*. These degenerations have distinctive characteristics. They are distinguished from one another by certain morbid causes that profoundly affect the organism, producing this degeneration rather than that one; and they form groups or families [criminality, imbecility, etc. – N.R.] that draw their characteristics from the cause that produces them. . . .

The clearest statement we can make about degeneration in the human species is to say that it is *a morbid deviation from a primitive type*. . . . Degeneration and morbid deviation from the normal type of humanity are, in my thought, one and the same.

Causes of degeneration

. . .

- *Degenerations from poisons.* The man who lives in a swampy area is an involuntary victim of forces that destroy his health and lead to state of heredity chronic illness; he has no choice but to suffer from poisonous phenomena. In other cases, however, the degeneration of the species is connected more directly with depravity of the moral sense, with violations of the laws of hygiene, and with failures to form educative habits. This is what one sees in the abuse of alcohol and of certain narcotics such as opium. These toxic agents produce such marked perversions in the functions of the nervous system that they give rise to true degenerations, whether through the direct influence of the toxic agent or through their impact on heredity. . . .
- *Degenerations caused by the social environment: Industries, unhealthy professions, misery.* . . . The practice of dangerous or unhealthy professions, and living in centers that are over-populated or unhealthy, expose the organism to new causes of decay and consequently of degeneration. . . .

- *Degenerations caused by a previous morbid affliction or by a morbid temperament.* . . . .
- *Degenerations caused by congenital disability or those acquired in infancy.* . . . .
- *The relationship of degeneration to hereditary influences.* . . . Those who inherit vicious predispositions reveal their bad heredity not only through typical external signs that are more or less easy to detect, such as small stature or bad skull conformation, morbid temperament, deformities, anomalies in the structure of their organs, and sterility; they also reveal it through strange aberrations in the use of the intellectual faculties and the moral sentiments. . . .

Degeneration can be congenital or acquired, complete or incomplete, susceptible to modification or entirely incurable.

Mental illnesses, suicides, crimes

I purposefully link these three terms that are so fundamental in statistical research. Indeed, there exist among the causes of mental illness, suicide, and criminality such similarities that the most common cause of mental illness, for example, leads to an increase in suicides, and vice versa. I hope that I will not be accused of confusing crime with madness, for I have made numerous efforts to establish the line of demarcation between them. But it is always a good idea to recognize that many individuals are sentenced for misdeeds committed during the onset of madness; and that, on the other hand, immorality, misery, bad example, and drunkenness are the most powerful causes of intellectual problems. . . .

Sterility in the parents and premature deaths among infants are, generally speaking, the two precursor symptoms of the degeneration of nations and their impending decadence. . . .

There are various categories of degeneration. In the first we classify individuals or groups of individuals who are the direct victims of alcoholic poisoning and who have suffered, both physically and morally, through all of the pathological phases of this poisoning, sadly ending their existence in stupor and paralysis.

The second category consists of a very numerous class of demoralized and brutish people who indicate their depravity, often of very early onset, by the dimming of their intellectual faculties and the commission of acts that outrage morality. Laziness and vagabondage are the principle characteristics of these unfortunates. For the forensic physician, they sometimes pose issues that are very difficult to resolve regarding the assessment of acts considered criminal. People in this category frequently live in large cities, especially in industrial centers, where they fill the houses of detention, begging corners, and prisons until they finally arrive at insane asylums, often after having been a source of endless trouble, scandal, and danger.

Understanding the heredity of degenerations

. . . By "heredity" I mean not merely the transmission of a parental malady to a child who develops similar physical and moral symptoms; I also mean the transmission of organic predispositions from parents to children. It is not necessary that the malady of the parents be *identically reproduced* in the children: *it suffices that the latter inherit an unfortunate organic predisposition to produce new morbid phenomena, be they physical, moral, or both.*

Note

1   See Daniel Pick, *Faces of Degeneration: A European disorder, c. 1848–c. 1919* (Cambridge: Cambridge University Press, 1989).

Chapter 17

J. Bruce Thomson: The psychology of criminals, 1870

In 1870, J. Bruce Thomson, resident surgeon at the General Prison for Scotland, published two highly influential articles in the *Journal of Mental Science*. Drawing on his long experience with criminals and familiarity with French degenerationist literature, Thomson argued that criminals are morally insane, forming something close to a separate group or race of people marked by physical and mental deterioration. Although his work drew on the concepts of moral insanity and degeneration, by virtue of its identification of the physical and mental characteristics of criminals, it also came close to criminal anthropology.

In "The psychology of criminals," Thomson begins by reporting on a recent book by Prosper Despine (see Chapter 15), the French psychologist and philosopher who in 1868 had published *Psychologie naturelle (Natural Psychology)*, a work that, like Morel's *Treatise*, drew on degeneration theory to explain crime. Thomson goes on to set forth his own views on the nature of criminals – views that influenced Lombroso and other criminal anthropologists. He hovers between environmental and hereditarian explanations in a way typical of degeneration theorists. This type of reasoning is today again becoming acceptable in the sense that geneticists believe that environment affects the way in which genes express themselves.

For this section, I extracted from the first half of Thomson's "Psychology of criminals," *Journal of Mental Science* 16 (1870): 321–50, in which he builds the bridge between degeneration theory and criminal anthropology. His argument here that criminals are intellectually weak re-emerged at the end of the nineteenth century, when the "feeblemindedness" explanation took hold and went on to dominate early twentieth-century Anglo-American criminology. In Part VII, on Habitual Criminals, I extract from the second half of this same article, in which Thomson argues that the characteristics of criminals almost force them to be remorseless repeat offenders. Passages from Thomson's second influential article, "The hereditary nature of crime," appear in Part VI, on Criminal Anthropology.

J. BRUCE THOMSON: THE PSYCHOLOGY OF CRIMINALS

That great criminals are wholly without the moral sense, that violent and habitual criminals are, as a class, moral imbeciles – are startling propositions; but, nevertheless, they have been adopted and advocated with singular show of truth and much ability of late years. Such views are quite opposed to all the doctrines of divines, and philosophers, speculative and practical. . . .

The bold propositions in regard to criminals have been propounded, defended, and supported, with a great array of facts, by Dr. Despine, in a work recently published, entitled, *Psychologie Naturelle*. . . . The present paper shall be confined almost entirely to the characteristics of the criminal classes, and to Dr. Despine's views of their moral insensibility. The writer here offers his extensive observation and experience among criminals, by way of comparison with the facts and conclusions arrived at by Dr. Despine; and however new and startling the results may be, if the facts are authentic, they must be received honestly. "We must take things as they really are, and not as we think them to be," is a maxim well stated by the philosophic Virchow.

Dr. Despine has given us a most elaborate and interesting treatise on moral insanity in relation to crime, accompanied with a vast mass of details of illustrative cases gathered from criminal records in France.

It is quite clear, however, that all his knowledge of criminals is gleaned from these records, and little or none from personal knowledge of criminals themselves. In this respect I hold a vantage ground, being enabled to offer facts and figures drawn from acquaintance with criminals for the last 12 years in the General Prison for Scotland, of which convict establishment I have medical charge. It seemed interesting to compare notes with the author of Psychologie Naturelle, who looks at his study from a different standpoint, and to run a parallel betwixt our respective observations and deductions. His business has been to read up the subject of criminals; the writer of this paper has had to see them, to speak with them, to observe their characteristics, physical, mental, moral; to visit them by day and night; and listen, in dreary solitudes and awful cells, to their plaints, echoing through the long corridors of the prison,

"The still sad music of humanity."

Moral insanity, where the intellect keeps sound for a time, deserves the most earnest and grave study of the lawyer, the divine, the psychologist, and the practical legislator; but such a disease as moral insanity is only being slowly allowed by even the medical profession. . . .

In our day the opinions held by Plato and Aristotle of the kinship of crime and madness are only being revived by psychologists, among whom we rank chief Pinel, Esquirol, and Prichard. On the subject of this paper – *"Criminals"*

– we have the following testimony in the beginning of this century by the zealous and observing Pinel: – "One of the great objects of my life shall be to demonstrate to the judges of the land, that numbers of persons brought before them, found guilty and convicted as criminals, were only insane." And again he says further, "Can mania exist without lesion of the understanding? I have seen many madmen, who at no time had manifested any lesion of the understanding, and who were under the dominion of a sort of instinctive fury, as if the affective faculties had been alone diseased." To shew that these views are advocated by the best psychologists of the present day, the following quotation may be given from Dr. Maudsley in one of his Gulstonian Lectures just published: – "Another group (of the insane) might be made of those persons of unsound mental temperament who are *born with an entire absence of the moral sense, destitute of the possibility even of moral feeling*; they are as truly insensible to the moral relations of life, as deficient in this regard as a person colour blind is to certain colours, or as one who is without ear for music is to the finest harmonies of sound." This strong statement by the eminent professor of medical jurisprudence in University College, London, and distinguished psychologist, deserves much respect; and all the more that it concurs largely with the study of Dr. Despine, who, of all writers, has propounded the boldest dogmas on the subject of moral insanity.

The gist of the three volumes of Dr. Despine lies in the following passage of his introduction, which it is meant should form the text of the present paper (auct. loq.). "*In reading without any preconceived notions the reports of criminal trials, I was struck with the constant recurrence, among those who committed great crimes in cold blood, of a mental condition marked by the absence of all moral remonstrance, before the act premeditated, and the absence, not less complete, of all remorse after the accomplishment thereof.*" Pursuing this inquiry, after long and diligent search into the details of crime, the author says he found the mental condition above described absolutely and invariably present, indeed an indispensable concomitant of crime. The conclusion is, of course, that great criminals are wholly destitute of the moral sense. . . .

The moral sense is absent in certain races of men, as the Bosjesman [Bushman – N.R.] and the Australian, who simply follow their desires and objects of interest; and not only in certain races, but persons in the best races are moral idiots; and further, sex and age and religious training modify the moral nature.

Criminals, who do great crimes in cold blood (*sang froid*), and betray no remonstrance before or remorse afterwards, are without the moral sense.

The intellect may be sane, and not the moral sense. . . .

Of the physical characteristics of criminals

. . . Criminals form a variety of the human family quite distinct from civil and social men. There is a low type of physique indicating a deteriorated character which gives a family likeness to them all. . . . In a recent report of the State Charities of America, it is stated – "There has sprung up *a criminal class just as distinctly marked as the slave class.*" Physical deterioration in the criminal as well as in the pauper class is strongly insisted on, and in America as well as here reports note the extreme nervous debility and defective vital energy peculiar to both. When a director or prison manager goes his rounds visiting each criminal in his cell, it is curious how readily he at once detects a prisoner of the better sort – not an *habitué* with the stamp of the caste upon him, not –

> "A fellow by the hand of Nature marked,
> Quoted and signed to do a deed of shame."

The reason, no doubt, of this likeness in the class is that they form a community – never levelling up by intercourse in marriage or otherwise, but retrograding from generation to generation by geometrical retrogression. They are a tribe, like the Ishmaelites, opposed to all others, whose *hand* is against civilised men . . .

Who can doubt that the poor and the criminal classes, born and brought up amidst the foul and poisoned air of the lanes, wynds, and closes of overcrowded cities, have a physical deterioration, and are a class of men and women totally different from the rich and great communities in the well ventilated streets and squares of the West End? Some recent reports show that the low haunts of the wretched poor and the criminal afford only 120 cubic feet of air (and such air!) to each person. The barrack soldier has recently been advanced from 400 to 600 cubic feet, which is little enough; the prisoners' cells are from 700 to 900 cubic feet. Such a depression of the vital powers as is necessarily consequent on the atmosphere and low living of the poorer classes, is clearly a great engendering cause of poverty and crime; the physical state breeding moral degeneration. . . .

The physical peculiarities of criminals are very easily explained by their low living, their associating in a community forming as it were but an enlarged family circle, and almost entire isolation from the higher classes of civilised beings. The same family likeness and occasional degeneration belong to the gipsy tribes, the miners, the fishermen on some of the Scottish coasts, who for generations have inhabited the same region, followed the same vocation, and intermarried only with those of the same race or tribe.

The physical organization of criminals is marked by a singularly stupid and insensate look. The expression in the countenance is not that of the "human face divine," but stupid, sullen, and diabolical. The colour of the complexion is bad, as if the "sweet juices of life" were poisoned, and no doubt bad passions and bad living will do this. The heads and outlines are harsh, angular, clumsy. The women are positively ugly in features, form, and action; beauty of colour, regularity of features, or grace of mien is rarely seen among them. We are speaking of the *habitués* born in crime, born into crime, and whose vocation is crime, by a physical and psychical proclivity in general quite irresistible.

The diseases of criminals are a proof of their low type and deteriorated systems. On examination of the physical diseases and causes of death, it is found that the tubercular class of diseases stands prominent in numerical importance, and next to this diseases of the nervous system. Most of the criminal class die before the meridian of life, and scarcely any see old age. More than 50 per cent, according to my mortality bills, die in prisons below 30 years of age, and only 1 per cent in old age. The post-mortem inspections show a series of morbid appearances very remarkable, almost every vital organ of the body being more or less diseased, few dying of one disease, but generally "worn out" by a complete degeneration of all the vital organs.

These observations lead us to the conclusions: –

That there is a physique distinctively characteristic of the criminal class, and

That their physical condition is indicative of a deteriorated organisation. The causes of this seem to be not only habitual vices, privations, and imprisonments, but chiefly hereditary deterioration. In all the old countries of Europe it is very evident that we have a community of crime which, if not stayed by extirpation or transportation, must extend; and by the abolition of transportation in Great Britain it is of late years becoming more distinct. Even in the new American States this association of criminals is attracting much notice by the transmission of a marked hereditary breed. The same tendency to degeneration has been clearly proved among the pauper as well as the criminal population, and demands state-attention. What is the cure? Improvement or abolition of the parent stock. . . .

The lesson lies in the laws of natural selection so well set forth by Mr. Darwin. When a race of plants is to be improved, gardeners "go over their seed beds and pull up the *rogues*, as they call the plants that deviate from the proper standard. With cattle this kind of selection is in fact always followed; for hardly any one is so careless as to allow his worst animals to breed." Why, then, should incorrigible criminals, at the healthy, vigorous period of life, be at large; why should they go into prison for short periods only, to be sent out again in renovated health, to propagate a race so low in physical organization?

One of the most marked physical characteristics of female prisoners in the General Prison for Scotland is the luxuriant heads of hair which they have. The observing matron first drew my attention to this fact. The hair does not seem so silky and fine as that belonging to the better classes, but thinness and deficiency are very rare in criminals. Except where fevers, and sometimes syphilis, have affected the scalp, baldness is rare among the male, and scantiness of hair among the female prisoners.

The Low State of Intellect among criminals, as a class, is one of those distinguishing characteristics obvious to all who know them. Under this head we do not mean to refer to those certified Insane, but to the numbers who, in various degrees, manifest a low calibre of intelligence. The low physique naturally points to this result. . . .

My own statistics, taken from a prison population in Scotland of nearly 6,000 prisoners, show that 12 per cent. appear on my register, for mental weakness – imbecile, suicidal, epileptic; and all this, besides those afterwards to be noted who becoming insane were sent to the Lunatic Department for criminals.

Some reasonable doubts may be entertained whether long and frequent imprisonment, rather than natural infirmity of mind, may have led to this. To shed some light on this question it was shewn that of 323 who were found imbecile or weak-minded and unfit to stand the separate confinement of a prison, the weakmindedness was chiefly *congenital*, appearing on admission or shortly after admission to prison. . . .

There is little doubt that if medical testimony were received by judges, especially in regard to old incorrigible offenders, the law would recognise doubtful responsibility and a low state of intellect in many habitual criminals, to such a degree as to affect the sentences awarded. One class above all

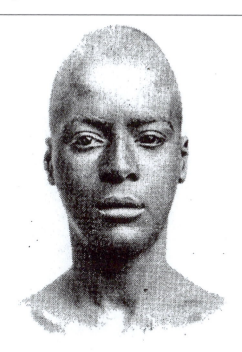

Figure 17.1 Negro with a Type of Degeneracy. According to Talbot, an American dentist concerned with degeneration, Negroes tend to long-headedness, but this young man has a wedge-shaped head due to "synostosis of the sagittal suture, with compensatory growth in region of the large fontanelle" – a sign of degeneracy. Eugene S. Talbot, *Degeneracy: Its causes, signs, and results* (London: Walter Scott, Ltd., 1898), Fig. 13, p. 170.

others – the epileptics – labours under actual disease and mental debility, especially about the time of the epileptic seizure. . . .

One more example from Morel, shewing how crime and mental disease alternate in families; of five children from an insane mother and a drunken father, one was suicidal, two suffered imprisonment, a daughter became insane, the other imbecile. Such cases explain how a class of criminals propagate – as we shall afterwards more clearly show – not only a class of criminals, but a community of men and women low in intelligence, and being originally weak in mind, lapsing in large numbers into insanity. Without enlarging further here, we conclude there is ample proof in this country and in America that, as a class, criminals are of low intellectual calibre; and that in many cases, and especially in the case of epileptics, the low degree of intellect calls for inquiry how far many criminals ought to be held responsible in the eye of the judges and legal authorities.

Chapter 18

Charles Darwin: The moral sense, 1871

In *The Origin of Species* (1859), the book in which he argued that evolution occurs through a process of natural selection, Charles Darwin (1809–82) avoided speaking specifically of human evolution; and while he could not avoid discussing change, he refrained from equating change with progress. In his 1871 book *The Descent of Man*, Darwin spoke more specifically about the evolution of mankind and here, especially when discussing the emergence of morality, he sometimes did equate developmental change with progress. Subscribing to a "soft" hereditarian position, he argued that acquired characteristics such as the desire to steal or a tendency to lie can become hereditary; similarly, moral tendencies such as chastity and kindness to animals can become "inherited habits." Moreover, he adopted an evolutionary perspective on the spread of moral characteristics, arguing that insofar as these traits confer an evolutionary advantage, they will "tend slowly to advance and be diffused throughout the world."

The following extracts come from Charles Darwin, *The Descent of Man* (London: J. Murray, 1871), pp 101–3 and 161–3.

CHARLES DARWIN: THE MORAL SENSE

Our great philosopher, Herbert Spencer, has recently explained his views on the moral sense. He says, "I believe that the experiences of utility organised and consolidated through all past generations of the human race, have been producing corresponding modifications, which, by continued transmission and accumulation, have become in us certain faculties of moral intuition – certain emotions responding to right and wrong conduct, which have no apparent basis in the individual experiences of utility." There is not the least inherent improbability, as it seems to me, in virtuous tendencies being more or less strongly inherited; for, not to mention the various dispositions and habits transmitted by many of our domestic animals, I have heard of cases in which a desire to steal and a tendency to lie appeared to run in families of the upper ranks; and as stealing is so rare a crime in the wealthy classes, we can hardly account by accidental coincidence for the tendency occurring in two or three members of the same family. If bad tendencies are transmitted, it is probable that good ones are likewise transmitted. Excepting through the principle of the transmission of moral tendencies, we cannot understand the differences believed to exist in this respect between the various races of mankind. We have, however, as yet, hardly sufficient evidence on this head.

Even the partial transmission of virtuous tendencies would be an immense assistance to the primary impulse derived directly from the social instincts, and indirectly from the approbation of our fellow-men. Admitting for the moment that virtuous tendencies are inherited, it appears probable, at least in such cases as chastity, temperance, humanity to animals, &c., that they become first impressed on the mental organisation through habit, instruction, and example, continued during several generations in the same family, and in a quite subordinate degree, or not at all, by the individuals possessing such virtues, having succeeded best in the struggle for life. . . .

In order that primeval men, or the ape-like progenitors of man, should have become social, they must have acquired the same instinctive feelings which impel other animals to live in a body; and they no doubt exhibited the same general disposition. They would have felt uneasy when separated from their comrades, for whom they would have felt some degree of love; they would have warned each other of danger, and have given mutual aid in attack or defence. All this implies some degree of sympathy, fidelity, and courage. Such social qualities, the paramount importance of which to the lower animals is disputed by no one, were no doubt acquired by the progenitors of man in a similar manner, namely, through natural selection, aided by inherited habit. When two tribes of primeval man, living in the same country, came into competition, if the one tribe included (other circumstances being equal) a greater number of courageous, sympathetic, and faithful members, who were always ready to warn each other of danger, to aid and defend each other, this tribe would without doubt succeed best and conquer the other. Let it be borne in mind how all-important, in the never-ceasing wars of savages, fidelity and courage must be. The advantage which disciplined soldiers have over undisciplined hordes follows chiefly from the confidence which each man feels in his comrades. Obedience, as Mr. Bagehot has well shewn, is of the highest value, for any form of government is better than none. Selfish and contentious people will not cohere, and without coherence nothing can be effected. A tribe possessing the above qualities in a high degree would spread and be victorious over other tribes; but in the course of time it would, judging from all past history, be in its turn overcome by some other and still more highly endowed tribe. Thus the social and moral qualities would tend slowly to advance and be diffused throughout the world.

Chapter 19

Henry Maudsley: The borderland, 1874

Henry Maudsley (1835–1918), the leading psychiatrist in Victorian England, served as medical superintendent of several insane asylums and as an editor of the *Journal of Mental Science*, Britain's premier journal in the field of mental illness. He also conducted a highly successful private practice and was a professor of medical jurisprudence at University College London. Toward the end of his life he founded the Maudsley Hospital, an institution that remains an important center for research on deviance and mental disease.

Among Maudsley's many books, one of the most successful was *Responsibility in Mental Disease*, from which the following material was extracted. In it he argues that there is a "borderland" between sanity and insanity populated by people with such disabilities as epilepsy, dipsomania, idiocy, imbecility, and criminality. Although Maudsley uses *mental derangement* as a generic term for fundamental physiological decay, the phenomenon he discusses closely resembles Morel's *degeneration*. Moreover, like Morel, Maudsley believes that mental derangement and other types of pathological decay can be inherited: some people have a "hereditary predisposition" to insanity which evolves through generations. But mental derangement can be studied and perhaps corrected by medical men and other scientists; thus criminals "rightly come within the scope of positive scientific research."

Responsibility in Mental Disease carries forward discussions of key criminological themes, some first articulated earlier, others that gained currency later. One is the notion of moral insanity, which Maudsley defines as a form or mental derangement closely allied to other forms of insanity and caused by defective organization of the brain. (Similarly, some of today's neurologists trace serious criminality to abnormal brain structures.)[1] Another is the idea of the hereditary born criminal, which Maudsley explored several years before Cesare Lombroso published his first work on "criminal man." When Maudsley writes of the evolution of the moral sense, he anticipates not only later works by Darwin and other nineteenth-century theorists, but also today's evolutionary psychologists. Finally, a decade before Francis Galton coined the term *eugenics*, Maudsley recommends eugenic solutions to criminality and other social problems, writing that human breeding offers a way to regenerate or improve human stock.

These passages come from the 1898 edition of *Responsibility in Mental Disease* (New York: D. Appleton), pp. 30–7, 62–7, 183–96, and 299–305.

HENRY MAUDSLEY: THE BORDERLAND

Introductory

Not until comparatively lately has much attention been given to the way in which criminals are produced. It was with them much as it was at one time with lunatics: to say of the former that they were wicked, and of the latter that they were mad, was thought to render any further explanation unnecessary and any further inquiry superfluous. It is certain, however, that lunatics and criminals are as much manufactured articles as are steam-engines and calico-printing machines, only the processes of the organic manufactory are so complex that we are not able to follow them. They are neither accidents nor anomalies in the universe, but come by law and testify to causality; and it is the business of science to find out what the causes are and by what laws they work. There is nothing accidental, nothing supernatural, in the impulse to do right or in the impulse to do wrong; both come by inheritance or by education; and science can no more rest content with the explanation which attributes one to the grace of Heaven and the other to the malice of the devil, than it could rest content with the explanation of insanity as a possession by the devil.

The few and imperfect investigations of the personal and family histories of criminals which have yet been made are sufficient to excite some serious reflections. One fact which is brought strongly out by these inquiries is that crime is often hereditary; that just as a man may inherit the stamp of the bodily features and characters of his parents, so he may also inherit the impress of their evil passions and propensities: of the true thief as of the true poet it may be indeed said that he is born, not made. This is what observation of the phenomena of hereditary action would lead us to expect; and although certain theologians, who are prone to square the order of nature to their notions of what it should be, may repel such a doctrine as the heritage of an *immoral* in place of a *moral* sense, they will in the end find it impossible in this matter, as they have done in other matters, to contend against facts. To add to their misfortunes, many criminals are not only begotten, and conceived, and bred in crime, but they are instructed in it from their youth upwards, so that their original criminal instincts acquire a power which no subsequent efforts to produce reformation will ever counteract.

All persons who have made criminals their study, recognize a distinct criminal class of beings, who herd together in our large cities in a thieves' quarter, giving themselves up to intemperance, rioting in debauchery, without regard to marriage ties or the bars of consanguinity, and propagating a criminal population of degenerate beings. For it is furthermore a matter of observation that this criminal class constitutes a degenerate or morbid variety of mankind, marked by peculiar low physical and mental characteristies. They are, it has been said, as distinctly marked off from the honest and well-bred operatives as "black-faced sheep are from other breeds," so that an experienced detective officer or prison official could pick them out from any promiscuous assembly at church or market. Their family likeness betrays them as fellows "by the hand of nature marked, quoted and signed to do a deed of shame." They are scrofulous, not seldom deformed, with badly-formed angular heads; are stupid, sullen, sluggish, deficient in vital energy, and sometimes afflicted with epilepsy. As a class, they are of mean and defective intellect, though excessively cunning, and not a few of them are weak-minded and imbecile. The women are ugly in features, and without grace of expression or movement. The children, who become juvenile criminals, do not evince the educational aptitude of the higher industrial classes: they are deficient in the power of attention and application, have bad memories, and make slow progress in learning; many of them are weak in mind and body, and some of them actually imbecile. Mr. Bruce Thomson, who in his official capacity as surgeon to the General Prison of Scotland had observed thousands of prisoners, declared that he had not known one to exhibit any æsthetic talent; he had never seen a pen-sketch, a clever poem, or an ingenious contrivance produced by one of them. Habitual criminals are, he says, without moral sense – are true moral imbeciles; their moral insensibility is such that in the presence of temptation they have no self-control against crime; and among all the murderers he had known, amounting to nearly five hundred, only three could be ascertained to have expressed any remorse. . . .

We may accept then the authority of those who have studied criminals, that there is a class of them marked by defective physical and mental organization, one result of their natural defect, which really determines their destiny in life, being an extreme deficiency or complete absence of moral sense. In addition to the perversion or entire absence of moral sense, which experience of habitual criminals brings prominently out, other important facts disclosed by the investigation of their family histories are, that a considerable proportion of them are weak-minded or epileptic or become insane, or that they spring from families in which insanity, epilepsy, or some other neurosis exists, and that the diseases from which they suffer and of which they die are chiefly tubercular diseases and diseases of the nervous system. Crime is a sort of outlet in which their unsound tendencies are discharged; they would go mad if they were not criminals, and they do not go mad because they are criminals.

Crime is not then in all cases a simple affair of yielding to an evil impulse or a vicious passion, which might be checked were ordinary control exercised;

it is clearly sometimes the result of an actual neurosis which has close relations of nature and descent to other neuroses, especially the epileptic and the insane neuroses; and this neurosis is the physical result of physiological laws of production and evolution. No wonder that the criminal *psychosis*, which is the mental side of the *neurosis*, is for the most part an intractable malady, punishment being of no avail to produce a permanent reformation. The dog returns to its vomit and the sow to its wallowing in the mire. A true reformation would be the *re*-forming of the individual nature; and how can that which has been forming through generations be *re*-formed within the term of a single life? Can the Ethiopian change his skin or the leopard his spots? . . .

There is a borderland between crime and insanity, near one boundary of which we meet with something of madness but more of sin, and near the other boundary of which something of sin but more of madness. A just estimate of the moral responsibility of the unhappy people inhabiting this borderland will assuredly not be made until we get rid of the metaphysical measure of responsibility as well as of the theological notion that vices and crimes are due to the instigation of the devil, and proceed by way of observation and induction to sound generalizations concerning the origin of the moral sentiments, the laws of their development, and the causes, course and varieties of moral degeneracy. Here as in other departments of nature our aim should be the discovery of natural laws by patient interrogation of nature, not the invention of theories by invoking our own minds to utter oracles to us. It must be received as a scientific axiom that there is no study to which the inductive method of research is not applicable; every attempt to prohibit such research by authority of any kind must be withstood and repelled with the utmost energy as a deadly attack upon the fundamental principle of scientific inquiry. With a better knowledge of crime we may not come to the practice of treating criminals as we now treat insane persons, but it is probable that we shall come to other and more tolerant sentiments, and that a less hostile feeling towards them, derived from a better knowledge of defective organization, will beget an indulgence at any rate towards all doubtful cases inhabiting the borderland between insanity and crime; in like manner as within living memory the feelings of mankind with regard to the insane have been entirely revolutionized by an inductive method of study.

The borderland

There is one occasional consequence of descent from an insane stock . . . which is of special interest in our present inquiry – namely, an entire absence of the moral sense. To those who take the metaphysical view of mind, it will no doubt seem improbable that absence of moral sense should ever be a congenital fault of mental organisation, but if we are to put any trust in observation, we must acknowledge such a defect to occur sometimes in consequence of parental insanity. It may be witnessed, even in young children, who, long before they have known what vice meant, have evinced an entire absence of moral feeling with the active display of all sorts of immoral tendencies – a genuine moral imbecility or insanity. As there are persons who cannot distinguish certain colours, having what is called colour-blindness, and others who, having no ear for music, cannot distinguish one tune from another, so there are some few who are congenitally deprived of moral sense. Associated with this defect there is frequently more or less intellectual deficiency, but not always; it sometimes happens there is a remarkably acute intellect with no trace of moral feeling.

Here, then, we are brought back to the connection between crime and insanity. A person who has no moral sense is naturally well fitted to become a criminal, and if his intellect is not strong enough to convince him that crime will not in the end succeed, and that it is, therefore, on the lowest grounds a folly, he is very likely to become one. As I have pointed out in the first chapter, criminals often do come of families in which insanity or some other neurosis exists, and instances are met with in which one member of a family becomes insane, and another reckless, dissipated, depraved, or perhaps even criminal. Several striking instances of the kind are related by Morel, who has traced and set forth in an instructive manner the course of human degeneracy in the production of *morbid varieties* of the human kind. Dr. Prichard mentions the case of a family, several members of which were afflicted with insanity, and were confined in asylums; they resembled each other; and the disease showed itself when they attained nearly the same period of life. A younger brother had a different organisation of body from the rest, and seemed likely to escape. There was only one other instance of immunity from the disease in the family – one, as he remarks, of still greater calamity. It was that of a brother who had never been, nor was thought to be, actually insane, but who was through life a reckless and depraved reprobate, and occasioned the greatest distress and vexation to his friends. If the secrets of their natures were laid open, how many perverse and wrongheaded persons, whose lives have been a calamity to themselves and others, how many of the depraved characters in history, whose careers have been a cruel chastisement to mankind, would be found to have owed their fates to some morbid predisposition! . . .

The medical psychologist must hold that the best of the argument concerning the origin of the moral sense is with those who uphold its acquired nature. That the sentiments of common interest in the primitive family and tribe, and the habitual reprobation of certain acts by individuals as injurious to the family or tribe, should finally generate a sentiment of right and wrong in regard to such acts, and that such sentiment should in the course of generations be transmitted by hereditary action as a more or less marked instinctive feeling, is in entire accordance with what we know of the results of education and of hereditary action. Time was, we know, when men wandered about the country in families or tribes. In order that they might rise from this nomadic state to a national existence, the acquisition and development of a moral sense must clearly have been essential conditions – not, however, as preformed agents, but as concomitant effects, of evolution. This development is still going slowly on; but the proof how little moral sense itself instigates progress is seen in the absence of it between nations. Men have risen to a national existence, but they have not yet risen to an international existence. With moral principles that have not changed within historical times, nations still laud patriotism, which is actually a mark of moral incompleteness, as the highest virtue; and statesmen sometimes think it a fine thing to sneer at cosmopolitanism. But it cannot be doubted that the time will come, though it may be yet afar off, when nations will know and feel their interests to be one, when moral feeling shall be developed between them, and when they shall not learn war any more; it will come as a step in evolution and as a condition of universal brotherhood, not otherwise than as, coming between tribes, it bound them into nations, and made patriotism the high virtue which it is believed to be.

If other arguments were needed in support of the opinion that conscience is a function of organization – the highest and most delicate function of the highest and most complete development thereof – they might be drawn from observation of conditions of moral degeneracy. Let it be noted how it is perverted or destroyed sometimes by disease or injury of brain. The last acquired faculty in the progress of human evolution, it is the first to suffer when disease invades the mental organization.

Moral insanity

This is a form of mental alienation which has so much the look of vice or crime that many persons regard it as an unfounded medical invention. Much indignation therefore has been stirred up when it has been pleaded to shelter a supposed criminal from the penal consequences of his offences; and judges have repeatedly denounced it from the bench as a "a most dangerous medical doctrine," "a dangerous innovation," which in the interests of society should be reprobated. The doctrine has no doubt been sometimes used improperly to shelter an atrocious criminal, but of the actual existence of such a form of disease no one who has made a practical study of insanity entertains a doubt. . . .

Notwithstanding prejudices to the contrary, there is a disorder of mind in which, without illusion, delusion, or hallucination, the symptoms are mainly exhibited in a perversion of those mental faculties which are usually called the active and moral powers – the feelings, affections, propensities, temper, habits, and conduct. The affective life of the individual is profoundly deranged, and his derangement shows itself in what he feels, desires, and does. He has no capacity of true moral feeling; all his impulses and desires, to which he yields without check, are egoistic; his conduct appears to be governed by immoral motives, which are cherished and obeyed without any evident desire to resist them. There is an amazing moral insensibility. The intelligence is often acute enough, being not affected otherwise than in being tainted by the morbid feelings under the influence of which the persons think and act; indeed they often display an extraordinary ingenuity in explaining, excusing, or justifying their behaviour, exaggerating this, ignoring that, and so colouring the whole as to make themselves appear the victims of mis-representation and persecution. Their mental resources seem to be greater sometimes than when they were well, and they reason most acutely, appar-ently because all their intellectual faculties are applied to the justification and gratification of their selfish desires. One cannot truly say, however, that the intellect is quite clear and sound in any of these cases, while in some it is manifestly weak. A sane person who is under the influence of excited feelings is notably liable to error of judgment and conduct; and in like manner the judgment and conduct of an insane person who is under the dominion of morbid feelings are infected. Moreover, the reason has lost control over the passions and actions, so that the person can neither subdue the former nor abstain from the latter, however inconsistent they may be with the duties and obligations of his relations in life, however disastrous to himself, and however much wrong they may inflict upon those who are the nearest and should be the dearest to him. He is incapable of following a regular pursuit in life, of recognising the ordinary rules of prudence and selfinterest, of appreciating the injury to himself which his conduct is. He is as distrustful of others as he is untrustworthy himself. He cannot be brought to see the culpability of his conduct, which he persistently denies, excuses, or justifies; has no sincere wish to do better; his affective nature is profoundly deranged, and its affinities are for such evil gratifications as must lead to further degeneration, and finally render him a diseased element which must either be got rid of out of the social organization, or be sequestrated and made harmless in it. He has lost the deepest instinct of organic nature, that by which an organism assimilates that which is suited to promote its growth and well-being, and he displays in lieu thereof perverted desires, the ways of which are ways of destruction. His alienated desires betoken a real alienation of nature.

It may be said that this description is simply the description of a very wicked person, and that to accept it as a description of insanity would be to confound all distinction between vice or crime and madness. No doubt, so far as symptoms only are concerned, they are much the same whether they are the result of vice or of disease; but there is considerable difference when we go on to inquire into the person's previous history – when we pass from psycho-logical to medical observation. The vicious act or crime is not itself proof of insanity; it must, in order to establish moral insanity, be traced from disease through a proper train of symptoms, just as the acts of a sane man are deduced from his motives; and the evidence of disease will be found in the entire history of the case. What we shall often observe is this – that after some great moral shock, or some severe physical disturbance, in a person who has a distinct hereditary predisposition to insanity, there has been a marked change of character; he becomes "much different from the man he was" in feelings, temper, habits, and conduct. We observe, in fact, that after a sufficient and well-recognised cause of mental derangement – a combination of predisposing and exciting causes which are daily producing it – a person exhibits symptoms which are strangely inconsistent with his previous character, but which are consistent with moral insanity. Or it may appear that there has been an attack of paralysis or epilepsy, or a severe fever, and that the change of character and the symptoms of moral alienation have followed one of these physical causes. In all cases, as Dr. Prichard, who was the first to describe the disease, has remarked, there has been an alteration in the temper and habits in consequence of disease or of a sufficient cause of disease. . . .

If the question be raised whether persons suffering from moral insanity should in every case be exempted from all responsibility for what they do wrong, I should shrink from answering it in the affirmative without qualification. They certainly have not the capacity of moral responsibility in its true sense; all the responsibility which they are capable of feeling is that which springs from a fear of punishment. But experience shows that this apprehension does influence some of them beneficially, and that the actual infliction of punishment may do them good; that in some few instances at any rate it is the best treatment which can be used. A diseased mind, like a diseased heart, may not incapacitate an individual for all actions, though it may positively incapacitate him for some; as he may do a day's quiet work with disease of the heart, although he cannot run a race, so he may be equal to some of the lesser responsibilities of life when he is not quite sane, and not capable of bearing the strain of great obligations. In other instances there can be no question that the persons are not proper objects of punishment in any form; and perhaps in any case the truest justice would be the admission of a modified responsibility, the degree thereof, where it existed, being determined by the particular circumstances of each case.

Assuredly moral insanity is disorder of mind produced by disorder of brain. In examining the conditions of its occurrence we have seen how plainly it follows the recognized causes of insanity; how it may precede for a time the outbreaks of various forms of unequivocal general alienation; how it accompanies intellectual insanity in most of its varieties; how it may follow other forms of general insanity; how it may precede or follow epilepsy, or occur as a masked epilepsy; how it may supervene at puberty on congenital moral imbecility; and how it may finally pass into dementia. These are facts of observation. Taking them fairly into consideration, and giving them the weight which they deserve, can we doubt that moral insanity is a form of derangement as genuine as any other form of mental derangement? If the law cannot adjust the measure of punishment to the actual degree of responsibility, and in its regard to the welfare of society cares not greatly to trouble itself about the individual, that is no reason why we should shut our eyes to facts; it is still our duty to place them on record, in the confident assurance that the time will come when men will be able to deal more wisely with them.

The prevention of insanity

It would be a hard and unwelcome thing to lay down rules for the prevention and regulation of marriages in accordance with what might seem to be the sober dictates of reason, even if, which is not the case, science had arrived at such a degree of development as to be able to do so with exactness and authority. Moreover, we are not sure how great may be the compensating advantages of seemingly unwise marriages. It will be easier and more agreeable to admit that for the present men must go on marrying and giving in marriage without much reflection, and to "trust the universal plan will all protect."

Nevertheless there is a certain amount of definite knowledge which we are bound to recognise, however we may deal with it. It is a fact that a pathological evolution – or, more correctly, a pathological degeneration – of mind does take place through generations. The course of events may be represented as something in this wise: in the first generation we perhaps observe only a predominance of the nervous temperament, irritability, a tendency to cerebral congestion, with passionate and violent outbreaks; in the second generation there is an aggravation of the morbid tendencies, displaying itself in cerebral hæmorrhages, idiopathic affections of the brain, and in the appearance of such neuroses as epilepsy, hysteria and hypochondria; in the third generation, if no check has been opposed to the downward course, we meet with instinctive tendencies of a bad nature, exhibiting themselves in eccentric, disorderly and dangerous acts, and with attacks of some forms of mental derangement; and finally, in the fourth generation, matters going from bad to worse, we meet with deaf-mutism, imbecility and idiocy, and sterility, the terminus of the pathological decline being reached. Such is the course of degeneration when it proceeds unchecked.

But an opposite course of regeneration of the family by happy marriages, wise education, and a prudent conduct of life is possible; the downward tendency may be thus checked, and even perhaps effaced in time. As things are at present, such regeneration is always accidental, is never designed and deliberately aimed at. How it may be done designedly and systematically is certainly a most complex and difficult enquiry, but it is one which lies within the range of human faculty. The first condition of the enquiry is that men should realise that such apparently capricious events as the imbecility of one child and the genius of another child are effects of natural laws, that they are not less so than are the complex chemical combinations and decompositions which at one time were as obscure, and seemed as irregular, uncertain and meaningless, but which are now known to take place with unfailing uniformity under the same conditions. Let the same amount of patient observation and laborious investigation which has been applied by a succession of distinguished men to unravel the mysteries of chemical combinations, be applied to the observation and investigation of the more complex mysteries of the degeneration and regeneration of families, and there can be no doubt that light will be thrown upon the phenomena. . . .

If we refer to the enumerated causes of insanity in any book which treats of the subject, or in the first asylum report which comes to hand, we shall find that hereditary predisposition, intemperance, and mental anxieties and troubles of some kind or other cover nearly the whole field of causation. These are causes which it should be the work of mankind to remove, or, if not to remove entirely, at any rate to abate considerably: hereditary predisposition, by abstention from marriage or by prudent intermarriage; intemperance, by temperance in living; mental anxieties, by the wise cultivation of the mind and by the formation of habits of self-government. Avoiding intemperance and other excesses, we shall cut off not only the insanity which is directly produced by it, but we shall prevent its indirect effects by cutting off a fruitful cause of hereditary predisposition to physical and mental degeneracy in the next generation; and by cutting off such native infirmities of brain and mind, we shall prevent the emotional agitations and explosions which are the consequences of such infirmities and which act as the so-called moral causes of the disease.

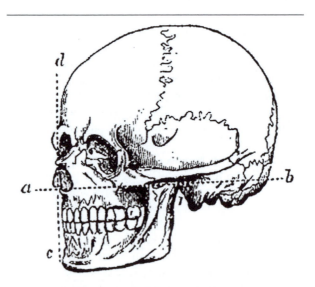

Figure 19.1 The Facial Angle of the Well Developed Skull and Face. The vertical forehead, according to scientific racists, is one of the traits distinguishing the civilized white man from inferior types, with their sloping foreheads. Eugene S. Talbot, *Degeneracy: Its causes, signs, and results* (London: Walter Scott, Ltd, 1898), Fig. 19, p. 181.

Note

1   See, for example, Adran Raine, Todd Lencz, Susan Bihrle, Lori laCasse, and
    Patrick Colletti, "Reduced prefrontal gray matter volume and reduced autonomic
    activity in antisocial personality disorder," *Archives of General Psychiatry* 57 (Feb.
    2000): 119–27.

Chapter 20

Richard L. Dugdale:
The "Jukes" family, 1877

Richard Dugdale, a New York City merchant, discovered the criminalistic "Jukes" family while doing volunteer research for the Prison Association of New York. In the following extract, he first describes how he happened upon this family, breeding promiscuously on the shores of the Finger Lakes. Eventually he traced the Jukes back to an ancestor, Max, born in the mid-eighteenth century. By collecting biographical data from jail, hospital, and poorhouse records, Dugdale believed he could trace and estimate the differential impact of heredity and environment on Max's descendants. He dubbed those descendants the "Jukes," even though they in fact had a variety of family names, and he designated all those with whom the Jukes married or cohabited as members of the "X" blood. These groupings gave the impression of two vast, monolithic family groups whose heredity could be traced through generations.

"The Jukes" is not a long book – just seventy pages – but it had immense impact. Dugdale's table-studded work heralded the advent of statistical methods in social scientific research. His fold-out charts on Max's five (hypothetical) daughters seemed to show disabilities like pauperism and criminality coursing through the generations, increasing in frequency in the third, fourth, and fifth generations, but finally disappearing as the Jukes succumbed to "exhaustion." (Like Morel, Dugdale believed that degenerate "stock" would simply die out through debilitude.) His statistical tables appeared to prove that blindness, drunkenness, insanity, criminality, epilepsy, and other degenerate traits are closely interrelated. Although Dugdale was probably unaware of the work of Morel and other European degenerationists, he came up with very similar results, apparently "inventing" a form of degeneration theory on his own.[1] And like Morel, he endorsed a "soft" hereditarianism, maintaining that the results of bad heredity can be modified by environmental improvements, although it may take several generations to restore bad stock to normality. Criminal tendencies, according to Dugdale, can be minimized or even eradicated by environmental changes – industrial training for wayward youths, for example, and removing children from criminalistic families as soon as they are weaned.

Dugdale became the darling of eugenicists, who thought that he had proved the inheritance of pauperism, criminality, and other social problems, and his work helped to inaugurate the eugenics movement. More conservative social reformers rushed to document the evolution of other bad families and to clamp down on their reproduction.[2]

These extracts come from Richard L. Dugdale, *"The Jukes": A study in crime, pauperism, disease, and heredity; also further studies of criminals* (New York: G. P. Putnam's Sons, 1877), pp. 7–15, 65–70.

RICHARD L. DUGDALE: THE "JUKES" FAMILY

In July, 1874, the New York Prison Association having deputed me to visit thirteen of the county jails of this State and report thereupon, I made a tour of inspection in pursuance of that appointment. No specially striking cases of criminal careers, traceable through several generations, presented themselves till—county was reached. Here, however, were found six persons, under four family names, who turned out to be blood relations in some degree. The oldest, a man of fifty-five, was waiting trial for receiving stolen goods; his daughter, aged eighteen, held as witness against him; her uncle, aged forty-two, burglary in the first degree; the illegitimate daughter of the latter's wife, aged twelve years, upon which child the latter had attempted rape, to be sent to the reformatory for vagrancy; and two brothers in another branch of the family, aged respectively nineteen and fourteen, accused of an assault with intent to kill, they having maliciously pushed a child over a high cliff and nearly killed him. Upon trial the oldest was acquitted, though the goods stolen were found in his house, his previous good character saving him; the guilt belonged to his brother-in-law, the man aged forty-two, above mentioned, who was living in the house. This brother-in-law is an illegitimate child, an habitual criminal and the son of an unpunished and cautious thief. He had two brothers and one sister, all of whom are thieves, the sister being the contriver of crime, they its executors. The daughter of this woman, the girl aged eighteen above mentioned, testified at the trial which resulted in convicting her uncle and procuring his sentence for twenty years to State prison, that she was forced to join him in his last foray; that he had loaded her with the booty, and beat her on the journey home, over two miles, because she lagged under the load. When this girl was released, her family in jail and thus left without a home, she was forced to make her lodging in a brothel on the outskirts of the city. Next morning she applied to the judge to be recommitted to prison "for protection" against specified carnal outrages required of her and submitted to. She has since been sent to the house of refuge. Of the two boys, one was discharged by the Grand Jury; the other was tried and received five years' imprisonment in Sing Sing.

These six persons belonged to a long lineage, reaching back to the early colonists, and had intermarried so slightly with the emigrant population of the old world that they may be called a strictly American family. They had lived in the same locality for generations, and were so despised by the reputable community that their family name *had come to be used generically as a term of reproach.*

That this was deserved became manifest on slight inquiry. It was found that out of twenty-nine males, in ages ranging from fifteen to seventy-five, the immediate blood relations of these six persons, seventeen of them were criminals, or fifty-eight per cent; while fifteen were convicted of some degree of offense, and received seventy-one years of sentence. Fuller details are shown in the table opposite [omitted here], the name "Juke" standing for the blood relations of those found in the jail, the capital "X" for relations by marriage or cohabitation.

The crimes and misdemeanors they committed were assault and battery, assault with intent to kill, murder, attempt at rape, petit larceny, grand larceny, burglary, forgery, cruelty to animals. With these facts in hand, it was thought wise to extend the investigation to other branches of the family, and explore it more thoroughly.

The sheriff communicated the names of two gentlemen – life-long residents of the county, one of them 84 years old and for many years town physician – who gave me the genealogies of many of the branches of this family, with details of individual biographies. This opened up so large a field of study, that I then had no idea of its extent and still less of the unexpected results which a subsequent analysis disclosed. . . .

Having brought back a very incomplete genealogical tree including 100 persons, Dr. Elisha Harris, the Corresponding Secretary of the Association, urged me to push the inquiry, and I returned to the country to resume the search. . . .

The habitat of the "Jukes"

The ancestral breeding-spot of this family nestles along the forest-covered margin of five lakes, so rocky as to be at some parts inaccessible. It may be called one of the crime cradles of the State of New York; for in subsequent examinations of convicts in the different State prisons, a number of them were found to be the descendants of families equivalent to the "Jukes," and emerging from this nest. Most of the ancestors were squatters upon the soil, and in some instances have become owners by tax-title or by occupancy. They lived in log or stone houses similar to slave-hovels, all ages, sexes, relations and strangers "bunking" indiscriminately. One form of this bunking has been described to me. During the winter the inmates lie on the floor strewn with straw or rushes like so many radii to the hearth, the embers of the fire forming a centre towards which their feet focus for warmth. This proximity, where not producing illicit relations, must often have evolved an atmosphere of suggestiveness fatal to habits of chastity. . . .

The origin of the stock of the "Jukes"

Between the years 1720 and 1740 was born a man who shall herein be called Max. He was a descendant of the early Dutch settlers, and lived much as the back-woodsmen upon our frontiers now do. He is described as "a hunter and fisher, a hard drinker, jolly and companionable, averse to steady toil," working hard by spurts and idling by turns, becoming blind in his old age, and entailing his blindness upon his children and grandchildren. He had a numerous progeny, some of them almost certainly illegitimate. Two of his sons married two out of six sisters (called "Jukes" in these pages) who were born between the year 1740 and 1770, but whose parentage has not been absolutely ascertained. The probability is they were not full sisters, that some, if not all of them, were illegitimate. The family name, in two cases, is obscure, which accords with the supposition that at least two of the women were half-sisters to the other four, the legitimate daughters bearing the family name, the illegitimate keeping either the mother's name or adopting that of the reputed father. Five of these women in the first generation were married; the sixth one it has been impossible to trace, for she moved out of the county. Of the five that are known, three have had illegitimate children before marriage. One who is called in these pages Ada Juke, but who is better known to the public as "Margaret, the mother of criminals," had one bastard son, who is the progenitor of the distinctively criminal line. . . .

Tentative generalizations on heredity and environment

1. Where the organization is structurally modified, as in idiocy and insanity, or organically weak as in many diseases, the heredity is the preponderating factor in determining the career; but it is, even then, capable of marked modification for better or worse by the character of the environment. In other words, capacity, physical and mental, is limited and determined mainly by heredity. This is probably because it is fixed during the period of ante-natal organization.

2. Where the conduct depends on the knowledge of moral obligation (excluding insanity and idiocy), the environment has more influence than the heredity, because the development of the moral attributes is mainly a post-natal and not an ante-natal formation of cerebral cells. The use to which capacity shall be put is largely governed by the impersonal training or agency of environment, which is itself very variable.

3. The tendency of heredity is to produce an environment which perpetuates that heredity: thus, the licentious parent makes an example which greatly aids in fixing habits of debauchery in the child. The correction is change of environment. For instance, where hereditary kleptomania exists, if the environment should be such as to become an exciting cause, the individual will be an incorrigible thief; but if, on the contrary, he be protected

from temptation, that individual may lead an honest life, with some chances in favor of the entailment stopping there.

4. Environment tends to produce habits which may become hereditary, especially so in pauperism and licentiousness, if it should be sufficiently constant to produce modification of cerebral tissue.

If these conclusions are correct, then the whole question of the control of crime and pauperism become possible, within wide limits, if the necessary training can be made to reach over two or three generations. . . .

The social damage of the "Jukes" estimated

Passing from the actual record, I submit an estimate of the damage of the family, based on what is known of those whose lives have been learned. The total number of persons included in the foregoing statement reach 709; besides these 125 additional names have been gathered since the text of this *essay* was prepared, whose general character is similar. If all the collateral lines which have not been traced could be added to the 709 here tabulated, the aggregate would reach at least 1,200 persons, living and dead. . . . Over a million and a quarter dollars of loss [occurred] in 75 years, caused by a single family 1,200 strong, without reckoning the cash paid for whiskey, or taking into account the entailment of pauperism and crime of the survivors in succeeding generations, and the incurable disease, idiocy and insanity growing out of this debauchery, and reaching further than we can calculate. It is

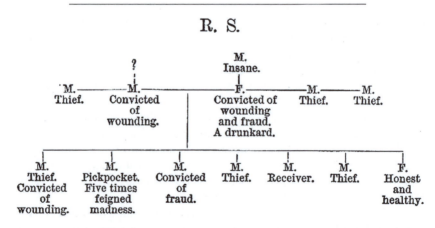

Figure 20.1 The Inheritance of Criminality. In his popular book on heredity, the British psychiatrist S. A. K. Strahan used the genealogy of R. S. to show that "criminality follows the same lines as most other family degenerations. In some cases, it is transmitted, like the suicidal impulse, unchanged through several generations." S. A. K. Strahan, *Marriage and Disease* (London: Kegan Paul, Trench, Trubner, & Co. Ltd, 1892), p. 288.

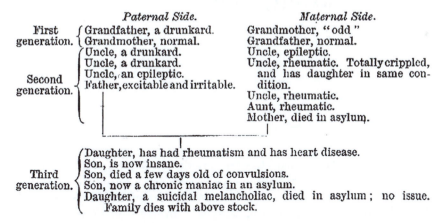

J. G. A.'s FAMILY HISTORY.

	Paternal Side.	*Maternal Side.*
First generation.	Grandfather, a drunkard. Grandmother, normal.	Grandmother, "odd" Grandfather, normal.
Second generation.	Uncle, a drunkard. Uncle, a drunkard. Uncle, an epileptic. Father, excitable and irritable.	Uncle, epileptic. Uncle, rheumatic. Totally crippled, and has daughter in same condition. Uncle, rheumatic. Aunt, rheumatic. Mother, died in asylum.
Third generation.	Daughter, has had rheumatism and has heart disease. Son, is now insane. Son, died a few days old of convulsions. Son, now a chronic maniac in an asylum. Daughter, a suicidal melancholiac, died in asylum; no issue. Family dies with above stock.	

Figure 20.2 Proof of Degeneracy. This chart of the family history of one J. G. A. illustrates degeneration theory, according to which any disability is a sign of underlying decay. S. A. K. Strahan, *Marriage and Disease* (London: Kegan Paul, Trench, Trubner, & Co. Ltd, 1892), p. 231.

getting to be time to ask, do our courts, our laws, our alms-houses and our jails deal with the question presented?

Notes

1   Nicole Rafter, *The Criminal Brain* (New York: New York University Press, 2008).
2   Other bad family studies appear in Nicole H. Rafter, *White Trash: The eugenic family studies, 1877–1919* (Boston: Northeastern University Press, 1988).

Chapter 21

Max Nordau: Decadence and degeneration, 1895

The Hungarian Max Nordau (1849–1923), the last of the great degeneration theorists, was a famous critic of fin-de-siècle art and what he saw as debased tendencies in contemporary cultural life. Morel's definition of degeneration as "a morbid deviation from an original type" provided Nordau with a tool to condemn what he saw as the decadence of late nineteenth-century art and fashion. Moreover, Lombroso's extension of the concept of degeneration into the realms of "psychiatry, criminal law, politics, and sociology," as Nordau explains in his dedication, inspired him to apply the concept of degeneration to "the domain of art and literature."

Impressionist painting, Wagner's operas, Zola's novels, fashion consciousness, gay culture, free thinking, and a rejection of traditional morals and art forms – Nordau condemned all such signs of change for what he saw as their egotism, hysteria, and intellectual exhaustion. Those who propagated such decadence, he felt sure, would be marked by the somatic stigmata of degeneration, just as their criminalistic fellow degenerates were marked; but it would be difficult to confirm this, and besides, he could just as well find the signs of degeneration in their art and social practices. Nordau is far more concerned with artistic degeneration than criminality, but in a final passage on what may lie ahead in the twentieth century, he warns that if degeneration is allowed to go unchecked, the results will be clubs for mutual assassination, drug houses on every corner, gay marriages, and random murders on city streets.

In addition to being an author and social critic, Nordau practiced medicine and became a leader of the Zionist movement. *Degeneration*, a massive work of 560 pages, was his most successful book and made his reputation. Originally published in German in 1892, it was translated and published in English in 1895 (New York: D. Appleton). I have extracted from the dedication (to Lombroso), the introductory section on "Fin-de-siècle" (pp. 15–18), and the concluding section on "The twentieth century" (pp. 537–57).

MAX NORDAU: DECADENCE AND DEGENERATION

TO PROFESSOR CÆSAR LOMBROSO, *TURIN*

DEAR AND HONOURED MASTER,

I dedicate this book to you, in open and joyful recognition of the fact that without your labours it could never have been written.

The notion of degeneracy, first introduced into science by Morel, and developed with so much genius by yourself, has in your hands already shown itself extremely fertile in the most diverse directions. On numerous obscure points of psychiatry, criminal law, politics, and sociology, you have poured a veritable flood of light, which those alone have not perceived who obdurately close their eyes, or who are too short-sighted to derive benefit from any enlightenment whatsoever.

But there is a vast and important domain into which neither you nor your disciples have hitherto borne the torch of your method – the domain of art and literature.

Degenerates are not always criminals, prostitutes, anarchists, and pronounced luna-tics; they are often authors and artists. These, however, manifest the same mental characteristics, and for the most part the same somatic features, as the members of the above-mentioned anthropological family, who satisfy their unhealthy impulses with the knife of the assassin or the bomb of the dynamiter, instead of with pen and pencil. . . .

Now I have undertaken the work of investigating (as much as possible after your method) the tendencies of the fashions in art and literature; of proving that they have their source in the degencracy of their authors, and that the enthusiasm of their admirers is for manifestations of more or less pronounced moral insanity, imbecility, and dementia.

Thus, this book is an attempt at a really scientific criticism, which does not base its judgment of a book upon the purely accidental, capricious, and variable emotions it awakens – emotions depending on the temperament and mood of the individual reader – but upon the psycho-physiological elements from which it sprang . . . .

Max Nordau

Fin-de-siècle

. . . The physician, especially if he have devoted himself to the special study of nervous and mental maladies, recognises at a glance, in the *fin-de-siècle* dis-position, in the tendencies of contemporary art and poetry, in the life and conduct of the men who write mystic, symbolic and "decadent" works, and the attitude taken by their admirers in the tastes and æsthetic instincts of fashionable society, the confluence of two well-defined conditions of disease, with which he is quite familiar, viz. degeneration (degeneracy) and hysteria, of which the minor stages are designated as neurasthenia. These two condi-tions of the organism differ from each other, yet have many features in com-mon, and frequently occur together; so that it is easier to observe them in their composite forms, than each in isolation.

The conception of degeneracy, which, at this time, obtains throughout the science of mental disease, was first clearly grasped and formulated by Morel. . . .

"The clearest notion we can form of degeneracy is to regard it as *a morbid deviation from an original type*. This deviation, even if, at the outset, it was ever so slight, contained transmissible elements of such a nature that anyone bearing in him the germs becomes more and more incapable of fulfilling his functions in the world; and mental progress, already checked in his own person, finds itself menaced also in his descendants."

When under any kind of noxious influences an organism becomes debilitated, its successors will not resemble the healthy, normal type of the species, with capacities for development, but will form a new sub-species, which, like all others, possesses the capacity of transmitting to its offspring, in a continuously increasing degree, its peculiarities, these being morbid deviations from the normal form – gaps in development, malformations and infirmities. That which distinguishes degeneracy from the formation of new species (phylogeny) is, that the morbid variation does not continuously subsist and propagate itself, like one that is healthy, but, fortunately, is soon rendered sterile, and after a few generations often dies out before it reaches the lowest grade of organic degradation.

Degeneracy betrays itself among men in certain physical characteristics, which are denominated "stigmata," or brandmarks – an unfortunate term derived from a false idea, as if degeneracy were necessarily the consequence of a fault, and the indication of it a punishment. Such stigmata consist of deformities, multiple and stunted growths in the first line of asymmetry, the unequal development of the two halves of the face and cranium; then imperfection in the development of the external ear, which is conspicuous for its enormous size, or protrudes from the head, like a handle, and the lobe of which is either lacking or adhering to the head, and the helix of which is not involuted; further, squint-eyes, hare-lips, irregularities in the form and position of the teeth; pointed or flat palates, webbed or supernumerary fingers (syn-and poly-dactylia), etc. In the book from which I have quoted, Morel gives a list of the anatomical phenomena of degeneracy, which later observers have largely extended. In particular, Lombroso has conspicuously broadened our knowledge of stigmata, but he apportions them merely to his "born criminals" – a limitation which from the very scientific standpoint of Lombroso himself cannot be justified, his "born criminals" being nothing but a subdivision of degenerates. Féret expresses this very emphatically when he says, "Vice, crime and madness are only distinguished from each other by social prejudices."

There might be a sure means of proving that the application of the term "degenerates" to the originators of all the *fin-de-siècle* movements in art and literature is not arbitrary, that it is no baseless conceit, but a fact; and that would be a careful physical examination of the persons concerned, and an inquiry into their pedigree. In almost all cases, relatives would be met with who were undoubtedly degenerate, and one or more stigmata discovered which would indisputably establish the diagnosis of "Degeneration." Of course, from human consideration, the result of such an inquiry could often not be made public; and he alone would be convinced who should be able to undertake it himself.

Science, however, has found, together with these physical stigmata, others of a mental order, which betoken degeneracy quite as clearly as the former; and they allow of an easy demonstration from all the vital manifestations, and, in particular, from all the works of degenerates, so that it is not necessary to measure the cranium of an author, or to see the lobe of a painter's ear, in order to recognise the fact that he belongs to the class of degenerates.

Quite a number of different designations have been found for these persons. Maudsley and Ball call them "Borderland dwellers" – that is to say, dwellers on the borderland between reason and pronounced madness. Magnan gives to them the name of "higher degenerates" (*dégénérés supérieurs*), and Lombroso speaks of "mattoids" (from *matto*, the Italian for insane), and "graphomaniacs," under which he classifies those semi-insane persons who feel a strong impulse to write. In spite, however, of this variety of nomenclature, it is a question simply of one single species of individuals, who betray their fellowship by the similarity of their mental physiognomy. . . .

The twentieth century

. . . Hysteria and degeneration have always existed; but they formerly showed themselves sporadically, and had no importance in the life of the whole community. It was only the vast fatigue which was experienced by the generation on which the multitude of discoveries and innovations burst abruptly, imposing upon it organic exigencies greatly surpassing its strength, which created favourable conditions under which these maladies could gain ground enormously, and become a danger to civilization. Certain micro-organisms engendering mortal diseases have always been present also – for example, the bacillus of cholera; but they only cause epidemics when circumstances arise intensely favourable for their rapid increase. In the same way the body constantly harbours parasites which only injure it when another bacillus has invaded and devastated it. For example, we are always inhabited by staphylococcus and streptococcus, but the influenza bacillus must first appear for them to swarm and produce mortal suppurations. Thus, the vermin of plagiarists in art and literature becomes dangerous only when the insane, who follow their own original paths, have previously poisoned the *Zeitgeist*, weakened by fatigue, and rendered it incapable of resistance.

We stand now in the midst of a severe mental epidemic; of a sort of black death of degeneration and hysteria, and it is natural that we should ask anxiously on all sides: "What is to come next?" . . .

It is possible that the disease may not have yet attained its culminating point. If it should become more violent, gain yet more in breadth and depth, then certain phenomena which are perceived as exceptions or in an embryo condition would henceforth increase to a formidable extent and develop consistently; others, which at present are only observed among the inmates of lunatic asylums, would pass into the daily habitual condition of whole classes of the population. Life would then present somewhat the following picture:

Every city possesses its club of suicides. By the side of this exist clubs for mutual assassination by strangulation, hanging, or stabbing. In the place of the present taverns houses would be found devoted to the service of consumers of ether, chloral, naphtha, and hashish. The number of persons suffering from aberrations of taste and smell has become so considerable that it is a lucrative trade to open shops for them where they can swallow in rich vessels all sorts of dirt, and breathe amidst surroundings which do not offend their sense of beauty nor their habits of comfort the odour of decay and filth. A number of new professions are being formed – that of injectors of morphia and cocaine; of commissioners who, posted at the corners of the streets, offer their arms to persons attacked by agoraphobia, in order to enable them to cross the roads and squares; of companies of men who by vigorous affirmations are charged to tranquillize persons afflicted with the mania of doubt when taken by a fit of nervousness, etc.

The increase of nervous irritability, far beyond the present standard, has made it necessary to institute certain measures of protection. After it has frequently come to pass that over-excited persons, being unable to resist a sudden impulse, have killed from their windows with air-guns, or have even openly attacked, the street boys who have uttered shrill whistles or piercingly sharp screams without rhyme or reason; that they have forced their way into strange houses where beginners are practising the piano or singing, and there committed murder. . . .

Sexual psychopathy of every nature has become so general and so imperious that manners and laws have adapted themselves accordingly. They appear already in the fashions. Masochists or passivists, who form the majority of men, clothe themselves in a costume which recalls, by colour and cut, feminine apparel. Women who wish to please men of this kind wear men's dress, an eyeglass, boots with spurs and riding-whip, and only show themselves in the street with a large cigar in their mouths. The demand of persons with the "contrary" sexual sentiment that persons of the same sex can conclude a legal marriage has obtained satisfaction, seeing they have been numerous enough to elect a majority of deputies having the same tendency. Sadists, "bestials," nosophiles, and necrophiles, etc., find legal opportunities to gratify their inclinations. Modesty and restraint are dead superstitions of the past, and appear only as atavism and among the inhabitants of remote villages. The lust of murder is confronted as a disease, and treated by surgical intervention, etc. . . .

It would be easy to augment this picture still further, no feature of which is invented, every detail being borrowed from special literature on criminal law and psychiatria, and observations of the peculiarities of neurasthenics, hysterics, and mattoids. This will be, in the near future, the condition of civilized humanity, if fatigue, nervous exhaustion, and the diseases and degeneration conditioned by them, make much greater progress.

Will it come to this? Well, no; I think not. And this, for a reason which scarcely perhaps permits of an objection: because humanity has not yet reached the term of its evolution; because the over-exertion of two or three generations cannot yet have exhausted all its vital powers. Humanity is not senile. It is still young, and a moment of over-exertion is not fatal for youth; it can recover itself. Humanity resembles a vast torrent of lava, which rushes, broad and deep, from the crater of a volcano in constant activity. The outer crust cracks into cold, vitrified scoriæ, but under this dead shell the mass flows, rapidly and evenly, in living incandescence.

As long as the vital powers of an individual, as of a race, are not wholly consumed, the organism makes efforts actively or passively to adapt itself, by seeking to modify injurious conditions, or by adjusting itself in some way so that conditions impossible to modify should be as little noxious as possible. Degenerates, hysterics, and neurasthenics are not capable of adaptation. Therefore they are fated to disappear. . . .

The disease of degeneracy consists precisely in the fact that the degenerate organism has not the power to mount to the height of evolution already attained by the species, but stops on the way at an earlier or later point. The relapse of the degenerate may reach to the most stupendous depth. As, in reverting to the cleavage of the superior maxillary peculiar to insects with sextuple lips, he sinks somatically to the level of fishes, nay to that of the arthropoda, or, even further, to that of rhizopods not yet sexually differentiated; as by fistulæ of the neck he reverts to the branchiæ of the lowest fishes, the selacious; or by excess in the number of fingers (polydactylia) to the multiple-rayed fins of fishes, perhaps even to the bristles of worms; or, by hermaphrodism, to the asexuality of rhizopods – so in the most favourable case, as a higher degenerate, he renews intellectually the type of the primitive man of the most remote Stone Age; or, in the worst case, as an idiot, that of an animal far anterior to man. . . .

It is the sacred duty of all healthy and moral men to take part in the work of protecting and saving those who are not already too deeply diseased.

The underclass and the underworld

The underclass and the underworld

Introduction to Part V

It is unlikely that any society has ever lacked criminals, as Emile Durkheim argues in a passage at the end of this book (Chapter 59). But to develop an underclass, a society needs conditions of gross inequality; and to develop a more or less stable criminal underworld, with specialized kinds of work and specialized lifestyles, a society needs not only inequality, but also a large population. These conditions – inequality and population size – were not unique to the nineteenth-century city, but industrialization and population growth, together with rapid migration from rural to urban areas, almost guaranteed that the nineteenth-century city would become a prolific breeding ground for the poor and the criminal.

What was unique to the nineteenth century was that journalists, novelists, travelers, and reformers started writing analytically about the underclass and underworld, identifying the inequalities that generated a hopelessly marginalized and self-replicating underclass and explaining why it produced crime. Few of these writers, aside from W. E. B. DuBois (Chapter 26), would have thought of themselves as sociologists, but they were inventing urban sociology as they went along: collecting data, analyzing it, and generating hypotheses. (Sometimes they even proposed a hypothesis only to test and reject it, as Henry Mayhew and John Binny do in Chapter 56, when they first blame prostitution on prostitutes' shamelessness, but then push on to identify social causes.) At the same time, these investigators were inventing criminology.

Of the Western world's "great cities," to use Fredrich Engels' term for areas that were more large than admirable, London and New York attracted the most commentary from the new chroniclers of the urban underclass and underworld. Thus, to avoid repetition, this section omits some of the best-known examples, such as those by Thomas Beames (*The Rookeries of London*, London: 1850), Charles Loring Brace (*The Dangerous Classes of New York, and Twenty Years' Work Among Them*, New York: Wynkoop and Hallenbeck, 1872), and Charles Booth (*Life and Labour of the People in London*, London: Macmillan, 1902–3 – slightly out of this volume's timeframe in any case). However, this part does include the fascinating example of a rural area with an underclass (Chapter 22), another of a particular group within the urban underclass (Chapter 26), and a third of Manchester, England, a very early and particularly brutal industrial city (Chapter 23), as well as representatives of the literature on London (Chapter 24) and New York (Chapter 25).

Elizabeth Fry and Joseph John Gurney: On the condition of the Irish people, 1827

Elizabeth Gurney Fry (1780–1845) became one of the best-known women in the United Kingdom for her work in prison and social reform. Even Queen Victoria met with her and financially supported her work. A Quaker, Fry was extremely devout and active in the Society of Friends, which she used as a base for improving prisons throughout the United Kingdom. She was particularly interested in reforming the management of women's prisons and abolishing capital punishment. Together with Joseph John Gurney, her younger brother, Fry composed this address to Richard Colley Wellesley, who had been appointed Lord Lieutenant of Ireland in 1821, a time when the English were beginning to rethink their exploitation of Ireland and cruel subjugation of its poor Catholic population. Fry and Gurney tried to push the reforms along.

This excerpt comes from Elizabeth Fry and Joseph John Gurney, *Report addressed to the Marquess Wellesley, Lord Lieutenant of Ireland*, originally published in 1827. I worked from the third edition, of 1847 (Norwich: Josiah Fletcher), extracting from the third and final section of the *Report*, titled "On the state of the people" (using pp. 66–7, 80–8).

ELIZABETH FRY AND JOSEPH JOHN GURNEY: ON THE CONDITION OF THE IRISH PEOPLE

. . . Now, what is the effect of all this grinding and oppression? The poor people on the estates of such landlords gradually sink into the extremity of wretchedness, listlessness, and want. They are deprived of all their motives to an honest industry, and are loosened from every tie of attachment to their superiors. They become thievish and idle servants – violent and dangerous neighbours – and miserably discontented subjects. But the most remarkable fact respecting them is this – that notwithstanding all those supposed *checks to population* which are said to arise from sickness, misery, and want, their numbers are perpetually increasing. Sensible that they can sink no lower in the scale of wretchedness, and anxious to secure to themselves the few natural enjoyments of which society has not deprived them, they are uniformly found to give themselves up to early and improvident marriages – and the lands on which the whole scene is acted, are presently overrun by a starving and angry population.

A state of overwhelming physical distress, in any people, is for the most part closely associated with a degraded condition of morals; partly because beggary and immorality produce and confirm each other, and partly because unsound principles of action are equally productive of *both*. This observation is, we fear, fully justified by the condition and character of the lower orders of the people in many parts of Ireland. We confess that we were deeply affected, as we passed through many of the villages and towns, by observing in the appearance and deportment of the populace, the too evident traces of a disordered state of morals; and this impression could not fail to be very much deepened by our visits to the jails. There, as we have already hinted, we were brought into contact with a vast variety, as well as quantity, of crime, and an opportunity was afforded us of studying the darker side of the character of the population – of observing what are their peculiar propensities to evil – and what the particulars of their natural temperament which most obviously require counteraction.

A great proportion of the offences committed in Ireland, are such as arise from the violent and often sudden impulse of unsubdued passion – inflamed probably by the intemperate use of spirituous liquors. Assaults of various descriptions are the most usual *misdemeanors*, for which Irishmen are sent to jail – and these instances are, in every part of the country, extremely numerous. Another large and more serious class of offenders appeared to have been engaged in acts of violence, and sometimes of great cruelty, from motives of *settled revenge*; and, as far as we could ascertain, this disposition was excited, almost universally, by private, rather than political, causes. When a gentleman, in any of the more disturbed districts, dispossesses a tenant – though for the fairest reasons – and lets his farm to a person who may not be quite so pleasing to the surrounding population – and even when no such distinction can be drawn – he exposes the new occupant of his farm to the revenge, not only of the individual supposed to be aggrieved, but to that of almost the whole neighbouring community: and we are sorry to be obliged to believe that this revenge is in general most difficult to appease. The result, perhaps, is the conflagration of his haystack or barn, or more probably, a combined attack upon his house, his family, or his person.

It is a melancholy fact, that these desperate attempts are too often consummated by the murder of the individual who is thus exposed to the vengeance of the people. It was, in the highest degree, awful and affecting to our feelings to find, in many of the jails, *several* individuals imprisoned under charge of murder. Some of these, we believe, were cases in which the sudden gusts of passion, or excess of intoxication, had led to the destruction of human life; but, for the most part, the offence appeared to have assumed the more formidable character of cruel deliberation, usually in order to gratify revenge, but in some instances for the purpose of robbery. . . .

If we are led to inquire into the origin of that violence and immorality which has now been described, it is obvious enough that it is to be found in the natural propensity of man to indulge his passions, in spite of the dictates of reason and conscience; but undoubtedly, in the case of the lower Irish, there are several circumstances which impart to this general source of evil a double vigour. We have, in the first place, a state of misery and degradation, by which every motive to sobriety, honesty, and virtue, is undermined, and a recklessness engendered, which leads, in the most easy manner, to the commission of crime: secondly, a national mind impatient of control, and liable, in the greatest degree, to strong and lively emotions; thirdly, a constant and cheap supply, and universal consumption, of ardent spirits: and lastly, in some parts of Ireland, an almost incredible ignorance and want of mental culture.

If these are some of the principal causes of the debased morals and violent crimes prevailing amongst the lower part of the population, it will not perhaps be very difficult to point out the best methods of counteracting their operation. This work of counteraction, however, must necessarily be a very slow one, and it is rather from a reliance on the *ultimate* efficacy of certain great principles, than from the expectation of any rapid change for the better, that we venture to throw before the Lord Lieutenant a few remarks on what appear to us the most important points connected with the subject.

If a state of great physical misery, and the degradation and despair connected with it, are one fertile source of the moral evils which abound in Ireland, it is evident that every sound plan for relieving and employing the poor, and of raising them to a condition of respectability, will not only produce its direct effect in alleviating distress, but will tend, though indirectly, yet certainly, to check the progress of immorality and crime. Nothing, indeed, can be of greater importance, in order to ensure the peace of Ireland, than a combined effort, on the part of the reflecting and cultivated portion of society, more completely to *civilize* the lower orders; to give them an interest, a stake, in the country; and, while relief and employment are afforded them, to lead them forward to habits of outward decency and comfort. These, when once formed, will preclude all temptation to a life of lawlessness and outrage.

Were the poor of Ireland, instead of being reduced by high rents, miserably low wages, uncertain tenure, and want of employment, to a condition of misery and disaffection – and then in the end driven off the lands in a state of despair – were they, instead of suffering all this oppression, kindly treated, properly employed and remunerated, and encouraged to cultivate small portions of land, at a moderate rent, on their own account, there can be little question that they would gradually become valuable members of the community, and would be as much bound to their superiors by the tie of gratitude, as they are now severed from them by ill-will and revenge. . . .

If partiality and corruption in magistrates are dangerous every where, we are persuaded that they are doubly dangerous in Ireland; and we have no doubt that the notorious existence of these evils, in some parts of the island, has been one of the most fruitful sources of disaffection and disturbance. Nothing, indeed, can be conceived more calculated than a partial and corrupt execution of the law, to inflame the passions of a most acute and sensitive people. We hope we may take the liberty of congratulating the Lord Lieutenant on the improvement which is universally allowed to have taken place, in this respect, within the last few years; nor ought it to be forgotten that, while the character and conduct of the local magistracy, where they have hitherto been defective, has been undergoing, we trust, an essential reform, the higher judicial offices are now generally filled with men whose humane and enlightened views are singularly well adapted to the state of the country.

But it is not justice and impartiality *alone* that the Irish people require at our hands. If we would conciliate their good will towards Great Britain and her government; if we would render them a satisfied and contented people; if we would turn their lively emotions of mind into the channel of love and gratitude, we must treat them with kindness and tenderness; we must be actuated, in all our transactions with them, by the most *patient* and *persevering* benevolence. Their wounds are too deep, and their irritation too much confirmed, to be very speedily healed; but a determinate adoption and *uniform maintenance* of such a line of conduct towards them will, doubtless, be found, in the end, efficacious and triumphant. These remarks are intended to apply not merely to the public acts of Government, but more particularly to the general conduct and demeanor of the upper classes towards those who are placed under their influence and authority. We were often pained, as we passed through the country, by hearing so much of the unqualified command and rough rebuke; nor could we wonder that, on the part of inferiors, sullenness and obstinacy were the consequence. We long to see the most degraded part of the people raised from the condition of slaves – treated as men of understanding and feeling – and ruled with that civility and tenderness which are sure to meet (in the Irishman especially) with a corresponding return of grateful and devoted affection.

Chapter 23

Friedrich Engels: The English working class, 1845

Friedrich Engels (1820–95), the German social theorist and philosopher, collaborated with Karl Marx to develop the political theory of communism. Born in Prussia, he was sent in 1842 by his father's textile company to work in Manchester, England, where he did the research for his first book, *The Condition of the Working Class in England*. Later he worked with Marx to write the *Communist Manifesto*.

The Condition of the Working Class in England, first published in German, in 1845, did not appear in English until 1887. I worked from an edition edited by David McLellan (Oxford: Oxford University Press, 1993); the extracts come from pp. 126–7 and 136–43 in that volume.

FRIEDRICH ENGELS: THE ENGLISH WORKING CLASS

He [the proletarian] is poor, life offers him no charm, almost every enjoyment is denied him, the penalties of the law have no further terrors for him; why should he restrain his desires, why leave to the rich the enjoyment of his birthright, why not seize a part of it for himself? What inducement has the proletarian not to steal? It is all very pretty and very agreeable to the ear of the bourgeois to hear the "sacredness of property" asserted; but for him who has none, the sacredness of property dies out of itself. Money is the god of this world; the bourgeois takes the proletarian's money from him and so makes a practical atheist of him. No wonder, then, if the proletarian retains his atheism and no longer respects the sacredness and power of the earthly God. And when the poverty of the proletarian is intensified to the point of actual lack of the barest necessaries of life, to want and hunger, the temptation to disregard all social order does but gain power. This the bourgeoisie for the most part recognizes. Symons observes that poverty exercises the same ruinous influence upon the mind which drunkenness exercises upon the body; and Dr Alison explains to property-holding readers, with the greatest exactness, what the consequences of social oppression must be for the working class. Want leaves the working man the choice between starving slowly, killing himself speedily, or taking what he needs where he finds it – in plain English, stealing. And there is no cause for surprise that most of them prefer stealing to starvation and suicide.

True, there are, within the working class, numbers too moral to steal even when reduced to the utmost extremity, and these starve or commit suicide. For suicide, formerly the enviable privilege of the upper classes, has become fashionable among the English workers, and numbers of the poor kill themselves to avoid the misery from which they see no other means of escape.

But far more demoralizing than his poverty in its influence upon the English working man is the insecurity of his position, the necessity of living upon wages from hand to mouth, that in short which makes a proletarian of him. The smaller peasants in Germany are usually poor, and often suffer want, but they are less at the mercy of accident, they have at least something secure. The proletarian, who has nothing but his two hands, who consumes today what he earned yesterday, who is subject to every possible chance, and has not the slightest guarantee for being able to earn the barest necessities of life, whom every crisis, every whim of his employer may deprive of bread, this proletarian is placed in the most revolting, inhuman position conceivable for a human being. The slave is assured of a bare livelihood by the self-interest of his master, the serf has at least a scrap of land on which to live; each has at worst a guarantee for life itself. But the proletarian must depend upon himself alone, and is yet prevented from so applying his abilities as to be able to rely upon them. Everything that the proletarian can do to improve his position is but a drop in the ocean compared with the floods of varying chances to which he is exposed, over which he has not the slightest control. . . .

There is nothing to be done with the bourgeois; he is essentially conservative in however liberal a guise, his interest is bound up with that of the property-holding class, he is dead to all active movement; he is losing his position in the forefront of England's historical development. The workers are taking his place, in rightful claim first, then in fact.

All this, together with the correspondent public action of the workers, with which we shall deal later, forms the favourable side of the character of this class; the unfavourable one may be quite as briefly summed up, and follows quite as naturally out of the given causes. Drunkenness, sexual irregularities, brutality, and disregard for the rights of property are the chief points with which the bourgeois charges them. That they drink heavily is to be expected. Sheriff Alison asserts that in Glasgow some 30,000 working men get drunk every Saturday night, and the estimate is certainly not exaggerated; and that in that city in 1830, one house in twelve, and in 1840, one house in ten, was a public house. . . .

On Saturday evenings, especially when wages are paid and work stops somewhat earlier than usual, when the whole working class pours from its own poor quarters into the main thoroughfares, intemperance may be seen in all its brutality. I have rarely come out of Manchester on such an evening without meeting numbers of people staggering and seeing others lying in the gutter. On Sunday evening the same scene is usually repeated, only less noisily. And when their money is spent, the drunkards go to the nearest pawnshop, of which there are plenty in every city – over sixty in Manchester, and ten or twelve in a single street of Salford, Chapel Street – and pawn whatever they possess. . . .

Next to intemperance in the enjoyment of intoxicating liquors, one of the principal faults of English working men is sexual licence. But this, too, follows with relentless logic, with inevitable necessity out of the position of a class left to itself, with no means of making fitting use of its freedom. The bourgeoisie has left the working class only these two pleasures, while imposing upon it a multitude of labours and hardships, and the consequence is that the working men, in order to get something from life, concentrate their whole energy upon these two enjoyments, carry them to excess, surrender to them in the most unbridled manner. When people are placed under conditions which appeal to the brute only, what remains to them but to rebel or to succumb to utter brutality? And when, moreover, the bourgeoisie does its full share in maintaining prostitution – and how many of the 40,000 prostitutes who fill the streets of London every evening live upon the virtuous bourgeoisie! How many of them owe it to the seduction of a bourgeois, that they must offer their bodies to the passers-by in order to live? – surely it has least of all a right to reproach the workers with their sexual brutality.

The failings of the workers in general may be traced to an unbridled thirst for pleasure, to want of providence, and of flexibility in fitting into the social order, to the general inability to sacrifice the pleasure of the moment to a remoter advantage. But is that to be wondered at? When a class can purchase few and only the most sensual pleasures by its wearying toil, must it not give itself over blindly and madly to those pleasures? A class about whose education no one troubles himself, which is a play-ball to a thousand chances, knows no security in life – what incentives has such a class to providence, to "respectability", to sacrifice the pleasure of the moment for a remoter enjoyment, most uncertain precisely by reason of the perpetually varying, shifting conditions under which the proletariat lives? A class which bears all the disadvantages of the social order without enjoying its advantages, one to which the social system appears in purely hostile aspects – who can demand that such a class respect this social order? Verily that is asking much! But the working man cannot escape the present arrangement of society so long as it exists, and when the individual worker resists it, the greatest injury falls upon himself.

Thus the social order makes family life almost impossible for the worker. In a comfortless, filthy house, hardly good enough for mere nightly shelter, ill-furnished, often neither rain-tight nor warm, a foul atmosphere filling rooms over-crowded with human beings, no domestic comfort is possible. The husband works the whole day through, perhaps the wife also and the elder children, all in different places; they meet night and morning only, all under perpetual temptation to drink; what family life is possible under such conditions? Yet the working man cannot escape from the family, must live in the family, and the consequence is a perpetual succession of family troubles, domestic quarrels, most demoralizing for parents and children alike. Neglect of all domestic duties, neglect of the children, especially, is only too common among the English working people, and only too vigorously fostered by the existing institutions of society. And children growing up in this savage way, amidst these demoralizing influences, are expected to turn out goody-goody and moral in the end! Verily the requirements are naïve, which the self-satisfied bourgeois makes upon the working man!

The contempt for the existing social order is most conspicuous in its extreme form – that of offences against the law. If the influences demoralizing to the working man act more powerfully, more concentratedly than usual, he becomes an offender as certainly as water abandons the fluid for the vaporous state at 80 degrees, Réaumur. Under the brutal and brutalizing treatment of the bourgeoisie, the working man becomes precisely as much a thing without volition as water, and is subject to the laws of Nature with precisely the same necessity; at a certain point all freedom ceases. Hence with the extension of the proletariat, crime has increased in England, and the British nation has become the most criminal in the world. From the annual criminal tables of the Home Secretary, it is evident that the increase of crime in England has proceeded with incomprehensible rapidity. The numbers of arrests for *criminal* offences reached in the years: 1805, 4,605; 1810, 5,146; 1815, 7,898; 1820, 13,710; 1825, 14,437; 1830, 18,107; 1835, 20,731; 1840, 27,187; 1841, 27,760; 1842, 31,309 in England and Wales alone. That is to say, they increased sevenfold in thirty-seven years. Of these arrests, in 1842, 4,497 were made in Lancashire alone, or more than 14 per cent of the whole; and 4,094 in Middlesex, including London, or more than 13 per cent. So that two districts which include great cities with large proletarian populations, produced one-fourth of the total amount of crime, though their population is far from forming one-fourth of the whole. Moreover, the criminal tables prove directly that nearly all crime arises within the proletariat. . . . The offences, as in all civilized countries, are, in the great majority of cases, against property, and have, therefore, arisen from want in some form; for what a man has, he does not steal. . . .

In this country, social war is under full headway, every one stands for himself, and fights for himself against all comers, and whether or not he shall injure all the others who are his declared foes, depends upon a cynical calculation as to what is most advantageous for himself. It no longer occurs to any one to come to a peaceful understanding with his fellow-man; all differences are settled by threats, violence, or in a law-court. In short, every one sees in his neighbour an enemy to be got out of the way, or, at best, a tool to be used for his own advantage. And this war grows from year to year, as the criminal tables show, more violent, passionate, irreconcilable. The enemies are dividing gradually into two great camps – the bourgeoisie on the one hand, the workers on the other. This war of each against all, of the bourgeoisie against the proletariat, need cause us no surprise, for it is only the logical sequel of the principle involved in free competition. But it may very well surprise us that the bourgeoisie remains so quiet and composed in the face of the rapidly gathering storm-clouds, that it can read all these things daily in the papers without, we will not say indignation at such a social condition, but fear of its consequences, of a universal outburst of that which manifests itself

TICKET-OF-LEAVE MEN.
(From a Photograph by Herbert Watkins, of Regent Street.)

Figure 23.1 Ticket-of-Leave Men. These recently released prisoners look ready to dive right back into the underworld. From Henry Mayhew and John Binny, *The Criminal Prisons of London and Scenes of Prison Life* (orig. 1862; repr. London: Frank Cass and Co., 1968), p. 33.

symptomatically from day to day in the form of crime. But then it is the bourgeoisie, and from its standpoint it cannot even see the facts, much less perceive their consequences. One thing only is astounding, that class prejudice and preconceived opinions can hold a whole class of human beings in such perfect, I might almost say, such mad blindness. Meanwhile, the development of the nation goes its way whether the bourgeoisie has eyes for it or not, and will surprise the property-holding class one day with things not dreamed of in its philosophy.

Chapter 24

Henry Mayhew and John Binny: A meeting with the criminal lads of London, 1862

The journalist and social scientist Henry Mayhew (1812–87) massively documented the miseries of the poor and criminal of Victorian London. He used remarkably innovative approaches, combining ethnographic investigations with statistical research and sociological analyses. Mayhew, one of the earliest cartographers of crime, also created maps showing the distribution of social problems; these anticipated the famous crime maps of the U.S. Chicago School of sociology by seven decades. Over the period 1851–62, Mayhew published a series of volumes on *London Labour and the London Poor*; it was followed, in 1862, by another huge study, *The Criminal Prisons of London and Scenes of Prison Life*. John Binny, an investigative journalist who had worked with Mayhew on *London Labour*, completed *Criminal Prisons* for him.

The present volume offers several examples from *The Criminal Prisons of London*, starting with this extract describing a meeting with juvenile delinquents that Mayhew organized as part of his research. This passage shows how he would go directly to his sources and conduct interviews with underworld characters. It derives from the original edition (London: Griffin, Bohn, and Company, 1862), pp. 43–4.

HENRY MAYHEW AND JOHN BINNY: A MEETING WITH THE CRIMINAL LADS OF LONDON

That vagrancy is the nursery of crime, and that the habitual tramps are first beggars then thieves, and finally the convicts of the country, the evidence of all parties goes to prove.

But we cannot give the reader a better general idea of the character and habits of this class than by detailing the particulars of a meeting of that curious body of people which we once held, and when as many as 150 were present. Never was witnessed a more distressing spectacle of squalor, rags, and wretchedness. Some were young men, and some were children. One, who styled himself a "cadger," was six years of age, and several who confessed themselves as "prigs" were only ten. The countenances of the boys were of various character. Many were not only good-looking, but had a frank ingenuous expression, that seemed in no way connected with innate roguery. Many, on the other hand, had the deep-sunk and half-averted eye, which is so characteristic of natural dishonesty and cunning. Some had the regular features of lads born of parents in easy circumstances. The hair of most of the lads was cut very close to the head, showing their recent liberation from prison; indeed, one might tell, by the comparative length of the crop, the time that each boy had been out of gaol. All but a few of the elder lads were remarkable, amidst the rags, filth, and wretchedness of their external appearance, for the mirth and carelessness impressed upon the countenance.

At first their behaviour was very noisy and disorderly, coarse and ribald jokes were freely cracked, exciting general bursts of laughter; while howls, cat-calls, and all manner of unearthly and indescribable yells threatened for a time to render all attempts at order utterly abortive. At one moment, a lad would imitate the bray of the jackass, and immediately the whole hundred and fifty would fall to braying like him. Then some ragged urchin would crow like a cook; whereupon the place would echo with a hundred and fifty cock-crows! Next, as a negro-boy entered the room, one of the young vagabonds would shout out swe-ee-p; this would be received with peals of laughter, and followed by a general repetition of the same cry. Presently a hundred and fifty cat-calls, of the shrillest possible description, would almost split the ears. These would be succeeded by cries of, "Strike up, catgut scrapers!" "Go on with your barrow!" "Flare up, my never-sweats!" and a variety of other street sayings.

Indeed, the uproar which went on before the commencement of the meeting will be best understood, if we compare it to the scene presented by a public menagerie at feeding time. The greatest difficulty, as might be expected, was experienced in collecting the subjoined statistics as to the character and condition of those present on the occasion. By a persevering mode of inquiry, however, the following facts were elicited: –

With respect to age, the youngest boy present was six years old; he styled himself a cadger, and said that his mother, who was a widow, and suffering from ill health, sent him into the streets to beg. There were 7 of ten years of age, 3 of twelve, and 3 of thirteen, 10 of fourteen, 26 of fifteen, 11 of sixteen, 20 of seventeen, 26 of eighteen, and 45 of nineteen.

Then 19 had fathers and mothers still living, 39 had only one parent, and 80 were orphans, in the fullest sense of the word, having neither father nor mother alive.

Of professed beggars, there were 50; whilst 66 acknowledged themselves to be habitual "prigs;" the anouncement that the greater number present were thieves pleased them exceedingly, and was received with three rounds of applause.

Next it was ascertained that 12 of them had been in prison once (2 of these were but ten years of age), 5 had been in prison twice, 3 thrice, 4 four times, 7 five times, 8 six times, 5 seven times, 4 eight times, 2 nine times (and 1 of these thirteen years of age), 5 ten times, 5 twelve times, 2 thirteen times, 3 fourteen times, 2 sixteen times, 3 seventeen times, 2 eighteen times, 5 twenty times, 6 twenty-four times, 1 twenty-five times, 1 twenty-six times, and 1 twenty-nine times.

The announcements in reply to the question as to the number of times that any of them had been in gaol, were received with great applause, which became more and more boisterous as the number of imprisonments increased. When it was announced that one, though only nineteen years of age, had been incarcerated as many as twenty-nine times, the clapping of hands, the cat-calls, and shouts of "bray-vo!" lasted for several minutes, whilst the whole of the boys rose to look at the distinguished individual. Some chalked on their hats the figures which designated the sum of the several times they had been in gaol.

Chapter 25

Edward Crapsey: The criminals and paupers of New York, 1872

In *The Nether Side of New York; or, the Vice, Crime and Poverty of the Great Metropolis*, the crime journalist Edward Crapsey reported the results of investigations he had conducted in the period 1868–71. Crapsey had systematically traversed lower Manhattan, accompanied most of the time by a patrolman-guide, to investigate harbor crime as well as violations committed in the areas now known as Greenwich Village and the Lower East Side. His purpose, he explains in his preface, is to "furnish a basis of fact for the operations of the social reformers of the future." *The Nether Side of New York* is organized into twenty chapters, most of which deal with a type of criminal (harbor thieves, fences, prostitutes) or with some closely related aspect of life in the city's underworld (tenement life, outcast children, haunts of vice). Crapsey is sometimes as hard on the criminal justice system as he is on offenders, accusing officials of laziness, senseless procedures, and corruption.

The following extracts from *The Nether Side of New York* are taken from the original edition (New York: Sheldon & Company, 1872), pp. 19–20 (professional criminals), 24–5 and 30–4 (casual criminals), 119–21 (outcast children), 138–40 (prostitution), and 147–8 (abortionists). Lacking Mayhew's verve and sympathy for the downtrodden, Crapsey produced rather ordinary investigative journalism, yet he gives vivid pictures of the underclass of lower Manhattan in a time of municipal squalor and economic depression, images that trace the interconnections of poverty and crime. Crapsey finds that for the most part, New York City's crime problem is caused not by professional criminals, but by "casual criminals," people who drop in and out of crime, leading disorganized lives on the brink of starvation, including drunks who get into brawls, petty thieves, and beggars (at the time, the act of begging was a crime), these casual offenders are not truly "depraved." More predatory are the prostitutes who play the "badger" game and the abortionists who cater to respectable, middle-class women happy to "sacrifice a newly-quickened life to avoid any interruption of their giddy pleasures" (p. 147).

EDWARD CRAPSEY: THE CRIMINALS AND PAUPERS OF NEW YORK

Professional criminals

Pickpockets in New York are almost without equal as cunning, daring criminals. They have, too, the great virtue of industry, and ply their trade with such unintermitting zeal that each one of them seems multiplied by a score. There are not more than three hundred of these light-fingered operators, notwithstanding a prominent detective lately announced his belief in the existence of a thousand. Nor would his statement seem incredible to the casual observer who should spend a day at the Central Detective Office and listen to the many "squeals for stuff," as the singular language of the place styles complaints that pockets have been picked. But when this casual observer learns that the New York pick-pockets are the most industrious thieves upon earth; that a pair of them will "work" half a dozen different lines of stages and street cars in the course of the same day, and then be on hand in the

A GROUP OF ITALIANS LANDED AT NEW YORK

Figure 25.1 Italian Immigrants Landed at New York. By the late nineteenth century, social reformers tended to be mistrustful of everyone who seemed strange, including immigrants from Southern and Eastern Europe. Here Boies, a Pennsylvania welfare official, uses Italian immigrants to demonstrate the degeneracy of the underclass. Henry Boies, *Prisoners and Paupers* (New York: G. P. Putnam's Sons, 1893), photograph following p. 58.

evening in places of public resort, he will, perhaps, begin to wonder why the three hundred do not every day steal every watch and wallet in the city. The adroitness and impudence of our pickpockets are matchless; and although they are so often arrested that many of them are probably in custody several times in every year, it is so difficult to fix their crimes upon them that it is a rare event for any expert professional to be convicted. In "mobs" of two or three, they infest the street cars, when they are overcrowded. Standing upon the rear platform where every one passing in or out must push past them, when a good watch-chain is discovered upon a vest they hustle the passenger violently about under pretence of making room for him, and, in the ensuing confusion, the watch and chain abruptly change owners. Sometimes they repeat this operation several times upon the same car, within as many minutes, and when they leave a car it is only to get upon another, and continue to ply their trade. They are so rarely taken in the act of crime that during the year 1868 only twenty-five persons were brought to trial for assaults with intent to steal as pickpockets, and of this small number two escaped conviction by reason of the insufficiency of the proof. About one-fourth of the pickpockets are females, who frequent dry-goods shops, churches, funerals, fairs, and other places crowded with ladies. These females are equally gifted with the males in the stealthy, light-fingered art. . . .

Shoplifters constitute another grand division of the army of rogues, and number not more than two hundred persons, fully one-half of whom are females, who are by far the most successful in this line of business, as, from their costume, they have better opportunities for carrying away the stolen goods from under the very eye of the owner. These female shoplifters always operate in pairs, and one of the two invariably has under her dress an immense pocket, sustained by a girdle around her waist, which will easily swallow two or more pieces of muslin, or packages of similar bulk. Entering a shop together, one of them engages the attention of the shopkeeper, the other slips a package of goods from the counter into her capacious pocket. . . .

Casual criminals

No class is more costly or in a certain way more offensive to the metropolis than that which drops into crime, as Mr. Wegg did into poetry, as an occasional interlude to more reputable employment. In consequence of the intense energy of its journals in collecting and commenting upon news, New York has acquired a reputation for lawlessness which, upon a candid consideration of all the facts, is found to be in a measure undeserved; and it is further to the credit of the city that nearly all the bad repute which rightfully belongs to it is due to its amateur instead of its professional criminals.

In every great community made up of heterogeneous materials, there are always a large number constantly hovering on the outermost edge of the law, where only the slightest influence is required to push them beyond it; and this is especially true of New York. No modern city has a population so mixed and in some portions more dense, or is so liable, from certain peculiarities in its system of government, to foster the disorderly classes which produce all of the casual crimes and much of the squalor of the great city. A population in which all nationalities are not only represented but intermingled, which is struggling with bitter intensity for bare subsistence, and which imbibes from a vicious political system a dangerous disregard for the rights both of person and property, is not one which can be expected to rigidly observe all the obligations of the law. . . .

There is the high authority of a proverb for the declaration that "when wine is in, wit is out," and it is not strange that the stuff sold in the bar-rooms of New York impels men to play such fantastic tricks with the established usages of society as occasionally get them inside a prison. These constitute the most numerous, as they are the least reprehensible and most unfortunate, of our casual criminals. . . .

There is another class of casual criminals, and it is the one, with perhaps a single exception, which is "more sinned against than sinning." In a single year 7,031 persons have been arrested in the city for the crime of theft, of which number 2,122 were accused of grand larceny, and 4,909 of petty pilfering. In the former case, sympathy would in nearly every instance be wasted if bestowed upon any of these prisoners, as they are offenders who have subsisted by crime for years and are beyond the chance of reformation. To one of any experience in the methods and appearance of criminals, there is gener- ally little difficulty in recogizing these veterans in warfare on mankind; but when a number of alleged petty thieves are arraigned at the bar of a minor tribunal, the casual is liable from mere carelessness to be considered as a professional and thus suffer gross injustice. The hardened thief is always so ready with a harrowing tale of pinching want and sudden temptation, that when it is the saddest truth that ever fell from human lips it comes to incredulous and unsympathetic ears. Yet in a city so over-crowded with struggling poor as this, a large proportion of the petty thefts are committed by persons more deserving of charity than censure. The professional outlaw who is worthy of being ranked as a public danger strikes at higher game than the unfortunate who, urged to crime by starvation, purloins some trifling article; and although it would not be safe to say that the pettiness of the theft removes it in a moral sense from the list of crimes, these cases are always sufficiently questionable to claim more careful investigation than they often receive. I have seen more of such cases than I desire to ever see again; for whether the plea be true, or, being false, is so told as to appear true, there is more pleasant entertainment than to hear it unavailingly uttered at the bar of justice, and I have heard it so uttered scores and scores of times.

Once it was a woman whose rags and gaunt face, made terrible by the wolfish eyes, ought to have been full confirmation of her story, who told of a husband dying more from want than sickness, and of three children crying for bread. She had begged for it without avail, and at last had stolen it. The crime was a venial one at best, but the outraged law that could be so merciful at times to the brawler or murderer could not forgive this trivial transgression, and the suffering woman was sent to jail. Again it was a boy, not more than ten years old, who, dwarfed by penury, was small and puny. He, too, had the ravenous eyes and hollow cheeks which the full-fed professional thief cannot counterfeit, and he, too, told a story that, corroborated as it was by his appearance, ought to have gained him forgiveness rather than punishment. In this case it was a shop boy who toiled sixteen hours in each twenty-four for a pittance barely sufficient to keep life in his little body, and who had struggled hopefully until his widowed mother, stricken down by sickness, was starving at home. Then he stole a dollar from the till of the shop, and being detected by his master was handed over to the police and sent to the House of Refuge as an incorrigible young rascal. What became of the mother I never knew, but most probably she starved to death, which is by no means an uncommon occurrence. Only yesterday, when looking over the mortuary tables for the week, I found marasmus credited with the taking of three lives, two of them being adults; want of proper food was most likely the origin. . . .

There is yet one other class of these incidental doers of evil that is apt to make a man of common humanity snap his fingers in the face of the law that is responsible for its existence. Poverty is closely akin to crime the world over, but an ordinance of the city of New York makes it an offence punishable with arrest and imprisonment to beg in the public streets. It is pleaded in extenuation of this device for the propagation of crime, that the city bountifully provides for its really poor, and the law is intended to suppress only the charlatans who have made beggary a profession. Whatever its purpose, it has worked evil and evil only. It is more often enforced against children, who have been sent into the streets by their parents to beg than against any one else. It is freely granted that these children are a great annoyance in public places, and that the parents spend the money thus obtained in rum, and yet the wisdom of the ordinance is denied. For it happens when the law is put into practice that it is chiefly used to rid the fashionable theatres of these children, who gather at the entrances to solicit alms of the arriving patrons. This is, of course, at an early hour of the evening, when the courts are closed for the day, and the child then arrested is necessarily taken to a station house. If held, as many of them are, they are locked up for the night in cells, where they are surrounded with thieves, prostitutes, and drunkards, and where they are exposed in a single night to more corrupting influences than any child ought ever to encounter. . . .

The casual criminals are entitled more to pity than censure. They are the victims of circumstances, or of a recklessness born of a legal blunder, and their crimes, even when so serious as the shedding of blood, never have their origin in total depravity.

Outcast children

Ten thousand human beings under the age of fourteen years are adrift in the streets of New York. Four-fifths of them are confirmed vagrants, and the majority are growing up in ignorance of everything but the depravity which is gleaned from the city slums, and all of them are being pushed by the relentless force of untoward circumstances into the criminal practices in which many have become adepts in the dawn of their blighted lives. The major portion are boys rapidly preparing for the almshouses, prisons, and gallows; but hundreds are girls, who have before them the darker horror of prostitution as well as those appliances of civilization for the care or repression of the pauperism and lawlessness which it creates. It is this juvenile army of vagabondage and crime hanging upon the flanks of society, and occasionally startling it from its propriety by manifestations of an immeasurable capacity for mischief, which is a prominent peril and the most sorrowful of the nether aspects of the city. . . .

Juvenile delinquents are infantile mendicants ripened by time and circumstances. Foremost among them are the boy-burglars and thieves who have become at least a grave annoyance of metropolitan life. There is nothing too trivial to escape the attention of these young marauders, and their physical insignificance is to their advantage in their work of depredation. They go with nonchalant ease where bolder spirits would fear to tread and larger bodies fail to penetrate. Having none of the caution of experience, and able to crawl into the crevices of buildings, all the vagaries of theft are laid to their charge. . . . Their particular depredation is to enter unoccupied houses and strip them of whatever they can conveniently carry away. The summer months, when large numbers of families go into the country for weeks, leaving their homes entirely unprotected, offer an opportunity to burglars which is never neglected, and very few of these houses escape pillage. Sometimes a clean sweep of everything portable is made, which is satisfactory evidence that adults have been at work; and sometimes only a few trifling articles are missing, but much wanton damage is done to what is left, which is sure proof that boys have been about. But the especial field of juvenile burglars is found in houses which are to let, and are therefore left to care for themselves by the police. The boys easily gain entrance, and once in are secure in the intrusion, however protracted it may be. There is nothing to operate upon apparently but the bare floors and walls, but the boys find portable plunder in the gas and water fixtures. Not only do they wrench off faucets and burners, but they pull the pipes out of the walls, and frequently do a damage of hundreds of dollars in obtaining plunder for which they get only a few cents from the junkmen. . . .

Prostitution

To see the worst, stand for the hour before midnight on the corner of Houston and Greene streets. In that time a hundred women apparently will pass, but the close observer will notice that each woman passes the spot on an average of about twice, so that in fact there are not more than fifty of them. This frequency of appearance leads to the supposition that they do not go far, which is the fact. Each set of prostitutes has its metes and bounds laid down by an unwritten code of its own enactment, which is rarely violated. The set now under consideration travels Houston, Bleecker, Wooster, and Greene streets, with occasional forays upon Broadway, which is the common property of all. But these poor fallen creatures rarely go there to put themselves in fruitless competition with more attractive sin. They are poorly dressed, have nothing of beauty in form or face, and are always uncouth or brazenly vulgar in manner. They are miserably poor, herding in garrets or cellars, and are driven by their necessities to accost every stranger they meet with what the silly law of New York calls "Soliciting for the purpose of prostitution." When a woman offers to sell her body to a man she never saw before, for fifty cents, she has fallen low indeed. . . .

There is yet another grade of these night-walkers, and it can be best seen at Broadway and Washington Place, or Broadway and Twenty-fourth street. But whoever wishes to observe this class must go earlier, as these women have nearly all retired from the tramp by ten o'clock, and can be seen in greatest numbers only between eight and nine in winter or nine and ten in summer. Almost without exception, they seem in the faint light of the streets to be dressed with elegance and taste, to be handsome in feature and form, and to have left in them something of womanly reserve and modesty. True, they are out in the streets at unseemly hours without male escort, but walking quickly as they do, without looking to the right or the left, the unpractised observer doubts that they belong to the *demi-monde*, and charitably supposes that they have been compelled to leave the shelter of their homes by sudden sickness in the family or by some equally urgent necessity. If the stranger is bold enough to accost one of them, he is even less sure than before of her character. She does not exactly repel his advances, but she does not invite them, and is sufficiently adroit to assume a maidenly reserve that perplexes while it allures him. She will not stop to talk with him, but if he walks beside her she will converse on ordinary topics and use language to which no exceptions can be taken. There is nothing essentially vulgar, much less indelicate, about her words, demeanor, or appearance, and by the time a novice has walked a block in her company he is in a tremor of apprehension that he has committed the grave indiscretion of speaking to a lady who happened to be unprotected, and who is luring him on to be cowhided by her brother or husband. If she succeeds in getting him to her home he finds it a house of respectable exterior and furnished within with some pretensions to elegance. As there was nothing indecent about the woman herself, so there is nothing bawdyish about her home. The pictures which adorn the walls are not, as in houses of a lower grade, suggestive of the vile lives of the inmates; the furniture is handsome and of a kind to give an impression of a quiet, reputable life. Under such circumstances as these the chances are that the stranger has been lured to the lair of a "badger" and is about to undergo the operation known as the panel game.

As this species of robbery must be described somewhere in this volume, I may as well pause here and have done with the disagreeable task. No kind of theft is so commonly practised, none yields such large returns, nor is any so safe to the spoilers as this. Formerly it was achieved by a contrivance by which it gained its name, but latterly it has been much more simple in its operation, as a consequence of its more general use. When thieving by prostitutes first became a distinct branch of criminal art, it was done only by mechanism specially prepared for the purpose. A whole house, or at least a floor of a house was hired, and one room was prepared with a secret door called a "panel," which could not be seen by even the closest scrutiny of the walls, and which, opening into another room, gave easy access to the "badger," as the male confederate of the prostitute is called. When the woman had lured a stranger to this room she always created a sense of safety in his mind by an ostentatious locking of all doors. She was always troubled with a modest reserve, and would proceed no further until the lights had been extinguished, and the victim rarely objected to a proceeding so manifestly proper. When the proper time arrived, of which he could easily judge, the "badger" stole into the room through the secret door, which opened without making the slightest noise, and having rifled the clothes of the stranger, which had been placed upon a chair, of all they contained, crept back to his hiding-place and closed the panel behind him, without having betrayed his presence by the faintest sound. Having succeeded in effecting the robbery, it was a matter of entire indifference to both the badger and his confederate when it was discovered. If the victim found his pockets empty before leaving the room, he might make as much outcry as he chose, as it would avail nothing; he had seen all the doors locked, he was sure no one but the woman and himself had been in the room, and she, while indignantly denying that he been robbed there, was extremely anxious that her innocence should be thoroughly established by a strict search of the room, where, as she well knew, none of the valuables would be found. Sometimes this was done, but more frequently the victim said nething whatever about his loss, either before or after he had parted with his frail companion. His mouth was closed by the disreputable circumstances attending the robbery, as he was usually a married man, and always one who would submit to any loss rather than compromise his character by admitting that he had been in such company. . . .

Abortionists

While there are many phases of nether life more sensational because more open to the public view, there is none more sickening than the work of the abortionists, who ply their infamous trade to a far greater extent than is believed by those who have not studied the matter. . . .

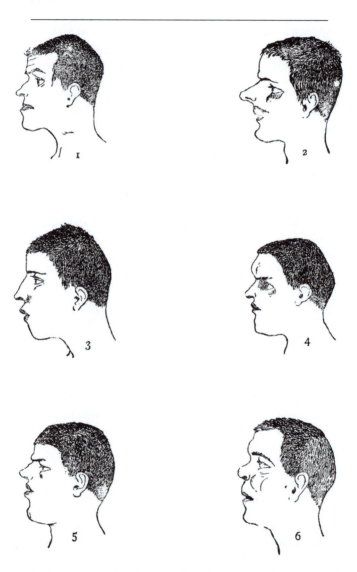

Figure 25.2 Profiles of Criminals. These profiles of criminals indicate the misshapen and indeed deformed nature of members of the underclass. From Havelock Ellis, *The Criminal* (London: Walter Scott, 1890), Plates IV and V, following p. 54.

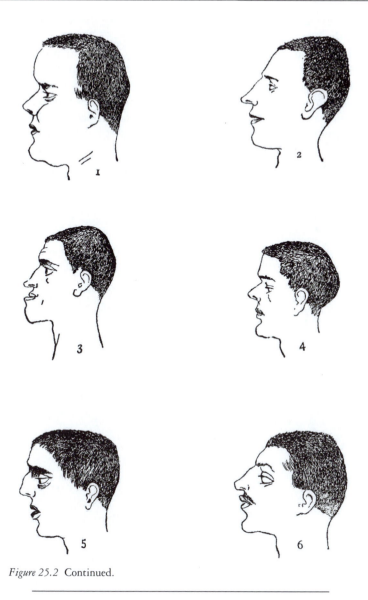

Figure 25.2 Continued.

The prevailing profligacy of the age is perhaps best shown by the fact that the majority of the patrons of these rascals are unmarried women who move in respectable society. This is a fact of which I am sure if the abortionists themselves can be believed, and there are occasionally cases which so drag the terrible business out into public view, as to convince the most skeptical that these vile practitioners do speak the truth. The most startling of all these instances was that of Alice A. Bowlsby, which became the celebrated crime of 1871, as the Nathan murder had been that of the previous year. This young girl had always moved in the most reputable circles, and had never been suspected, even by her most intimate friends, of any impropriety. Yet she was forced, in order to be rid of the consequences of her transgressions, to resort to the man in whose hands she died. Up to the moment when the identity of the corpse found in the trunk at the Hudson River Railroad dépôt was established, there was no young woman of fairer reputation; but the revelations following her death rolled away the closing stone from a whited sepulchre, so that all the world looked in upon a mass of corruption. . . .

Chapter 26

W. E. B. DuBois: The Negro criminal, 1899

William Edward Burghardt DuBois (1868–1963) was one of the first American criminologists to be formally trained in sociology. He first attended Fisk University, an all-black institution in Nashville, Tenn.; then he transferred to Harvard, where he studied with some of the country's most eminent social scientists; and finally he studied in Europe for two years with Max Weber, the great German sociologist. While still young, DuBois was commissioned by white Philadelphia reformers to undertake a study of Negro life in their city; this became his book *The Philadelphia Negro: A Social Study*. Looking back in 1940, DuBois wrote of this work:

> The fact was that the city of Philadelphia at that time had a theory; and that theory was that this great, rich, and famous municipality was going to the dogs because of the crime and venality of its Negro citizens, who lived largely centered in the slum at the lower end of the seventh ward. Philadelphia wanted to prove this by figures and I was the man to do it. Of this theory back of the plan, I neither knew nor cared. I saw only here a chance to study an historical group of black folk and to show exactly what their place was in the community. . . . [The study] revealed the Negro group as a symptom, not a cause; as a striving, palpitating group, and not an inert, sick body of crime; as a long historic development and not a transient occurrence.[1]

For this section, I have extracted passages dealing with criminality, pauperism, and alcoholism from W. E. B. DuBois, *The Philadelphia Negro* (Philadelphia: University of Pennsylvania Press, 1899), pp. 235–96. DuBois reports very little on the cultural life of Philadelphia's black criminals, although he does describe the circumstances under which the poorest blacks lived. Later in the present book (Chapter 61), I extract other material from *The Philadelphia Negro* to exemplify DuBois's sociological approach to the study of crime.

W. E. B. DUBOIS: THE NEGRO CRIMINAL

From his earliest advent the Negro, as was natural, has figured largely in the criminal annals of Philadelphia. Only such superficial study of the American Negro as dates his beginning with 1863 can neglect this past record of crime in studying the present. Crime is a phenomenon of organized social life, and is the open rebellion of an individual against his social environment. Naturally then, if men are suddenly transported from one environment to another, the result is lack of harmony with the new conditions; lack of harmony with the new physical surroundings leading to disease and death or modification of physique; lack of harmony with social surroundings leading to crime. . . .

Throughout the land there has been since the war a large increase in crime, especially in cities. This phenomenon would seem to have sufficient cause in the increased complexity of life, in industrial competition, and the rush of great numbers to the large cities. It would therefore be natural to suppose that the Negro would also show this increase in criminality and, as in the case of all lower classes, that he would show it in greater degree. His evolution has, however, been marked by some peculiarities. For nearly two decades after emancipation he took little part in many of the great social movements about him for obvious reasons. His migration to city life, therefore, and his sharing in the competition of modern industrial life, came later than was the case with the mass of his fellow citizens. The Negro began to rush to the cities in large numbers after 1880, and consequently the phenomena attendant on that momentous change of life are tardier in his case. His rate of criminality has in the last two decades risen rapidly, and this is a parallel phenomenon to the rapid rise of the white criminal record two or three decades ago. Moreover, in the case of the Negro there were special causes for the prevalence of crime: he had lately been freed from serfdom, he was the object of stinging oppression and ridicule, and paths of advancement open to many were closed to him. Consequently the class of the shiftless, aimless, idle, discouraged and disappointed was proportionately larger. . . .

Let us now turn from the crime to the criminals [541 Negroes committed to Eastern Penitentiary, 1885–1895 – N.R.]. 497 of them (91.87 per cent) were males and 44 (8.13 per cent) were females. 296 (54.71 per cent) were single, 208 (34.45 per cent) were married, and 37 (6.84 per cent) were widowed. . . .

Altogether 21 per cent were natives of Philadelphia; 217 were born in the North, and 309, or 57 per cent, were born in the South. Two-thirds of the Negroes of the city, judging from the Seventh Ward, were born outside the city, and this part furnishes 79 per cent of the serious crime. 54 per cent were born in the South, and this part furnishes 57 per cent of the crime, or more, since many giving their birthplace as in the North were really born in the South. . . .

From this study we may conclude that young men are the perpetrators of the serious crime among Negroes; that this crime consists mainly of stealing and assault; that ignorance, and immigration to the temptations of city life, are responsible for much of this crime but not for all; that deep social causes underlie this prevalence of crime and they have so worked as to form among Negroes since 1864 a distinct class of habitual criminals; that to this criminal class and not to the great mass of Negroes the bulk of the serious crime perpetrated by this race should be charged. . . .

Pauperism and alcoholism

Emancipation and pauperism must over go hand in hand; when a group of persons have been for generations prohibited from self-support, and self-initiative in any line, there is bound to be a large number of them who, when thrown upon their own resources, will be found incapable of competing in the race of life. Pennsylvania from early times, when emancipation of slaves in considerable numbers first began, has seen and feared this problem of Negro poverty. . . .

We have already seen that in the Seventh Ward about 9 per cent of the Negroes can be classed as the "very poor," needing public assistance in order to live. From this we may conclude that between three and four thousand Negro families in the city may be classed among the semi-pauper class. Thus it is plain that there is a large problem of poverty among the Negro problems; 4 per cent of the population furnish according to the foregoing statistics at least 8 per cent of the poverty. Considering the economic difficulties of the Negro, we ought perhaps to expect rather more than less than this. Beside these permanently pauperized families there is a considerable number of persons who from time to time must receive temporary aid, but can usually get on without it. In time of stress as during the year 1893 this class is very large.

There is especial suffering and neglect among the children of this class of people. . . .

Several typical families will illustrate the varying conditions encountered:

No. 1. – South Eighteenth street. Four in the family; husband intemperate drinker; wife decent, but out of work.

No. 2. – South Tenth street. Five in the family; widow and children out of work, and had sold the bed to pay for expense of a sick child.

No. 3. – Dean street. A woman paralyzed; partially supported by a colored church.

No. 4. – Carver street. Worthy woman deserted by her husband five years ago; helped with coal, but is paying the Charity Organization Society back again.

No. 5. – Hampton street. Three in family; living in three rooms with three other families. "No push, and improvident." . . .

The intemperate use of intoxicating liquors is not one of the Negro's special offences; nevertheless there is considerable drinking and the use of beer is on the increase. . . .

The rents paid by the Negroes are without doubt far above their means and often from one-fourth to three-fourths of the total income of a family goes in rent. This leads to much non-payment of rent both intentional and unintentional, to frequent shifting of homes, and above all to stinting the families in many necessities of life in order to live in respectable dwellings. Many a Negro family eats less than it ought for the sake of living in a decent house. . . .

Much of the Negro problem in this city finds adequate explanation when we reflect that here is a people receiving a little lower wages than usual for less desirable work, and compelled, in order to do that work, to live in a little less pleasant quarters than most people, and pay for them somewhat higher rents.

Note

1   W. E. B. DuBois, *Dusk of Dawn: An essay toward an autobiography of a race concept*, orig. 1940, as quoted by Elijah Anderson, "Introduction to the 1996 edition," *The Philadelphia Negro* (Philadelphia: University of Pennsylvania Press, 1996), p. xvi.

Criminal anthropology

Criminal anthropology
Introduction to Part VI

Criminal anthropology – the theory that the criminal is a being apart, marked by anomalies that signify his or her physical, mental, and social backwardness – was the first independent theory of crime. Earlier explanations of criminal behavior had been incidental to another theory such as phrenology or degeneration; criminal anthropology, however, was an explanation in its own right.

While criminal anthropology was anticipated by earlier thinking about crime, evolution, and degeneration (Chapter 27), it was first clearly formulated by the Italian psychiatrist Cesare Lombroso in his book *L'uomo delinquente* or *Criminal Man*, published in 1876 and revised four times thereafter. At the heart of Lombroso's work lay the idea of the born criminal, an atavism or throwback to an earlier evolutionary stage. Scarred with the stigmata of crime – small skull, slanting forehead, jutting jaw, jug ears, insensitivity to pain, vanity, religiosity, a tendency to insanity – the primitive born criminal is doomed to repeat crime for his entire life. Lombroso was at first vague about heredity, but later, when he folded in the idea of degeneration, his born criminal became a hereditary criminal as well as a throwback. As Lombroso refined his theory, he concluded that born criminals comprise only 35 to 40 percent of the total criminal population, with other types – the occasional criminal, hysterical criminal (especially common among women), political criminal, and so on – being shaped less by biological than by sociological factors such as nationality and education. He also decided that women and children are essentially born criminals – children because they have not yet been trained to control their savage instincts, women because they are inferior to the highest evolutionary type, the European male. But women and children were sidelines; Lombroso's basic interest lay with the menacing figure of the male born criminal.

What made criminal anthropology particularly significant was that Lombroso perceived, as no one before him had, that criminology could become a science, one that could accumulate empirical data, use control groups, test theories, and in other ways, too, incorporate the tenets of positivist social science. To this end he measured criminals' crania (Chapter 28), tested their arm strength, recorded their reactions to shocks, analyzed their handwriting, and studied their mental states. His criminal anthropology, an amalgam of anthropology, medicine, psychiatry, psychology, and sociology, became the foundation for the Positivist or Italian school of criminology, which included his students and associates. (For the work of Enrico Ferri, one of his most able followers, see Chapters 53 and 60.) It attracted followers from all over Europe and the United States (Chapters 30, 31, 32, and 33). It also attracted critics, especially among the French (Chapters 34 and 35), who were more socio-logical in orientation, but also among Americans (Chapter 36). Criminal anthropology eventually fell by the wayside, but it dominated criminological thinking for the last quarter of the nineteenth century, and it established the idea that crime and criminals could be studied scientifically.

Chapter 27

J. Bruce Thomson: The hereditary nature of crime, 1869

Six years before Lombroso introduced the world to criminal anthropology, the Scottish prison physician J. B. Thomson anticipated the new science of the criminal with his 1869 article on "The hereditary nature of crime." In it he made the radical claim that there is a hereditary criminal class with its own physical and mental traits. Here we almost have Lombroso before Lombroso. All that was missing was Lombroso's demonstrations that the study of crime could become a bona fide science and the brilliance of his packaging – his presentation of his claims as an anthropology of criminal man.

Thomson's "Psychology of Criminals" was extracted earlier in the present volume, in the section on degenerationism (Chapter 17). That it is possible to include another influential Thomson essay, "The Hereditary Nature of Crime," written about the same time, in this section on criminal anthropology demonstrates, again, the closeness of degeneration theory to criminal anthropology, and the emergence of the latter out of the former. Here Thomson begins by insisting on "the alliance of crime and insanity" and claiming that both afflictions fall in "the border-land of lunacy." This is pure degenerationism. However, he quickly moves on to the physical and mental inferiority of criminals and to proofs that crime is hereditary. This is pure criminal anthropology.

This article first appeared in *The Journal of Mental Science* 15 (72) (January 1870): 487–98.

J. BRUCE THOMSON: THE HEREDITARY NATURE OF CRIME

On the border-land of Lunacy lie the criminal populations. It is a debateable region; and no more vexed problem comes before the Medical Psychologist than this – viz: where badness ends and madness begins in criminals. The inmates of Asylums and of Prisons are so nearly allied that "thin partitions do their bounds divide." From large experience among criminals I have come to the conclusion, that the principal business of Prison Surgeons must always be with mental diseases; that the number of physical diseases are less than the psychical [mental – N.R.]; that the diseases and causes of death among prisoners are chiefly of the nervous system; and in fine that the treatment of crime is a branch of psychology. . . .

The proposition that crime is generally committed by criminals hereditarily disposed to it, I shall try to prove by shewing:

1 That there is a *criminal class* distinct from other civilized and criminal men.
2 That this criminal class is marked by peculiar physical and mental characteristics.
3 That the hereditary nature of crime is shewn by the *family* histories of criminals.
4 That the *transformation* of other nervous disorders with crime in the criminal class, also proves the alliance of hereditary crime with other disorders of the mind – such as epilepsy, dipsomania, insanity, &c.
5 That the *incurable* nature of crime in the criminal class goes to prove its hereditary nature.

1. When it is averred that *there is a criminal class sui generis* it is not denied that now and then crop out criminals of all kinds from all classes of men – from the lowest stratum to the upper ten. Such are not the criminal class proper. . . . The criminal class have a *locale* and a community of their own in our great cities. You never find them pursuing an honest trade or an honourable profession. They do not mingle in markets, and engage in commerce with civilized business men. The greatest number are thieves, Ishmaelites, whose hand is against every civilized man. There is a thieves' quarter – a devil's den, for these city Arabs. There is their Alsatia; in the midst of foul air and filthy lairs they associate and propagate a criminal population. They degenerate into a set of demi-civilized savages, who in hordes prey upon society, and of them the historian says, "In the hearts of our great capitals are a race as fierce as those who followed Attila, or marched in the ranks of Genseric." These communities of crime, we know, have no respect for the laws of marriage – are regardless of the rules of consanguinity; and, only connecting themselves with those of their own nature and habits, they must beget a depraved and criminal class hereditarily disposed to crime. Their moral disease comes *ab ovo*. They are born into crime, as well as reared, nurtured, and instructed in it; and habit becomes a new force – a second nature, superinduced upon their original moral depravity.

2. That there *is a distinctive Criminal Class is shewn by the typical, physical, and mental peculiarities of the class*. . . .

The physical characters of the criminal class indicate a low type of men and women, and walking through a large prison, if one of a better class is there, even in the prison garb, he is easily known from the common criminal. A decent industrial operative, a cottar, a clerk, a railway official, an inspector of poor, and such like, stand out from the others by a better physical appearance. The common thief, or robber, or garrotter (thieves being the chief prisoners), have all a set of coarse, angular, clumsy, . . . features and dirty complexion. The women are all ugly in form and face and action, without the beauty of colour, or grace, or regularity of features, and all have a sinister and repulsive expression in look and mien. . . .

From such physical we naturally expect low *psychical characteristics*. Physical degeneration must beget mental and moral depravity.

The writer has visited the great prisons of England, Ireland, and Scotland; and in all these the authorities, governors, chaplains, surgeons, warders, concur in stating that prisoners, as a class, are of mean and defective intellect, generally stupid, and many of them weak minded and imbecile.

Not to heap up proofs which are ample, I shall only add to this my own testimony as a prison surgeon, as to the mental condition of prisoners generally. Out of a population of 5,432 no less than 673 were placed on my registers as requiring care and treatment on account of their mental condition. The forms of mental disorder were –

Weak-mindedness or Imbecility in   580
Ditto and Suicidal   36
Epileptic   57

This table showed 12 per cent. mentally weak in different degrees, and all this, exclusive of those prisoners who had become insane, and had been transferred to the lunatic department for criminals. One remarkable feature of the above table of weak-minded prisoners is that the greatest number were seen to be weak minded on admission, or a few weeks thereafter, apparently *from congenital causes*. Similar observations as to the low mental calibre of criminals are well known in the Irish and English prisons also, but have been attributed to the effects of imprisonment rather than hereditary deterioration.

3. *The Family Histories of the Criminal Class indicate that crime in them is Hereditary.*

Many who cannot deny physical heritages of infirmities and diseases hesitate to admit the heritage of immorality, and yet the relations of mind and matter, body and soul, are now pretty generally received by the schools of philosophy and theology. . . .

One of the most remarkable examples of a criminal family I know of is as follows: –

Three brothers had families amounting to 15 members in all. Of these 14 were utterers of base coin; the fifteenth appeared to be exceptional, but was at length detected setting fire to his house after insuring it for four times its value. The importance of checking, if possible, by legal restrictions such criminal tendences is brought out in this case, when it is calculated that thousands of offences might have been prevented by these three brothers being *permanently* imprisoned before they became fathers of families, and thereby perpetuated crime by heritage.

The family history of criminals shows their hereditary tendencies as a class. This kind of information is not very easily got at, for they are constantly changing their names; and the following is a very imperfect approximation to entire facts. In the prison, under my medical charge, I ascertained the following: –

At the same time 109 prisoners were known to be in the same prison out of 50 families. Of one family eight were known – often two or three at the same time. The father had been several times under long sentences; and since 1843 this family had been chiefly supported at the public expense in prisons. The relations I found in prison were the father, two sons, three daughter, [sic] one daughter-in-law, and a sister-in-law. Doubtless other connections not discovered were there also. When these notes were taken there were in this prison three cousins (two being sisters), two aunts, and two uncles of the same family. Of two families, six were in prison about the same time, viz. – four brothers and two sisters. . . .

4. *The Hereditary taint and tendency to crime further appears from the resemblance in the transmission to other Hereditary Maladies.*

One of the leading characters in the natural history of hereditary depravity is the singular transmutation from physical to psychical diseases; and to diversities of these diseases, interchanging often with crime. Esquirol says, that of all diseases insanity is the most hereditary, and one-third or one-fourth of the cases of insanity are found so. But if we were to take into account the various transformations cropping out in abnormal states of the body, in weak-mindedness, in epilepsy, in paralysis, and even in crime, the heritage would still more appear. Various writers have proved that the *lower forms* of mental disease as silliness and imbecility are, in the most remarkable degree, transmissible. . . .

Dipsomania shows in the psychological history of families the same curious *transformation* of diseases, and my enquiries lead me to the belief that in almost all cases hereditary causes lead to dipsomania. This is a disease where we are often puzzled to distinguish between the disease and the vice; the mental and moral malady running into each other. The hereditary tendency, although ignored by the legal mind, is a most valuable guide to the medical inquirer. Some years ago, in a rural district where the families do not fluctuate, and their history for generations could be got at, I examined into the cases of insane drinking which occurred, and the singular interchange or transformation into other mental disorders was brought out as by the following facts I tabulated out of ten families: –

Dipsomaniacs living	19
Dipsomaniacs dead	18
Epileptics	3
Insane	10

In one of these families there were four brothers who fell victims to insane drinking, and three of these died in the meridian of life. One became paralytic, several sisters were intemperate, one granddaughter insane, and vicious and criminal acts transpired among them. There also were physical deformities, and silliness, and eccentricity at times in one or more of the branches of these families. As among the criminal class so among these families, and among the cretins, epilepsy is a prevalent malady. . . .

5. *The incurable nature of crime in the criminal class.*

This is the great corollary from the whole study, viz., that crime is intractable in the highest degree, and must be so because it is hereditary. Crime is "bred in the bone," and how can it be got out of the flesh? The criminal class are born in crime, and what treatment in such cases can be made available? . . .

The painful fact is before us that time after time the criminal classes lapse into crime, and are rarely improved by any form of prison discipline. When extending these notes, I looked at the calendar of crime in this city, and of persons to be tried before the Circuit Court, ten out of twelve were known to be offenders – old offenders of the criminal class. Such facts press it strongly on my mind that crime (in the general) is a moral disease of a chronic and congenital nature, intractable in the extreme, because transmitted from generation to generation. . . .

I offer the following conclusions from the foregoing examen: –

1   That crime being hereditary in the criminal class, measures are called for to break up the *caste* and community of the class.
2   That transportation and long sentences of habitual criminals are called for in order to lessen the criminal offenders.
3   That old offenders can scarcely be reclaimed, and that juveniles brought under very early training are the most hopeful; but even these are apt to lapse into their hereditary tendency.
4   That crime is so nearly allied to insanity as to be chiefly a psychological study.

Chapter 28

Cesare Lombroso: "Criminal craniums," from *Criminal Man*, 1876

This extract comes from the first chapter of the first edition of Lombroso's *Criminal Man*. It illustrates his love of "facts" and his fixation on physical abnormalities, including his famous discovery, in the cranium of a brigand from Calabria named Villella, of a median occipital fossetta or indentation that reminded Lombroso of the skulls of rodents, lemurs, undeveloped human fetuses, and people with dark skins ("the colored and inferior races"). Such abnormalities lead him to ask rhetorically, "Is it possible that individuals with such an enormous variety of cranial anomalies can have the same level of intelligence and sense of responsibility as men with perfectly normal skulls?"

This selection comes from Cesare Lombroso, *Criminal Man*, translated and with a new introduction by Mary Gibson and Nicole Hahn Rafter (Durham, NC: Duke University Press, 2006), pp. 45–9.

CESARE LOMBROSO: CRIMINAL CRANIUMS

I thought it best to begin this study of criminal man with an anatomical table to facilitate a thorough examination of criminal craniums, amounting to a total of sixty-six skulls. Of these

> 16 were provided by Calori, from his superb Anatomical Museum in Bologna;
> 8 were provided by Mantegazza, from the Anthropological Museum of Florence;
> 5 were provided by Zoja, from the Anatomical Museum of Pavia;
> 6 came from the Anthropological Museum of the Academy of Medicine at Turin;
> 18 came from Dr. Roggero's valuable private collection at the town prison of Alessandria;
> 12 were collected by me and form part of my Anthropological-Psychiatric Museum;
> 1 was donated by my esteemed friend, Dr. Golgi.

As shown in table 1 [omitted here – N.R.], measurement of cranial circumference found very few criminal skulls that were particularly large (one of 580 mm [millimeters], two of 560 mm, one of 550 mm, two of 540 mm) or even normal in size (eight of 530 mm, thirteen of 520 mm), but a high incidence of craniums that were microcefalic or abnormally small: thirty-nine out of sixty-five. More precisely, there were nineteen at 510 mm, twelve at 500 mm, and eight at 490 mm.

The cranial sutures or joins in the bones of the skull were normal in only seventeen cases. In five cases, they were still open at the age of seventy-five or eighty. This was true of men like Villella, Pietrotto, and Soldati, who were famous for committing crimes into old age and repeatedly eluding capture. A few of the skulls with open sutures had a large cranial capacity, but others had a small one accompanied by many monkeylike anomalies. The cranial sutures were completely closed in thirty-eight cases – so thoroughly in seven of these that they had become invisible.

In another study of fifty-six criminal craniums, I found that thirteen had one of the most serious of all anomalies, a median occipital fossetta or indentation at the base of the skull. A brigand from Calabria, Villella, had a median occipital fossetta of extraordinary dimensions, 34 mm long, 23 mm wide, and 11 mm deep. He also exhibited atrophy of the lateral occipital openings, absence of the occipital crest, and two boney parallel projections that gave the occipital opening a trapezoidal shape that ended in a small triangular protrusion near the occipital aperture. From these features, comparative anatomy and human embryology can induce that we are dealing with a fairly small cerebellum. Such a brain suggests not the sublimity of the primate, but the lower level of the rodent or lemur, or the brain of a human fetus of three or four months.

If we compare criminals with the insane, we find the former exhibit a similar or perhaps greater number of cranial abnormalities. This is not surprising, given that most of the insane are not born so, but become mad, while criminals are born with evil inclinations. At the moment I will not go into all the reasons for these cranial abnormalities in criminals, but I cannot avoid pointing out how closely they correspond to characteristics observed in normal skulls of the colored and inferior races.

Criminals have the following rates of abnormality: 61 percent exhibit fusion of the cranial bones; 92 percent, prognathism or an apelike forward thrust of the lower face; 63 percent, overdevelopment of the sinuses; 27 percent, cranial thickness; 9 percent, an open mediofrontal suture; 20 percent, a large jawbone; 25 percent, a receding forehead; 74 percent, wide or overdeveloped cheekbones; 45 percent, overly large wisdom teeth; 59 percent, small cranial capacity, among which 10 percent show true microcephaly; and 14 percent, too many wormian bones. These features recall the black American and Mongol races and, above all, prehistoric man much more than the white races.

These abnormalities are almost always found in large clusters in individual criminals like Villella. Is it possible that individuals with such an enormous variety of cranial anomalies can have the same level of intelligence and sense of responsibility as men with perfectly normal skulls? Note, moreover, that the cranial variations discussed here represent only the most obvious lesions of the brain, that is, alterations of volume and form.

Chapter 29

Cesare Lombroso and Guglielmo Ferrero: The moral sense in criminal women, 1893

Like many European men of his day, Lombroso took it for granted that women were inferior to men biologically, intellectually, and morally. In *Criminal Woman*, he argues that women's crime rates are lower than those of men because they are inferior creatures, less well developed than men (also see Chapter 14). In *Criminal Man*, however, Lombroso had argued that those who commit crime do so because they are inferior creatures, so he now found himself making a contradictory argument about the relationship between inferiority and crime rates, a contradiction he tries to resolve, as near the end of this extract, by claiming that women's maternal traits help to tamp down their inherent savagery.

This Lombroso extract also illustrates his strong interest in evolutionary explanations. Through his efforts to apply evolution theory to criminality, he in effect tried to become the Darwin of criminology.

This extract comes from Cesare Lombroso and Guglielmo Ferrero, *Criminal Woman, the Prostitute, and the Normal Woman*, originally 1893, translated and with a new introduction by Nicole Hahn Rafter and Mary Gibson (Durham, NC: Duke University Press, 2004), pp. 77–81.

CESARE LOMBROSO AND GUGLIELMO FERRERO: THE MORAL SENSE IN CRIMINAL WOMEN

Lying

To demonstrate that lying is habitual and almost physiological in woman would be superfluous, since it is confirmed even by popular sayings. The proverbs we refer to are innumerable and turn up in all languages.

- "Tears of women, a fountain of malice" (Tuscany)
- "Women always tell the truth, but they don't tell all of it" (Tuscany)
- "The horse that sweats, the man who swears, the woman who cries: do not believe any of them" (Tuscany)

- "False as a woman" (Rome)

Women have something close to what might be called an instinct for lying. Caught at something unexpectedly, they start concocting a lie (though some do this better than others). Their first move, even when they are not guilty, is to dissimulate. This is so organic that they are unaware of it, and they are never able to be entirely sincere. Unconsciously, all are a little false.

That women lie habitually is confirmed by the common custom of refusing to accept, or to accept much of, women's testimony. This custom grew out of not only primitive man's disdain for woman's weakness but also his experience with her untruthfulness. Woman's incapacity for criminal responsibility was recognized in the laws of ancient Greece and Rome and in the codes of many Germanic peoples. Even today the Ottoman Code (article 355) provides that the deposition of a man should be worth that of two women. . . .

A sequence of causes contributed to the development of women's ability to lie:

1   Weakness. The oppressed and servile, having no power, need to use cunning and lies. Openness can be a virtue only of the strong.
2   Menstruation. When menstruation became an object of disgust for man, woman had to hide it. Today, too, it is the first lie that one teaches girls; we train them to hide their real condition by simulating other illnesses. This means that women must lie for two or three days each month; perhaps we should call it an exercise in periodic dissimulation.
3   Shame. "The drawback of shame," writes Stendhal, "is that it gets one used to lying." And if *shame* [*pudore*] comes from *putere* [to stink], one can easily see how from earliest times it must have habituated women to lying. Moreover, women are not allowed to reveal any feelings of love. . . .
4   The sexual struggle. Woman must hide her defects, her age, her illnesses – everything that could harm her in men's eyes. She often needs to pretend to have wealth and comfort that she in fact lacks; often, too, she finds it necessary to hide certain superior qualities that men dislike in female companions, such as intelligence, generosity, and scorn for ludicrous social formalities. Rouge, hair dyes, toiletries: at base these are only lies in action, used by women as ammunition in the sexual battle.
5   The desire to be interesting. Woman, like the child, is weak and thus has an instinctive need to be protected; in man's protection she finds her pride and joy. As a result, as Mantegazza and various proverbs note, she often feigns sadness. She cries or pretends to be sick to attract the attention and kindness of others; this is the source of the traditional misconception that women are more sensitive than men. One of the most common forms of malice in woman appears when she does not know how to extricate herself from an embarrassing situation: She pretends to

faint. In hysterics, woman's natural need for protection becomes morbid, giving rise to strange and often inexcusable artifices.

6   Suggestibility. Women are extremely suggestible, overresponding to the ideas of others and even themselves. They easily accept the reality of things about which they are told or which they themselves invent. What is more, they experience things inexactly. Because they grasp the truth with less intensity than men, women are able to let go of it easily.

7   The duties of maternity. Maternity obliges women to dissimulate because child raising depends on a series of clever or stupid lies designed to hide information about sex, to camouflage mothers' own ignorance of things, to guide children on the paths of morality through fear of God and the devil, and so on.

Woman is, in conclusion, a great child, and children are liars par excellence. It is all the easier for women to lie in that they have more reasons for lying than we do.

Vanity

With the advent of civilization, the vanity of men started to decline while that of women began to grow. The principal means through which women express vanity is clothing – a fact so well known that there is almost no need to demonstrate it. . . .

The savage is vain about the trophies of the hunt and war and about simple ornaments. For him, small changes of face or person comprise aesthetic pleasure, constituting a sign of superiority. Savage woman was not yet (or was less) vain. So long as she was man's slave and not yet involved in the sexual competition for men, she had no need to put herself forward. She was like the peahen, which lacks fancy tail feathers and is sought out by the male. She had no need to turn cartwheels.

With evolution and social experience, vanity disappears from the man. Woman, as she evolves, acquires the trait of vanity, the sexual struggle now requiring that she put her attractions on display. This impulse is egotistical, as in savages, and involves the same defect of intelligence. Thus at festivals every woman hopes that every man will be interested only in her. Female vanity expresses itself specifically in clothing because modesty constrains women to cover the entire body, except for the hands and face (sometimes it calls for the face to be covered too). Clothing becomes even more important than corporeal beauty. . . .

Synthesis

In sum, in women, as in children, the moral sense is inferior. Some would say that in a commercial period such as ours, honor, loyalty, and the like are losing their worth for men, and that false stock market tips fabricated by businessmen are as bad as anonymous rumors fabricated by ladies. We would respond that there is as much difference between one and the other as between a soldier who kills an enemy who threatens him and a soldier who kills an unarmed prisoner who happens to offend him. The dishonesty of a banker is a necessity occasioned by the commercial struggle – if he does not set a trap for his rival today, he will fall in it himself tomorrow. It is relatively normal behavior because it is adapted to the conditions, however transitory, of life. On the other hand, the vengeful fury directed by a lady against a rival who is better dressed at a celebration is immoral because it flows from her own excessive egoism and is aimed at someone who is merely exercising a right.

Here we find ourselves led back to the psychology of primitive man, who is happy if the smearings on his face attract the attention of his companions, and who is so vindictive that for him revenge constitutes a religious duty. We are also back to the psychology of the child who, when a favor is given to a companion but not to him, cries as if his rights had been violated.

That which differentiates woman from the child is maternity and compassion; thanks to these, she has no fondness for evil for evil's sake (unlike the child, who will torture animals, and so on). Instead – as we demonstrated in the section on cruelty – she develops a taste for evil only under exceptional circumstances, as for example when she is impelled by an outside force or has a perverse character.

But woman is always fundamentally immoral, and oftentimes her immorality is even a by-product of her compassion. We do not hesitate to deem immoral (even while we are touched by its signs of the dawning of civilization) the warnings savage women gave to European travelers to stay on guard against the plots of their husbands and brothers, because these were contrary to the interests of their social group. Similarly, we deem it immoral for criminal women to denounce their own accomplices, for by turning in their companions, they, too, demonstrate an inability to adapt to social life, albeit a life of crime.

Normal woman has many characteristics that bring her close to the level of the savage, the child, and therefore the criminal (anger, revenge, jealousy, and vanity) and others, diametrically opposed, which neutralize the former. Yet her positive traits hinder her from rising to the level of man, whose behavior balances rights and duties, egotism and altruism, and represents the peak of moral evolution.

Chapter 30

Moriz Benedikt: The brains of criminals, 1881

Moriz Benedikt (1835–1920), a professor of neurology at the University of Vienna, wrote his book *Anatomical Studies upon Brains of Criminals*, he tells us, "to furnish the foundation stones toward a Natural History of Crime." Like Lombroso, with whose work he was familiar, Benedikt began with the assumption that "a defective, atypically-constructed brain, cannot function normally." He dissected the brains of various executed criminals, describing them in minute detail and also, in the original edition, in photographical detail. (E. P. Fowler's English translation converted the photographs to line drawings.) Given his premise and interest in criminal anthropology, it is not surprising that Benedikt concluded, as in this extract, that criminals have abnormal brains and should be considered a separate, anthropological variety of the human species.

But while this conclusion is clearly stated, the rest of Benedikt's book is nearly incomprehensible. A contemporary reviewer (*The New England Medical Gazette* 16, August 1881, p. 250) wrote that "This is one of the very last books we should think of recommending . . . . Almost the entire book is occupied with dry, detailed explanations of the author's efforts at mapping out each individual gyrus, lobulus, fissura, sulcus, etc. on the surfaces of a score or more brains of criminals and comparing them with the external appearances of brains of those who were supposed to be morally superior." I have included a little material in addition to Benedikt's statement of his major finding to give readers the flavor of the work. Its significance to criminology lies in the evidence it gives of the spread of criminal anthropology through Europe, not necessarily in the form taught by Lombroso, but in other anatomical studies that reached similar conclusions about the criminal body.

This extract comes from Moriz Benedikt, *Anatomical Studies upon Brains of Criminals*, translated from the German by E. P. Fowler, M.D. (orig. 1881, reprint New York: Da Capo Press, 1981), pp. 156–8, (grammar as in original translation).

BALÁZS—Murderer and Robber.

(Roumanian.)

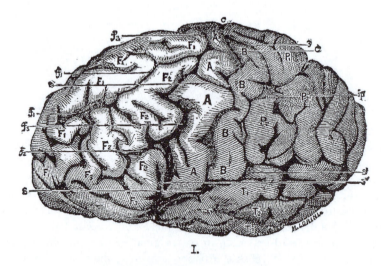

Figure 30.1 Brain of Balázs, a Roumanian Murderer and Robber. The criminal anthropologist Moriz Benedikt dissected the brains of executed criminals to discover
their anomalies. From Moriz Benedikt, *Brains of Criminals* (orig. 1881; repr. New
York: Da Capo Press, 1981), p. 34.

MORIZ BENEDIKT: THE BRAINS OF CRIMINALS

In these brains (of criminals) which were perhaps conspicuously Sclavonic, it seemed especially noticeable that the *sulcus interparietalis* communicated very frequently with the *fossa Sylvii*, and the *parieto-occipitalis* (po) with the *horizontalis* (ho) and the *interparietalis* (ip).

Zernoff "seldom" observed a union of the frontal sulci with the *fossa Sylvii*. In his collection of one hundred brains, the *sulcus centralis* seems to have had connection in but one instance and then with the *fissura Sylvii*.

He seems to have observed a connection with the *scissura hippocampi* (h) with the *calloso-marginalis* (cm), the *parieto-occipitalis* (po), and *collateralis* (cl) and of this last with the *occipitalis* (po); the same also as regards a communication between the *calloso-marginalis* (cm) and the *parieto-occipitalis* (po).

At all events, I hope that these very questions which I here present for debate, will serve as a spur to somewhat promote a knowledge of brain anatomy as it exists in European races; and it especially devolves upon the Austrian, Hungarian, and Russian physicians, to complete this work.

The authority of Betz and the work of Zernoff enable us to reject – as being insufficient at least – the idea that the specimens of criminals' brains which we have portrayed, represents but a deviating type of a normal Sclavonian brain.

The fact also that in the brains of five different races such great deviations from the normal type are found in common, forbids us, *a priori*, to consider these brains as expressing no more than deviations incident to comparative race-anatomy.

There remains nothing more, for the present at least, but to express the proposition:

THE BRAINS OF CRIMINALS EXHIBIT A DEVIATION FROM THE NORMAL TYPE, AND CRIMINALS ARE TO BE VIEWED AS AN ANTHROPOLOGICAL VARIETY OF THEIR SPECIES, AT LEAST AMONGST THE CULTURED RACES.

This proposition is calculated to create a veritable revolution in Ethics, psychology, jurisprudence, and criminalistics. For this very reason it should be handled with the greatest prudence; it should not yet serve as a premise; and for the present it should not leave the hands of expert anatomists.

In matters of fact it must yet be repeatedly proven and that from many different points of view, until it can finally rank as an undoubted addition to human science.

The variety of conditions which we may expect to meet in the different races, will assign to this proposition a little halting place in the history of Science, and worthless as well as valuable contributions will, for a time to come, give rise to oscillations of opinion.

Chapter 31

Pauline Tarnowsky: The anthropology of prostitutes and female thieves, 1889

Pauline Tarnowsky published two books, *Étude anthropométrique sur les prostituées et les voleuses* (*Anthropological Study of Prostitutes and Female Thieves*, 1889) and *Les Femmes homicides* (*Women Who Kill*, 1908). Little is known of her or her work, although she was clearly one of Europe's leading criminal anthropologists. Her books, while cited frequently and admiringly at the turn of the century, were never translated into English. Today she is known mainly through Lombroso's frequent references to her in *Criminal Woman*, to which she contributed data and photographs of female offenders.[1] Tarnowsky seems to have been born in Russia (in both books, the criminals are Russian prisoners, and the prostitutes of the first book were patients in a Russian hospital); and she was a physician.

Tarnowsky's study of prostitutes and thieves was standard criminal anthropology in its assumptions and methods. Describing her work as "anthropometric research" in anthropology and social pathology, she records data on hair and eye color, measures crania, counts anomalies, and offers images of abnormal ears. She reports being heavily influenced by Lombroso's belief that much can be discovered by studying criminals by offense type – thus her selection of thieves, a category she then subdivides into prostitute-thieves, psychopathic thieves, occasional thieves, and so on.

Interest in Tarnowsky is picking up today as she is being recognized as the first female criminologist, an early student of female sexuality, and a pioneer in public-health issues. Research is needed to determine her relationships with other criminal anthropologists; her attitudes toward the women she studied; her findings on menstruation and crime (a topic that fascinated her contemporaries and later criminologists); and her influence (if any) on the French school of criminal anthropology.

For this extract I translated the final pages (201–4) of *Étude anthropométrique sur les prostituées et les voleuses* (Paris: Bureax du Progrès and E. Lecrosnier et Babé, 1889).

PAULINE TARNOWSKY: THE ANTHROPOLOGY OF PROSTITUTES AND FEMALE THIEVES

To summarize our work on prostitutes and female thieves, we offer the following conclusions:

1   Professional **prostitutes** are incomplete beings, arrested in development and marked by a morbid heredity; they bear signs of physical and psychological degeneration that demonstrate their imperfect evolution.
2   The signs of physical degeneration show up among prostitutes mainly in deformities of the head, abnormalities of the cranium (41.33 percent) and the face (42.66 percent), numerous anomalies of the ears (42 percent), and defective teeth (54 percent).
3   Their psychological defects may show up in a more or less pronounced weakness of the intelligence, in a neuropathic constitution, or in a notable absence of the moral sense. It is confirmed by their abuse of the procreative function as well as by their attraction to their dishonorable

Figure 31.1 Gabrielle Bompard. This notorious French prostitute, found guilty of premeditated murder, was deemed a born criminal by Cesare Lombroso, the founder of criminal anthropology. Cesare Lombroso and Guglielmo Ferrero, *La donna delinquente* (Turin: Roux, 1893), p. 343. Image used courtesy of Mary Gibson and Duke University Press.

profession, to which they return voluntarily even after they have been liberated.

4   The stigmata of degeneration are most pronounced among prostitutes and thieves whose mothers abandoned themselves to alcohol. This confirms the hypothesis that it is the mother's influence in particular that determines the infant's physical constitution.

5   Sterility and extinction of the line, so often observed among professional prostitutes, will afflict them to the degree that the individual's abnormal state is rich in hereditary defects; moreover, sterility and extinction seem to confirm that these women are degenerates.

6   Habitual prostitutes, whose work would make it difficult to classify them as healthy and normal beings, fill the large gap that crime statistics have established in favor of women.[2]

7   **Thieves**, while equally marked by the physical and moral signs that differentiate them from honest women, nonetheless are closer than prostitutes to the normal type. This is because:

   a   Thieves are less burdened by hereditary defects.
   b   There are fewer signs of physical degeneration among thieves.
   c   The number of births is larger among thieves.
   d   The main diameters of the cranium, along with the total horizontal circumferences, are larger among thieves than prostitutes (assuming the two belong to the same race).
   e   The cheekbones and mandibles of prostitutes are larger than those of thieves.
   f   The intellectual and moral level of thieves surpasses that of prostitutes. The thief has more self-esteem, her spirit is livelier; and she is more energetic and better prepared for the struggle of life. She is much less lazy and is not afraid of work.
   g   Although theft and selling one's body are both repulsive phenomena, the professional thief, no matter how incorrigible she may be or how numerous her misdeeds, is unable to commit and repeat her offenses at every hour of the day, as the prostitute does. . . . The thief only sins in intervals, according to the occasion, while the brothel prostitute traffics her body without respite, abdicating the right to chose and refuse; she basks in her miserable profession and does not want to change.

8   The anthropological facts, together with research on the heredity of prostitutes and thieves, the circumstances of their birth, and their subsequent social lives, plus the study of their intellectual and moral levels – all these unite to prove that prostitutes and thieves belong to a class of abnormal women, degenerate and degenerating.

   They are the product of slums, the dregs of society, who will diminish in number as the circumstances of biological evolution improve in society.

To halt the evil produced by these strays of civilization, it is not enough to punish as we do now. It would be necessary to get at the evil at its very source: to improve the environmental conditions where these abnormal women are born and live; to reduce their misery by broadening the means of honest and remunerative work for women; and to admit them to the manifold professions and trades dominated by men. New opportunities for honest labor by women would automatically reduce the difficulty that they experience in finding a livelihood; such opportunities would enable them to leave misery behind and turn their backs on bad advisors who counsel debauchery and vice, quite contrary to their own innate inclinations.

To remove children from the pernicious influence of vicious relatives and debauched incorrigibles, it is indispensable to organize educational opportunities for abandoned children. To diminish the ravages caused by drunkenness, syphilis, and other debilitating illnesses and make it possible to have, in a word, a sufficient number of alive-and-kicking offspring to produce a healthy generation, undamaged by morbid heredity – that must be the aim of truly enlightened and careful philanthropic efforts.

Figure 31.2 Delinquent Girls. While all children are inherently criminalistic, according to Lombroso, some are more likely than others to commit crime, as shown by their anomalies. Here Lombroso points to the facial asymmetry of the girl to the left and the overdeveloped cheekbones of the girl to the right. Cesare Lombroso, *Atlante* (vol. 4 of the 5th edition of *L'uomo delinquente*, Turin: Fratelli Bocca Editori, 1897), p. XIII. Image used courtesy of Mary Gibson and Duke University Press.

Notes

1   The photographs are reproduced in Cesare Lombroso and Guglielmo Ferrero, *The Female Offender* (New York: D. Appleton & Company, 1895).

2   Editor's note: Like many other nineteenth-century criminologists, Tarnowsky argues that, although crime statistics show women to be much less criminal than men, they are equally bad if one includes prostitution. Earlier in the book she wrote (p. 97) that although statistics show the criminal tendency to be four or five times lower in women than men, "it is hard to see why woman would be morally superior to man to such a marked degree. . . . Habitual prostitutes, whom one would hardly classify among healthy, normal, honest human beings, fill in the large hole that criminal statistics establish in favor of women. We believe therefore that habitual prostitutes constitute the counterweight that equalizes the balance of criminality, and shares out a more just and uniform measure between the two sexes."

Chapter 32

Havelock Ellis: The results of criminal anthropology, 1890

Havelock Ellis (1859–1939) was the first Englishman to write a book solely on criminology. Although he derived nearly all of the data for *The Criminal* from works by Lombroso and other criminal anthropologists, he was able to synthesize this information in a more readable style than that of most of the researchers themselves. Moreover, *The Criminal*, as the first purely criminological text in English, became the source to which readers in Great Britain and America turned when they wanted to learn about the new science of the criminal. It was reprinted numerous times on both sides of the Atlantic and was one of the most significant works of criminal anthropology after those of Lombroso himself.

Ellis studied medicine, but never practiced it, as his goal was to study sexuality. The scientific study of human sexual behavior had been founded by Krafft-Ebing (see Chapter 12), but Ellis broadened the focus to include not only deviant but also normal sexual behavior, and, famously, he helped normalize homosexuality. A leading advocate of eugenics, or human breeding, Ellis also worked on social reform; and he was a prolific author.

I worked from the 1892 edition of Ellis's *The Criminal* (London: Walter Scott and New York: Charles Scribner's Sons). I have entirely skipped the early chapters, in which he reports various research on the physical and psychical (meaning psychological or mental) characteristics of the criminal, but include parts of Ellis's summary, "The results of criminal anthropology" (pp. 202–31).

HAVELOCK ELLIS: THE RESULTS OF CRIMINAL ANTHROPOLOGY

So far I have been summarising the chief results obtained in the investigation of the criminal up to the present date by many workers in various lands. There is not very much doubt about the results here recorded; even when they do not agree among themselves, it is still generally possible to account for the divergency by the special character of the group to which the individuals examined belong. But when we come to consider the significance of the facts we are no longer on such safe and simple ground. There is, however, no reason here for surprise when we remember how youthful a science criminal anthropology is. Even the related science of general anthropology is still young, and much of our progress in it still lies in the unlearning of our errors, so that as Virchow recently remarked, we know considerably less about anthropology to-day than we knew some years ago. The same is true of another related science, the study of insanity. If therefore my conclusions as to the place of the criminal in nature may seem to be somewhat cautious and tentative, it must be remembered that we are still slowly feeling our way to firm ground. Few as are the general conclusions which we may boldly assert, they are yet sufficient to throw a flood of new light on the nature of the criminal, and on his treatment and prevention.

I purpose to touch briefly on certain relationships of crime and the criminal, the consideration of which will lead us naturally to a clearer view of the criminal's position. We will glance at (a) the biological beginnings of crime, (b) crime among children, (c) the criminal woman as distinct from the criminal man, (d) the relation of crime to vice, (e) crime as a profession, (f) the relations of crime to epilepsy and insanity.

(a) The biological beginnings of crime have been examined by Lombroso, Lacassagne, and Ferri; and by some have even been traced as far back as the vegetable world. Thus Lombroso seems to claim those insectivorous plants studied by Darwin and others as belonging to the category of criminals. I doubt whether by any tenable definition of the criminal such a classification can be upheld, and Lombroso himself speaks with less than his usual decision. An act which is common to a whole species cannot reasonably be described as criminal. It may be unjust, even cruel, but it does not thereby necessarily become criminal. . . . It is only when we are dealing with animals of the very highest order of intelligence that we find any manifestations that can be at all fairly described as criminal. . . .

We have to realise clearly what constitutes criminality when we turn to the lower human races. To say, as has been asserted, that among savages criminality is the rule rather than the exception, is to introduce confusion. Among many savages infanticide, parricide, theft and the rest, far from being anti-social, subserve frequently some social end, and they outrage, therefore, no social feeling. These acts are not anti-social; and many recent investigations, such as those of Élie Reclus, show that there is under the given conditions a certain reasonableness in them, although among us they have ceased to be reasonable, and have become criminal. On the other hand, many acts which the needs or traditions of a barbarous society have caused to be criminal become in a higher phase of society trivial or beneficial. . . .

If we are wise we shall be very tender in arousing our indignation against the social habits of lower races, even when these involve such an act as parricide, for the distance between ourselves and even the lowest races is quite measurable. Our social code is not far removed from that of the Maori who considered that it was murder to kill the man to whom he had given hospitality, but not murder to run his spear through the stranger whom he met on his morning walk. We to-day regard it as a great crime to kill our own fathers or children; but even the most civilised European nation – whichever that may be – regards it as rather glorious to kill the fathers and children of others in war. We are not able yet to grasp the relationship between men. In the same way, while we resent the crude thefts practised by some lower races, we are still not civilised enough to resent the more subtle thefts practised among ourselves which do not happen to conflict with the letter of any legal statute.

Criminality, therefore, cannot be attributed indiscriminately even to the lowest of races. It consists in a failure to live up to the standard recognised as binding by the community. The criminal is an individual whose organisation makes it difficult or impossible for him to live in accordance with this standard, and easy to risk the penalties of acting anti-socially. By some accident of development, by some defect of heredity or birth or training, he belongs as it were to a lower and older social state than that in which he is actually living. It thus happens that our own criminals frequently resemble in physical and psychical characters the normal individuals of a lower race. This is that "atavism" which has been so frequently observed in criminals and so much discussed. . . .

(b) The development of crime is precocious. Rossi ascertained at what age 46 of his 100 criminals commenced their criminal career. Of these 46, no less than 40 began before the age of twenty – i.e., 1 at four years of age, 2 at seven, 6 at eight, 1 at nine, 5 at ten, 1 at eleven, 3 at twelve; and so on. The evidence from France, from England, and from America gives very similar results. Children may even become expert professional criminals, and not in Europe alone. . . .

There is a certain form of criminality almost peculiar to children, a form to which the term "moral insanity" may very fairly be ascribed. This has been described by Krafft-Ebing, Mendel, Savage, and others, and is characterised by a certain eccentricity of character, a dislike of family habits, an incapacity for education, a tendency to lying, together with astuteness and extraordinary cynicism, bad sexual habits, and cruelty towards animals and companions. It shows itself between the ages of five and eleven, and is sometimes united with precocious intellectual qualities. There can be no doubt that many of these develop into instinctive criminals. . . . Both child and criminal are subject to such impulses.

In the criminal, we may often take it, there is an arrest of development. The criminal is an individual who, to some extent, remains a child his life long – a child of larger growth and with greater capacity for evil. This is part of the atavism of criminals. . . .

(c) It is interesting to consider the sexual variations of criminality. Women are everywhere less criminal than men. . . .

While men criminals are everywhere in a more or less marked majority, there are certain crimes which both sexes commit about equally, and these are usually the most serious. Thus, as Quetelet remarked, nearly as many women are poisoners as men, and of parricides 50 per cent. are women. The crimes of women are essentially domestic, against fathers and husbands and children. A very large proportion are, directly or indirectly, of a sexual character. . . .

Prostitution exerts an undoubted influence in diminishing the criminality of women, in spite of the fact that the prostitute generally lives on the borderland of crime. If, however, it were not for prostitution there would be no alternative but crime for the large numbers of women who are always falling out of the social ranks. As it is, in those families in which the brothers become criminals, the sisters with considerable regularity join the less outcast class of prostitutes; sometimes in league with their criminal brothers, but yet possessing a more recognised means of livelihood. There will be something more to say on this point a little later on.

The strongest barrier of all against criminality in women is maternity. The proportion of criminals among young women with children is very small. . . .

(d) One is inclined on first approaching the subject to make the clear line of demarcation between crime and vice, which is necessary in practical life. From the anthropological point of view, however, it appears on closer examination impossible to draw this clear line.

In the course of Lombroso's investigations he was surprised to find in the examination of supposed normal persons certain individuals who presented in a marked form those anthropologic signs of a low and degenerate type which he had usually found among criminals. On further inquiry it appeared that those individuals were of vicious character. Again, it is a remarkable fact that prostitutes exhibit the physical and psychic signs associated usually with criminality in more marked degree than even criminal women. While criminal women correspond on the whole to the class of occasional criminals, in whom the brand of criminality is but faintly seen, prostitutes correspond much more closely to the class of instinctive criminals. Thus their sensory obtuseness has been shown to be extreme, and it is scarcely necessary to show that their psychical sensitiveness is equally obtuse. Several valuable series of observations recently made on prostitutes in Italy and elsewhere have brought out interesting results in this respect. Thus, for example, Dr. Praskovia Tarnovskaia [Pauline Tarnowsky – N.R.] examined at St. Petersburg fifty prostitutes who had been inmates of a brothel for not less than two years, and she also examined, for the sake of comparison, fifty peasant women of so far as possible the same age and intellectual development. She found (1) that the prostitutes presented a shortening, amounting to half a centimetre, of the anterior, posterior, and transverse diameters of skull; (2) 84 per cent. showed various signs of physical degeneration – irregular skull, asymmetry of face, anomalies of hard palate, teeth, ears, etc. . . . Dugdale, in his valuable and thorough study of the "Jukes" family of criminals in America, shows that while the eldest sons in a criminal family carry on the criminal tradition, the younger sons become paupers or vagabonds, and the sisters become prostitutes. . . .

(e) We saw in Chapter I. that there is a fairly well-marked class of professional criminals. They are the *élite* of the criminal groups; they present a comparatively small proportion of abnormalities; their crimes are skillfully laid plots, directed primarily against property and on a large scale; they never commit purposeless crimes, and in their private life are often of fairly estimable character. They flourish greatly in a civilisation of rapidly progressing material character, where wild and unprincipled speculation is rife, as in the United States; their own schemes have much of the character of speculations, with this difference, that they are not merely unprincipled but are against the letter of the law; notwithstanding the ability and daring they require, they are a relatively unskilled kind of speculation. . . .

(f) The morbid element in criminality has sometimes been too strongly emphasised, but it would be idle to attempt to deny its importance. The frequency with which insanity appears among criminals, even when the influence of imprisonment may with considerable certainty be excluded, is well ascertained. Of recent years also the close connection between criminality and epilepsy and general paralysis has often been shown. I have several times pointed out that the resemblances between criminals considered as a class and the insane so considered are by no means great; at many points they are strongly contrasted. The resemblances with epileptics, on the other hand, are anthropologically very marked, as Lombroso was the first to point out in detail. . . .

Up to recent times the criminal has been regarded as a kind of algebraic formula, to use Professor Ferri's expression; the punishment has been proportioned not to the criminal but to the crime. We are now learning to regard the criminal as a natural phenomenon, the resultant of manifold natural causes. We are striving to attain to scientific justice.

Chapter 33

Arthur MacDonald: Evolution, crime, and criminals, 1893

Arthur MacDonald's *Criminology* was the first book-length text on the causes of crime published in the United States.[1] It carried a short introduction by Cesare Lombroso himself, who was always ready to promote his ideas and no doubt attracted by MacDonald's plan to establish a laboratory in Washington D.C. for the study of abnormality and criminality.[2] In fact, Lombroso may have known MacDonald personally, for the latter claimed to have studied criminal anthropology in Turin, Italy, where Lombroso taught.

MacDonald (1856–1936) studied theology, medicine, and law and spent time at five European universities, but he earned no further degrees beyond an M.A. from the University of Rochester, and whatever his training, in *Criminology* he seems uncertain about the nature of science. He himself did no research on the causes of crime and so he has to repeat what others have said. He leans especially heavily on Lombroso, whose sentences he repeats frequently and almost verbatim; and in contrast to Havelock Ellis, he makes no effort to evaluate the material he reports. (Also in contrast to Ellis, MacDonald could not write very well.) In his preface he states that "There is . . . no defined theory advocated," meaning that the book is not pushing a specific theory of crime, but that is disingenuous, for his data and approach assume the validity of criminal anthropology. He takes for granted that humans are evolving as Lombroso and other scientific racists said, with the white, law-abiding males having reached the peak of perfection that criminals, savages, women, and children have not yet attained on the evolutionary ladder.

MacDonald's preface describes *Criminology* as a second edition, but the "first edition" consisted of no more than a pamphlet reprint of an article published earlier that year. Part I of the book, entitled "General Criminology," covers the evolution of crime and the biology, psychology, and intelligence of criminals. It concludes with material on hypnotism and recidivism. Part II, "Special criminology," consists of three case histories and Part III of various bibliographies of crime, some lifted from other books. The overall impression is of an author who is out of his depth and foundering, trying to produce a work on a topic he does not fully understand.

For this extract I used the 1893 edition of *Criminology* (New York: Funk & Wagnalls), pp. x, 18–19, 23–4, 32–3, 40–3, and 97–8.

ARTHUR MACDONALD: EVOLUTION, CRIME, AND CRIMINALS

Preface to second edition

In the first edition of this work, issued some three months ago, a full statement of the purpose of the author was not made. A few of the criticisms seem to indicate some misapprehensions.

The purpose in the general part is to give the most trustworthy opinions and the results of *original* investigations. In a subject of such recent development it would be premature to introduce a system or theory of criminology, or to enter into the philosophy of crime or any form of criminological polemics. There is, therefore, no defined theory advocated. Many problems, including that of the criminal "type," are not considered by the author. In a strict sense, criminology is, of course, not yet a science any more than sociology is; but it may prove to be an important step in the direction of a scientific study of humanity; for investigations of normal humanity with scientific instruments and methods can best begin in prison. At least half of the prisoners are as normal as persons outside, and they are much easier reached and much more likely to confess truths that individuals in free life would conceal. . . .

The evolution of crime

. . . The plant, the animal, the savage, the child of civilized man, and civilized man himself, are stages in nature, which pass imperceptibly one into the other, and form one synthetic whole. According, then, to the natural-history method nature may be studied in her lower realms in order to gain an insight into her more developed stages; for although the processes of elimination may be more direct and severe in the beginnings of nature, yet they are in essence the same throughout her whole extent, reaching into the highest spheres of action and thought. From these points of view, many of the acts of nature are the most cruel and immoral. The insectivorous plants commit the equivalents of murder. . . .

As we pass from the vegetable to the animal, the number of equivalents of crime increases in variety. Thus taking of life in order to procure food or to command the tribe has been observed among horses, bulls, and stags. It is a familiar fact that cannibalism is sometimes practiced among wolves. . . . There are birds who break their eggs and destroy their nests; monkeys who dash the heads of their young against a tree when they are tired of carrying them. Cats, hares, and dogs furnish the equivalents of infanticide, and the young of foxes practice parricide. There is in animals, as in men, an irresistible impulse for over-excitement of passions. . . .

In passing from animals to man we find, as is natural to expect, the lowest degree of savagery in prehistoric races. Without discussing tertiary man, we know in general the manner of life of quartenary man; it was the lowest degree of savagery. . . .

Among the savages crime was the rule. . . . The large number of homicides in savage life is explained by the fact that excessive increase of population, in comparison with natural means of subsistence was a constant peril. Such homicides were often ordained by morality and religion, and furnished a title to glory. Abortion, unknown to the animals, is common among savages. Some tribes in Central Africa frequently used their children as a bait to catch lions. . . .

Cruelty is common among children; they delight in breaking inanimate objects, tearing things, hitting animals, smashing caterpillars; tramping on anything to kill it. Among the lower classes boys from 5 to 10 years of age are notoriously cruel.

But murder, no less than anger, vengeance, and cruelty, is found in children. Caligula at 13 had a slave cast into an oven for a slight offense. . . .

The physical side of the criminal

. . . The criminal, as to æsthetical physiognomy differs little from the ordinary man, except in the case of women criminals, who are most always homely, if not repulsive; many are masculine, have a large, ill-shaped mouth, small eye, large, pointed nose, distant from the mouth, ears extended and irregularly implanted. The intellectual physiognomy shows an inferiority in criminals, and when in an exceptional way there is a superiority, it is rather of the nature of cunning and shrewdness. The inferiority is marked by vulgarity, by meager cranial dimensions, small forehead, dull eyes. The moral physiognomy is marked in its lowest form with a sort of unresponsiveness; there is little or no remorse; there is sometimes the debauched, haggard visage. . . . Those guilty of rape (if not cretins) almost always have a projecting eye, delicate physiognomy, large lips and eyelids; the most of them are slender, blond, and rachitic. The pederasts often have a feminine elegance, long and curly hair, and, even in prison garb, a certain feminine figure, a delicate skin, childish look, and abundance of glossy hair, parted in the middle. Burglars who break into houses have, as a rule, woolly hair, deformed craniums, powerful jaws, and enormous zygomatic arches, are covered with scars on the head and trunk, and are often tattooed. . . .

Intelligence of criminals

In intelligence the criminal is below the average. It must be remembered that the wandering and uncertain life of a criminal and his knocking about in the world favor a development of his intelligence. The first in Europe to investigate and establish an average were the Spaniards. Out of 53,600 about 67 per cent. had a fair intelligence, 10 per cent. were below the average, and 18 per cent. were depraved mentally; less than 1 per cent. possessed hardly any intelligence, and 2¾ per cent. could not be classified.

The majority feel themselves unqualified for any constant work, and their purpose is to escape every kind of occupation. . . .

Levity, mobility, and inconstancy of mind are characteristics of criminals. In Switzerland it is calculated that 44 per cent. of the condemned have been led to crime by their levity.

The prostitutes are so light-minded, as not to be able to hold their attention on any idea; it is difficult to reason with them; thus comes their lack of foresight, which aids their patrons to retain them and impoverish them.

Notes

1 Nicole Hahn Rafter, "Criminal anthropology in the United States," *Criminology* 30 (4) (1992): 525–45.
2 In fact, the laboratory was never established, although MacDonald spent most of his life trying to realize the plan. See James B. Gilbert, "Anthropometrics in the U.S. Bureau of Education: The case of Arthur MacDonald's 'laboratory'," *History of Education Quarterly* 17 (2) (Summer, 1977): 169–95.

Chapter 34

Léonce Manouvrier: Are there anatomical traits peculiar to criminals? 1890

Léonce Manouvrier (1850–1927) was one of the leading French anthropologists of his generation and an implacable foe of the anatomical excesses of Italianate criminal anthropology. In contrast to other French anthropologists who hoped to confine the field to anatomy, Manouvrier defined the newly developing area of anthropology to include "the science of human beings in all their aspects."[1]

Manouvrier was responsible for the day-to-day operations of the famous Laboratory of Anthropology, in Paris, which had been founded by the leader of the previous generation of French anthropologists, Paul Broca. A liberal, Manouvrier argued against not only biological determinism but also, for example, the prevailing anthropological view that women must be less intelligent than men (closer to gorillas, according to one authority) because their skulls were lighter and smaller. Using anthropology, Manouvrier demonstrated that women's craniums were in fact heavier than those of men.

In 1889, the second International Congress of Criminal Anthropology convened in Paris and there, away from their home territory, Lombroso and his Italian followers took a beating at the hands of Manouvrier and other French scientists who defined the study of crime much more sociologically.[2] The following extract shows Manouvrier using logic and wit to critique the Italians' strict determinism and their search for the physical anomalies or stigmata of crime.

For this extract, I translated from Léonce Manouvrier, "Deuxième question: Existe-t-il des caractères anatomiques propres aux criminels?" *Actes du Deuxième Congrès International d'Anthropologie Criminelle, Biologie et Sociologie, Paris, 1889* (Lyon: Storck, 1890), using pp. 28–32.

LÉONCE MANOUVRIER: ARE THERE ANATOMICAL TRAITS PECULIAR TO CRIMINALS?

The aim of this report is to show where anatomical anthropology is with regard to criminals, to critique the work done to date, and to encourage new research which will avoid the errors made in the past. I have to be general, for details would take up a large amount of space, but there will be opportunities for other such efforts aimed, as was this one, at determining the truth.

The anatomical study of criminals cannot be conducted without preliminary psychological analyses to guide it. It is hardly a new type of research, for it involves the connections between body and morality, the links among character, aptitude, moral habits, and physical constitution—matters studied without interruption for nearly a century by a great number of more or less scientific observers who, under the banner of phrenology, enjoyed a popularity much greater than those who today conduct the same type of research under the banner of criminal anthropology, reinvigorating and yet diminishing it. Their rashness and lack of competence or scientific rigor have discredited the phrenological tradition and stunted its development. . . .

Acts can vary from the sociological point of view without varying physiologically or anatomically. In other words, the same organs can produce an infinity of acts appreciable through sociology. A single individual can act in a thousand different ways, bending to the influences to which he is subjected without varying physiologically or anatomically and without ceasing to react in conformity with his constitution: that is, his physiology. Man is an instrument put in play by an infinitely variable environment.

Crime, a serious violation of the law, is a sociological, not a physiological, matter. To analyze criminal anatomy, one would have to break crimes down into physiological elements, referring only to anatomy. Such an analysis would not be easy, but one could use it to avoid the sort of investigations that today use averages to discover if criminals differ anatomically from honest men, or if categories of criminals differ from one another. As soon as one recognized the existence of special anatomical characteristics, or the most frequent, or the most pronounced in criminals in general or in this or that category of criminals, then one would be on the way to the sort of psychological analysis that today is vaguely called the tendency to crime or the tendency to this or that crime in particular. . . .

It is easy to anticipate that one will discover a multitude of anatomical characteristics, for anatomic variations are innumerable, and criminals, whether or not they have a sort of bump of crime, will also present all the anatomical variations found in all sorts of men. How to bring order to this jumble? The classification of criminals into thieves, killers, arsonists, etc., would not constitute a sufficient means of analysis, and here we find evidence for the justice of a remark made earlier: that crime is not a direct function of anatomy. Thus we would need to try to sort criminals into groups that would make the links clearer. For example, one might consider separately:

1   Strange crimes, acts that would be inexplicable in the case of men who are healthy and normally constituted, that is to say offenses committed

by madmen, epileptics, idiots, those who are deliriously ill or anatomical monsters. . .;

2 Crimes accomplished under the influence of a transient problem (anger, drunkenness, jealousy, fear, etc.). . . . One would expect many offenders in this group to be degenerates and weak in spirit, inferiors of all sorts, psychologically and anatomically;

3 Crimes accomplished in cold blood, whether habitually or professionally, or perhaps occasionally, under the influence of inauspicious sociological conditions and from motives that are susceptible to regulation among men who are healthy and normal.

These distinctions, based on physiological analysis and distinctions between normal and pathological states, are indispensable. . . . Without them, the social class of criminals is nothing but a physiological mess to which corresponds a scientifically useless anatomical mess.

It is also good to try to distinguish normal and abnormal states from one another, physiologically and anatomically. . . It is abnormal to kill and steal without reason or, rather, without any other reason than the pleasure of watching someone who did us no harm suffer. But one would have to be strongly optimistic or a really enthusiastic admirer of normal humanity to believe that it is abnormal to lust after the goods of others and, so lusting, to try to appropriate them for oneself. . . . One is thus not obliged to suppose that ordinary crimes are associated with a morbid or abnormal physiology.

Then one must consider that many distinctive physiological traits can, according to circumstances, be either virtues or blemishes. A loving temperament might be highly appreciated in one situation but considered dangerous in others. The audacity that causes a smashing action by a soldier might become the object of disadvantageous remarks in the case of a criminal. . . .

One conceives, in sum, not only that crime is not necessarily allied with particular psychological abnormalities or disadvantages, but even that it might be determined, everything else held equal, by truly good qualities that are short-circuited by true defects.

Finally we must not forget that the healthy and normal man is not a man without flaws or a tendency to vice. Such a man would be hard to find even among honest people. A flaw or a vice does not become an anomaly solely because it is observed in a criminal, even one who is abnormal. . . .

Has anyone found an anatomical trait that characterizes criminals exclusively, or a certain category of criminals (thieves, con artists, killers, etc.) exclusively? No, there is perhaps only one anthropologist who believes in the existence of such a trait. . . .

Notes

1   Jennifer Michael Hecht, *The End of the Soul: Scientific modernity, atheism, and anthropology in France* (New York: Columbia University Press, 2003), p. 79.
2   Robert A. Nye, "Heredity or milieu: The foundations of modern European criminological theory," *Isis* 47 (238) (1976): 335–55.

Chapter 35

Alexandre Lacassagne: Social milieu and criminality, 1894

The French physician, criminal anthropologist, and forensic scientist Alexandre Lacassagne (1843–1924) led the French rivals of Lombroso's Italian School of criminology. Like Lombroso, Lacassagne founded an important criminological journal, the *Archives de l'Anthropologie Criminelle*, editing it from Lyon, France, where he held the university's chair of Legal Medicine.[1]

Although he was deeply influenced by Lombroso's work, Lacassagne opposed the Italian positivists on key points. He was less deterministic and less hereditarian, insisting on greater attention to environmental circumstances that cause crime. Moreover, he rejected the Italians' fixation on biological and anthropological factors, calling for the study of such influences in their social context.

This passage, originally a speech ("Speech of the President," as it is listed in the *Archives*) that Lacassagne delivered at the second congress of the Patronage des Libérés, in 1894, was printed in his *Archives de l'Anthropologie Criminelle*, vol IX: 404–10. I have translated pp. 405–8, an extract that includes Lacassagne's famous comparison of the criminal to a microbe floating in a culture: "the social milieu is a bouillon, a culture for criminality. The microbe is the criminal, an element of no importance until the day he finds the bouillon which he makes ferment."

ALEXANDRE LACASSAGNE: SOCIAL MILIEU AND CRIMINALITY

We must consider men not as specific individuals, isolated beings, but instead as parts of the same organism. Given this conviction, it follows that my ideas about crime and criminals differ from those of my colleague Lombroso.

The professor of legal medicine at Turin attributes a large role to heredity and even to the most remote kinds of atavism. At first Lombroso argued that the criminal is a savage who has mistakenly wandered into our civilization. He is suddenly a new specimen from prehistoric times, reappearing among us with the instincts and passions of a man of the quarternary period.

A few years later, having closely studied his topic, Lombroso modified this first impression, and, greatly reinforced by measurements, statistics, and percentages, he held that the born criminal was a pathological man with the same anatomical dispositions or distinctive qualities that one finds, but less frequently, among honest men. Finally, in a third stage, Lombroso merged criminals with the morally insane and proclaimed that the born criminal was nothing more than an epileptic.

The French school, which flowed from Gall, Broussais, Morel, and Despine, has proposed different laws and arrived at other results. Rejecting Lombroso's fatalism and idea of an original blot, we rather believe that it is society which makes and prepares the way for criminals.

There are two factors: the individual and the social. It is the latter which is most important. The individual factor has limited influence. Without doubt, one could take note of criminals' anomalies or physical and moral defects. But this shows only that these signs are not themselves characteristic of criminality but rather can be found among other men as well.

When the pathological side predominates or has great influence, one is dealing with a madman and not a criminal. It is the will to carry out an act, and not the act itself, which characterizes crime. The horror of a crime or the monstrous circumstances which accompanied it are not sufficient for us to conclude that the acts were committed by a madman or someone who was unbalanced. The most atrocious of destructive instincts cannot allow us to conclude that the actor was ill.

Man is born with abilities, instincts, and passions, but not with that which is called the *moral sense*.[2] This ability to distinguish that which is good or bad in a society is an effect, a consequence of adaptation and of life in this particular social circumstance. That is why the moral sense changes with time and place. This social sense, with its virtues and its shortcomings, varies with the virtues and errors of the times, with the customs or even the prejudices of an epoch.

Thus we can define crime as *all acts injurious to the existence of a human collectivity*. We know that the moral personality demonstrates itself through manifestations of feelings, intelligence, and activity. For a long time popular parlance recognized the predominance of one or the other of these manifestations by speaking of men of spirit, of character, of heart. Similarly, we speak of criminals of thought, action, or feeling.

One also says that society produces virtues and vices, just as it manufactures vitriol and sugar. But it is more exact to say that like most living bodies, society has its parasites and its microbes. Those are the criminals.

Given this framework, comparisons are easy. You have heard of aerobic microbes that live in the presence of air, and of anaerobic microbes that reproduce in milieus deprived of oxygen. Do we not similarly have criminals who exercise their profession in broad daylight and others that practice it only at night, living in thick shadows and seething hovels?

There are pathological microbes which act on the organism by causing functional problems and through the detritus that they leave. This detritus is the violent poison called ptomaine. Do you believe that frantic speculation, bizarre financial enterprises, and a passion for gambling on races or games of chance can occur without leaving the dregs of moral disorganization? Here, it seems to me, are the social ptomaines.

We also know that there are microbes which provoke putrefaction and others which live without effect in the organism until time or accident makes them proliferate or provokes their toxicity.

Similarly the social milieu is a bouillon, a culture for criminality. The microbe is the criminal, an element of no importance until the day he finds the bouillon which he makes ferment.

Enough of these analogies that come so naturally to a medical criminologist. I wanted to show you that the health of a society can better be judged by its mores than by its laws.

Notes

1   The *Archives* and a rich trove of other materials on French criminal anthropology can be found online at www.criminocorpus.cnrs.fr
2   Note how different this assertion is from the earlier belief in moral insanity, which assumed that everyone aside from remorseless criminals is born *with* a moral sense – N.R.

Chapter 36

Frederick Howard Wines: Criminal anthropology, 1895

Frederick Howard Wines (1838–1912), a census official, chaplain, criminologist, prison reformer, and sociologist, was as active as anyone of his day in developing a picture of America's social problems and finding solutions to them. In 1895 he published *Punishment and Reformation*, a popular text with a chapter that politely tore criminal anthropology to shreds on methodological grounds. Wines was well situated to write such a critique: the son of a famous prison reformer, Enoch Wines, he himself had long served as head of the Illinois Board of Public Charities, the organization in charge of the state's prisons and other institutions for what were at the time called the "dependent, defective, and delinquent classes." In addition, he had been in charge of collecting and analyzing the statistics on crime and pauperism for the Tenth and Eleventh U.S. Censuses (1880 and 1890).

Punishment and Reformation was designed, Wines states in his preface, "to be an aid to legislation and to the formation of a correct public opinion." He had been lecturing about criminal anthropology, the new European science that had stirred up prison reformers, and so he included a chapter exposing its flaws in his book. *Punishment and Reformation* was revised at least once and frequently reprinted.

This extract comes from the chapter on "Criminal anthropology" (pp. 229–65) in the first edition: Frederick Howard Wines, *Punishment and Reformation* (New York: Thomas Y. Crowell & Company, 1895). I reprint material from pp. 254–61.

FREDERICK HOWARD WINES: CRIMINAL ANTHROPOLOGY

. . . Criminal anthropology, as thus outlined, occupies the debatable ground between science and philosophy. As a science, it is positive and aggressive. As a philosophy, it consists almost wholly of negations, the chief of which are the negation of spirit, of freedom of the will, and of moral responsibility. Its philosophical conceptions will be commented upon in another chapter. Some remarks upon its scientific validity are here in place.

The value of scientific investigation depends upon a variety of considerations, such as the competency of the observer, the number and extent of the observations, and the methods employed. No observations, however numerous, are of any scientific value (except as material for science) until they are reduced to order by classification and comparison. Observations of the abnormal are of no value without comparison with the normal.

The test of the adequacy and accuracy of the observations themselves is the agreement or disagreement of the observers in statements of fact. In the declarations regarding convicts made by criminologists, disagreements like those above cited as to their color-blindness or their hearing prove that the examination made was superficial, on the one side or the other, or else that the groups examined were of insufficient size to insure correspondence in the statistical result. This inquiry of necessity assumes largely a statistical form. The opportunities of police and prison officers to obtain, by means of daily contact with the criminal class, more accurate impressions and a better general notion respecting their appearance and character, exceed those of any scientific enthusiast; but they are apt to be unskilled observers, incapable of conducting an investigation after the systematic methods followed in an anthropological laboratory, or of pursuing it to the point of medical interrogation of the vital organs; and the commonplaces of the prison need statistical verification, for which records are necessary, which it is not usual to keep. Now every statistician knows that the limits of variation in the percentages obtained by the mathematical subdivision of any two corresponding groups of observed facts, if the groups are only large enough, are extremely narrow. Where the groups are large, and the percentages do not closely approximate each other, group for group, the difference is the result of causes operating locally, which are either known or can be searched out. Until a sufficient number of criminological statistical tables shall have been made and compared with each other to demonstrate their substantial agreement, without reference to the personality of the observer or the observed, the elementary facts of criminal anthropology can have no scientific authority, for want of an adequate scientific basis.

In the second place, the comparisons which must be made, in order to have any bearing upon the question of the existence or non-existence of a distinct and recognizable criminal type, must be comparisons not of isolated phenomena, but of groups of phenomena. A type, whatever else it may be, is "an *ensemble* of characters." It is not enough to know that certain characters exist in detail in more abundant measure in the criminal than in the non-criminal class; their tendency to repeat themselves in certain specific combinations must be proved, and the combinations themselves described. The new science, if it is a science, is not yet in position to attempt anything of the sort.

The extreme difficulty of such a comparison is probably unsuspected by the great majority of its votaries.

Furthermore, if every criminal in the world were listed, examined, a truthful report made of all his essential peculiarities, and an accurate count made, showing all the important groupings of such peculiarities, so that the result could be tabulated and the percentages calculated, it would still be necessary to have a corresponding report exhibiting the same groupings of the same characters in an equal number of persons never convicted of crime, as a background for comparison, before the assertion that any particular grouping is even *primâ facie* evidence that its subject belongs to a separate anthropological type. The case is here put strongly, in order to impress this point upon the imagination. It would not in fact be necessary to carry the investigation so far. But it is necessary to carry it far enough to secure credibility in the result, and it must be carried as far for the innocent as for the guilty. It is said that red-haired criminals are relatively more rare than honest people with red heads. How is this known? How can it be known, without a statistical inquiry too extended to be attempted by private initiative? Suppose that the reverse were true; would it be allowable to entertain a suspicion of the honesty of all blondes? The peculiarities recorded in the case of convicts are also observable in honest men and women. Much has been made of cranial asymmetry, about which every hatter who uses a *formateur* can give a criminologist points which would possibly correct his estimate of the value of this particular stigma. A photographer could do the same with reference to asymmetry of the countenance; if he knows his business, he makes every subject sit with the worst side of his face in shadow.

Anatomical remarks are of course the most palpable; for this reason the writings of the anthropologists exhibit the greatest affluence of statistics upon the precise points which are of the smallest relative significance. Of greater importance is the study of physiological peculiarities, especially if they are at the same time pathological and reveal a nervous diathesis analogous to that of the insane or epileptic. But, after all, the most important characters demanding investigation are the psychical. If a criminal type in fact exists, it can be discovered and brought to light only by a demonstration of the uniform or approximately uniform coexistence of certain combinations of physical and psychical manifestations, which are rarely if ever found to be dissociated from each other. Such a demonstration would afford a trustworthy basis for scientific prevision and prediction. The perfection of any science is shown by the capacity of those who have mastered it to read the future, as astronomers, for instance, are able to foretell the precise moment of an eclipse, while meteorologists can rarely foretell the weather twenty-four hours in advance. Judged by this standard, criminal anthropology is still in the state of adolescence, if not of infancy.

Finally, what is a type? The word is employed in two very different senses. Popularly, perhaps, it is used to express the fact that certain groups of characters repeat themselves in numbers of individuals, without reference to the question whether they are accidental and due to environment, education, or habit, or whether they are transmissible by inheritance. Every such group of individuals bearing a marked resemblance to each other in appearance, habits, tastes, occupations, and so forth, is said to be a type. Even in this sense a single character does not constitute the type, but an aggregation of characters – an *ensemble*. In the strictly scientific sense, on the contrary, an anthropological type cannot be said to exist, where it does not tend in a high degree to reproduce itself in offspring. The *ensemble* of characters which, taken together, express it, must be recognized in a majority at least of the members of a family, a tribe, or a nation, united by ties of blood. They must be inherited from a common ancestor. In the first of these two senses, the existence of a criminal type is admitted, though it may be difficult to define with precision all the elements of which it is composed. In the more restricted and accurate signification of the term, the existence of an anthropological criminal type has not been proved, and it is doubtful whether it can be proved.

In order to prove it, it will be necessary to push the inquiry a step further, and to ascertain, in a sufficient number of individual instances, whether any special group of peculiarities demonstrably attaching to criminals and more rarely found in combination in virtuous, peaceable, honest citizens, did in fact characterize either or both the parents of the criminals in question; or, if not, whether they characterized some more remote progenitor; and whether they are repeated in any considerable number of the near relations of the aforesaid criminals, who may be supposed to have in their veins a large proportion of the same vicious or degenerated blood. Here we touch upon the vexed question, still in suspense, of the transmissibility of acquired characters, into which we cannot here enter, but which is the vital question of evolution, and the central point of this particular controversy.

From these statements the reader may form an adequate notion of the difficulty, as well as of the importance of the task to which these gentlemen have devoted their talents and their energies. The obstacles to be overcome are enormous, if not insuperable. They are enhanced by the ignorance, stupidity, indifference, suspicion, and inveracity of the convicts, who alone, in many cases, can give the desired family history, (which a large percentage of them cannot do), and whose statements regarding themselves require verification, before science can predicate any conclusions from them. When the facts shall have been collected and verified, the work of interpretation will be in order; but it involves so much hypothetical, speculative reasoning, particularly upon the point of the relative importance of heredity and environment in the production of the specific characters included in each type, that the conclusions formulated will differ with the personal convictions and prejudices of the writer. From the description of an anthropological type should be excluded all characters which are not hereditary, or at least transmissible – cuts and scars, for instance, of which there is a fearful percentage among old, habitual convicts; and yet one observer with little notion of perspective gives undue prominence in his picture of typical crime to the wrinkled faces of prisoners.

Among the questions on which students are by no means agreed is that of normality: what is normal? and what is abnormal? . . .

The pretensions of the new science are therefore out of all proportion to its achievements and its claims . . .

Habitual criminals and their identification

Habitual criminals and their identification
Introduction to Part VII

Today's criminologists have come to focus on a hard core of repeat offenders, the small group that seems to be responsible for a large proportion of street crime. Similarly, nineteenth-century criminologists came to focus on habitual criminals, the repeaters who seemed to be incorrigible and whose behavior, some thought, might be explained by Lombroso's theory of the born or hereditary criminal (Chapter 39). Throughout Western Europe and the United States, attention turned to understanding habitual criminals (Chapters 37 and 38) and identifying them. Alphonse Bertillon, a Frenchman, devised a complex means of detecting repeat offenders when they were rearrested (Chapter 40); meanwhile the Englishman Francis Galton investigated the possibilities of fingerprinting (Chapter 41), pioneering the development of the system that eventually replaced *bertillonage*.

Chapter 37

Henry Mayhew and John Binny: Habitual criminals, 1862

An earlier extract (Chapter 24) drew on Mayhew's and Binny's great survey of the London underworld for a portrait of the underclass, specifically, a view of a rowdy gathering of delinquent boys. Here I return to *The Criminal Prisons of London* for Mayhew's and Binny's comments on habitual criminals. Although they view habitual criminals as an anthropologically distinct form of people, Mayhew and Binny show nothing like the scientific interest in the anatomy of habitual criminals that we find in criminal anthropological works just a few years later. Nor, despite their references to Hottentots and Kaffirs, do they indulge in scientific racism. Indeed, some of the habitual criminals whom they describe are highly skilled – "professionally dishonest," as Mayhew and Binny put it.

This passage comes from the 1862 edition of *The Criminal Prisons of London* (London: Griffin, Bohn, and Company), pp. 89–90.

HENRY MAYHEW AND JOHN BINNY: HABITUAL CRIMINALS

The *habitual* criminals . . . are a distinct body of people. Such classes appertain to even the rudest nations, they being, as it were, the human parasites of every civilized and barbarous community. The Hottentots have their "*Son-quas*," and the Kaffirs their "*Fingoes*," as we have our "prigs" and "cadgers." Those who object to labour for the food they consume appear to be part and parcel of every State – an essential element of the social fabric. Go where you will – to what corner of the earth you please – search out or propound what new-fangled or obsolete form of society you may – you will be sure to find some members of it more apathetic than the rest, who will object to work; even as there will be some more infirm than others, who are unable, though willing, to earn their own living; and some, again, more thrifty, who, from their prudence and their savings, will have no need to labour for their subsistence.

These several forms are but the necessary consequences of specific differences in the constitution of different beings. Circumstances may tend to give an unnatural development to either one or the other of the classes. The criminal class, the pauper class, or the wealthy class may be in excess in one form of society as compared with another, or they may be repressed by certain social arrangements – nevertheless, to a greater or less degree, there they *will*, and, we believe, *must* ever be.

Since, then, there is an essentially distinct class of persons who have an innate aversion to any settled industry, and since work is a necessary condition of the human organization, the question becomes, "How do such people live?" There is but one answer – If they will not labour to procure their own food, of course they must live on the food procured by the labour of others.

The means by which the criminal classes obtain their living constitute the essential points of difference among them, and form, indeed, the methods of distinction among themselves. The "Rampsmen," the "Drummers," the "Mobsmen," the "Sneaksmen," and the "Shofulmen," which are the terms by which the thieves themselves designate the several branches of the "profession," are but so many expressions indicating the several modes of obtaining the property of which they become possessed.

The *"Rampsman,"* or *"Cracksman,"* plunders by force – as the burglar, footpad, &c.

The *"Drummer"* plunders by stupefaction – as the "hocusser."

The *"Mobsman"* plunders by manual dexterity – as the pickpocket.

The *"Sneaksman"* plunders by stealth – as the petty-larceny boy. And

The *"Shofulman"* plunders by counterfeits – as the coiner.

Now, each and all of these are a distinct species of the criminal genus, having little or no connection with the others. The "cracksman," or housebreaker, would no more think of associating with the "sneaksman," than a barrister would dream of sitting down to dinner with an attorney. The perils braved by the housebreaker or the footpad, make the cowardice of the sneaksman contemptible to him; and the one is distinguished by a kind of bull-dog insensibility to danger, while the other is marked by a low, cat-like cunning.

The "Mobsman," on the other hand, is more of a handicraftsman than either, and is comparatively refined, by the society he is obliged to keep. He usually dresses in the same elaborate style of fashion as a Jew on a Saturday (in which case he is more particularly described by the prefix "swell"), and "mixes" generally in the "best of company," frequenting, for the purposes of business, all the places of public entertainment, and often being a regular attendant at church, and the more elegant chapels – especially during charity sermons. The mobsman takes his name from the gregarious habits of the class to which he belongs, it being necessary for the successful picking of pockets that the work be done in small gangs or mobs, so as to "cover" the operator.

Among the sneaksmen, again, the purloiners of animals (such as the horse-stealers, the sheep-stealers, &c.) all – with the exception of the dog-stealers –

belong to a particular tribe; these are agricultural thieves; whereas the mobsmen are generally of a more civic character.

The shofulmen, or coiners, moreover, constitute another species; and upon them, like the others, is impressed the stamp of the peculiar line of roguery they may chance to follow as a means of subsistence.

Such are the more salient features of that portion of the habitually dishonest classes, who live by *taking* what they want from others. The other moiety of the same class, who live by getting what they want *given* to them, is equally peculiar. These consist of the "Flat-catchers," the "Hunters," and "Charley Pitchers," the "Bouncers," and "Besters," the "Cadgers," and the "Vagrants."

The *"Flat-catchers"* obtain their means by false pretences – as swindlers, duffers, ring-droppers, and cheats of all kinds.

The *"Hunters"* and *"Charley Pitchers"* live by low gaming – as thimblerig-men.

The *"Bouncers"* and *"Besters"* by betting, intimidating, or talking people out of their property.

The *"Cadgers,"* by begging and exciting false sympathy.

The *"Vagrants,"* by declaring on the casual ward of the parish workhouse.

Each of these, again, are unmistakably distinguished from the rest. The "Flat-catchers" are generally remarkable for great shrewdness, especially in the knowledge of human character, and ingenuity in designing and carrying out their several schemes. The "Charley Pitchers" appertain more to the conjuring or sleight-of-hand and black-leg class. The "Cadgers," on the other hand, are to the class of cheats what the "Sneaksman" is to the thieves – the lowest of all – being the least distinguished for those characteristics which mark the other members of the same body. As the "Sneaksman" is the least daring and expert of all the "prigs," so is the "Cadger" the least intellectual and cunning of all the cheats. A "Shallow cove" – that is to say, one who exhibits himself half-naked in the streets, as a means of obtaining his living – is looked upon as the most despicable of all creatures, since the act requires neither courage, intellect, nor dexterity for the execution of it. Lastly, the "Vagrants" are the wanderers – the English Bedouins – those who, in their own words, "love to shake a free leg" – the thoughtless and the careless vagabonds of our race.

Such, then, are the characters of the habitual criminals, or professionally dishonest classes – the vagrants, beggars, cheats, and thieves – each order expressing some different mode of existence adopted by those who hate work-ing for their living. The vagrants, who love a roving life, exist principally by declaring on the parish funds for the time being; the beggars, as deficient in courage and intellect as in pride, prefer to live by soliciting alms from the public; the cheats, possessed of considerable cunning and ingenuity, choose rather to subsist by fraud and deception; the thieves, distinguished generally by a hardihood and comparative disregard of danger, find greater delight in risking their liberty and taking what they want, instead of waiting to have it given to them.

Figure 37.1 Female Convict at Millbank Prison. From Henry Mayhew and John Binny, *The Criminal Prisons of London and Scenes of Prison Life* (orig. 1862; repr. London: Frank Cass & Co., 1968), p. 85.

Chapter 38

J. Bruce Thomson: The psychology of criminals, continued, 1870

The first part of J. B. Thomson's influential article on "The psychology of criminals" was extracted in Chapter 17, where I used it to illustrate degenerationist thinking. Thompson's work incorporated earlier ideas about moral insanity, human evolution, and the deteriorated condition of the underclass to propose that criminals are a breed apart from honest men and women. His analyses came close to those put forth a few years later by Lombroso and other criminal anthropologists who spoke of a born criminal, an evolutionary laggard backward in body, mind, and morals.

The born criminal, doomed to offend repeatedly throughout life, was a close cousin to the habitual or incorrigible offender of other writings, including the *habitués* whom Thomson describes here. Anticipating late twentieth-century criminologists, Thomson here discovers that a relatively small number of habitual offenders commit a majority of crimes.

This extract comes from J. Bruce Thomson, "The psychology of criminals," *Journal of Mental Science* 16 (1870): 321–50; here I use pp. 337–44.

J. BRUCE THOMSON: THE PSYCHOLOGY OF CRIMINALS, CONTINUED

By the frequent re-committals of the criminals we may judge of their extreme moral insensibility. . . .

The female convicts since 1855, in consequence of the abolition of transportation, have been all confined in penal servitude, and have been under my charge in the General Prison for Scotland. They go through their sentences from five years to life, and offer a complete study. The number admitted since 1855–68 amounted to 1034, of whom have been re-committed 458, known to have suffered repeated sentences to transportation or penal servitude in the General Prison, as follows : –

345 have been twice under convict sentences.
103 have been thrice under convict sentences.
  7 have been four times under convict sentences.
  3 have been five under convict sentences.

Therefore their number of re-committals as convicts must have been –

$$345 \times 2 = 690 \text{ times}$$
$$103 \times 3 = 309 \text{ ,,}$$
$$7 \times 4 = 28 \text{ ,,}$$
$$3 \times 5 = 15 \text{ ,,}$$

Total re-committals of 458 } convicts since 1855 } = 1042

But the half is not told by this startling sum. The average number of committals to small local prisons of every female convict, I find to average at least four times before she is sent to suffer long confinement in the convict prison; and some have been ten, fifty, one hundred times under short sentences. Let us take four as an average for these 458, and we have –

458 × 4 times in local prisons   = 1832
To which add the re-committals to General } Prison or Transportation } = 1042

Total re-committals to local prisons – Transportation or Convict Prison – of 458 } = 2874 female convicts

Can anything express more strongly than these figures the extreme perversity and moral insensibility of the criminal class of *habitués?* What hope is there of disciplining such a set into honest ways of living? We earnestly enquire with Despine, are these utterly without the moral sense? Are not such anomalous states of mind proofs of moral insanity? . . .

Allow me to offer a remark or two on the foregoing figures.

First.   Note the fewness of our criminals compared with the reported numbers of committals. The admissions to prison were 1034, but of these 458 cases are more than once included in that number; so that the number of our female convicts in Scotland is only a few hundreds after all. If these *habituées* were confined for life, the residue outside would be small, and the propagation of the criminal class prevented.

Again.   Note the enormous expense these 458 habitual criminals cost the country. Their commitments amounted to 2874. I have tried to come at a reasonable estimate of the expense of each trial; taking into account police apprehensions, transference to seat of local prison, official fees for precognosing, reporting, and attendance on trials, time of judges, juries, and other officials valued, expense of witnesses, escorts to convict prison; all being calculated. The cost of each trial could not be less than £30, which being multiplied by the number of trials, 2,874 = £86,220. To this must be added the prison keep, considerably above £20 per annum, say for an average of five years, and we have :–

£20 for five years = £100 × 458	£45,800
Expenses before and after trial	86,220
Total expenses incurred by 458 female convicts	£132,020

What a stupendous expenditure is that for prisons and criminals, with what a poor and miserable result!

The moral insensibility of criminals is further shown by their continued tendency in prison to offences. The history of their punishments in prison is a most singular one, showing extreme perverseness, great irritability of temper, tendency to steal, to destroy articles, to strike, to do all manner of mischief, in fine, to show complete want of principle and self-control. Instead of penitence

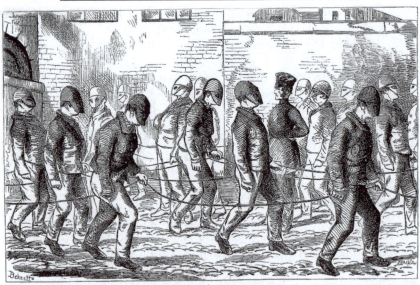

CONVICTS EXERCISING IN PENTONVILLE PRISON.

Figure 38.1 Convicts Exercising in Pentonville Prison. Convicts were masked so they would not recognize one another, but authorities worried that criminals, by giving false names, also masked their identities to avoid being identified as repeat offenders. From Henry Mayhew and John Binny, *The Criminal Prisons of London and Scenes of Prison Life* (orig. 1862; repr. London: Frank Cass & Co., 1968), p. 49.

we usually have sullen discontent, violence, arrogance, recklessness of disposition, indicative of moral insensibility. When I was first called to the charge of the convict prison for Scotland, I can well remember how I felt awed to enter by night to visit a patient, and in my simplicity thought how many hundreds of wretches lay around me, as I supposed, tossed on a troubled bed, haunted by the memories of the past. There is no such thing. The criminals seem to me to sleep upon their hammocks as soundly as other people. . . .

The last, and perhaps the strongest proof of the moral insensibility of criminals (the habitual criminals, I refer to), is that they seem not amenable to moral treatment. All the appliances of chaplains and teachers, with all the discipline of prison legislation, are not known to turn any from the error of their ways. The criminal goes out of and into prison many times, and the hopeless imbecile is not reformed if a professional criminal. Such are set at large, after short sentences, to my seeming, with as much judgment as guided the Knight of La Mancha, when he in his morbid philanthropy set at liberty the wild galley slaves going to punishment. I have asked all the principal governors of Scotland if they can point to a converted thief, but they never knew an habitual thief, man or woman, who became honest and industrious. A distinguished writer, who has, as he says, looked more criminals in the face than any man in Scotland, and has well studied their characteristics, says "*As to reforming old thieves, find me the man who has made an honest working man out of an old thief, and I'd next set him about turning old foxes into house dogs. The fact is impossible.*"

Would not life-confinements be at once a wise economy to the country and a mercy to the criminal?

Habitual criminals may be very justly regarded not only as incurable, but, viewed in the most humane and Christian light, their acts are inexpiable.

Chapter 39

Cesare Lombroso: Incorrigibles, 1878, 1889, and 1896–7

Lombroso used the terms "born criminal," "incorrigible," and "habitual criminal" almost interchangeably to refer to the type of offender who could not be reformed. The following passages are drawn from three editions of *Criminal Man* (those of 1878, 1889, and the final 1896–97 edition); all three can be found in Cesare Lombroso, *Criminal Man*, a new translation with introduction and notes by Mary Gibson and Nicole Hahn Rafter (Durham, NC: Duke University Press, 2006), pp. 145–6, 294–5, and 341–2.

CESARE LOMBROSO: INCORRIGIBLES

Prisons for incorrigibles (1878 edition)

Even the best possible prison system cannot completely eliminate recidivism. We need to establish institutions for those criminals who demonstrate a tendency to crime from childhood and have become continual repeat offenders, especially if they have no family (or an immoral family) or if they themselves request such treatment. Those deemed incorrigible should also display all the physical and mental characteristics typical of the true criminal. They should be sentenced to life imprisonment by a jury made up of the prison's director and doctors, as well as judges and members of the public.

These wretches should be held under a regime that is gentler than the normal prison, ideally on an island. They should work in the countryside, which is good both for their health and the state, especially if they work in harvesting teams as in Sweden (*Kronarbets*), under military discipline as road builders, or in land reclamation. They should be allowed to receive letters from relatives and to have a few hours a day for personal business; but they should be released only if they show exceptional improvement.

This type of life imprisonment can replace the death sentence, which public opinion, rightly or wrongly, wants removed from the penal code. Modern criminal anthropologists also oppose the death penalty. The establishment of prisons for incorrigibles would free up cells for less serious criminals, allowing the implementation of the cellular system in regular prisons on a much larger scale. Prisons for incorrigibles would offer a place to hold in perpetuity those recidivistic offenders and members of criminal organizations who most threaten society. Such institutions for incorrigibles would also give us a way to purge regular prisons of the gangs that, by glorifying vice, stymie efforts at correction. Furthermore, they would gradually reduce that not inconsiderable proportion of criminality that stems from hereditary factors and the bad example of relatives. There would be a return to the process of natural selection that has produced not only our race but the very justice that gradually came to prevail with the elimination of the most violent.

The expense of maintaining prisoners for life would be significant, for many would refuse to work; and yet it would be lower than that incurred by society as a result of more crimes and more trials. The latter often cost fabulous sums. Thomson has calculated that 458 Scottish recidivists cost £132,000, of which £86,000 alone went into their trials – a truly princely sum!

Whether biologically abnormal or not, recidivists are harmful to themselves and their offspring. Life imprisonment for incorrigible criminals is not more unjust than internment of the insane in mental hospitals – and possibly more useful.

Habitual criminals (1889 edition)

Most occasional criminals are born without any particular tendencies to crime over and above those inherent in all children. However, if children lack good upbringing and education, they will never mature into honest adults. Instead, their potential criminality grows stronger and worsens. Good upbringing and education can never transform the born criminal into a gallant fellow, but they can prevent normal children from developing into habitual criminals.

Occasional criminals have low crime rates early in life. Moreover, their crimes are minor, like petty theft, swindling, and assault. But once their latent tendency to crime begins to thrive, it becomes habitual, ingrained, and ever more serious. This criminal habit is aggravated by the anaesthetizing abuse of alcohol and by anger against society (which blindly punishes those who least deserve it, and vice versa). It is also aggravated by that vanity that is found in every occupation and every profession.

What does one of these wretched minor offenders do when, arrested initially for having attacked an adversary in a fit of rage or for roaming like a vagabond, he is thrown into prison? Baptized into the confraternity of inmates and welcomed into their ranks, he loses all sense of morality. What choice does he have but to join those who offer him a sort of family, a society in the midst of which crime brings not shame but fame? Is it not inevitable, given that human nature is inclined to crime, for him to persevere and perfect his abilities until he becomes indistinguishable from the born criminal?

Habitual criminals resemble born criminals in both recidivism and the early onset of their offending. Never having lost their infantile immorality, for them crime becomes an organic phenomenon, flesh of their own flesh. In an environment that encourages struggle against all, mutual defense, and seditious impulses, habitual criminals develop pride in their abilities. And then repetition reinforces their tendencies toward recidivism.

Punishment (1896–1897 edition)

Once we stop thinking of punishment as retaliation or as a sort of civil excommunication, we can see that it must change direction completely. The purpose of punishment should be not the infliction of pain on the criminal, but the well-being of society and restitution to the victim. Punishment should be proportional less to the gravity of the crime than to the dangerousness the criminal. There is a vast difference between the future threat posed by an individual who kills a man for honor, politics, or an ideal after leading a completely honest life and one who kills to rape or rob, crowning a life already full of crime. In the first case, punishment is almost unnecessary because the crime itself tortures the perpetrator, who will never repeat it. In the second case, every delay and mitigation of punishment endangers society. As Ferri aptly writes: "It is impossible to separate the crime from the person who commits it."

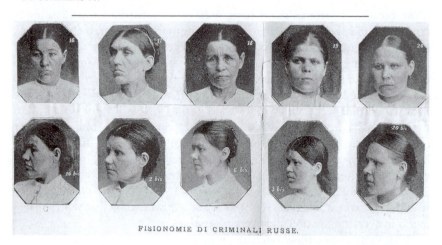

FISIONOMIE DI CRIMINALI RUSSE.

Figure 39.1 Physiognomy of Russian Female Criminals. Extending the physiognomical tradition of Lavater, criminal anthropologists believed that they could read criminality from the face and even photographs, as in the case of these hardened Russian women. Cesare Lombroso and Guglielmo Ferrero, *La donna delinquente* (Turin: Roux, 1893), Tav. VIB. Image used courtesy of Mary Gibson and Duke University Press.

Crime is like an illness that requires a specific remedy for each patient. It is the job of criminal anthropology to establish the relationship between criminals and their punishment. Punishment should vary according to the type of offender: the born criminal, the insane criminal, the habitual criminal, the occasional criminal, and the criminal of passion.

Chapter 40

Alphonse Bertillon: The Bertillon system of identification, 1891

The French forensic criminologist Alphonse Bertillon (1853–1914) invented the first scientific method for identifying criminals. His system, known as anthropometry or (after it become famous) *bertillonage*, involved taking measurements of people who had been arrested – their arm lengths, their head circumference, and so on – as well as making notations of (or photographing) their faces, ears, and scars. This system rested on the assumption that people's bodies do not change in basic characteristics. Bertillon introduced his system in 1882; it was adopted by the Parisian police and from there spread throughout much of the world. However, in the early twentieth century, anthropometry was replaced by fingerprinting, a more efficient and accurate method of identifying previously arrested criminals.

Bertillon did not advance a specific theory of crime, but his system, with its emphasis on the body and measurement, fostered an impression that criminal anthropology had been validated. Moreover, in a period when criminal justice officials and the public were alarmed about recidivism, anthropometry increased the possibility of identifying habitual offenders. (Previously, repeat offenders could be identified only by officers at the station house watching to see if they recognized someone.) In addition to his indirect contributions to criminology, Bertillon played a significant role in the development of scientific policing. Fingerprinting was already known at the time this article was written, but as he explains here, Bertillon did not think that it could "serve as a basis for the classification of several hundred thousand cases."

Bertillon described his system in detail in his book *Signaletic Instruction* (Chicago: The Werner Company, 1896), but also publicized it through shorter works, such as this article for *The Forum*, a journal read by criminal justice reformers. This extract reprints significant parts of the article "The Bertillon system of identification," *The Forum* 11 (3) (1891): 330–41.

ALPHONSE BERTILLON: THE BERTILLON SYSTEM OF IDENTIFICATION

In all ages questions of identity have excited the interest of men. Is it not at bottom a problem of this sort that forms the basis of the everlasting popular melodrama about lost, exchanged, and recovered children? . . .

But it is naturally the world of criminals that has furnished, and yet furnishes, the greatest number of such attempts at deceit. It is not generally known by the honest public how large a number of malefactors have recourse to concealment of identity. We may assert without exaggeration that there is not a single habitual criminal who does not seek to hide his individuality when the circumstances of his arrest permit. The immensity of modern cities and the increasing facility of communication make this course more and more easy. International criminals, such as bank-robbers and pickpockets, traverse two continents, changing their names from country to country. The greater, therefore, becomes the necessity of some methodical system of identification.

It was believed for a short time, thirty years since, that photography was to give the solution of the problem. But the collection of criminal portraits has already attained a size so considerable that it has become physically impossible to discover among them the likeness of an individual who has assumed a false name. It goes for nothing that in the past ten years the Paris police have collected more than 100,000 photographs. Does the reader believe it practicable to compare successively each of these with each one of the 100 individuals who are arrested daily in Paris? When this was attempted in the case of a criminal particularly easy to identify, the search demanded more than a week of application, not to speak of the errors and oversights which a task so fatiguing to the eye could not fail to occasion. There was need of a method of elimination analogous to that in use in botany and zoölogy; that is to say, one based on the characteristic elements of individuality, and not on the station and occupation of the accused, which may be erroneously given. . . .

The anthropometric method of description, of which I am the inventor . . . lends itself admirably to classification. That is its aim, its sole aim. It depends on the three following principles, which the experience of the past ten years has proved to be sound: 1. The facility and the rigorous exactitude with which the principal dimensions of the human skeleton are susceptible of being measured in the living subject, by means of a simply-constructed pair of compasses. 2. The extreme diversity presented by the human skeleton from one subject to another – such a diversity that it is impossible to find two individuals possessing frames, I will not say rigorously similar, but even sufficiently alike to be confounded with each other. 3. The almost absolute fixity of the skeleton after the twentieth year. The height alone or, at most, the length of the *femur*, continues to increase for two or three years, but so slightly that it is easy to take this growth into account; while the length and breadth of the head, the length of the fingers, of the hand, of the foot, of the

ABSTRACT OF

THE ANTHROPOMETRICAL SIGNALMENT

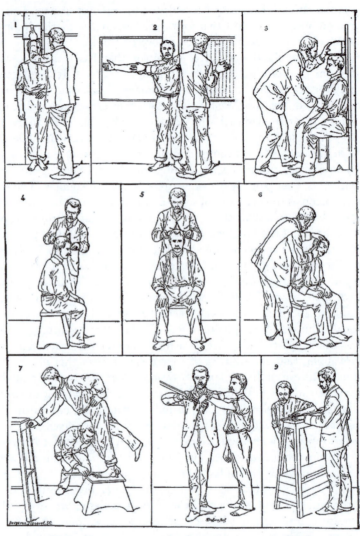

1. Height.	2. Reach.	3. Trunk.
4. Length of head.	5. Width of head.	6. Right ear.
7. Left foot.	8. Left middle finger.	9. Left forearm.

(ii)

Figure 40.1 Summary of Bertillon's Anthropometric Method. These diagrams summarize the measurement aspect of Bertillion's approach to identifying recidivists. From Alphonse Bertillon, *Signaletic Instructions, Including the Theory and Practice of Anthropometrical Identification* (Chicago: The Werner Company, 1896), Frontispiece.

Figure 40.2 Bertillon Classification by Head Shape. The Bertillon method involved not only measuring criminals, but also photographing them and classifying the photographs by head shape. Alphonse Bertillon, *Signaletic Instructions, Including the Theory and Practice of Anthropometrical Identification* (Chicago: The Werner Company, 1896), Plate 41.

forearm, and of the ear are unchangeable, whatever may be the development of muscle or of adipose tissue.

The measurements that have been mentioned have been made on the 120,000 subjects that have passed through the Paris prisons during the past ten years, and copied on as many bits of cardboard, which are filed away in pigeon holes. The principal features of the method adopted for the classification of this enormous mass of measurements are as follows: The cards containing descriptions of men are placed on one side; those of women on the other. The latter are much less numerous than the former, not exceeding 20,000. From the 100,000 masculine descriptions that remain, about 10,000 must be separated, because they relate to minors and require special classification. The remaining 90,000 measurements of adults are first divided, according to the length of head, into three classes, as follows:

1. Division of short heads, comprising about   30,000 cards.
2.   "   medium "   "   "   30,000   "
3.   "   long   "   "   "   30,000   "
                                                 ———————
            Total, ...   90,000 cards.

The measurements are correct within one millimeter, and experience has proved that it is possible, once for all, to fix the limits of the three classes in such manner that each shall always contain approximately the same number of cards. Each of these three great masses of 30,000 measurements is then redivided, without any more reference to the length of the head, into three groups based on the width of the head. These groups, nine in all, will, therefore, contain each about 10,000 cards. These subdivisions are themselves divided each into three groups, according to the length of the middle finger. Each of these last groups evidently contains only about 3,300 measurements. The length of the foot furnishes a fourth basis of division, by which each of the last-mentioned packets of cards is divided again into three groups of 1,100 each. Then come similar subdivisions based respectively on the length of the forearm, the height, the length of the little finger, and the color of the eye. The cards in these last groups, which contain only about 13 each, are arranged according to the length of the ear. Thus, thanks to six new anthropometric principles – those of sex, height, age, and color of the eyes having always figured in descriptions – the collection of 120,000 photographs in the Paris prefecture of police has been divided into groups containing a dozen pictures each.

Suppose, now, that we wish to find out whether a person who has just been arrested, and who says he has no criminal antecedents, has been previously measured and classified under a different name. An anthropometric measurement is first made. Then we seek, first, the primary division of cards corresponding to the length of head of the person measured; next the subdivision of this indicated by the width of his head; then the successive groups corresponding to the length of his middle finger, that of his foot, and that of his forearm. Thus, by a process of elimination, we arrive finally at the packet which ought to contain the measurement sought, if the man arrested has previously been convicted and measured. When one or several of the measurements taken fall on the dividing line between two groups, search has to be made in each, and followed out through all the successive branches of classification, exactly as one searches in a dictionary at different places for a word whose exact spelling escapes him. Comparison and discussion of the descriptions on the cards in any one of the final packets show that it is almost impossible to find two similar ones, so that the equivalence of the corresponding figures of two measurements constitutes almost a certainty of identity. Nevertheless, as in the pursuit of justice absolute certainty ought to be aimed at in all cases where it can be attained, anthropometric measurement, properly speaking, is always supplemented in practice by a descriptive identification, by noting the color of the eyes, hair, beard, and complexion; and by analyzing the contours of the profile, forehead, nose, lips, chin, and ear. . . . This descriptive part of our scheme of identification is replaced by photographs of the judicial type (face and profile side by side) whenever the necessities of the police or the magistracy render the preparation of a portrait desirable.

Finally, our cards of identification bear a third and last element of recognition – the record of particular marks. Every one bears, often unknown to himself, numerous external peculiarities of structure – pigmentary moles, or "grains of beauty," and the scars of cuts, boils, or wounds, not to speak of the tattooings so frequent among criminals. Three or four of these marks suffice to distinguish an individual from all other inhabitants of the earth, if they are described with anatomical precision. . . .

Let us now glance at the results obtained by this plan. Formerly the prefecture of police, to guard against concealments of identity, placed the recognition of habitual criminals on the footing of a kind of competitive contest. A prize of five francs was given to every police agent or prison official who recognized a criminal that was concealing his identity, and who could tell the prisoner's real name. In this way from 7,000 to 8,000 francs a year were paid out in exchange for the recognition of from 1,400 to 1,600 criminals. Nevertheless, in spite of the relative size of these figures, the magistrates and the prison directors admitted that more than half of the habitual criminals arrested escaped recognition. . . .

One of the curious consequences of the infallibility of anthropometry is the almost complete disappearance of international pickpockets from Paris. Eight years ago, 100 of them were arrested there yearly; by 1887, the number had fallen to 34; it did not exceed a dozen during the past year. Being satisfied that it has become impossible for them to hide their antecedents in case of arrest, and fearing also the increase of punishment inflicted on habitual

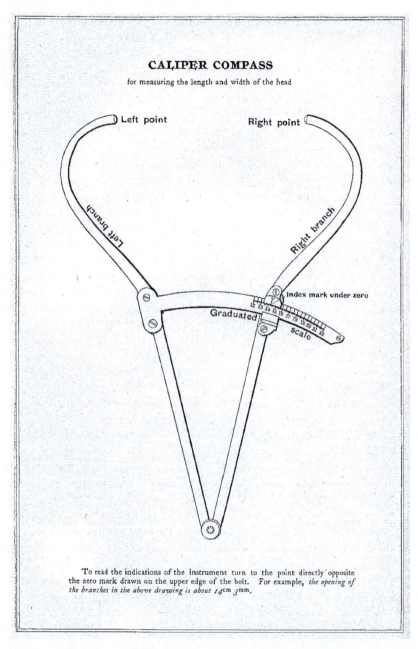

CALIPER COMPASS

for measuring the length and width of the head

Left point   Right point

Left branch   Right branch

Index mark under zero

Graduated   scale

To read the indications of the instrument turn to the point directly opposite the zero mark drawn on the upper edge of the bolt. For example, *the opening of the branches in the above drawing is about 14cm 3mm.*

Figure 40.3 Caliper Compass. Like Lombroso, Bertillon measured the length and width of criminals' heads. In Bertillon's case, however, the aim was to identify repeat offenders, not to make a criminological point. Alphonse Bertillon, *Signaletic Instructions, Including the Theory and Practice of Anthropometrical Identification* (Chicago: The Werner Company, 1896), Plate 2.

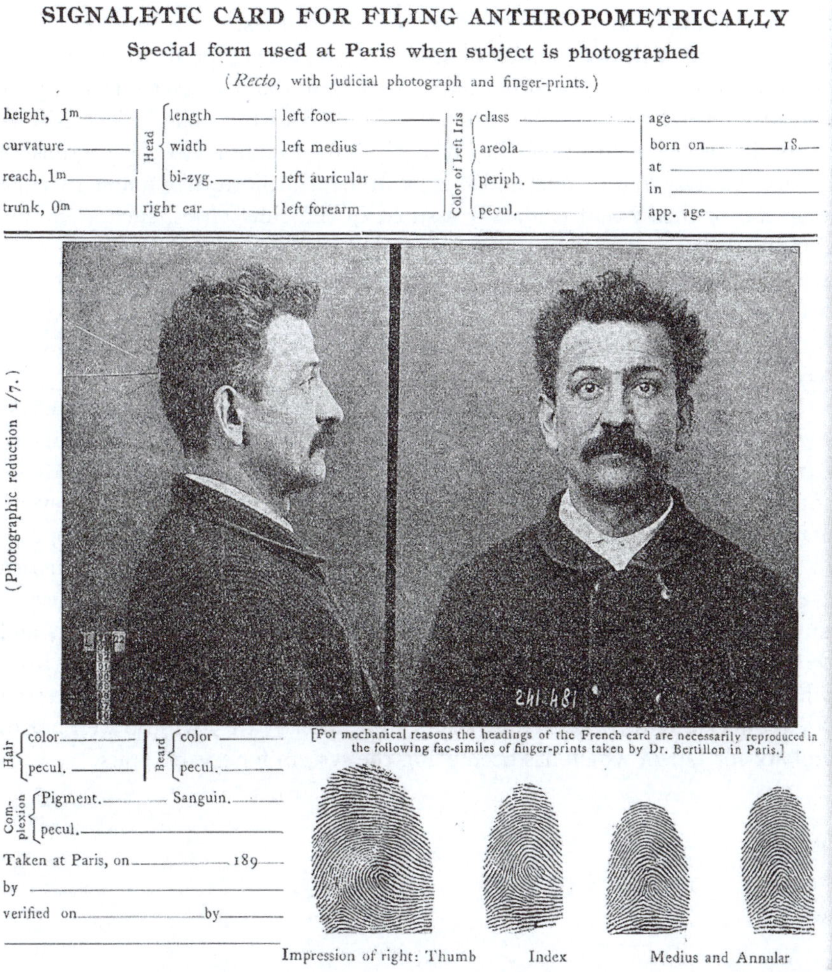

SIGNALETIC CARD FOR FILING ANTHROPOMETRICALLY

Special form used at Paris when subject is photographed

(*Recto*, with judicial photograph and finger-prints.)

height, 1m
curvature
reach, 1m
trunk, 0m

Head: length, width, bi-zyg.
right ear

left foot
left medius
left auricular
left forearm

Color of Left Iris: class, areola, periph., pecul.

age
born on 18
at
in
app. age

(Photographic reduction 1/7.)

Hair: color, pecul.

Beard: color, pecul.

Com-plexion: Pigment. Sanguin. pecul.

Taken at Paris, on 189
by
verified on by

[For mechanical reasons the headings of the French card are necessarily reproduced in the following fac-similes of finger-prints taken by Dr. Bertillon in Paris.]

Impression of right: Thumb Index Medius and Annular

Figure 40.4 Example of Bertillon File Card. Bertillon's method of identifying criminals was at first supplemented by fingerprinting, as shown here, and eventually replaced by it. Cards of this sort could be found in prisons throughout Europe and the United States in the early twentieth century. Alphonse Bertillon, *Signaletic Instructions, Including the Theory and Practice of Anthropometrical Identification* (Chicago: The Werner Company, 1896), Plate 79a.

criminals and on those who have disobeyed a decree of expulsion, they prefer now to remain, of their own accord, in foreign capitals. . . .

My country will not long enjoy its immunity alone, for anthropometry is being adopted rapidly by other nations. Belgium and Russia introduced it officially several years ago, and are quite satisfied with it. The Federal Minister of Justice of Switzerland has recently sent a circular to the cantons to induce them to do the same, and I know from an authoritative source that the adoption of the system is already assured in the chief cities, such as Berne, Zurich, and Geneva. Vienna, Berlin, and Rome are now trying it in their prisons. England alone has held back, in spite of the efforts of certain members of Parliament. But I have just learned that a bill giving to the police the legal power to measure criminals according to the Bertillon system has been recently introduced in the House of Commons.

So our poor international thieves are seeing all European countries successively closed to them. Will they be forced to cross the ocean, to take refuge in America? There also they will find something to talk about, for judicial anthropometry has been put into practice by legislative enactment in several States of the Union, and seems to be working its way toward general adoption in the United States and Canada. The National Prison Association of America even advocated it in 1887, several years before it came into general use in Europe. Among the republics of South America, Uruguay, Paraguay, and certain provinces of Brazil have adopted it and are applying it, judging from official documents that have reached me. Yet a few years and our interesting clients will have no other refuge than China; already they will do well not to embark for Japan, which has been using the system for several years.

Chapter 41

Francis Galton: Personal identification, 1892

Francis Galton's signficance to the development of criminology has not yet been fully assessed,[1] although it is clear that he played a crucial role, especially through his work on heredity. In Galton's day (1822–1911), genes had not yet been identified; but various scientists, including Gregor Mendel, were publishing results that pointed toward a reconceptualization of the "stuff" of heredity as not "soft" and malleable (as in degeneration theory), but rather "hard" and impervious (as in later genetic theory). Galton's work was part of this reorientation. His research on heredity led him to found the science of eugenics (he even coined the term; see Chapter 45), which developed its own highly influential theory of crime, in which law-breaking was the result of bad heredity. Galton also established the basis for later theories of intelligence and crime.

Furthermore, Galton contributed to the development of statistics and fingerprinting. The latter effort led, eventually, to the replacement of Bertillon's anthropometrical method of identifying recidivists. This extract comes from chapter 10 of Galton's pioneering work *Finger Prints* (London: MacMillan, 1892), pp. 146–69. In it Galton argues for the ease of fingerprinting relative to *bertillonage* and its usefulness. In addition, Galton concludes, fingerprinting is more accurate. However, at this point he goes no further than arguing that fingerprinting be used to supplement Bertillon's method.[2] Both procedures contributed to efforts to identify habitual offenders and explain their conduct.

FRANCIS GALTON: PERSONAL IDENTIFICATION

We shall speak in this chapter of the aid that finger prints can give to personal identification, supposing throughout that facilities exist for taking them well and cheaply, and that more or less practice in reading them has been acquired by many persons. . . .

In civilised lands, honest citizens rarely need additional means of identification to their signatures, their photographs, and to personal introductions.

The cases in which other evidence is wanted are chiefly connected with violent death through accident, murder, or suicide, which yield the constant and gruesome supply to the Morgue of Paris, and to corresponding institutions in other large towns, where the bodies of unknown persons are exposed for identification, often in vain. But when honest persons travel to distant countries where they have few or no friends, the need for a means of recognition is more frequently felt. The risk of death through accident or crime is increased, and the probability of subsequent identification diminished. There is a possibility not too remote to be disregarded, especially in times of war, of a harmless person being arrested by mistake for another man, and being in sore straits to give satisfactory proof of the error. A signature may be distrusted as a forgery. There is also some small chance, when he returns to his own country after a long absence, of finding difficulty in proving who he is. But in civilised lands and in peaceable times, the chief use of a sure means of identification is to benefit society by detecting rogues, rather than to establish the identity of men who are honest. Is this criminal an old offender? Is this new recruit a deserter? Is this professed pensioner personating a man who is dead? Is this upstart claimant to property the true heir, who was believed to have died in foreign lands?

In India and in many of our Colonies the absence of satisfactory means for identifying persons of other races is seriously felt. The natives are mostly unable to sign; their features are not readily distinguished by Europeans; and in too many cases they are characterised by a strange amount of litigiousness, wiliness, and unveracity. . . .

Whatever difficulty may be felt in the identification of Hindoos, is experienced in at least an equal degree in that of the Chinese residents in our Colonies and Settlements, who to European eyes are still more alike than the Hindoos, and in whose names there is still less variety. . . .

For most criminal investigations, and for some other purposes also, the question is not the simple one just considered, namely, "Is A the same person, or a different person from B?" but the much more difficult problem of "Who is this unknown person X? Is his name contained in such and such a register?" We will now consider how this question may be answered.

Registers of criminals are kept in all civilised countries, but in France they are indexed according to the method of M. Alphonse Bertillon, which admits of an effective search being made through a large collection. We shall see how much the differentiating power of the French or of any other system of indexing might be increased by including finger prints in the register. . . .

The scale on which the [Bertillon] service is carried on, is very large. It was begun in 1883, and by the end of 1887 no less than 60,000 sets of measures were in hand, but thus far only about one half of the persons arrested in Paris were measured, owing to the insufficiency of the staff. Arrangements were then made for its further extension. There are from 100 to 150 prisoners sentenced each day by the Courts of Law in Paris to more than a few days' imprisonment, and every one of these is sent to the Dépôt for twenty-four hours. While there, they are now submitted to *Bertillonage*, a newly coined word that has already come into use. This is done in the forenoon, by three operators and three clerks; six officials in all. About half of the prisoners are old offenders, of whom a considerable proportion give their names correctly, as is rapidly verified by an alphabetically arranged catalogue of cards, each of which contains front and profile photographs, and measurements. The remainder are examined strictly; their bodily marks are recorded according to a terse system of a few letters, and they are variously measured. Each person occupies seven or eight minutes. They are then photographed. From sixty to seventy-five prisoners go through this complete process every forenoon. . . .

The success of the system is considered by many experts to be fully proved, notwithstanding many apparent objections, one of which is the difficulty due to transitional cases: a belief in its success has certainly obtained a firm hold upon the popular imagination in France. Its general acceptance elsewhere seems to have been delayed in part by a theoretical error in the published calculations of its efficiency: the measures of the limbs which are undoubtedly correlated being treated as independent, and in part by the absence of a sufficiently detailed account of the practical difficulties experienced in its employment. Thus in the *Application pratique* [by Bertillon], p. 9: "We are embarrassed what to choose, the number of human measures which vary independently of each other being considerable." In the *Signalements* [by Bertillon], p. 19: "It has been shown" (by assuming this independent variability) "that by seven measurements, 60,000 photographs can be separated into batches of less than ten in each." (By the way, even on that assumption, the result is somewhat exaggerated, the figures having been arrived at by successively taking the higher of the two nearest round values.) In short, the general tone of these two memoirs is one of enthusiastic belief in the method, based almost wholly, so far as is there shown, on questionable *theoretic* grounds of efficiency. . . .

We will now separately summarise the results arrived at, in respect to the two processes [*Bertillonage* and finger-printing] that may both be needed in order to effect an identification.

First, as regards *search in an Index*. – Some sets of measures will give trouble, but the greater proportion can apparently be catalogued with so much certainty, that if a second set of measures of any individual be afterwards taken, no tedious search will be needed to hunt out the former set. Including the bodily marks and photographs, let us rate the Bertillon method as able to cope with a register of 20,000 adults of the same sex, with a small and definable, but as yet unknown, average dose of difficulty, which we will call x.

A catalogue of 500 sets of finger prints easily fulfils the same conditions. I could lay a fair claim to much more, but am content with this. Now the finger patterns have been shown to be so independent of other conditions that

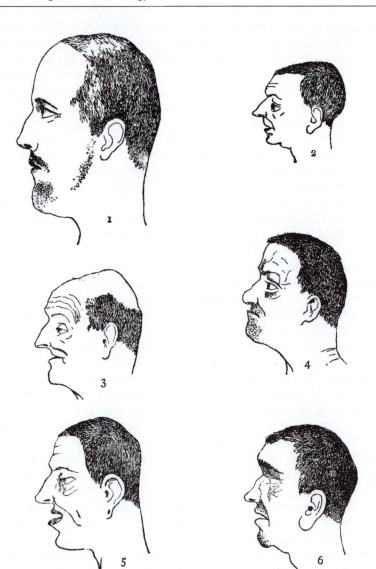

Figure 41.1 Repeat Offenders. Sketches 1 and 2 are of murderers who evidently had no previous record, but Ellis gives prior records for the other four men. No. 4, for example, a farm labourer from Nottingham serving a 10-year sentence for multiple petty thefts, had been convicted three times previously. Havelock Ellis, *The Criminal* (London: Walter Scott, 1890), Plate 1, following p. 54.

they cannot be notably, if at all, correlated with the bodily measurements or with any other feature, not the slightest trace of any relation between them having yet been found. . . . For instance, it would be totally impossible to fail to distinguish between the finger prints of twins, who in other respects appeared exactly alike. Finger prints may therefore be treated without the fear of any sensible error, as varying quite independently of the measures and records in the Bertillon system. Their inclusion would consequently increase its power fully five-hundred fold. Suppose one moderate dose of difficulty, x, is enough for dealing with the measurements, etc., of 20,000 adult persons of the same sex by the Bertillon method, and a similar dose of difficulty with the finger prints of 500 persons, then two such doses could deal with a register of 20,000 × 500, or 10,000,000.

We now proceed to consider the second and final process, namely, that of identification by *Comparison*. When the data concerning a suspected person are discovered to bear a general likeness to one of those already on the register, and a minute comparison shows their finger prints to agree in all or nearly all particulars, the evidence thereby afforded that they were made by the same person, far transcends in trustworthiness any other evidence that can ordinarily be obtained, and vastly exceeds all that can be derived from any number of ordinary anthropometric data. *By itself it is amply sufficient to convict. Bertillonage* can rarely supply more than grounds for very strong suspicion: the method of finger prints affords certainty. It is easy, however, to understand that so long as the peculiarities of finger prints are not generally understood, a juryman would be cautious in accepting their evidence, but it is to be hoped that attention will now gradually become drawn to their marvellous virtues, and that after their value shall have been established in a few conspicuous cases, it will come to be popularly recognised.

Let us not forget two great and peculiar merits of finger prints; they are self-signatures, free from all possibility of faults in observation or of clerical error; and they apply throughout life.

Notes

1 I make a preliminary effort to assess it in *The Criminal Brain* (New York: New York University Press, 2008), but much work remains to be done.
2 For more on the development of fingerprinting, see Simon A. Cole, *Suspect Identities: A history of fingerprinting and criminal identification* (Cambridge: Harvard University Press, 2001).

Eugenic criminology

Part VIII

Eugenic criminology

Eugenic criminology
Introduction to Part VIII

Throughout the nineteenth century, social theorists discussed eliminations of welfare programs and even prevention of reproduction as means of reducing the size of problematic populations, as indicated here by two extracts, one by the phrenologist Johann Gaspar Spurzheim and dating from 1828 (Chapter 42), the other by the great evolutionist Charles Darwin and dating from 1871. The specific idea of preventing reproduction by criminals came naturally to scientists immersed in degeneration theory and other evolutionary and hereditarian ideas. In the United States, the first step toward a eugenic solution to crime was taken in the early 1880s, when Josephine Shaw Lowell (Chapter 44), a social reformer from New York, established an "asylum" for feeble-minded women on the theory that if they were not locked up, they would give birth to illegitimate, feeble-minded and criminalistic children.[1] (She had been inspired in particular by Richard Dugdale's horrific study of the "Jukes" family; see Chapter 20.) Notably, many of these eugenic proposals were made, and Lowell's eugenic measure was implemented, before 1883, when Francis Galton invented the term *eugenics* to denote efforts to breed better human beings and prevent reproduction by the unfit (Chapter 45).

Eugenic ideas spread rapidly in the United States and Western Europe, shaping criminological theory in ways indicated here by extracts from two late nineteenth-century classics, Henry Boies's *Prisoners and Paupers* (Chapter 46) and W. Duncan McKim's *Heredity and Human Progress* (Chapter 47). Again, it is noteworthy that although both authors fervently recommend control of reproduction as a way of controlling crime, neither mentions Galton or his term "eugenics."

Note

1   See Nicole Hahn Rafter, "Claims-making and socio-cultural context in the first U.S. eugenics campaign," *Social Problems* 39 (1992): 17–34.

Chapter 42

Johann Gaspar Spurzheim: Hereditary descent and the prevention of crime, 1828

Johann Gaspar Spurzheim, the eminent phrenologist whose work was previously extracted in Chapter 4, first published his book on education, *A View of the Elementary Principles of Education,* in 1821, in Edinburgh, Scotland, a city where phrenology flourished. The book was reprinted many times thereafter. I used the 1828 edition (London: Treuttel, Wurtz, and Richter), pp. 41–52 and 280–4.

As these passages demonstrate, eugenics theory was formulated long before Francis Galton coined the term *eugenics.* To support his conclusions about inheritance in human families, Spurzheim reaches back into the late eighteenth century to quote Benjamin Rush's *Influence of Physical Causes upon the Moral Faculty* (see Chapter 8).

Biological theories of crime such as phrenology tended to reach eugenic conclusions for the extirpation of crime. Here Spurzheim urges that governments should be authorized to prevent criminals and the poor from reproducing.

JOHANN GASPAR SPURZHEIM: HEREDITARY DESCENT AND THE PREVENTION OF CRIME

On the laws of hereditary descent

The developement [*sic*] of the human body is favoured, retarded, or disordered, according to the general laws of organization, in the same way as that of other living beings. Consequently children participate in the bodily configuration and constitution of their parents, and also in their tendencies to particular manifestations of the mind, these being dependent on the individual parts of the brain. The elucidation of these subjects is indispensable to a sound system of education. Nay, I am convinced, that this condition exerts a greater and more permanent influence than any other which can be introduced with the view of perfecting mankind. Let us first consider how other organized beings are improved. . . .

In perfecting animals, or in promoting their peculiar qualities, such as the colour or figure of horses, the wool of sheep, the smell of dogs, &c. country people have recourse to the laws of propagation. By these means, farmers have succeeded in diminishing or increasing various parts of animals, such as their bones, muscles, &c.

We might naturally suppose, that it would be sufficient to mention the fact, that the organization of man is submitted to the same general laws as that of animals, to induce reasonable beings to take at least the same care of their own offspring as of their sheep, pigs, dogs and horses. But man wishes to make himself an exception from the immutable laws of the Creator, and the result of his ignorance and self-conceit is lamentable. As this subject is of the utmost importance, I shall enter into a few details upon it.

For the sake of bodily health, many natural philosophers, a long time ago, insisted on the necessity of a better regulation of marriage. Their benevolent desire was supported by the constant observation, that health depends on organization, and that the latter is propagated by birth. . . .

Those who have more confidence in facts than in speculative reasoning, cannot doubt that the qualities of the body are hereditary. There are family-faces, family-likenesses; and also single parts, such as bones, muscles, hair and skin, which resemble in parents and in children. The disposition to various disorders, as to gout, scrofula, dropsy, hydrocephalus, consumption, deafness, epilepsy, apoplexy, idiotism, insanity, &c. is frequently the inheritance of birth. There are few families where there is not one part of the body weaker than the rest, – the lungs, for instance, the eyes, the stomach, liver, intestines, some other viscus, the brain, &c.

Children born of healthy parents, and belonging to a strong stock, always bring into the world a system formed by nature to resist the causes of disease; while the children of delicate, sickly parents, are overpowered by the least unfavourable circumstance. . . .

The laws of hereditary descent should be attended to, not only with respect to organic life, but also to the manifestations of the mind, since these depend on the nervous system. There are many examples on record, of certain feelings, or intellectual powers, being inherent in whole families. Now, if it be ascertained that the hereditary condition of the brain is the cause, there is a great additional motive to be careful in the choice of a partner in marriage. No person of sense can be indifferent about having selfish or benevolent, stupid or intelligent children. . . .

The laws of degeneration belong to those of propagation, and deserve a peculiar attention. They again are general throughout all nature. Plants culti-vated on the same spot degenerate. Wheat must alternate with barley, flax, potatoes, or other plants. Where firs will no longer grow, beeches will succeed. The seed of plants that degenerate, ought not to be taken for propagation, for they at length perish entirely: nor ought the sickly organization of one tree to be engrafted on another. . . .

It is indeed a pity that the laws of propagation are so much neglected, whilst, by attention to them, not only the condition of single families, but of whole nations, might be improved beyond imagination, in figure, stature, complexion, health, talents, and moral feelings. . . .

"It is probable," says Dr. Rush, "that the qualities of body and mind in parents, which produce genius in children, may be fixed and regulated; and it is possible the time may come, when we shall be able to predict with certainty the intellectual character of children, by knowing the specific nature of the different intellectual faculties of their parents. The marriages of Danish men with the East Indian women produced children that had the countenances and vigorous minds of Europeans; but no such results appeared in the children of the East Indian women who intermarried with the males of any other European nation." ("On the Influence of Physical Causes on the Intellectual Faculties," p. 119.) . . .

Correction of malefactors

. . . The most important way of preventing crime, is that of improving mankind by every possible means, and especially by those spoken of in the preceding pages on education in general, and on that of nations in particular. Let the inferior races, whose actions are stigmatized by crimes or disorderly living, be prevented, as much as possible, from propagation; for it is a fact well known to those who have attended to the subject, that the organs of the animal passions, like those of the other faculties of the mind, are hereditary. Moreover, let ignorance, idleness, intemperance, and poverty, which are the principal causes of crimes, be prevented, and there will be little occasion for prisons. . . .

It is both more effectual towards promoting the welfare of society and more agreeable, to correct morals, than to punish crimes. To that end it ought to be a serious aim with governments, to adopt means to exclude idleness and intemperance from society. Children should be accustomed to sobriety, and intemperate persons despised. Every person found intoxicated in the streets should be taken up and confined for twenty-four hours, and fed on bread and water.

Persons when drunk are deprived of the use of their reason, and often inclined to abuse their animal propensities; and hence the welfare of society requires them to be placed in a situation where they can do no harm, and which may contribute to their correction. The criminal records of every country bear evidence of flagitious crimes committed, and much misery inflicted, of which drunkenness was the proximate cause. Governments are therefore wrong in licensing numberless alehouses and gin-shops, and in affording great facility of pawning. . . .

If the poor must be permitted to marry, after the consequences are pointed out to them, then, at least, let every one be equally free; let him who gets children provide for their subsistence; and let him who labours reap the whole fruits of his own industry.

But, it may still be said, that whoever lives has a right to the prolongation of his days, and that, hence, the necessitous must not be allowed to perish. Strictly speaking, there is no doubt that those who exist have a right to partake in whatever nature produces. But civil laws are destined to keep order, and to regulate property. Now, I am willing to admit, that humanity calls upon us to preserve those who actually exist; but it appears to me to be impossible permanently to ameliorate the condition of the poor, except by preventing them, by some means or other, from excessive propagation. In the first place, It [sic] is a general law in nature, and it holds good in the case of mankind, as well as in every other species of animals, that every germ produced is not permitted to prosper and to multiply. As things are now managed, however, the best and most considerate of the race, are those who are most restrained from multiplying; because they see the evils, and endeavour to avoid them, while the worthless and unreflecting indulge their propensities without fear, and fill the world with misery. This is exactly the reverse of what it ought to be. Moreover, for the sake of general order, sailors and soldiers are prohibited from living in matrimony, and why should not the same liberty be taken with the poor? If they can show that they have the means of supporting a family, they are no longer poor, and the interdict would not apply to them. Many things are forced upon, as well as interdicted to individuals, for the sake of general happiness; and this being the principal aim of society, I cannot conceive a reason why the abject poor may not be hindered from marrying, for the general good, just as they are excluded, for the same reason, from directing the government.

Chapter 43

Charles Darwin: On the development of the intellectual and moral faculties, 1871

A previous selection from Darwin's *Descent of Man* (Chapter 18) comprised material on the evolution of the moral sense; this passage extends the earlier argument. Charity saves the weak, Darwin observes, and in preserving those who would otherwise die out we thwart the process of natural selection. Thus it would be good to prevent "the weaker and inferior members of society" from reproducing. In fact, civilized nations already eliminate some badly-endowed individuals – through execution, for example. Darwin concludes this passage by wondering if the worst criminals might not be "reversions to a savage state," an idea Lombroso developed just a few years later into the idea of the atavistic born criminal.

As usual, Darwin carefully cites his sources; they are excised here but include "Mr. Wallace," i.e., Alfred Russel Wallace, who published a theory of evolution by natural selection at the same time as Darwin. (Here Darwin cites a Wallace paper of 1870.) He also acknowledges W. R. Greg, who in 1868 had published an article "On the failure of 'Natural Selection' in the case of man," *Fraser's Magazine* 78 (1868): 359, and the work of his half-cousin Francis Galton, *Hereditary Genius* (1869). Even to a meticulous scientist like Darwin, the evidence seemed to favor a policy of eugenics.

This extract comes from Charles Darwin, *The Descent of Man* (London: J. Murray, 1871), pp. 166–73.

CHARLES DARWIN: ON THE DEVELOPMENT OF THE INTELLECTUAL AND MORAL FACULTIES

. . . It must not be forgotten that although a high standard of morality gives but a slight or no advantage to each individual man and his children over the other men of the same tribe, yet that an advancement in the standard of morality and an increase in the number of well-endowed men will certainly give an immense advantage to one tribe over another. There can be no doubt that a tribe including many members who, from possessing in a high degree the spirit of patriotism, fidelity, obedience, courage, and sympathy, were always ready to give aid to each other and to sacrifice themselves for the common good, would be victorious over most other tribes; and this would be natural selection. At all times throughout the world tribes have supplanted other tribes; and as morality is one element in their success, the standard of morality and the number of well-endowed men will thus everywhere tend to rise and increase. . . .

Some remarks on the agency of natural selection on civilised nations may be here worth adding. This subject has been ably discussed by Mr. W. R. Greg, and previously by Mr. Wallace and Mr. Galton. Most of my remarks are taken from these three authors. With savages, the weak in body or mind are soon eliminated; and those that survive commonly exhibit a vigorous state of health. We civilised men, on the other hand, do our utmost to check the process of elimination; we build asylums for the imbecile, the maimed, and the sick; we institute poor-laws; and our medical men exert their utmost skill to save the life of every one to the last moment. There is reason to believe that vaccination has preserved thousands, who from a weak constitution would formerly have succumbed to small-pox. Thus the weak members of civilised societies propagate their kind. No one who has attended to the breeding of domestic animals will doubt that this must be highly injurious to the race of man. It is surprising how soon a want of care, or care wrongly directed, leads to the degeneration of a domestic race; but excepting in the case of man himself, hardly any one is so ignorant as to allow his worst animals to breed.

The aid which we feel impelled to give to the helpless is mainly an incidental result of the instinct of sympathy, which was originally acquired as part of the social instincts, but subsequently rendered, in the manner previously indicated, more tender and more widely diffused. Nor could we check our sympathy, if so urged by hard reason, without deterioration in the noblest part of our nature. The surgeon may harden himself whilst performing an operation, for he knows that he is acting for the good of his patient; but if we were intentionally to neglect the weak and helpless, it could only be for a contingent benefit, with a certain and great present evil. Hence we must bear without complaining the undoubtedly bad effects of the weak surviving and propagating their kind; but there appears to be at least one check in steady action, namely the weaker and inferior members of society not marrying so freely as the sound; and this check might be indefinitely increased, though this is more to be hoped for than expected, by the weak in body or mind refraining from marriage. . . .

In regard to the moral qualities, some elimination of the worst dispositions is always in progress even in the most civilised nations. Malefactors are executed, or imprisoned for long periods, so that they cannot freely transmit their bad qualities. Melancholic and insane persons are confined, or commit suicide. Violent and quarrelsome men often come to a bloody end. Restless men who will not follow any steady occupation – and this relic of barbarism is a great check to civilisation – emigrate to newly-settled countries, where they prove useful pioneers. Intemperance is so highly destructive, that the expectation of life of the intemperate, at the age, for instance, of thirty, is only 13.8 years; whilst for the rural labourers of England at the same age it is 40.59 years. Profligate women bear few children, and profligate men rarely marry; both suffer from disease. In the breeding of domestic animals, the elimination of those individuals, though few in number, which are in any marked manner inferior, is by no means an unimportant element towards success. This especially holds good with injurious characters which tend to reappear through reversion, such as blackness in sheep; and with mankind some of the worst dispositions, which occasionally without any assignable cause make their appearance in families, may perhaps be reversions to a savage state, from which we are not removed by very many generations. This view seems indeed recognised in the common expression that such men are the black sheep of the family.

Chapter 44

Josephine Shaw Lowell: One means of preventing pauperism, 1879

Josephine Shaw Lowell (1843–1905) was the first female member of New York's State Board of Charities, the body charged with supervising its public welfare institutions, and one of the leading social reformers of the late nineteenth century. At the time Lowell joined the Board, in 1876, pauperism, meaning chronic poverty, was being redefined as an inherited disability. Partly due to research such as that which Lowell describes in this report, and partly due to the heredity charts in Richard Dugdale's *"The Jukes"* (Chapter 20), it seemed impossible to deny the truth of the degenerationists' contention that disabilities were not only hereditary, but also interchangeable, so that, for instance, poor women might bear criminal children. "Hard" hereditarianism replaced the softer determinism of earlier degeneration theory, while pessimism supplanted the earlier optimism about human perfectibility that can be see in works by Benjamin Rush and phrenologists. Lowell and others began to promote eugenic solutions even though it would be years before Galton coined the specific term *eugenics* (Chapter 45).

In this address to a national conference of social workers, Lowell begins by describing the type of women found in state poorhouses – dependent on public welfare, mother to numerous illegitimate children, "debased and vagrant." Then she poses, rhetorically, her eugenical question: "What right have we to-day to allow men and women who are diseased and vicious to reproduce their kind?" Lowell establishes the state's "right" to prevent such women from breeding, for she is sure they will only beget offspring like themselves.

At the time, New York had a prison for women felons, but no state institution for minor female offenders (and certainly none for pauperized women, whom no one hitherto had considered criminalistic). Create reformatories for women, Lowell urges, penal institutions where perhaps they can be rehabilitated. But if they do not reform, she continues, then such women should be incarcerated for life – for their own good, as well as the good of the state.[1]

This passage comes from Josephine Shaw Lowell, "One means of preventing pauperism," in National Conference of Charities and Correction, *Proceedings for 1879*: 189–200.

JOSEPHINE SHAW LOWELL: ONE MEANS OF PREVENTING PAUPERISM

The legislature of New York, by concurrent resolution of May 27–29, 1873, directed the State Board of Charities to examine into the causes of the increase of crime, pauperism, and insanity in that State. In compliance with this resolution, an examination, which occupied the Secretary of the Board, with the assistance of various commissioners, for the greater part of two years, was made into the antecedents of every inmate of the poorhouses of the State, and the result submitted to the legislature in the Tenth Annual Report of the State Board of Charities. Even a casual perusal of that report will convince the reader that one of the most important and most dangerous causes of the increase of crime, pauperism, and insanity, is the unrestrained liberty allowed to vagrant and degraded women. The following are the records of a few only of the women found in the various poorhouses, – women who from early girlhood have been tossed from poorhouse to jail, and from jail to poorhouse, until the last trace of womanhood in them has been destroyed: –

"In the Albany County poorhouse, a single woman, forty years old, of foreign birth, and nine years in the United States, the mother of seven illegitimate children; the woman degraded and debased, and soon again to become a mother."

"In the Chautauqua County poorhouse, a woman, fifty-five years old, admitted when twenty-two as a vagrant; said to have been married, but the whereabouts of her husband is unknown; has been discharged from the house, and returned repeatedly, for the past thirty-three years, during which time she has had six illegitimate children." . . .

"In the Essex County poorhouse, a black woman, widowed, aged forty-nine years, and her daughter, single, aged twenty-four years, and her grandson, a mulatto, four years old, illegitimate, and born in the house. The first has been the mother of ten children, seven illegitimate; the second has had three illegitimate children. Both women are intemperate and thoroughly depraved, and quite certain to remain public burdens, each having already been nineteen years in the house. . . .

These women and their children, and hundreds more like them, costing the hard-working inhabitants of the State annually thousands of dollars for their maintenance, corrupting those who are thrown into companionship with them, and sowing disease and death among the people, are the direct outcome of our system. The community itself is responsible for the existence of such miserable, wrecked specimens of humanity. . . .

To begin at the beginning, what right had we to permit them to be born of parents who were depraved in body and mind? What right have we to-day to allow men and women who are diseased and vicious to reproduce their kind, and bring into the world beings whose existence must be one long misery to themselves and others? We do not hesitate to cut off, where it is possible, the entail of insanity by incarcerating for life the incurably insane: why should we not also prevent the transmission of moral insanity, as fatal as that of the mind?

Again, what right had we to leave these unhappy children to be reared in poorhouses, shut off from all that was good and pure, surrounded by all that was low and evil? . . .

These men and women are now constantly maintained by the public, sometimes for years at a time in the same institution, sometimes continually changing from one to another, but never failing to demand a support from their fellows. Why, then, should they not be maintained in institutions fitted to save them from their own weaknesses and vices, where in due time they may be formed anew in body and mind, and be ready to enter the ranks of free and intelligent men and women? . . .

In his essay on "The Jukes," Mr. Dugdale has computed that in seventy-five years the descendants of five vicious pauper sisters amounted to twelve hundred persons, and had cost the State of New York more than one million and a quarter dollars. The expense to which the thousand young women who last year entered the poorhouses and jails of the State, many of them already habitual offenders, prostitutes and confirmed drunkards, will subject the State during the next fifty years, becomes a serious question, and one which it is worth while to consider. . . .

To rescue these unfortunate beings and to save the industrious part of the community from the burden of their support, "Reformatories" should be established, to which all women under thirty, when arrested for misdemeanors, or upon the birth of a second illegitimate child, should be committed for very long periods (not as a punishment, but for the same reason that the insane are sent to an asylum), and where they should be subject to such a physical, moral and intellectual training as would re-create them. Such training would be no child's play, since the very character of the women must be changed, and every good and healthy influence would be rendered useless without the one element of *time*. It is education in every sense which they need, and education is a long process, tedious and wearing, requiring unfaltering hope and unfailing patience on the part of teacher and pupil. Consequently these Reformatories must not be prisons, which would crush out the life from those unfortunate enough to be cast into them; they must be *homes*, – homes where a tender care shall surround the weak and fallen creatures who are placed under their shelter, where a homelike feeling may be engendered, and where, if necessary, they may spend years. The unhappy beings we are speaking of need, first of all, to be taught to be women; they must be induced to love that which is good and pure, and to wish to resemble it; they must learn all household duties; they must learn to enjoy work; they must have a future to look forward to; and they must be *cured*, both body and soul, before they can be safely trusted to face the world again. . . .

Under such a system, many of the women, who with our present jail and poorhouse education are doomed, might without doubt be rescued. They need to be saved from temptation (which assails them from within and without), and to be guided aright, and many of them will respond joyfully to the efforts for their improvement.

If, however, there were no hope of reforming even one of the thousand young women now beginning what may be a long life of degradation and woe, if the State owed no debt to those whom it has systematically crushed and imbruted from their earliest years, even then it would be the *wisest economy* to build houses for them, where they might be shut up from the present day till the day of their death. They will all live on the public in one way or another for the rest of their lives, many of them will continue to have children, and to cut off this baneful entail of degenerate propensities would be an economy, even though the term of guardianship ended only with the unhappy life itself. For *self-protection*, the State should care for these human beings who, having been born, must be supported to the end; but every motive of humanity, justice, and self-interest should lead to the extinction of the line so soon as possible.

Even the weak State of Hawaii, in order to save its people from the contagion of a physical leprosy, has established an asylum for all who are tainted, on a separate island, to which all lepers of whatever rank are banished for life. Shall the State of New York suffer a moral leprosy to spread and taint her future generations, because she lacks the courage to set apart those who have inherited the deadly poison and who will hand it down to their children, even to the third and fourth generations?

Note

1   For more detail on Lowell's influence on the development of the U.S. women's prison system, as well as an analysis of her rhetoric in this particular talk, see Nicole Hahn Rafter, *Partial Justice: Women, prisons, and social control* (2d ed., New Brunswick, NJ: Transaction, 1990).

Chapter 45

Francis Galton: Breeding better humans, 1883

An earlier extract (Chapter 41) reproduced parts of Galton's book *Finger Prints*. This one focuses on Galton's suggestions in his 1883 book *Inquiries into Human Faculty and its Development* for breeding superior human beings. It begins with the passage in which (in a footnote) Galton coins the term *eugenics* and continues with a passage calling for human pedigree studies. The next passages, on criminals and the insane, invoke Dugdale's "Jukes" study to show that criminality is a hereditary trait. They are followed by materials on selection and race discussing steps to encourage "superior strains" (among whom Galton includes immigrants) to multiply. He also recommends marks for family merit. The extract ends with a fervent, almost religious, exhortation for man to use eugenics to further "the course of evolution."

With these suggestions, Galton set the stage for the eugenic approach to criminals that became popular in the late nineteenth century and dominated criminology in the early twentieth century. In the view of eugenic criminologists, criminals commit crimes due to their bad heredity; if they are prevented from reproducing, crime rates will fall in the next generation.

This extract comes from *Inquiries into Human Faculty and its Development* (London: Macmillan and Co., 1883), pp. 24–5 and 44–5 (coining of "eugenics"; its goals); 61–5 (criminals and their heredity); 307–17 (selection and race); 324–5 (marks for family merit); and 334–5 (conclusion).

FRANCIS GALTON: BREEDING BETTER HUMANS

. . . I do not propose to enter further into the anthropometric differences of race, for the subject is a very large one, and this book does not profess to go into detail. Its intention is to touch on various topics more or less connected with that of the cultivation of race, or, as we might call it, with "eugenic"[1] questions, and to present the results of several of my own separate investigations. . . .

The life histories of our relatives are prophetic of our own futures; they are far more instructive to us than those of strangers, far more fitted to encourage and to forewarn us. If there be such a thing as a natural birthright, I can conceive of none superior to the right of the child to be informed, at first by proxy through his guardians, and afterwards personally, of the life-history, medical and other, of his ancestry. The child is thrust into existence without his having any voice at all in the matter, and the smallest amend that those who brought him here can make, is to furnish him with all the guidance they can, including the complete life-histories of his near progenitors.

The investigation of human eugenics – that is, of the conditions under which men of a high type are produced – is at present extremely hampered by the want of full family histories, both medical and general, extending over three or four generations. There is no such difficulty in investigating animal eugenics, because the generations of horses, cattle, dogs, etc., are brief, and the breeder of any such stock lives long enough to acquire a large amount of experience from his own personal observation. A man, however, can rarely be familiar with more than two or three generations of his contemporaries before age has begun to check his powers; his working experience must therefore be chiefly based upon records. Believing, as I do, that human eugenics will become recognised before long as a study of the highest practical importance, it seems to me that no time ought to be lost in encouraging and directing a habit of compiling personal and family histories. If the necessary materials be brought into existence, it will require no more than zeal and persuasiveness on the part of the future investigator to collect as large a store of them as he may require. . . .

Criminals and the insane

Criminality, though not very various in its development, is extremely complex in its origin; nevertheless certain general conclusions are arrived at by the best writers on the subject, among whom Prosper Despine is one of the most instructive. The ideal criminal has marked peculiarities of character: his conscience is almost deficient, his instincts are vicious, his power of self-control is very weak, and he usually detests continuous labour. The absence of self-control is due to ungovernable temper, to passion, or to mere imbecility, and the conditions that determine the particular description of crime are the character of the instincts and of the temptation.

The deficiency of conscience in criminals, as shown by the absence of genuine remorse for their guilt, astonishes all who first become familiar with the details of prison life. Scenes of heartrending despair are hardly ever witnessed among prisoners; their sleep is broken by no uneasy dreams – on the contrary, it is easy and sound; they have also excellent appetites. But hypocrisy is a very common vice; and all my information agrees as to the utter untruthfulness of criminals, however plausible their statements may be. . . .

The perpetuation of the criminal class by heredity is a question difficult to grapple with on many accounts. Their vagrant habits, their illegitimate unions, and extreme untruthfulness, are among the difficulties of the investigation. It is, however, easy to show that the criminal nature tends to be inherited; while, on the other hand, it is impossible that women who spend a large portion of the best years of their life in prison can contribute many children to the population. The true state of the case appears to be that the criminal population receives steady accessions from those who, without having strongly marked criminal natures, do nevertheless belong to a type of humanity that is exceedingly ill suited to play a respectable part in our modern civilisation, though it is well suited to flourish under half-savage conditions, being naturally both healthy and prolific. These persons are apt to go to the bad; their daughters consort with criminals and become the parents of criminals. An extraordinary example of this is afforded by the history of the infamous Jukes family in America, whose pedigree has been made out, with extraordinary care, during no less than seven generations, and is the subject of an elaborate memoir printed in the Thirty-first Annual Report of the Prison Association of New York, 1876. [Dugdale originally published his "Jukes" study as a report to the sponsoring group. – N.R.] It includes no less than 540 individuals of Jukes blood, of whom a frightful number degraded into criminality, pauperism, or disease.

It is difficult to summarise the results in a few plain figures, but I will state those respecting the fifth generation, through the eldest of the five prolific daughters of the man who is the common ancestor of the race. The total number of these was 123, of whom thirty-eight came through an illegitimate granddaughter, and eighty-five through legitimate grandchildren. Out of the thirty-eight, sixteen have been in jail, six of them for heinous offences, one of these having been committed no less than nine times; eleven others led openly disreputable lives or were paupers; four were notoriously intemperate; the history of three had not been traced, and only four are known to have done well. The great majority of the women consorted with criminals. As to the eighty-five legitimate descendants, they were less flagrantly bad, for only five of them had been in jail, and only thirteen others had been paupers. Now the ancestor of all this mischief, who was born about the year 1730, is described as having been a jolly companionable man, a hunter, and a fisher, averse to steady labour, but working hard and idling by turns, and who had numerous illegitimate children, whose issue has not been traced. He was, in fact, a somewhat good specimen of a half-savage, without any seriously criminal instincts. The girls were apparently attractive, marrying early and sometimes not badly; but the gipsy-like character of the race was unsuited to success in a civilised country. So the descendants went to the bad, and such hereditary moral weaknesses as they may have had, rose to the surface and worked their mischief without check. Cohabiting with criminals, and being extremely prolific, the result was the production of a stock exceeding 500 in number, of a prevalent criminal type. Through disease and intemperance the breed is now rapidly diminishing; the infant mortality has of late been horrible, but fortunately the women of the present generation bear usually but few children, and many of them are altogether childless. . . .

Selection and race

. . . Whenever a low race is preserved under conditions of life that exact a high level of efficiency, it must be subjected to rigorous selection. The few best specimens of that race can alone be allowed to become parents, and not many of their descendants can be allowed to live. On the other hand, if a higher race be substituted for the low one, all this terrible misery disappears. The most merciful form of what I ventured to call "eugenics" would consist in watching for the indications of superior strains or races, and in so favouring them that their progeny shall outnumber and gradually replace that of the old one. Such strains are of no infrequent occurrence. It is easy to specify families who are characterised by strong resemblances, and whose features and character are usually prepotent over those of their wives or husbands in their joint offspring, and who are at the same time as prolific as the average of their class. These strains can be conveniently studied in the families of exiles, which, for obvious reasons, are easy to trace in their various branches.

The debt that most countries owe to the race of men whom they received from one another as immigrants, whether leaving their native country of their own free will, or as exiles on political or religious grounds, has been often pointed out, and may, I think, be accounted for as follows: – The fact of a man leaving his compatriots, or so irritating them that they compel him to go, is fair evidence that either he or they, or both, feel that his character is alien to theirs. Exiles are also on the whole men of considerable force of character; a quiet man would endure and succumb, he would not have energy to transplant himself or to become so conspicuous as to be an object of general attack. We may justly infer from this, that exiles are on the whole men of exceptional and energetic natures, and it is especially from such men as these that new strains of race are likely to proceed.

Influence of man upon race

. . . To this brief sketch of changes of population in very recent periods, I might add the wave of Arab admixture that has extended from Egypt and the northern provinces of Africa into the Soudan, and that of the yellow races of China, who have already made their industrial and social influence felt in many distant regions, and who bid fair hereafter, when certain of their peculiar religious fancies shall have fallen into decay, to become one of the most effective of the colonising nations, and who may, as I trust, extrude hereafter the coarse and lazy Negro from at least the metaliferous regions of tropical Africa.

It is clear from what has been said, that men of former generations have exercised enormous influence over the human stock of the present day, and that the average humanity of the world now and in future years is and will be very different to what it would have been if the action of our forefathers had been different. The power in man of varying the future human stock vests a great responsibility in the hands of each fresh generation, which has not yet been recognised at its just importance, nor deliberately employed. It is foolish to fold the hands and to say that nothing can be done, inasmuch as social forces and self-interests are too strong to be resisted. They need not be resisted; they can be guided. It is one thing to check the course of a huge steam vessel by the shock of a sudden encounter when she is going at full speed in the wrong direction, and another to cause her to change her course slowly and gently by a slight turn of the helm. Nay, a ship may be made to describe a half circle, and to end by following a course exactly opposite to the first, without attracting the notice of the passengers.

Marks for family merit

. . . The final object would be to devise means for favouring individuals who bore the signs of membership of a superior race, the proximate aim would be to ascertain what those signs were, and these we will consider first.

The indications of superior breed are partly personal, partly ancestral. We need not trouble ourselves about the personal part, because full weight is already given to it in the competitive careers; energy, brain, morale, and health being recognised factors of success, while there can hardly be a better evidence of a person being adapted to his circumstances than that afforded by success. It is the ancestral part that is neglected, and which we have yet to recognise at its just value. A question that now continually arises is this; a youth is a candidate for permanent employment, his present personal qualifications are known, but how will he turn out in later years? The objections to competitive examinations are notorious, in that they give undue prominence to youths whose receptive faculties are quick, and whose intellects are precocious. They give no indication of the direction in which the health, character, and intellect of the youth will change through the development in their due course, of ancestral tendencies that are latent in youth, but will manifest themselves in after life. Examinations deal with the present, not with the future, although it is in the future of the youth that we are especially interested. Much of the needed guidance may be derived from his family history. I cannot doubt, if two youths were of equal personal merit, of whom one belonged to a thriving and long-lived family, and the other to a decaying and short-lived family, that there could be any hesitation in saying that the chances were greater of the first-mentioned youth becoming the more valuable public servant of the two.

A thriving family may be sufficiently defined or inferred by the successive occupations of its several male members in the previous generation, and of the two grandfathers. These are patent facts attainable by almost every youth, which admit of being verified in his neighbourhood and attested in a satisfactory manner.

A healthy and long-lived family may be defined by the patent facts of ages at death, and number and ages of living relatives, within the degrees mentioned above, all of which can be verified and attested. A knowledge of the existence of longevity in the family would testify to the stamina of the candidate, and be an important addition to the knowledge of his present health in forecasting the probability of his performing a large measure of experienced work. . . .

On the one hand, we know that evolution has proceeded during an enormous time on this earth, under, so far as we can gather, a system of rigorous causation, with no economy of time or of instruments, and with no show of special ruth for those who may in pure ignorance have violated the conditions of life.

On the other hand, while recognising the awful mystery of conscious existence and the inscrutable background of evolution, we find that as the foremost outcome of many and long birth-throes, intelligent and kindly man finds himself in being. He knows how petty he is, but he also perceives that he stands here on this particular earth, at this particular time, as the heir of untold ages and in the van of circumstance. He ought therefore, I think, to be less diffident than he is usually instructed to be, and to rise to the conception that he has a considerable function to perform in the order of events, and that his exertions are needed. It seems to me that he should look upon himself more as a freeman, with power of shaping the course of future humanity, and that he should look upon himself less as the subject of a despotic government, in which case it would be his chief merit to depend wholly upon what had been regulated for him, and to render abject obedience.

The question then arises as to the way in which man can assist in the order of events. I reply, by furthering the course of evolution. He may use his intelligence to discover and expedite the changes that are necessary to adapt circumstance to race and race to circumstance, and his kindly sympathy will urge him to effect them mercifully.

Note

1   That is, with questions bearing on what is termed in Greek, *eugenes*, namely, good in stock, hereditarily endowed with noble qualities. This, and the allied words, *eugeneia*, etc., are equally applicable to men, brutes, and plants. We greatly want a brief word to express the science of improving stock, which is by no means confined to questions of judicious mating, but which, especially in the case of man, takes cognisance of all influences that tend in however remote a degree to give to the more suitable races or strains of blood a better chance of prevailing speedily over the less suitable than they otherwise would have had. The word *eugenics* would sufficiently express the idea; it is at least a neater word and a more generalised one than *viriculture*, which I once ventured to use.

Chapter 46

Henry M. Boies: Degeneration and regeneration, 1893

Henry Boies's book *Prisoners and Paupers* shows how easily degeneration theory and criminal anthropology flowed into demands for eugenic responses to crime. Boies, a member of Pennsylvania's Board of Public Charities, was also on the state's Lunacy Commission and active in prison reform on both the state and national levels. What distinguished him from other social reformers of his day were his books – *Prisoners and Paupers*, from which I extract here, and *Diseases of Society* (1901) – and the vigor with which he demanded eugenic measures.

Criminals and paupers are both degenerates, Boies writes; the fundamental problem lies not with their behavior, but with their condition, degeneracy, a disease that must be excised from society. "The gangrened member must be cut off from the body politic." Sterilization will "promptly and completely" stop "the horrid breed," and it will save the U.S. economy $60 million a year.

This extract comes from Henry M. Boies, *Prisoners and Paupers* (New York: G. P. Putnam's Sons, 1893), pp. 264–80 and 291.

HENRY M. BOIES: DEGENERATION AND REGENERATION

. . . So many writers have of late years been threshing out the wheat of valuable knowledge without winnowing it, that we are constrained to attempt to concentrate into a concise and intelligible summary, the results of the exhaustive and diversified investigations of learned men and philanthropists into the causes of the great increase of crime and pauperism, and the failure of the wonderful modern advance of civilization and growth of Christianity to check this.

The wide range of these investigations, and the interesting and useful results obtained, are very fully and impressively epitomized in Havelock Ellis' book entitled *The Criminal*, published in 1892. . . . While . . . no single peculiarity has been identified as a universal characteristic, these examinations have demonstrated beyond question the abnormality of all incorrigible

PORTRAITS FROM THE " ROGUES' GALLERY."
ILLUSTRATING ABNORMAL PHYSIOGNOMY.

Figure 46.1 Proof of Need for Sterilization. To reformers like Henry Boies, the "universal abnormality" of criminals and paupers proved the need for sterilization. Henry Boies, *Prisoners and Paupers* (New York: G.P. Putnam's Sons, 1893), photo following p. 180.

criminals. Every member of the actual criminal class diverges in some essential respects from the normal type of mankind. His physical constitution is a serious variation from, if not an actual deformity or malformation of the complete, healthy, human being, aptly illustrating the truth of the reversed Latin adage, "*insana mens insano corpore*"; so that abnormality becomes in itself an indicative characteristic of the class. Conversely, there is never found in the criminal or pauper class, except by accident, a normal, well developed, healthy adult. At least not in America, where the will of the majority is recognized as rational law by all rational beings, and the opportunities of self-support are ample for the healthy and strong.

We believe it is established beyond controversy that criminals and paupers, both, are degenerate; the imperfect, knotty, knurly, worm-eaten, half-rotten fruit of the race. In short, both criminality and pauperism are conditions and not dispositions. . . .

Omitting then from our present consideration the subject of secondary causes, let us limit ourselves to an effort to change the condition, for the condition requires distinct and different treatment from its causes. Vaccination will avert small-pox, but it is folly and wickedness to vaccinate a patient and let him go free, after he has broken out with the disease. We are to prescribe for the case already infected. Here is a gangrened member of the body politic: the question is not how it came to be so, but what shall be done to stop the spread of the poison, and save the life of the patient. There appears to be a remarkable confusion in the minds and practice of many penologists and philanthropists, of the methods of prevention, with remedial measures – a persistence of reliance upon vaccination after small-pox has developed. By thus confining ourselves to the treatment of the diseased member we shall greatly simplify our study, and limit it within comparatively narrow bounds. For while the causes of degeneracy are many and diverse, the rational treatment of a common, well-known case, is simple and plain. The gangrened member must be cut off from the body politic, or physical, and the system toned up to health. We do not propose to turn the criminal and pauper over to the executioner, as is done in some nations, but we do propose, in the utmost kindness of heart toward them, as well as toward society, to show how they may cut themselves off naturally by the processes of exhaustion. . . .

By carefully providing for its degenerates and abnormals in comfortable prisons, asylums, and almshouses, giving them the advantages of the highest knowledge and science of living, society unwittingly aggravates the evil it seeks to alleviate. It maintains alive those who would perish without its aid. It permits their reproduction and multiplication. It fosters, with more attention than it gives its better types, the establishment and increase of an abnormal and defective class. It not only perpetuates by care but encourages by permitting unrestricted "breeding in" among them the unnatural spread and growth of a social gangrene of fatal tendencies. It is assuming oppressive and alarming proportions which begins to be felt in the whole social organization. In terror our advancing civilization begins to inquire if there be no way of counteraction consistent with its highest benevolence, by which this abnormality of abnormalism may be avoided, criminality and pauperism restored to natural proportions, or to that ratio of increase which may be the inevitable result of ignorance and excess of living.

We believe that the progress of medical and surgical science has opened up such a way entirely practicable, humanitarian in the highest sense, unobjectionable except upon grounds of an absurd and irrational sentiment. The discoveries in the use of anæsthetics and antiseptics have rendered it possible to remove or sterilize the organs of reproduction of both sexes without pain or danger. This is the simplest, easiest, and most effectual solution of the whole difficulty. It promptly and completely stops the horrid breed where it begins and obviates the necessity of permanent seclusion otherwise imperative. This is another grain of wisdom to be separated for a profitable use. . . .

Such a removal would be a positive benefit to the abnormal rather than a deprivation, rather a kindness than an injury. This operation bestowed upon the abnormal inmates of our prisons, reformatories, jails, asylums and public institutions, would entirely eradicate those unspeakable evil practices which are so terribly prevalent, debasing, destructive, and uncontrollable in them. It would confer upon the inmates health and strength for weakness and impotence, satisfaction and comfort for discontent and insatiable desire.

Neither should the purpose of this operation, the prevention of reproduction, be objectionable to the subject. The abnormal does not want children, has no affection for them, and gets rid of them as soon as posssible if they come. . . .

Such a limitation of the unnatural increase of these classes would certainly reduce, in a short time, their public burden and cost more than one half, by mere reduction of their numbers. This would be a social economy in the neighborhood of sixty millions of dollars a year in the United States, equivalent to an annual addition to the wealth of the people of a dollar a head. . . .

The law that "like begets like" is by no means confined to criminals and paupers, but operates inexorably in all classes and conditions of people. A taint of hereditary drunkenness, insanity, suicide, epilepsy, idiocy, deaf-mutism, cancer, syphilis, gout, rheumatism, tuberculous or scrofulous diathesis in the blood is a symptom of degeneration, likely to be intensified by propagation in succeeding generations until the tainted family becomes extinct. Intermarriage with those tainted diffuses weakness, deformity, and abnormality through the social structure, deteriorates and contaminates all who issue from such unions. These things are well known and completely established. . . . The laws of heredity in respect to these more distinct forms of degeneration are now so well established, and the frightful consequences of their neglect so apparent, as to demand legislation for social self-preservation. There can no longer be any doubt that the degeneration of the race is due to the continual reproduction of humanity tainted to a greater or less[er] degree

A GROUP OF PAUPERS IN AN ALMSHOUSE.

Figure 46.2 Paupers in an Almshouse. More evidence in favor of sterilization. Henry Boies, *Prisoners and Paupers* (New York: G.P. Putnam's Sons, 1893), photo following p. 208.

with these common diseases and defects. Not only that all, absolutely all of the crime and pauperism, but most of the suffering and unnatural afflictions, sicknesses, loss of children, untimely deaths, and social loss and waste due to these, are to be attributed to misalliances of, or with, tainted stock. . . .

Let society, under the compulsion of the necessity which is upon it, cut the Gordian knot of its bondage with this sword of justice; take the control of its destiny into its own hand, regulate its reproduction with the wisdom of its experience, and the "ills which flesh is heir to" will vanish with the mists of its night of suffering and sorrow, dissatisfaction and jealous rage, before the glorious dawn of its millenial day of comfort, hope, peace, and promise.

W. Duncan McKim: Selecting the fittest and eliminating the unfit, 1900

The American physician W. Duncan McKim (1855–1935) was wealthy, well - educated (he held a Ph.D as well as a medical degree), and well con-nected. His popular eugenics tract *Heredity and Human Progress* was reprinted several times in his lifetime.

McKim here proposes death by gassing for a large proportion of the crim-inal population. While today he sounds like an arch conservative, eugenic solutions to crime were in fact progressive at the time. However, McKim was more radical than others who thought that eugenics might solve the crime problem; most eugenicists endorsed life incarceration as the best way to cut off the flow of degenerate germ plasm.

This extract comes from W. Duncan McKim, *Heredity and Human Progress* (New York: G. P. Putnam's Sons, 1900), pp. 75, 85–7, 119–20, and 184–93.

W. DUNCAN MCKIM: SELECTING THE FITTEST AND ELIMINATING THE UNFIT

The cause of human wretchedness

It has been held, from remote ages, that the fundamental cause of all our woe is an inborn tendency toward evil. In the light of modern knowledge, we still retain this old doctrine, although obliged to modify its current interpret-ation. By the term human evil we understand generally all that is hurtful to the best interests of man, as individual or race. The human tendency toward self-hurt is in part the result of undevelopment, in part of development in a wrong direction; but always it is incorporated within the physical structure where-with we enter upon this life, and the variations in the degree and peculiar character of this tendency are, in the main, a matter of inheritance. . . .

Not only are all constitutional diseases, dependent upon hereditary or congenital predisposition on the part of the patients, but this appears to be largely true, likewise, of certain germ-diseases, and many of the psychic and neurotic symptoms occurring during the course of infectious disease in general, or as a result of accidental wounds and other injuries, are clearly traceable to an abnormal inheritance. There is reason for believing that even such a disease as "writer's cramp," formerly regarded as purely an accidental result of excessive muscular exertion, is dependent upon an inherited predisposition – so marked in some persons that very ordinary use of the muscles involved may induce this diseased condition. The other professional cramps appear to require the same favoring circumstance of predisposition.

Quite as abundant and incontrovertible as in the case of disease is the evidence for the hereditary transmission of the taints of degeneracy. In them we must see evidence of defective nutrition during intra-uterine life, and except in very rare instances we must hold a blemished parental *vitality*, rather than an unfortunate maternal *environment*, as responsible. Somewhere among the ancestors of the degenerate family there has been bodily or mental impoverishment, and this has impaired the full developmental impulse normally transmitted from parents to offspring. As a result, there has been some interference with growth or development: some part of the body tissues has not attained to that perfection of structure which is the requisite basis for the perfect performance of function.

The abnormal structures and functions in the degenerate are termed "stigmata," and the degree of degeneracy is estimated by their number and intensity. They are weaknesses, and thus constitute *predispositions*; so that the degenerate often succumb to disease and stress of life amid which the "normal" pass unharmed; or they may appear as eccentricities of thought and action, marring the happiness of the individual and working much mischief to society. The condition of degeneracy appears, at times, to be induced in a normal individual through a reckless misuse of his powers and opportunities, but we have good reason for believing that in the great majority of such cases the individual has been, already, a degenerate unrecognized who, through the gratification of abnormal tendencies, has merely intensified his degeneracy to a degree at which it can no longer escape recognition. Almost invariably, if we search for it, we find the fundamental factor of a man's degeneracy to be a taint derived through inheritance.

During recent years, our conception of morbid heredity has become much clearer through a recognition of the great principle that the special defects of offspring are not necessarily identical in character with those existing in the nearer ancestry, but are merely the special manifestations of a transmitted abnormal vitality. In the degenerate, the defects which we see and those the existence of which we infer are all due to disturbances of nutrition. One structure has been insufficiently fed, and we find a dwarfing of its growth and a repression of its function; another has been superabundantly nourished, and displays an exuberance of growth with a consequent imperiousness of function. In such manner must we explain the very unstable equilibrium of the degenerate – the characteristic absence from mind and body of the normal balance. The essence of morbid inheritance being merely a tendency toward abnormal nutrition, the latter reveals itself under varying forms, according to conditions of which, as yet, we have little knowledge. Degeneracy has, as it were, a long array of masks from which to choose for its disguising, but many of these are well recognized by the trained eye. . . .

We must recognize . . . that the weak and the vicious who, a few centuries ago, were suffered to have a share in the world's parentage, have transmitted to us all some of their weakness and depravity; on the other hand, the "defectives" and criminals permitted, in this generation, to multiply their kind, are creating a stream of foulness which will surely, some day, mingle with and defile the blood of our own direct descendants. Generation after generation, the ever-widening circles of hereditary influence approach one another, those of the noblest and those of the vilest human progenitors, until they overlap and completely coincide, with the sad result that all of mankind are kept at one low level. A strong tendency toward reversion to the normal type is frequently manifested in heredity, and this influence has nullified, no doubt, much of the evil which, otherwise, would have been transmitted from remote ancestors; but we must remember that this tendency toward the normal is assisted by some, and combated by other, conjugal unions, and that, as said elsewhere, the affinities of the degenerate incline them toward unfavorable unions.

It is a general biological law that the lower the position of an animal in the scale of being, the greater its capacity for the reproduction of its kind. This law holds generally in the case of man, and goes far to explain the exceeding slowness of human progress. Not only are men of the superior type much more rare than those of the inferior, but the latter are very much more prolific. Cherishing, as we do, the offspring of the very worst of men, we thereby add to the already overwhelming odds against which the race struggles toward perfection.

It has now been sufficiently shown, I trust, that heredity is the fundamental cause of human wretchedness. Environment – essentially the influence of heredity in previous generations – is a mighty factor, too, but, as Kurella has remarked, it is no more the *cause* of the human tendencies which it influences than is digitalis, when it modifies the action of heart and arteries, the *cause* of the circulation of the blood. In our veins flows the blood of ancestral imbeciles, lunatics, and criminals: small wonder, then, that we should continually suffer, ourselves, and constantly harass our neighbors, through our weakness, our eccentricity, and our crime!

A remedy

That the methods as yet proposed for the betterment of our human condition are alarmingly inefficient is fast coming to be the general conviction. It is very clear that there are individuals innumerable who are destined, through their lack of development, to be lifelong burdens, whose influence for evil often becomes intensified in succeeding generations; and it is no less evident that there are many criminals who, in their very nature, must be incorrigible. As members of the first class I need mention only the idiots and imbeciles, and as of the second, the moral imbeciles, hysterical and epileptic criminals, and the criminals who are incurably insane. Against these two classes which curse the human race we have as yet no remedy.

But an inspiring idea is unfolding with the knowledge of these recent years. Poverty, disease, and crime are traceable to one fundamental cause, – *depraved heredity*; they are *not* a necessary human heritage, but result from our toleration of the weak and vicious. Such base scions of human kind not only vex their own generation, but contaminate posterity, in an ever-widening reach, until whole nations have partaken of the infection. The weakening and debasing ancestral elements thus transmitted are the ultimate cause with which we must do battle: we may hope to triumph in the degree that we cease to breed strains which are weak or vicious.

We must learn from nature's method for the preservation and elevation of races, – the selection of the fittest and the rejection of the unfit. The life of each organism waits upon nature's approval: if deemed unworthy, the creature is quickly resolved into its constituent atoms, usually before it has had opportunity to multiply its kind. I believe that our true progress as a people depends upon our application of this natural method. . . .

For the rejuvenation of the race, we need to multiply those individuals whose dominant craving is the altruistic sense, and to eliminate those whose lives are ruled by the baser selfishness. It is among the many defectives thrown upon the State for maintenance and the many vicious held in restraint by the State on account of their crimes, that a system of elimination seems practicable; and through it there would be given ever-increasing opportunity for the expansion of such lives as tend to advance the standard of the race.

It is thus by an artificial selection that it is proposed to elevate the human race. While not interfering with the general productiveness of our kind, I would limit the multiplication of the organically weak and the organically vicious, restricting the plan, however, to the *very* weak and the *very* vicious *who fall into the hands of the State, for maintenance, reformation, or punishment*. The surest, the simplest, the kindest, and most humane means for preventing reproduction among those whom we deem unworthy of this high privilege, is a *gentle, painless death*; and this should be administered not as a punishment, but as an expression of enlightened pity for the victims – too defective by nature to find true happiness in life – and as a duty toward the community and toward our own offspring. To change for the better human nature as found in vicious stocks would be, as we have seen, a slow and exceedingly difficult, if not hopeless, undertaking; but so to change it in stocks already good is but a hastening of the natural trend of human evolution.

Let us now unfold, somewhat more in detail, the plan under consideration, premising that an idea so radical and so replete with practical difficulties cannot at first be shaped into any great degree of definiteness. Indeed, for the reduction of the principles here enunciated into a form susceptible of practical application, no one individual is competent; but I believe that the task is not too grave for the aggregate wisdom of society.

The essential feature of the plan is the gentle removal from this life of such idiotic, imbecile, and otherwise grossly defective persons as are now *dependent for maintenance upon the State*, and of such criminals as commit the most heinous crimes, or show by the frequent repetition of crimes less grave, by their bodily and mental characters, and by their ancestry, that they are hopelessly incorrigible. But we may specify more minutely the individuals whom we should select for extinction.

It is clear that all idiots would require such a decision; and of imbeciles by far the greater number, and especially those who while intelligent gave sure indication of *moral* imbecility. The majority of epileptics would require extinction; but those in whom the disease has apparently been caused by injury or by some removable condition, and whose families give indication of but little degenerative taint, should first be detained for a time, to profit perhaps through the chance of cure by treatment.

Respecting habitual drunkards, the degree of addiction to drink which should necessitate extinction would best be decided through a physical and mental examination. The essential question being the degree to which the man might be dangerous to society, the answer would be found in the condition to which drink had reduced his bodily and mental powers, and not in the quantity of liquor consumed in a day, nor in the number of years through which the drunken habit had persisted. . . .

In the case of criminals, we should need to exercise much discrimination, but the general principles as to the selection of proper subjects for extinction might be laid down as follows: First, not so much the injury dealt to society by any single act, as the dangerous quality of the criminal should be the determining factor. In a sense, the criminal deed might be regarded merely as the inconsiderate act which had thrown a man whom society had had need to fear into its hands for judgment; and the deed itself might have little share in guiding us to our decision – for death or an attempt at reformation. Murder being still regarded as the greatest of all crimes, it would not follow that the life of every murderer should be taken from him. One murderer, in spite of the deliberateness of his deed, might still be a very useful member of society and one who, after the infliction of some penalty other than death, – for the sake of its deterrent influence, – would be thereafter far less likely than the average citizen to take a human life. Another murderer, less guilty than the first according to the old-time way of judging, might appear to be constitutionally of so dangerous a character, so irreclaimable, that in his case death would seem to be the only reasonable sentence.

There is a large class of offenders not murderers to whom, as it seems to me, the death-penalty should be awarded: these are the nocturnal house-breakers. There is no criminal more regardless of the rights of his fellow-men, more continually aggressive, more hardened, more ruthless, more incorrigible. . . .

Innumerable criminals are found to be idiots, imbeciles, epileptics, habitual drunkards, insane, or even to constitute some combination of these dangerously defective characters: all such, speaking generally, should receive the death-sentence. Finally, such prisoners, whatever their offence, who have shown themselves by their record in reformatory or prison to be hopelessly irreclaimable, should likewise undergo this condemnation.

The roll, then, of those whom our plan would eliminate consists of the following classes of individuals *coming under the absolute control of the State:* idiots, imbeciles, epileptics, habitual drunkards, and insane criminals; the larger number of murderers; nocturnal house-breakers; such criminals, whatever their offence, as might through their constitutional organization appear very dangerous; and, finally, criminals who might be adjudged incorrigible. Each individual of these classes would undergo thorough examination, and only by due process of law would his life be taken from him.

The painless extinction of these lives would present no practical difficulty: in carbonic acid gas we have an agent which would instantaneously fulfil the need.

Part IX

Criminal statistics

Criminal statistics
Introduction to Part IX

One of the most exciting aspects of nineteenth-century criminology was the development of statistics – first the stunning accomplishment of organizing national, ongoing censuses of criminals and then the feat of learning how to use the data to test both theories and the efficacy of new policies. Most important of all was the realization that statistics could reveal, as no number of case studies could, the social nature of crime – the social forces operating behind and on the individual that no one could begin to identify without statistical methods.

Andre-Michel Guerry (Chapter 48) organized the first of the annual collections of crime data, in France is the early 1830s. He was immediately struck, as were his followers at home and abroad, by the "fixity" of the figures year after year, a constancy indicating that crime was socially produced and for the most part unaffected by court decisions or prison policies. Here was the beginning of the French sociological tradition that, throughout the century, countered the more biological work on crime that emanated from Italy and the more reformist tracts produced in the United States. Adolphe Quetelet, another French statistician, followed up on Guerry's findings (Chapter 49), re-emphasizing the almost static nature of the annual figures and explaining, in terms that have rarely been equaled for their clarity and passionate logic, why numbers are better than individual cases when it comes to analyzing criminal behavior.

Shifting to England, the next two extracts (Chapters 50 and 51) show how crime statistics were used in that country to address the causes of crime and assess crime-prevention programs. Chapter 52 reproduces parts of the 1880 U.S. census on criminals, passages revealing that America was behind both in organizing a nationwide, ongoing survey of offenders and in analyzing crime data sociologically. It contrasts with Chapter 53, in which Enrico Ferri, the Italian jurist, outlines his vision of *criminal sociology*, a program of statistical research that will reveal the social causes of crime.

Chapter 48

Andre-Michel Guerry: The moral statistics of France, 1833

Andre-Michel Guerry (1802–66), the French lawyer and statistician, was born in Lyon, but in early adulthood moved to Paris, where he became involved in the Ministry of Justice's work of organizing the collection of crime statistics and reporting them in the annual *Compte général de l'administration de la justice criminelle en France* (*General Account of the Administration of Criminal Justice in France*). This was the first national database on crime and one to which many subsequent criminologists turned for material. Like Guerry himself, criminologists elsewhere were fascinated by the database's demonstration of "this fixity, this constancy in the reproduction of facts," by which Guerry meant that crime statistics varied little year by year, irrespective of actions by courts and prisons.

In his famous *Essai sur la statistique morale de la France* (*Essay on the Moral Statistics of France*), Guerry defines *moral statistics* as data aimed at the study of "intellectual man" – his faculties, customs, and feelings. It is a field that embraces moral philosophy, politics, religion, legislation, history, literature, and the arts.[1] In other words, he sees crime statistics as a means of understanding a broad range of human behavior – of creating a kind of sociology of man. He begins his essay by giving himself credit ("One owes it to M. Guerry of Champneuf") for the immense administrative task of organizing the new database; he also points out the significance of this essay as the first analysis of national crime statistics over a period of years. He then explains why he uses arrests, not convictions, for his baseline. This method had already been harshly criticized, and Guerry admits that it is not error-free. However, is has fewer errors than other methods do.

Next, Guerry takes on those who argue that statistics can never pin down the truths of crime, critics who want to cling to the older method of theorizing about crime on the basis of logic rather than numbers. In the central part of the *Essay*, which I summarize here, he methodically analyzes the latest data, much as today's national crime reports analyze the reports of the previous year. Guerry concludes that crime statistics are not yet capable of establishing "truth." However, they are valuable for encouraging a critical frame of mind about matters of crime and criminal justice, and their potential has as yet barely been mined.

Guerry's *Essay* is one of the founding documents of criminology and sociology. It is frequently referenced in histories of the social sciences, but because it is difficult to access, it is rarely read. I used A. M. Guerry, *Essai sur la statistique morale de la France* (*Essay on the Moral Statistics of France*) (Paris: Chez Crochard, 1833), translating from pp. 5–9 and p. 69.

ANDRE-MICHEL GUERRY: THE MORAL STATISTICS OF FRANCE

General Considerations: The first authentic documents published on the administration of criminal justice in France did not appear until 1825. . . . Today, each trimester, the procurers general send to the Keeper of the Seals information on criminal and correctional matters brought before the tribunals of their jurisdiction. . . . Their end-of-the-year analysis forms the *Compte général de l'administration de la justice criminelle*. Never in any land has there been a work of this type executed in so complete a fashion. One owes it to M. Guerry of Champneuf, the former director of criminal matters and of pardons, who for five years has worked steadily on its improvement. . . .

Instead of using the number of persons convicted for the base rate of our calculations, we have taken the number of persons accused, which more accurately represents the number of crimes committed. This method may be surprising and at first appear quite wrong. It generated lively criticism before publication of the *Compte général* of 1827, and thus we must explain why we decided to use it.

To be accused, they say, is not necessarily to be guilty; the number of crimes therefore cannot be deduced from the number of the accused, for the figure would count as criminals men later proclaimed innocent. Doubtless it would be wrong to regard as guilty the man who is later exonerated; but just because a crime was not committed precisely by the suspect, can one conclude that there was no crime? . . .

In using the number of persons accused as the baseline, we undeniably expose ourselves to errors; but those errors are less serious than if we took into consideration only people convicted of crimes. . . .

The first discussions of criminal statistics, presenting promising results and fitting well with popular theories, were greeted with great favor. People were tired of seeing the same old doctrines constantly attacked and defended by reasoning alone; it seemed that there had finally been found an instrument that would give quick solutions to difficult problems. But very soon the exactitude of these results was contested; and the results subverted those that other numbers had established. Consequently, criminal statistics inspired mistrust, and they were accused of constituting an unproductive, conjectural, and unreliable science.

In criminal matters, it was said, as in all those related to the moral sciences, facts are too mobile, too elusive, to be pinned down by numerical observation. Thus it is necessary to hang on, as in the past, to theories founded on logic, to rely on the examination of general facts and on individual experience.

To begin with, we ask how one can interpret the results of experience so long as experiences are neither categorized nor numerically recorded, and when they consequently shift in importance, not only from one individual to the next, but within the individual himself, according to whether he is more or less deterred and according to the particular and accidental circumstances. . . . How can we bring oneness to such disparate elements and compare them with one another? And then, indeed, what is a general fact? . . .

Before entering into the details of criminal statistics, it is important to give examples of this fixity, this constancy in the reproduction of facts, formerly considered elusive in their entirety, and subject to no law.

[Guerry proceeds to make his point by comparing different regions of France year by year for the period 1825–1830, examining crimes against the person and against property and showing that there is but small variation around the mean each year. Then he compares crime rates for men and women by year, to the same end, a demonstration followed by one for age and then the seasons. Having thus demonstrated the relative stability of crime rates, Guerry moves on to give tables for current crimes, discussing specific offenses such as rape, infanticide, and false witnessing. He lists the motives for capital offenses and presents maps – perhaps the first crime maps ever made – showing the distribution of various offenses for France's 86 departments. Arguing against the popular theory that ignorance causes crime, he shows statistically that areas with poor education are not those with high rates of crime against the person. He also gives information on rates of illegitimate births, charitable giving, and suicide. Then he concludes as follows. – N.R.]

These first efforts [at analyzing crime statistically] rarely lead to immediate applications. They undermine errors more than they establish truth, and their utility consists less in promoting theories than in spreading the spirit of doubt and critical scrutiny. Crime statistics are still too imperfect even to give an idea of the immense development that could be fostered by pursuing research of this type.

Note

1   Guerry, *Essai sur la statistique morale de la France* (Paris: Chez Crochard, 1833), p. 69.

Chapter 49

Adolphe Quetelet: Criminal statistics and what they show, 1835

Adolphe Quetelet (1796–1874) powerfully influenced the development of criminology by helping to establish the quantitative tradition and sociological approach that today dominate the field. It is difficult to assess the full range of his impact because few of Quetelet's works have been adequately translated. However, it is clear that at a time when Western nations were just starting systematically to gather crime statistics, Quetelet's sophisticated use of French judicial data (the annual *Comptes géneraux* or overall tallies) dramatically demonstrated the value of such record-keeping, and his work influenced nearly all other nineteenth-century criminologists. Havelock Ellis called Quetelet's book *On Man and the Development of his Faculties* the beginning of criminal sociology.[1]

Quetelet, a Belgian astronomer and mathematician, followed Guerry in discovering that the statistics of crime change little year by year – a realization that caused consternation among moralists and reformers who focused on redeeming the individual criminal, but that opened up the whole field of crime to sociological analysis. Quetelet's sophisticated approach also contradicted the love of anecdote and appeals to personal experience that were nearly ubiquitous in other aspects of nineteenth-century thinking about crime; in the face of these, Quetelet could present figures showing that, in a sense, crime pre-existed the individual in society, and while he did not deny that change could occur, he warned that it would occur only slowly, because society itself would have to change. As Piers Beirne points out in a helpful essay, "Quetelet's insertion of criminal behavior into a formal structure of causality was a remarkable advance over the ad hoc and eclectic speculations of his contemporaries."[2]

For this extract I translated from Quetelet's *Sur l'homme et le développement de ses facultés* (*On Man and the Development of his Faculties*), vol. 2 (Paris: Bachlier, 1835), pp. 100–4, 107–9, 160, and 242–9. In the first section, Quetelet explains why it is better to use a large number of cases than individual examples to analyze a phenomenon like crime. (He uses *courage* as an analogue.) In the second section, Quetelet sets forth conclusions based on his statistical analysis of crime data.

ADOLPHE QUETELET: CRIMINAL STATISTICS AND WHAT THEY SHOW

Determining the moral and intellectual characteristics of the average man

Suppose that two individuals were every day in a position to do acts of courage and that their ability to do these was exactly the same. Suppose, moreover, that each year one were to count approximately 500 acts of courage for one of the men and only 300 for the other; and that these acts, no matter how remarkable, could be collectively judged to have the same value because they were generally repeated under the same circumstances. Agreeing to this, it would be easy to say that these two individuals have courage in the ratio of 500 to 300, or five to three. A similar assessment might be more persuasive if the observations were made over a greater number of years and if the results varied within narrow limits. If the example seems absurd, the absurdity comes only from the *impossibility*, first, of putting two men in an equally favorable position to do acts of courage; second, of counting each time these acts were made; and third, of gathering a sufficiently large number so that one's judgment would deviate as little as possible from the truth. The relationship seems absurd only because we believe it *impossible* to determine.

Nevertheless suppose that there were taken from the French population two individuals, the first representing men from 21 to 25 years old and the other men aged 32 to 40; moreover, for the acts of courage let us substitute thefts sufficiently serious to be judged by criminal tribunals. In such a manner we are able to say with considerable confidence that the tendency to theft is in France around five for the man of 21–25 years and three for the man of 35–40 years. In effect, one can agree that the men between 21 and 25 years who, according to French population statistics, are equal in number to the men of 35–40 years, have the same ability as the latter to indulge in theft and that, moreover, thefts judged by criminal tribunals present them with equally serious circumstances. If someone objects that I am taking into consideration only thefts judged by tribunals, I would reply that when one calculates the mortality or fecundity of a nation, one also does not know all the facts, and that a great number might be omitted. The probability of these omissions, in any case, is just as large for individuals of 21-to-25 years as it is for those of 35-to-40 years. . . .

That which seems to me impossible to estimate is the absolute degree of courage (or that which is conventionally considered to be courage) of an isolated individual; for what unit of measure should be used? should one observe this individual for a long time and in a sustained manner, so as to reckon with all his actions, when one estimates the worth of his courageous acts? Will those acts be sufficiently numerous to enable us to conclude something worthwhile? And who will guarantee that, during the course of the observations, the individual might not have changed? But when one works with a large number of men, these problems nearly disappear, especially if one aims at determining relationships and not absolute values.

Thus one could estimate the tendency to certain vices or virtues, be it for men of different ages, or for the two sexes, when it involves the same nation. However, the difficulties grow when one compares different counties because many circumstances which are initially the same can differ greatly later on. . . .

It would be impossible to compare two specific men, one between 21 and 25 years, the other between 35 and 40, to determine (everything else being equal) their greater or lesser tendency to theft or even to crime, for this tendency might never reveal itself, even in a single act, during the course of the observation. But that does not matter when one studies all men of the same age collectively: the number of actions or their effects is sufficiently the same that one can, without large errors, ignore the different degrees of energy in the acts. If one finds, moreover, that the number of crimes remains nearly exactly the same from one year to the next, there is a large probability that the results deviate little from the truth. . . .

If exceptions are found to the rule ascertained for the average, as they are to all laws of nature, at least the exceptions will help us understand better what is happening in society, and that is what we particularly want to know. From birth man carries the germs of all the traits which he later develops, and in proportions more or less great: prudence predominates in one man, greed in another, imagination in the third. We find, moreover, an excess of height given age, or a precocious imagination, or an old age that is active and vigorous. The simple fact that we notice discrepancies shows that we already have the sense of a general law of development and that we actually make use of it in our judgments. I am not undertaking anything new, other than to bring more exactness to understandings that are usually quite vague, since they rest on incomplete or defective observations, and usually on observations that are too few in number.

All that being said, I know that it is not absurd but *possible* to calculate the traits of the average man of a nation or of the human race. The apparent absurdity of such research comes only from the lack of precise observations made in sufficiently large numbers that the results are likely to conform to the truth.

In the preceding volume I tried to determine the laws of the physical development of man. I am going to continue now, extending my research to the study of moral and intellectual traits.

On the development of the tendency to crime

Supposing men to share similar circumstances, I give the label *tendency to crime* to the probability of their committing a crime. My goal is to study in particular the influence that the seasons, climate, sex, and age have on this tendency.

. . .

Conclusions. The main observations of this chapter lead to these conclusions:

1   *Age* is undoubtedly the cause that acts with the most energy to develop or dampen the tendency to crime.
2   This unfortunate tendency seems to develop in proportion to the physical strength and passions in man; it attains its maximum at about the age of 25 years, the period at which physical development is nearly ended. Intellectual and moral development occurs more slowly, dampening the tendency to crime, which still later diminishes through weakening of physical force and the passions.
3   While it is toward the age of 25 years that we find the maximum in the number of crimes of the different types, nonetheless this maximum rises and falls in some years for certain crimes according to the rate of development of qualities which relate to crime. Thus a man, driven by the violence of his passions begins with rape and attacks against modesty; he starts at almost the same time on a career of theft which he seems to follow by instinct until his last gasp. The development of his strength carries him next to all acts of violence, homicide, rebellion, and highway robbery. Later, reflection converts murder into assassination and poisoning. Finally the man, advancing in his criminal career, substitutes little by little trickery for force, and he is now more likely to become a counterfeiter than at any other period in his life.
4   *The difference between the sexes* also has a great influence on the tendency to crime; usually only one woman comes before the tribunals for every four men.
5   The tendency to crime grows and decreases in almost the same degree for the two sexes; nevertheless the period of the maximum arrives a little later for women, around the age of thirty.
6   Woman, no doubt through her sense of weakness, commits more crimes against property than persons; and when she tries to destroy her fellow creature, she prefers poison. . . .
7   *The seasons* exercise a very marked influence on the tendency to crime. During summer the most crimes are committed against persons and the least against property; the opposite is true in winter.

. . .

12   *Education* is far from having such a strong influence on the tendency to crime as is commonly supposed. Moreover, one often confuses moral

education with the type of education that consists only of reading and writing, and that often provides new tools for committing crime.

13   The same is true of *poverty*; several areas of Frances reputed to be the most poor, are at the same time the most moral. . . .

I cannot finish this chapter without again mentioning my surprise at the constancy one finds in the results that present themselves, year after year, in the records of the administration of justice. . . . All observations confirm the truth of the proposition I enunciated long ago, that *when we look at the human species en masse, we find order in the physical facts*. The greater the number of individuals, the more the will of the individual disappears, enabling the general facts that hold society together to predominate. These are the causes which one seeks to apprehend; when one knows them, one can determine their influence on society, just as one determines the effects of causes in the physical sciences. . . .

All observations confirm the truth of the proposition, formulated by me long ago, that *when we look at the human species en masse, we find order in the physical facts*. . . . I am far from concluding, however, that man can do nothing for his amelioration. I believe, as I said at the opening of this work, that he possess a moral force capable of changing the rules that concern him. But this force acts only slowly, for the causes which influence the social system are unable to undergo rapid change. They have acted over a series of years and they continue to do so if we do not succeed in changing them. But I cannot repeat too often to all men who care about the well-being and honor of their fellow creatures, men who blush to equate a few francs more or less with a few heads more or less for the executioner's axe: there is a fee that one pays with a frightful regularity, that of the prisons, the work camps, and the scaffolds. It is that above all that we must strive to reduce.

Notes

1   Havelock Ellis, *The Criminal* (London: Walter Scott, 1892), p. 44.
2   Piers Beirne, "The rise of positivist criminology: Adolphe Quetelet's 'social mechanics of crime'," in Piers Beirne (ed.), *Inventing Criminology* (Albany, NY: State University of New York Press, 1993), p. 87.

Chapter 50

Joseph Fletcher: Statistics of crime in England and Wales, 1849

Joseph Fletcher, a barrister and honorary secretary to the Statistical Society of London, was initially interested in determining the effects of "Christian education" on crime rates, but he ended up studying a wide variety of influences. For over 270 pages his report on "Moral and educational statistics of England and Wales" examines the impact on crime of such variables as pauperism, urbanization, industrialization, food costs, education, crime type, race, and bastardy, displaying the data in county-to-county breakdowns. Fletcher's discussions are often difficult to follow and his conclusions seldom crystalline. However, he did statistically map social conditions in England and Wales in the mid-nineteenth century, creating models for the sociological investigation of crime and preserving a goldmine of data for historians. Moreover, he uses crime statistics to test theories about the causes of crime and to suggest new ones.

Fletcher begins with a problem. He wants to show that education reduces crime, and a comparison of an earlier three-year period (1842–4) with the most recent one (1845–7) shows that crime did indeed go down. However, it declined most in the areas where instruction was weakest, not strongest. Fletcher gets around the problem by explaining that an economic uptick has suppressed crime among the "poorer and more ignorant classes," veiling the impact of education on them.

After bemoaning the failure of education statistics to clarify the benefits of instruction, Fletcher moves on to lambaste a new book he has heard of by Andre-Michel Guerry (Chapter 48), in which the French statistician maintains that in England, as in France, instruction has no effect on crime rates. Indignant, Fletcher touts his own work as superior to Guerry's and suggests that France take a closer look at England's superior educational system.

Fletcher goes on to discuss problems in the collection of crime data by "statists" (statisticians) like himself: the occasional, arbitrary dropping of "whole classes of the minor offences" from reports; changes in the classification of crimes necessitated by changes in the criminal law; and inconsistencies in reporting by district. He objects to the distinction between personal and property crimes because "under the former head are . . . a cloud of common assaults, which entirely obscure the numerical data relating to more serious forms of offence", while the "property crime" category masks the fact that some property crimes are caused not by greed, but malice. Thus, Fletcher devises a new three-fold categorization of offenses. He also frets over whether to count court commitments or convictions and how to best to compare counties with one another. (He calculates national three-year averages and compares the counties' three-year averages with them.) These passages show Fletcher grappling with key issues in the collection and reporting of crime statistics.

In the final passage, Fletcher moves on to discuss the causes of crime, which he locates in "the constitution of society" – here, in economic depression and lack of employment for the poor. He concludes that "*steadiness* in the price of food, in credit, and in employment" are crucial for "the moral welfare of modern society." In other words, unregulated capitalism can cause crime.

This extract comes from pp. 151, 154, 158, 163–5, and 169 in Joseph Fletcher, "Moral and educational statistics of England and Wales," *Journal of the Statistical Society of London* 12 (May, 1849): 151–77, 189–336.

JOSEPH FLETCHER: STATISTICS OF CRIME IN ENGLAND AND WALES

Having made the progress of education among those committed for criminal offences the subject of former investigation, I would now beg permission to put on record the accompanying summary of that progress, as tested by the average proportion in each district, showing each degree of instruction in 1842–3–4, compared with that showing the same degree of instruction in 1845–6–7. It will be found to present some peculiar features, which appear, at the first glance, to be quite anomalous; but a closer inspection will show that they support the conclusions that have been drawn from the more detailed evidence.

Thus it appears a fatal blow to the reputation of good influences from education to find that, in the total decline of 13.2 per cent in the criminal commitments there has been a decline of 19.7 per cent, in the least instructed, and only 2.1 per cent in the most instructed districts. But this will be explained by observing further that the greatest decline in the total number of commitments is also coincident (one district alone excepted) with the greatest apparent *progress* in education, and the least decline with the least apparent progress in instruction during the period under observation. Whence it is obvious that this disturbance of the figures from their arrangement in the tables representing the preceding period of five years, is but the result of the universal breeze of real or fancied prosperity which accompanied cheaper food and the development of the railway system, and found ample employment for the poorer and more ignorant classes generally. The decline of commitments from these classes in the districts of mere labour, thus throws the more instructed districts, which contain the metropolis and the towns of the south, into a comparatively invidious relief; while the metropolis itself appears positively to exhibit an increase in every feature of depravity. . . .

M. Guerry has long maintained that in France, the moral features of different districts present no general coincidence with the varying amount of technical instruction prevailing in them. But how he can have arrived at the same conclusion in regard to England, as it is said he has, except through very rude and imperfect processes, I cannot conceive. The results which I am now submitting are derived from an analysis of every recent evidence on the subject, pursued in the most legitimate methods, with every available correction; and since they differ from those of M. Guerry, I am led to doubt whether those put forth in his original work on the Moral Statistics of France would not be considerably altered by a correction in the distribution of crime for the differences in the ages of the population in the different departments. If this be not the case, it is the more important for both countries to understand what are the influences which unite an element of moral improvement with all vigorous instruction in England but are wanting to that which prevails in France; for that they may be wanting I can very well conceive; and statistical evidence to their absence under a highly elaborate system of public instruction is of an importance too grave to be received with vague incredulity, or met by any denial which does not satisfactorily subvert such formal testimony. If it be well founded, it is a warning to our neighbours to seek for the rising generation in their own country the character of instruction, and the beneficial influences generally associated with it, which are observed in extensive operation among the people of England. . . .

The classification of crime adopted in the Criminal Returns of the Home Office is avowedly imperfect; and it is by no means easy to make one which shall be simple, and yet serve the purposes at once of administrative justice and abstract science; the latter imperfect, and the former encumbered with arbitrary classifications and designations of crime inherited from every age of our legislation and legal practice. It is our present duty, however, to make the best of the classification already in use, rather than suggest a better; and we are under great obligation, as Statists, to our fellow labourer, Samuel Redgrove, Esq., of the Home Office, for the superiority of that which he has employed ever since the year 1834, when the Criminal Returns first came under his superintendence, as compared with the rude and imperfect catalogue for the kingdom at large, and for the metropolis alone in detail, which they previously presented; whole classes of the minor offences, such as assaults, riots, &c., being arbitrarily omitted by the compiler. This classification was the subject of much debate in our Society soon after its first publication; and in a paper by Mr. Symons, which was abstracted in our proceedings, many desiderata were suggested. But the officers of our Courts necessarily refuse to make any distinctions which the Courts themselves do not; and those who compile from their data cannot change their integral character. Changes are, however, constantly taking place in these returns, not to meet the views of the man of science, but as a necessary result of even minor changes in our criminal law, which occasion a mutability in the classification of offences under the heads now employed, though these be not themselves changed, which would invalidate any work, however elaborate, if it assumed that the figures found under each head always described exhaustively the same thing, and attempted by their means its separate exhibition during a long course of years. It is only the great groups that can safely be employed for comparison between one time or place and another; and as these groups supply a sufficient basis of observations without wandering over any lengthened period, it is the averages of the two several periods of three years each, last put on record, that I have employed for the purpose of the present comparisons between one county or district and another. . . .

By following arbitrarily the distinction between offences against the person and offences against property, the totals under the former head are made to embrace a cloud of common assaults, which entirely obscure the numerical data relating to more serious forms of offence; while, on the other hand, the malicious offences against property, entered in the midst of those whose object is purely the desire of gain, cause the total of offences against property to involve very discordant elements. I have, therefore, although the change still leaves various minor discrepancies, brought into one group the offences which are principally the result of uncontrolled or disordered lust and revenge, by placing side by side all the offences against the person, with the exception of assaults, and all the malicious offences against property, and bringing them to common totals. This leaves in perfectly distinct relief the three great classes of crime which result from a desire of dishonest gain, in so far as they become the subject of criminal proceedings; viz., first, offences against property committed with violence: second, offences against property committed without violence; and third, forgery and offences against the currency, which might well have been included among the latter. We have then remaining the assaults, which will, in the main, arise from the ebullitions of ungoverned temper, even those upon police officers in the execution of their duty; and the class of "other offences." These, except the offences against the State, might have been grouped with one or other of the preceding classes; but they are all offences common to the people at large, and not to any special localities, except those of smuggling and poaching. . . .

The three cardinal groups to which we are thus brought are: –

1   Serious offences against persons and offences against property, chiefly from lust and revenge. . . .
2   Offences against property, with and without violence, from the desire of dishonest gain. . . .

3   Miscellaneous offences, as assault, riot, misdemeanor, &c., in great part
     from ebullitions of temper. . . .

The propriety of taking records of *commitments* instead of convictions as
the foundation of statistical calculations in criminal matters has often been
discussed, and as often decided in favour of the former, as being a better
index to the number of crimes actually committed than the latter. . . . It is
always difficult, however, to determine the allowance to be made for the
differing manners, habits, and police of the more polished and populous
places, as compared with the more rude and remote, in which, unheeded by
any public tribunal, occur petty disorders, which, in a well-policed town,
would be the subject of criminal proceedings. Neither, it may be argued, is
it possible, from existing data, to know how many of the persons committed
in one district may be immigrants from another. But when it is considered
that the great body of those whose cases are sent to assizes and sessions,
instead of being summarily treated, are not mere wanderers, they must be
regarded as forming essentially a part of the community in which they are
found. . . .

It would appear that fluctuations in the supply of food, and with it, sooner
or later, of employment and profit, act upon the social constitution generally,
and deprave or embitter its moral tone throughout, to an extent from which it
has not the elasticity to recover before the attack, in the course of nature, is
renewed. It is worthy of remark, too, that there is an obvious tendency, in the
aggravated uneasiness of the periods of depression to find some general cause
in the constitution of society for the various forms of unhappiness by which it
is assailed; sometimes, perhaps, to the destruction of an arrangement already
condemned by sound judgment, but always with a blindness of passion which
it must sometimes prove difficult either to guide, to humour, or to resist.
Steadiness in the price of food, in credit, and in employment, is obviously,
therefore, one of the first desiderata for the moral welfare of modern
society. . . .

Recognising, then, the disastrous moral effects of this reeling in the edifice
of industry, what are we to conclude from the augmented leaven of crime and
burthen of criminals which it entails upon society at every assault of the
seasons? Is it that the social fabric is yielding, or merely, that, by our mal-
administration, we convert the weak, who become bad at such periods, into a
class of permanent and professional delinquents, from whom we are not freed
by their vices, by the hulks, by transportation, or by the gallows, before we
undertake the education of a new accession of recruits for the same wretched
disservice? These questions will be answered with vehement readiness,
though not with exact accord, by those who imagine that they see intuitively
through the labyrinth of social influences; but our presumptions do not
extend beyond legitimate hypotheses, to be answered "yea" or "nay," by
further observation and analysis; and these I would now push into a

comparison of the several counties and districts, in reference to the relative progress of population and commitments in each, during thirty years, from 1811 to 1841, or rather from 1810–11–12 to 1840–1–2; for three years are taken to give a securer basis to the results.

Chapter 51

Mary Carpenter: On the importance of statistics to the Reformatory Movement, 1857

Mary Carpenter (1807–77), the British social reformer, author, and social scientist, had international impact on the reformatory movement and prison policy. She is best known for her book *Our Convicts*, a founding document in the movement to establish reformatories for not only juvenile delinquents, but also adult offenders. In the address extracted here (originally a paper read at a meeting of the British Association for the Advancement of Science), Carpenter argues that the government must gather accurate statistics upon the operation of its reformatories to assess "the actual success or failure of the plans adopted." In other words, better crime statistics can make possible evaluation research on crime control policies.

Carpenter lays out the inadequacies of current statistics. Whether they keep track of commitments or convictions, they overestimate the number of delinquents, since many children move in and out of the criminal justice system several times over the course of a year. Over-counting makes it impossible to estimate the deterrent influence of legislation, such as that of a new law ordering parents to contribute to the upkeep of incarcerated children; this law may well be having a deterrent effect on parents who used to send their children out to commit felonies, but current statistics make it difficult to tell. Moreover, Carpenter continues, accurate figures can tell us which regions of the country need reformatories, and they can show when institutions are needed for girls or older delinquents. Better statistics can help the government monitor cities to see which are failing to commit delinquents to reformatories. Finally, accurate statistics can help determine the causes of crime. Using data collected by the institutions, Carpenter argues that few delinquents are orphans, although most have a parent of bad or unkind character. Thus not orphanage but bad parentage is a cause of crime.

This extract comes from pp. 33–7 of Mary Carpenter, "On the importance of statistics to the Reformatory Movement, with returns from female reformatories, and remarks on them," *Journal of the Statistical Society of London* 20(1) (1857): 33–40.

MARY CARPENTER: ON THE IMPORTANCE OF STATISTICS TO THE REFORMATORY MOVEMENT

The position which Reformatory Schools at present hold with regard to the State, renders it of the first importance that as much light as possible should be thrown by statistics on the real numbers of the juvenile criminal population of the country, and that official returns should be henceforth so arranged that accurate information may be obtained as to the actual success or failure of the plans adopted.

The want of such information has led to very serious and alarming apprehensions relative to the inadequacy of any possible supply of reformatories to cope with the enormous multitude of young thieves which is supposed to exist. Reference has been made to criminal returns of convictions, throughout the country, of young persons under the age of 16, and it has been imagined that we must make provision for such an annual supply. Two points have, however, been left out of view: first, that the number of either *commitments* or *convictions* by no means shows the number of criminal individuals, since many have been committed several times during the year; and secondly, that according to the old system of imprisonment for juveniles, the same individual not only would be recommitted two or three times in the same year, but might remain from year to year until transported, not only himself swelling the annual list of convicts, but drawing others into his vortex, and thereby multiplying crime in a fearful ratio; whereas, when the reformatory system is fully carried out, no young person will be allowed to be more than a second time convicted, and frequently all who are likely to be exposed to a second will be removed at the first, and thus each year the list must be greatly lessened numerically. Not only so, but it has been found that a deterring influence has already been exerted in those towns where the Juvenile Offenders' Act has been carried into active operation. At the late meeting in Bristol of the National Reformatory Union, an important communication was made by the chief constable of Berwick, that there had been considerable diminution in juvenile crime since the Juvenile Offenders' Act came into operation; and it was stated by the chaplain of the Liverpool Gaol, "that since the Liverpool magistrates began to act with their present determination of availing themselves of the Youthful Offenders' Act in all its provisions, both for the protection of the child and for enforcing the parental responsibility in every suitable case, a manifest anxiety amongst the criminal population had been created, and that the number of juveniles in the gaol, of which he had been for some years chaplain, is less than during any period within his recollection."

An analysis of one of the tables in the Liverpool Police Report for 1855 will present an important illustration of the points on which there should be careful entries in all such returns, and of the erroneous impressions which may arise from a want of such well arranged tables.

We learn from this table, that in the year 1855 there were 1140 apprehensions of boys and 304 of girls, altogether 1344 apprehensions of juveniles under the age of 16. But of these, 372, in the case of boys, and 75, in the case of girls, were repetitions of previous apprehensions, making the actual number of individual boys apprehended only 768, and of girls 229. Again, of these, 290 boys and 85 girls had been apprehended in previous years, and these 290 boys had had among them 259 re-apprehensions, the 85 girls, 39 re-apprehensions. Now when the Youthful Offenders' Act has come into full operation, the old offenders will all be removed, and, consequently, instead of the enormous amount of 1140 apprehensions of boys and 304 of girls, we shall have, on the same average, only 478 of boys and 144 of girls, somewhat more than one-third.

A similar process applied to a table of *commitments*, during the same year, presents even more striking results. We here find 489 commitments of boys and 110 of girls; but after making the same reductions as before, 95 represents the number of boys now committed who were not known to have been so before, and 37 the number of girls. In the case of the commitments, a very large proportion is of individuals who are known to have been previously in custody, viz. 377 of the boys and 70 of the girls. If all these old offenders had been removed, it cannot be doubted that the number of new commitments would have been very greatly diminished; but even as the case now stands, the number of known delinquents is not so great but that it may be well grappled with, viz., 132 of both sexes, for the town of Liverpool, which, from its position and circumstances, may be expected to be more prolific of juvenile vice than any place out of the metropolis. There cannot be a doubt that a still greater reduction will take place when reformatories have been longer in operation. Such a result is strongly evidenced by the following extract from the Liverpool Police Report for 1856, just issued: –

> Since the reformatories have been in operation, a diminution in juvenile crime has taken place in this borough; for it is known to the police that some parents who formerly sent out their children for the purpose of committing felonies, upon the proceeds of which they subsisted, are now aware that should their children be detected in crime, they would be taken from them, sent to a reformatory, and they themselves charged a weekly sum, varying according to their circumstances, for their maintenance; *greater care is taken by such parents of their children, as it is now their interest to prevent what was formerly encouraged by them.*

The returns show a very considerable diminution in the number of juveniles taken into custody.

It is of great importance to the reformatory movement that such tables as these, with the addition of tables of convictions and sentences of all young persons under 16 (not 17 as heretofore), should be kept universally throughout the country, and that further means should be taken, as in France, to record all cases of relapse in young persons who have been in reformatories, including the Government Reformatory, at Parkhurst, Isle of Wight. There will thus be the means afforded of ascertaining to some extent the wants of the country in the establishment of reformatories; the degree in which the intentions of the government are carried out in the substitution of reformatories for prisons, in the case of young persons under 16; and the effect of the mode of management adopted in each establishment.

The managers of reformatories must also carefully perform their part in keeping careful and regular records on all points which will be likely to throw light on the subject, and must be particularly exact in all matters concerning the disposal of the children, and their subsequent course.

At the commencement of the movement the reformation of boys only was the object of much attention; but it is now beginning to be understood that there exists in the country a large number of girls, marked with the prison brand, whose condition is far worse than that of boys, and who, if left unreformed, will be the teachers of vice to the next generation. A commencement has been recently made of schools for these, as will be shewn by the following table, from which some important facts may be elicited. [Omitted here are two tables on girls sent to reformatories – N.R.]

Several striking facts may be elicited from the foregoing table: –

First. – While the schools are capable of containing 254 girls, we find only 155 actually in them, and of these one-half are volunteers. Knowing then that a very large number of young girls are annually convicted of crimes, it follows that during the two years the schools have been in operation, magistrates and judges have not availed themselves of the provisions of the Act as fully as they might have done.

Secondly. – The list of the places, from which girls have been sent to the schools, shows that, while an interest in the movement is extending into even remote parts of the kingdom, the large towns, which are the great centres of juvenile delinquency, have shown a remarkable backwardness in sentencing girls to reformatories, and thus bringing these institutions to bear on their criminal population. Liverpool is the only town which has done this, and we have already recorded the testimony of the chaplain as to the results. The magistrates of Manchester and Bristol have never sentenced a single girl to a reformatory (the two sent from these towns to Red Lodge were volunteers), though the former had so good an example near, and the latter has two large reformatories within its own precincts.

Thirdly. – The bulk of the children in these reformatories are under 14 years of age. Several of the schools, and among them that at Chelsea, decline receiving children above that age, conceiving justly that it is very undesirable, for many reasons, that older and younger girls should be in the same establishment. Separate schools are much required for older girls, whose condition greatly needs the saving help of a Christian hand.

Fourthly. – The educational condition of the delinquent class, in a large town like Liverpool, is much lower than the general average throughout the country. While about half of the whole number of the delinquents had a slight knowledge, at least, of reading, only three or four of the 67 Liverpool girls had any education beside what they had acquired in the gaol.

Fifthly. – Orphanage is not the cause of crime among these children, little more than one-tenth of them having lost both parents. Nearly one-half, however, have lost one parent, and a large proportion of these have a step-father or mother. In almost all cases which have been investigated, the delinquency of the child is directly traceable to the bad character of the parents, or, if the surviving parent is respectable, to the unkind treatment of a step-mother.

These few remarks will show how rich a mine of instruction, as to the causes of juvenile crime and the condition of the children, may be worked by an examination of the histories of those who fill the reformatory schools.

Chapter 52

Frederick Howard Wines: Crime in the 1880 U.S. census, 1888

The gathering and analysis of statistics on crime for the 1880 U.S. dicennial census were the responsibility of Frederick Howard Wines, a leading social reformer and man closely familiar with the misuses of crime data (see Chapter 36). That statistics on criminals ["delinguents"] were reported in the same census volume with statistics on "defectives" (the blind, deaf-mute, and idiotic) and "dependents" (paupers and the insane) was a legacy of degeneration theory, which conceived of the three as interrelated and indeed interchangeable categories.

Wines begins his commentary with straightforward analysis of the figures: there are fewer prisoners than insane, idiots, or paupers; there are ten times more men than women in prison; and the rates for foreigners and "colored" are higher than for native-born whites. Prisoners are mainly between 20 and 30 years of age and they tend to stop committing crimes as they grow older (the aging-out effect much remarked by today's lifecourse criminologists). There are many elderly prisoners who, in Wines' opinion, should be released "on the ground of humanity," just as children in prison should be removed to better surroundings.

Wines deplores the inadequacies of the federal government's crime statistics, and he all but begs for the creation of something like today's Uniform Crime Reports, a compilation that will give a national overview of crime in the United States. He himself attempts to put togther such an overview here; in its general patterns, the picture he constructs of crime in 1880 is similar to that of the early twenty-first century.

Wines estimates the extent to which the "colored" population is over-represented in prison and tries to explain it. In addition, he attacks the lease system practiced in the South, whereby states lease their prisoners to private farmers and businessmen instead of housing them in jails. Another criminal justice practice that comes under attack here is what Wines discovers to be over-arrest – police abusing their power of arrest.

This extract comes from pp. xix–xxviii and xlvi–liv of Wines's "Introductory remarks" to the *Report on the Defective, Dependent, and Delinquent Classes of the Population of the United States, as Returned at the Tenth Census (June 1, 1880)* (Washington: Government Printing Office, 1888).

FREDERICK HOWARD WINES: CRIME IN THE 1880 U.S. CENSUS

There are more insane in proportion to the population than there are of any other class. After the insane follow, in order, the idiots, the paupers, the prisoners, the blind, and the deaf.

The male sex is more liable to each of the forms of misfortune enumerated, except insanity, than the female sex. The preponderance of insanity is among women. . . .

The general facts here stated affect the geographical distribution of misfortune by states and territories. In the northern states, with their large foreign population, the ratio of insanity, pauperism, and crime is naturally larger than in the south. But the negro population is also more largely criminal and more subject to idiocy than are the foreign-born. Where the female sex preponderates, as it does in the northeastern states, the ratio of insanity is of necessity increased. . . .

Broadly speaking, the ratio of prisoners of the male sex is ten times as great as that of the female; the ratio among foreigners is nearly twice as great as among the native-born; and among the colored nearly three times as great as among whites. It is considerably greater among the colored than among the foreign population. These statements are true of the table as a whole, but with variations, and with an occasional exception. (Observe the native and foreign ratios in Dakota, Delaware, Nebraska, North Carolina, and Utah; and the white and colored ratios in New Mexico. The ratio of foreign prisoners is also greater than that of colored in Alabama, Florida, Georgia, Louisiana, Mississippi, Montana, New Mexico, Virginia, and Washington.)

The states and territories which have the largest percentage of prisoners are Wyoming, Nevada, and California; next to them are the District of Columbia and Massachusetts; then Texas, Colorado, and Montana; which are followed by New York. Leaving the "far" west out of view, if the number of prisoners is any indication of the volume of crime, crime is more prevalent in the east than in the west, and in the north than in the south.

In respect to female prisoners, Massachusetts, New York, and the District of Columbia are away in the lead.

It is worthy of remark that the ratio of colored prisoners in the south is much less than in the north; it is greater in the "border" states than in those farther south, with the exception of Texas. . . .

The average age of prisoners is twenty-nine years and a little more than seven months. A little more than one-fourth of them are under twenty-three years of age; rather more than one-third of them are under twenty-five; and more than one-half of them are under twenty-eight. Their youth is a very striking fact. It indicates that, even under our imperfect prison system, a very large number of criminals, after reaching middle life, either abandon a career of crime as unprofitable, or they become more cautious and induce or compel younger men to take the active risk of the criminal enterprises in which they are interested, or their lives are cut short by habits of vicious self-indulgence. But the youth of the great majority of those detained in prisons ought to be regarded as an incentive and an inspiration to more earnest efforts for their reformation. Very nearly one-half of them have passed their twentieth birthday, but are still under the age of thirty years.

The very young reported as prisoners are, as previously suggested, not prisoners in fact, but are probably the children of prisoners, who have been permitted to remain with their mothers undergoing sentence. Some of them were no doubt born in prison. It is true, nevertheless, that too many children are committed to prison for alleged offenses who have no business to be there. Some of them have not reached the age of legal liability; and, in any event, their place is in a reformatory institution for children. And the detention of children in jails, while awaiting commitment to a reformatory institution, is an outrage, from the effects of which they can scarcely be expected to recover; especially where the county authorities have failed to make provision for their separate detention, and they are thrown into immediate and unrestricted contact with old and hardened offenders.

The number of very aged prisoners reported is surprising: There are, over ninety years old, 8; over eighty, 46; over seventy, 283; and over sixty, 1,376. Most of these are probably life-prisoners, or they have been sentenced for very long terms, amounting, in some instances, to a life sentence. It is, on the ground of humanity, desirable that the law should provide some method of terminating the imprisonment of aged convicts, who are no longer capable of any injury to society.

The number of children of school age in prison is between seven and eight hundred; but there are between four and five thousand children of school age and about as many more who are under school age in the almshouses of this country, where they are compelled to associate with the dregs of humanity. No public duty is more imperative than that of removing these children from their debasing and degrading surroundings, and placing them either in suitable institutions or in private families, in order to afford them the chance of success in life to which they are entitled. . . .

No part of this entire investigation, in my opinion, is more important than that which relates to crime and punishment. The question of crime, in its relation to government, is fundamental; to deal with crime is the primary purpose of government, and its efficiency may be said to be measured by the degree of its success in preventing and repressing it. Yet the statistics of crime are deplorably meager and inadequate. When compared with the judicial statistics of England and with the criminal statistics of many of the continental nations, they may almost be said to be a disgrace to us as a people. No doubt their imperfection is due in part to the refusal of the general government to deal with crime directly (with the exception of a few offenses against the federal statutes), and the relegation of this particular function to the governments of the several states. A study which I have caused to be made of the criminal statutes of the states and territories, for the purpose of comparing the character and amount of penalty prescribed by them for particular offenses, but which, unfortunately, is still incomplete, shows the most striking and illogical variations, not only in respect of the definition of crime, but in the methods of dealing with them. The imperfection of our criminal statistical records for the past one hundred years may further be attributed to the sparseness of the population and the infrequency of crime in our early history. None of the founders of the republic seem to have appreciated the benefit to posterity of complete information respecting crime and criminal procedure, in tabular form, year by year, upon a uniform system, such as to admit of easy and instructive comparison. I venture to express the wish that the government, through its Department of Justice, or some special bureau of the Department of the Interior, could be induced, even at this late day, to begin the collection of criminal statistics from all the states and territories, and their publication in an annual blue-book. . . .

Of all the crimes charged, 59 per cent. are against property, 20.5 per cent. against the person, 18.2 per cent. against society, and 2.3 per cent. against the Government. . . .

The crimes charged against men and boys number 48,845; against women and girls, 4,324. The men outnumber the women, very nearly twelve to one. This is partly because women are better than men, and partly because they are more timorous and less aggressive; if a wicked woman wants a crime committed, she can usually get a man to do it for her. Partly, too, the smaller proportion of women who are prisoners is due to the leniency of the officers of the law in dealing with them. Most of the offenses committed by women are not of a serious character. . . .

The crimes charged against white prisoners number 38,538; against colored prisoners, 14,631. The ratio of the colored population in prison is two and a half times as great as that of whites, being, for the latter, 964 to 1,000,000, but for the former 2,480. . . . The tendency manifested by them to commit crimes against property is 50 per cent. greater, and against the person it is 100 per cent. greater than among the native white population. But, if they are much more thievish than the whites and very much more violent, they are at least far more orderly. Their disregard for the rights of property is a natural consequence of the previous condition of slavery. Their propensity to murderous assaults and affrays may be attributed partly to their strongly emotional nature and partly to the fact that, in their new condition of personal freedom, they have not yet learned to adjust their relations with the stronger race. . . .

Taking the entire population together, the offense of most frequent occurrence is larceny; next on the list is burglary; assaults and affrays of all sorts rank third; then follow drunkenness and disorder, murder and manslaughter, offenses against chastity, and vagrancy, highway robbery, forgery, rape, and arson, in the numerical order here indicated. . . .

The ratio of crimes against the person, in comparison with the crimes against property, is greater among the foreign population than it is even among the negroes, and very much greater than among the native whites. The only nationalities which show a smaller ratio of crimes of passion and a larger one of crimes of interest than the native whites are British America, England, and Scotland. Those most given to crimes of violence are, in the order named: Italy, Spain, Russia, Switzerland, South America, Holland, and Ireland. The ratio among the Germans is less than among foreigners generally, but greater than among the Americans. . . .

The leasing of prisoners to private persons, for a pecuniary consideration, is the greatest blot upon our American prison system. It is, so far as it goes, a virtual abdication of the direct responsibility of the government for the treatment to be accorded to convicts. The best that can be said of it is that the states which have adopted it do not know what better to do. The leased prisoners are all in southern states. . . . Their condition is for the most part deplorable in the extreme, especially in the county chain-gangs. Of this class of convicts, 4,404, or nine-tenths, are negroes, and it is urged, in extenuation of the system, that the states named are unable to furnish suitable labor for negroes inside of prison walls. It is also said that the negro lacks pride of character, and that he does not regard confinement in the penitentiary as particularly disgraceful, nor does he dread it, as white prisoners do. The system is, however, so inherently vicious, involving, as it does, an enormous death-rate and an extraordinary number of successful attempts at escape, that it does not meet the approval of the better class of citizens in the southern states, and it is undoubtedly doomed to speedy extinction.

The presence of 350 insane convicts in hospitals for the insane is another unpleasant fact to contemplate. The insane who have not committed any crime ought not to be compelled to associate with convicts, sane or insane, and the necessity for their doing so is felt by themselves and by their friends to be an outrage. The excuse offered for the continuance of this practice is that the number of insane convicts in any given state is so small that it is impracticable to erect special hospitals for their accommodation. But this is not true of all states; and if it were, it would seem to me to be a very proper thing for the general government to construct and maintain an institution for insane convicts, to which they might be sent by the states to which they belong, and these states might pay an equitable charge for their custody and care. . . .

By dividing the total number of years of imprisonment assigned to each of these subdivisions by the number of convicts in each we obtain the average sentences, as follows: Native white, (male) 4.95 years, (female) 3.75; foreign-born white, (male) 5.23, (female) 2.78; colored, (male) 6.41, (female) 5.50; for all classes, 5.45. The colored convict receives, on the average, a sentence one year longer than that given to a white convict. The average sentence of the foreign-born white convict is, on the whole, a trifle shorter than that pronounced against the native white. If the foreign-born prisoner is a man he receives a somewhat longer sentence; but a foreign-born woman receives one year less than her native sister. . . .

The number of arrests exceeds 650,000, or 50 to each patrolman, or more than 1 to every 20 inhabitants. The enormous number of arrests, compared with the prison population, suggests the thought that either too many persons are arrested who are innocent of any actual offense, or too few are punished of those really guilty. Probably both statements are true; but there can be no question, in the minds of those who have given this subject attention, that the police are too free in the exercise of the power of making arrests which is vested in them. Many persons are undoubtedly arrested on suspicion without warrant, and after having been subjected to this ignominy are allowed to go free without trial; many more are hauled before the police magistrates and dismissed on the ground that the charges against them are of trivial consequence or not sustained by legal evidence. The injury done in this way to the self-respect of those arrested is beyond calculation, and doubtless many persons have been thus led into a life of crime who might otherwise have remained in a state of legal innocence. The practice followed in some cities of paying fees for arrests, or otherwise rewarding patrolmen for making them, is inherently vicious, and wherever it exists should be summarily suppressed.

Chapter 53

Enrico Ferri: The data of criminal statistics, 1884

Enrico Ferri (1856–1929), a professor of criminal law and socialist deputy in the Italian Parliament, was the most important of Lombroso's followers in terms of the development of criminology, for he emphasized the statistical and sociological side of research on crime – what he called *criminal sociology*. With Lombroso and another of Lombroso's students, Raffaele Garofalo, Ferri founded the Positivist school of criminology, a loose group of scholars who emphasized empiricism, science, and the gathering of statistics. While Ferri published a number of books, the best known was *Criminal Sociology* (originally 1884), a work that, because it was translated into English by 1884 (well before most of Lombroso's own works), became one of the conduits through which European criminological ideas traveled to England and the United States. Ferri's ideas shaped criminal justice policies in Argentina as well as Italy.

Ferri devotes a long central chapter of *Criminal Sociology* to "the data of criminal statistics," praising statistics as one of "the most efficacious instruments" for the study of crime. Only statistics can reveal to us the nature of crime as a social (as opposed to an individual) phenomenon. The levels of crime oscillate, partly from annual variations in factors such as food supplies and weather, partly from more general factors related to the "fundamental conditions of each nation." The Classical school (see Chapter 2), blind as it is to social influences on crime rates, traces crime to problems with penal systems and other aspects of punishment. (Ferri wittily dubs those who, when faced with increases in crime, demand more severity, "laxativists" – people who think a dose of punishment will provide a remedy.[1]) Similarly, politicians think that short-term governmental measures can reduce crime, but criminal statistics show that, in fact, deterrence has but a small effect on crime rates. Following Lombroso, Ferri insists that the solution to crime lies not in deterrence, but in crime prevention.

This extract comes from Enrico Ferri, *Criminal Sociology* (New York: D. Appleton and Company, 1898 [orginally 1884]), pp. 51–2, 65–6, 76–8, and 80–2.

ENRICO FERRI: THE DATA OF CRIMINAL STATISTICS

For moral and social facts, unlike physical and biological facts, experiment is very difficult, and frequently even impossible; observation in this domain brings the greatest aid to scientific research. And statistics are amongst the most efficacious instruments of such observation.

It is natural, therefore, that criminal sociology, after studying the individual aspect of the natural genesis of crime, should have recourse to criminal statistics for the study of the social aspect. Statistical information in the words of Krohne, "is the first condition of success in opposing the armies of crime, for it discharges the same function as the Intelligence department in war."

From statistics, in fact, the modern idea of the close relation between offences and the conditions of social life, in some of its aspects, and above all in certain particular forms, has most directly sprung.

The science of criminal statistics is to criminal sociology what histology is to biology, for it exhibits, in the conditions of the individual elements of the collective organism, the factors of crime as a social phenomenon. And that not only for scientific inductions, but also for practical and legislative purposes; for, as Lord Brougham said at the London Statistical Congress in 1860, "criminal statistics are for the legislator what the chart and the compass are for the navigator." . . .

In the movement of crime in each country it is necessary to distinguish special oscillations, more or less prolonged, of increase or decrease, from its general and permanent tendency. The latter is determined by the fundamental conditions of each nation, physical and social, apart from the purely artificial section of transgressions brought into existence by new laws. The special oscillations, on the other hand, are determined by the annual variations in this or that factor of the more numerous offences; that is to say, by abundance or scantiness of the harvests, by the annual variations of temperature, by industrial and political crises, and the like.

The oblivion of this marked distinction, coupled with the prejudices of the scientific schools, and even of political parties, leads to some curious disagreements, and to lively discussions on the results of criminal statistics. For on one side the champions of the classical school plainly see that the persistent increase of crimes and offences amounts to a proof of that breakdown of penal systems, practical and theoretical, which have hitherto been applied – as was admitted by Holtzendorff. And on the other hand, the increase of crimes is denied or affirmed for the purpose of supporting or attacking some particular ministry. For, in parliaments more than elsewhere, there is always a deep-seated and vivacious prejudice, a kind of social artificiality, which causes men to think that the condition of States, moral and economic, is fundamentally determined far more by the action of this or that government than by natural factors, which are mainly superior to and outside of governments and politicians. . . .

Criminal statistics show that crime increases in the aggregate, with more or less notable oscillations from year to year, rising or falling in successive waves. Thus it is evident that the level of criminality in any one year is determined by the different conditions of the physical and social environment, combined with the hereditary tendencies and occasional impulses of the individual, in obedience to a law which I have called, in analogy with chemical phenomena, *the law of criminal saturation.*

Just as in a given volume of water, at a given temperature, we find a solution of a fixed quantity of any chemical substance, not an atom more or less, so in a given social environment, in certain defined physical conditions of the individual, we find the commission of a fixed number of crimes.

Our ignorance of many physical and psychical laws and of innumerable conditions of fact, will prevent us from obtaining a precise view of this level of criminality. But none the less is it the necessary and inevitable result of a given physical and social environment. Statistics show us, indeed, that the variations of this environment are always attended by consequential and proportional variations of crime. In France, for instance (and the observation will be found to apply to every country which possesses an extended series of criminal statistics), the number of crimes against the person varies but little in sixty-two years. The same thing holds good for England and Belgium, because their special environment is also less variable, by reason that hereditary dispositions and human passions cannot vary profoundly or frequently, except under the influence of exceptional disturbances of the weather, or of social conditions. In fact, the more serious variations in respect of crimes against the person in France have taken place either during political revolutions, or in years of excessive heat, or of exceptional abundance of meat, grain, and wine. This is illustrated by the exceptional increase of crime from 1849 to 1852. Minor offences against the person, on the contrary, which are more occasional, assaults and wounding, for example, vary in the main, as to their annual oscillations, with the abundance of the wine harvest, whilst in their oscillations from month to month they display a characteristic increase during the vintage periods, from June to December, notwithstanding the constant diminution of other offences and crimes against the person.

On the other hand, crimes against property, and still more offences against property, show wide oscillations on account of the variability of the special environment, which is almost always in a condition of unstable equilibrium, as in periods of scarcity, and of commercial, financial and industrial crises, and so forth, whilst they are subject also to the influence of the physical environment. Crimes and offences against property display extraordinary increases in the severest winter seasons, and diminutions in milder winters.

And this correspondence between the more general, powerful, and variable physical and social factors of crime, as well as its more characteristic manifestations such as thefts, wounding, and indecent assaults, is so constant and so direct that, when I was studying the annual movement of criminality in

France, and perceived some extraordinary oscillation in the crimes and offences, I foresaw that in the annals of the year I should find mention of an agricultural or political crisis, or an exceptional winter or summer in the records of the weather. So that with a single column of a table of criminal statistics I was able to reconstruct the historical condition of a country in its more salient features. In this way psychological experiment again confirmed the truth of the law of criminal saturation. . . .

Two fundamental conclusions of criminal sociology may be drawn from this law of criminal saturation.

The first is that it is incorrect to assert a mechanical regularity of crime, which from Quetelet's time has been much exaggerated. There has been a too literal insistance on his famous declaration that "the budget of crime is an annual taxation paid with more preciseness than any other"; and that it is possible to calculate beforehand how many homicides, poisoners, and forgers we shall have, because "crimes are generated every year in the same number, with the same punishments, in the same proportions." And one constantly meets with this echo of the statisticians, that "from year to year crimes against the person vary at the most by one in twenty-five, and those against property by one in fifty"; or, again, that there is "a law of limitation in crime, which does not vary by more than one in ten."

This opinion, originated by Quetelet and other statisticians after an inquiry confined to the more serious crimes, and to a very short succession of years, has already been refuted, in part by Maury and Rhenisch, and more plainly by Aberdare, Mayr, Messedaglia and Minzloff.

In fact, if the level of criminality is of necessity determined by the physical and social environment, how could it remain constant in spite of the continual variations, sometimes very considerable, of this same environment? That which does remain fixed is the proportion between a given environment and the number of crimes: and this is precisely the law of criminal saturation. But the statistics of criminality will never be constant to one rule from year to year. There will be a dynamical but not a statical regularity.

Thus the element of fixity in criminal sociology consists in asserting, not the fatality or predestination of human actions, including crimes, but only their necessary dependence upon their natural causes, and therewith the possibility of modifying effects by modifying the activity of these causes. And, indeed, even Quetelet himself recognised this when he said, "If we change the social order we shall see an immediate change in the facts which have been so constantly reproduced. Statisticians will then have to consider whether the changes have been useful or injurious. These studies therefore show how important is the mission of the legislator, and how responsible he is in his own sphere for all the phenomena of the social order."

The second consequence of the law of criminal saturation, one of great theoretical importance, is that the penalties hitherto regarded, save for a few platonic declarations, as the best remedies for crime, are less effectual than they are supposed to be. For crimes and offences increase and diminish by a combination of other causes, which are far from being identical with the punishments lightly written out by legislators and awarded by judges.

Note

1   Enrico Ferri, *Criminal Sociology* (New York: D. Appleton and Company, 1898), p. 97.

Sociological approaches to crime

Sociological approaches to crime

Introduction to Part X

Biological theories dominated nineteenth-century criminology, and eugenics, a particularly virulent biological theory, dominated late nineteenth-century discussions of solutions to crime, at least in English-speaking countries (Chapters 46 and 47). However, this preference for biological answers and solutions was supplemented by a strong undercurrent of sociological criminology. One example can be found in an 1833 commentary on female crime and the causes of crime more generally by the political scientist Francis Lieber (Chapter 54). Another appears in a mid-century discussion of urbanization and crime by Friedrich Engels (Chapter 55). Henry Mayhew's and John Binny's study of *The Criminal Prisons of London*, too, includes sociological passages such as the one reproduced here on the causes of female criminality (Chapter 56). But indeed, many of the earlier extracts in the present volume illustrate sociological approaches to crime, including Lacassagne's much-quoted metaphor for criminals' relationship to their social milieu (Chapter 35) and all of the material on statistics (Part IX).

Toward the century's end, several sophisticated sociologists moved beyond analysis of specific variables like sex and urbanization to locate crime in larger contexts. For example, the multi-competent Gabriel Tarde, a French lawyer and sociologist, proposed a theory of imitation to explain criminal behavior (Chapter 57). In the United States, the famous sociologist Edward Alsworth Ross focused not on crime, but social control, the forces involved in maintaining order (Chapter 58). Again, in France, the sociologist Émile Durkheim courageously concluded that crime is far from the destructive force it is usually pictured; rather, Durkheim writes (Chapter 59), crime is a normal and indeed useful phenomenon. In Italy, Enrico Ferri projected a program of punishment based on sociological reasoning (Chapter 60). The section ends with an extract (Chapter 61) from the work of W. E. B. DuBois, an analysis of the causes of Negro crime and poverty, which in some respects continues to apply to racial differences in crime rates.

Chapter 54

Francis Lieber: Sex differences in crime, 1833

Francis Lieber (1798–1872) was one of the first American theorists to approach crime and criminal justice sociologically. Born in Germany, Lieber participated in various political movements before moving to Boston in 1827, where he helped to found the *Encyclopedia Americana*. He soon published a book on penology, and it was during this period in his long life that he befriended Beaumont and Tocqueville, the Frenchmen who were sent from Europe to gather information on the American prison system. When Beaumont and Tocqueville produced *On the Penitentiary System in the United States*, Lieber translated it, adding his own introduction and appending voluminous notes that made the book almost as much his as it was the authors'. Lieber went on to teach political science and history at what is now the University of South Carolina and became influential as a diplomat, economist, and legal theorist.

In the first part of this extract, Lieber discusses the causes of female crime; this was perhaps the first extended sociological analysis of that topic in the United States. Later, in his introduction, Lieber speaks of the causes of crime more generally.

The extract comes from a reprint of Gustave de Beaumont and Alexis de Tocqueville, *On the Penitentiary System in the United States and its Application in France* (originally Philadelphia: Carey, Lea & Blanchard, 1833; repr. New York: Augustus M. Kelley, 1970), pp. vi, xiii–xvii, and xxiv–xxv.

FRANCIS LIEBER: SEX DIFFERENCES IN CRIME

In the work of which I offer a translation, the authors give the result of their minute inquiry into an institution {prisons – N.R.}, which, besides its importance to all mankind, has for Americans the additional interest of having originated with them, and been brought to a high degree of perfection. . . .

I have added numerous notes, sometimes when I differed in opinion with the authors, sometimes further to elucidate their statements. . . .

There is one point . . . connected with this special topic, to which I should invite the reader's attention for a few moments longer – the imprisonment of women. It is a branch of administration of penal justice, much and unfortunately neglected in our country.

In all countries women commit less crimes than men, but in none is the disproportion of criminals of the two sexes so great as in ours. The authors of the present work have given some interesting comparative tables on this subject, and I have stated my views on some of the causes of this fact. Unhappily, the small number of crimes committed in our country by women, has caused a comparative neglect of female criminals. Public attention has hardly turned itself toward this subject, and yet none claims it in a higher degree.

The influence of women, as wives and mothers, upon their family, and also, if they stand single in society, upon those who are in some connexion with them, is, generally speaking, greater than that of men, as husbands, fathers, or single, upon the morals of those who surround or are connected with them. The influence of woman upon manners in society, is not greater than that which she may exercise on morals, and even upon crimes, in those classes whose wants expose them more to commit offences than others. A prudent and moral mother, may, in a great degree, counteract in her family the unhappy consequences of her husband's intemperate or dissolute life, much more than it is possible for an honest and industrious husband to counteract the melancholy effects of the bad conduct of an immoral wife. The wife's sphere is supremely that of domestic life; there is the circle of activity for which she is destined, and there, consequently, she has the greatest influence; and the lower we descend in the scale of society, the greater the influence of woman in her family. If she is unprincipled, the whole house is lost, whilst, if she walks on the path of virtue and religion, she is the safest support of a son, thrown upon the agitated sea of life, or of a husband, oppressed by misfortune or misery, and beset by a thousand temptations. That tender age, in which the very seeds of morality must be sown and fostered in the youthful soul, is much more dependant upon the mother's care, than upon that of the father – in all working classes it is almost solely dependant upon the former. A woman given to intemperance, and, what is generally connected with it, to violence and immoral conduct in most other respects, is sure to bring up as many vagabonds and prostitutes as she has male and female children; and I believe I am right in stating, that the injury done to society by a criminal woman, is in most cases much greater than that suffered from a male criminal. . . .

To all this must be added the fact, known to all criminalists, that a woman once renouncing honesty and virtue, passes over to the most hideous crimes which women commit, with greater ease than a man proceeds from his first offence to the blackest crimes committed by his sex. There is a shorter distance between a theft committed by a woman and her readiness to commit murder by poison, or arson, from jealousy or hatred, than between forgery or theft committed by a man, and murder or piracy. A male criminal may be a thief for a long series of years, and yet as unwilling to steep his hands in the blood of a fellow man, as many honest men; a person may commit depredation upon public property for his whole life, and yet shudder at the idea of highway robbery. With women this is not often the case. It seems, moreover, that the majority of those characters in the annals of crimes at which we shudder most, have been females. That crime, the most revolting to human nature – poisoning, has found its blackest and foulest adepts among the women. . . .

It appears, then, from the preceding observations, that a woman, when she commits a crime, acts more in contradiction to her whole moral organization, i. e. must be more depraved, must have sunk already deeper than a man. She abandons shame as much as a man, who commits the same; but shame is of still greater moral importance to her than to him.

I have thought I found in these arguments also, the reasons why, in all countries, girls, in houses of refuge for juvenile offenders, are so much more difficult to be reclaimed than boys; and that it is almost impossible to reclaim them, if they have been prostitutes. . . .

We should be wrong in concluding from the small number of crimes committed by women, compared with those committed by men, that there is a greater moral capacity in women in general; and thence again, that penitentiaries for females are comparatively unimportant. Women commit fewer crimes from three causes chiefly: 1. because they are, according to their destiny and the consequent place they occupy in civil society, less exposed to temptation or to inducement to crime; their ambition is not so much excited, and they are naturally more satisfied with a dependant situation; 2. they have not the courage or strength necessary to commit a number of crimes which largely swell the lists of male convicts, such as burglary, robbery, and forcible murder; 3. according to their position in society they cannot easily commit certain crimes, such as bigamy, forgery, false arrest, abuse of official power, revolt, &c. There are some crimes they cannot commit at all, such as rape; but there are on the other hand, crimes which men cannot commit, as abortion; or to which they are not so easily induced, as infanticide. According to the *Compte général de l'Administration de la Justice criminelle* (in France) for 1826 and 1827, we find that in 1826, 5712 men, and 1276 women were accused of crimes. . . .

Are we then justifiable, after all these considerations, in not providing more effectually for the correction of female convicts? The only remaining question can be; are separate penitentiaries for females required? I believe they are, if the Pennsylvania penitentiary system is not adopted, and with that system a matron at least will be necessary for the special superintendence of the female prisoners; she is quite indispensable if the Auburn system is applied to women as well as men; she alone can enforce the order of this system, whilst it is nearly impossible for male keepers. The whole spirit of opposition in womankind is raised against him. . . .

A minute knowledge of all co-operating circumstances is nowhere more indispensable, in order to arrive at just conclusions, than in the statistics of crimes. There are certain laws which experience teaches us, and if we disregard them we shall continually be liable to draw false conclusions; for instance, that certain causes, as an unusually cold winter, famine, stagnation of business, and poverty, caused by war, &c., never fail to effect a rapid increase of crimes, whilst the ceasing of these causes by no means effects a proportionally rapid decrease of crime. These considerations respecting the increase or decrease of crime, are not only important in regard to prison discipline, but also as to the progress of morality, or the demoralization of mankind in general.

Civilization certainly increases the number of tried crimes and offences, for two very simple reasons: 1. because it increases the opportunity of crime, since it increases the variety of pursuits and mutual relations between men; every progress in industry offers naturally to the wicked a new opportunity for abusing this industry, or the new relations which it creates between men; civilization, moreover, increases our wants and our ambition; 2. because it increases at the same time the means and opportunities for prosecutions of crime. It sounds paradoxical, when Pangloss [a character in *Candide*, a novel by Voltaire – N.R.], shipwrecked on the coast of Portugal, drew the inference from seeing men in chains that he was in a civilized country; yet he was right considering his time, and it may be safely said, that a community of any magnitude, within which no crime is committed, cannot be far advanced in civilization. There is a latent criminality in such communities, which shows itself whenever opportunity offers. If the wants of men are reduced to the simplest food which the field offers, and to clothing which is provided by their own flocks, they are easily satisfied, and hardly an opportunity exists for the numerous crimes and offences committed against property in a civilized and active society. There is or may be an absence of crime, but between this and positive morality there is yet a vast difference. Mankind are destined for civilization, and the great problem is to arrive through civilization at morality.

Chapter 55

Friedrich Engels: Urbanization and crime, 1845

An earlier passage (Chapter 23) reproduced parts of Friedrich Engels's description of the life of the industrial proletariat and its criminogenic consequences. This extract reprints some of his remarks on capitalism as an ultimate cause of crime. Engels describes the anomic condition of people who "have been forced to sacrifice the best qualities of their human nature" and wrung dry by two primary effects of capitalism: urbanism and industrialization.

Engels's *Condition of the Working Class in England* appeared in German in 1845, but was not published in English until 1887. This extract comes from pp. 36–8 of an edition edited by David McLellan (Oxford: Oxford University Press, 1993).

FRIEDRICH ENGELS: URBANIZATION AND CRIME

The great towns

A town, such as London, where a man may wander for hours together without reaching the beginning of the end, without meeting the slightest hint which could lead to the inference that there is open country within reach, is a strange thing. This colossal centralization, this heaping together of two and a half millions of human beings at one point, has multiplied the power of this two and a half millions a hundredfold; has raised London to the commercial capital of the world, created the giant docks and assembled the thousand vessels that continually cover the Thames. I know nothing more imposing than the view which the Thames offers during the ascent from the sea to London Bridge. The masses of buildings, the wharves on both sides, especially from Woolwich upwards, the countless ships along both shores, crowding ever closer and closer together, until, at last, only a narrow passage remains in the middle of the river, a passage through which hundreds of steamers shoot by one another; all this is so vast, so impressive, that a man cannot collect himself, but is lost in the marvel of England's greatness before he sets foot upon English soil.

But the sacrifices which all this has cost become apparent later. After roaming the streets of the capital a day or two, making headway with difficulty through the human turmoil and the endless lines of vehicles, after visiting the slums of the metropolis, one realizes for the first time that these Londoners have been forced to sacrifice the best qualities of their human nature, to bring to pass all the marvels of civilization which crowd their city; that a hundred powers which slumbered within them have remained inactive, have been suppressed in order that a few might be developed more fully and multiply through union with those of others. The very turmoil of the streets has something repulsive, something against which human nature rebels. The hundreds of thousands of all classes and ranks crowding past each other, are they not all human beings with the same qualities and powers, and with the same interest in being happy? And have they not, in the end, to seek happiness in the same way, by the same means? And still they crowd by one another as though they had nothing in common, nothing to do with one another, and their only agreement is the tacit one, that each keep to his own side of the pavement, so as not to delay the opposing streams of the crowd, while it occurs to no man to honour another with so much as a glance. The brutal indifference, the unfeeling isolation of each in his private interest becomes the more repellent and offensive, the more these individuals are crowded together, within a limited space. And, however much one may be aware that this isolation of the individual, this narrow self-seeking is the fundamental principle of our society everywhere, it is nowhere so shamelessly barefaced, so self-conscious as just here in the crowding of the great city. The dissolution of mankind into monads, of which each one has a separate principle and a separate purpose, the world of atoms, is here carried out to its utmost extreme.

Hence it comes, too, that the social war, the war of each against all, is here openly declared. Just as in Stirner's recent book, people regard each other only as useful objects; each exploits the other, and the end of it all is, that the stronger treads the weaker under foot, and that the powerful few, the capitalists, seize everything for themselves, while to the weak many, the poor, scarcely a bare existence remains.

What is true of London, is true of Manchester, Birmingham, Leeds, is true of all great towns. Everywhere barbarous indifference, hard egotism on one hand, and nameless misery on the other, everywhere social warfare, every man's house in a state of siege, everywhere reciprocal plundering under the protection of the law, and all so shameless, so openly avowed that one shrinks before the consequences of our social state as they manifest themselves here undisguised, and can only wonder that the whole crazy fabric still hangs together.

Since capital, the direct or indirect control of the means of subsistence and production, is the weapon with which this social warfare is carried on, it is clear that all the disadvantages of such a state must fall upon the poor. For him no man has the slightest concern. Cast into the whirlpool, he must struggle through as well as he can. If he is so happy as to find work, i.e. if the bourgeoisie does him the favour to enrich itself by means of him, wages await him which scarcely suffice to keep body and soul together; if he can get no work he may steal, if he is not afraid of the police, or starve, in which case the police will take care that he does so in a quiet and inoffensive manner. During my residence in England, at least twenty or thirty persons have died of simple starvation under the most revolting circumstances, and a jury has rarely been found possessed of the courage to speak the plain truth in the matter. Let the testimony of the witnesses be never so clear and unequivocal, the bourgeoisie, from which the jury is selected, always finds some back door through which to escape the frightful verdict, death from starvation. The bourgeoisie dare not speak the truth in these cases, for it would speak its own condemnation. But indirectly, far more than directly, many have died of starvation, where long continued want of proper nourishment has called forth fatal illness, when it has produced such debility that causes which might otherwise have remained inoperative brought on severe illness and death. The English working men call this "social murder", and accuse our whole society of perpetrating this crime perpetually. Are they wrong?

Chapter 56

Henry Mayhew and John Binny: Female criminality, 1862

Earlier, Chapter 24 reproduced Mayhew's and Binny's vivid description of London's jail-hardened delinquents; and Chapter 37 extracted from their material on habitual offenders. Much of their *Criminal Prisons of London* comprises descriptive sociology, but elsewhere, as in the passage selected here, they go beyond descriptive to analytical sociology, identifying social factors that breed crime.

In this commentary on female criminality, the authors begin by reaching the conclusions that follow from statistics and observation: women are less criminal than men, and most female criminals are prostitutes. At first Mayhew and Binny seem to be locating the causes within the individual criminals, citing laziness and shamelessness as the primary causes. As they go on, however, they grapple with the causes of shamelessness in prostitutes, tracing them to the women's social condition. They then embark on a remarkably sympathetic analysis of the relationship of prostitutes to their "fancy-men" or pimps.

This extract comes from the original edition of *The Criminal Prisons of London* (London: Griffin, Bohn, and Company, 1862): pp. 454–6 and 466–7.

HENRY MAYHEW AND JOHN BINNY: FEMALE CRIMINALITY

Female prisoners generally

As a body, women are considerably less criminal than men. We know not whether this be due to the fact of the female nature being more kindly or less daring than that of the male; but so it is – the returns of the country, for a long series of years, showing that in every 100 prisoners there are but some 20 odd women; so that males would appear to be, at least, four times more vicious than females; for, according to the tables in the census, there is a greater proportion of the latter than the former in the country; and therefore, if the criminal tendencies were equal in either sex, our criminal records should exhibit a greater number of women than men annually accused of crime.

Moreover, if it could be possible to obtain accurate returns as to the number of "public women" throughout the country, it would be found that by far the greater proportion of the female offenders is derived from that class; and thus it would be proven, that among the chaste portion of the female sex crime is comparatively unknown.

There would appear, then, to be, generally speaking, but one great vice appertaining to the gentler sex, viz., prostitution; and the reason of this would seem to be two-fold. The great mass of crime in the country we have shown, by an analysis of the Government returns, to be pursued regularly as a means of subsistence by criminals. Hence, what theft is to the evil-disposed among men, street-walking is to the same class among women – an easy mode of living; so that those females, among the poorer classes of society, who are born to labour for their bread, but who find work inordinately irksome to their natures, and pleasure as inordinately agreeable to them, have no necessity to resort to the more daring career of theft to supply their wants, but have only to trade upon their personal charms in order to secure the apparent luxury of an idle life. . . .

The other reason why prostitution constitutes the chief delinquency of the female sex, is because the indulgence in it demands the same insensibility to shame on the part of woman as dishonesty in man. Mandeville, long ago, showed that society was held together chiefly by the love of approbation and dread of disapprobation among mankind; and, though the philosopher endeavoured to prove, what is obviously absurd, that there is no right nor wrong, except such matters as have come, by general consent, to be universally praised or blamed, nevertheless, all must admit, that the desire to be admired, and the disinclination to be despised, which exists in the breast of all people, is one of the most important instruments in the machinery of human society.

Indeed, it is this continual fear of what the world will say – this ever-active sensibility as regards public opinion – the perpetual craving for credit and reputation and standing among the various classes of people – that prompts and keeps the great mass of mankind to righteous courses, far more than any moral sense or any aspiration to fashion their actions according to the standard of the Great Exemplar and Teacher; for the eye, which men fancy to be ever watching and weighing their conduct, is that of this same public opinion rather than of All-perfection and Justice. An external standard of admiration, instead of an internal principle of righteousness, rules the world – a dread of shame among men, rather than an innate hatred of what is iniquitous – whilst what is termed civilization consists principally in the development of human vanity to an inordinate degree; and hence the *polite* and artificial form of society, though apparently more moral, is assuredly more false and dishonest than the natural and barbaric mode of life. . . . But those whose powers are the weakest, and who are, therefore, the most diffident as to their own endowments, not only require to have their faith continually sustained, but naturally find the greatest delight in approbation. Hence it is that the weakest people are the vainest, or most open to flattery, as well as alive to shame; whilst those who have the greatest confidence in themselves are ever the proudest, and but little affected even by the contempt of others.

Thus, then, it is that women, being the weaker portion of humanity, are naturally not only more fond of being admired, but more bashful or morally timid than men; so that shame is the great ruling principle of their lives; whilst those who become callous to it, as well as reckless as to how their acts are regarded by others, are viewed by the rest of the world as creatures in whom the brightest feminine qualities have been effaced, and whose natures and passions are subject to none of the ordinary principles of restraint. The reason, therefore, why prostitution is the one chief delinquency of the female sex is because it is the one capital act of shamelessness, and that which consequently fits the creature for the performance of any other iniquity. Hence we can readily understand how it is that the great mass of female criminals are drawn from the ranks of the street-walkers of the country; for, as juvenile delinquency constitutes the apprenticeship of the habitual male offender, so prostitution is the initiatory stage of criminality among women. . . .

Shame is *as* unnatural to woman as it is for mankind to love their enemies, and to bless those that persecute them. It is *as much* an educated sentiment as is the appreciation of the beautiful and the good, and *as thoroughly* the result of training as is a sense of decency and even virtue; for in the same manner as the conscience itself remains dormant in our bosoms till developed, like the judgment, or indeed any other faculty, by long teaching and schooling; so shame itself, though the main characteristic of civilized woman, may continue utterly unawakened in the ruder forms of female nature.

Many of the wretched girls seen in our jails have, we verily believe, never had the sentiment educated in them, living almost the same barbarous life as they would, had they been born in the interior of Africa. . . .

And yet they who have studied the idiosyncrasy of these degraded women know that they are capable, even in their degradation, of the very highest sacrifices for those they love. The majority of the *habitual* female criminals are connected with some low brute of a man who is either a prize-fighter, or cab-driver, or private soldier, or pickpocket, or coiner, or costermonger, or, indeed, some such character. And for this lazy and ruffian fellow, there is no indignity nor cruelty they will not suffer, no atrocity that they are not ready to commit, and no infamy that they will hesitate to perform, in order that he may continue to live half-luxuriously with them in their shame. A virtuous woman's love is never of the same intensely passionate and self-denying character as marks the affection of her most abject sister. To comprehend this, we must conceive the wretched woman shunned by almost all the world for her vice –

we must remember that, in many instances, she has lost every relative and friend, and that even her parents (whose love and care is the last of all to cease) have cast her from them, and that she is *alone* in the great wilderness of life and care – friendless at the very time when she needs and longs most for a friend to protect and console her. We must endeavour, too, to conceive what must be the feelings of such a woman for the *one* person, amid all mankind, who seems to sympathize with her, and who is ready to shield her from the taunts and cuffs of the world; for most strange indeed it is, that those who seem to be the least like women of all, and appear to be the least loving and self-denying in their natures, should be characterized even in their debasement by the tenderest attribute of the female constitution, and remarkable for a love that is more generous, more devoted, more patient, and more indomitable than any other. . . .

Chapter 57

Gabriel Tarde: Imitation and crime, 1890

Gabriel Tarde (1843–1904) was one of the leaders of the French criminologists who, in the late nineteenth century, undertook to discredit the biological positivism of the Lombrosians and, alternatively, develop a social understanding of the causes of crime. A judge, statistician, sociologist, and scholar, Tarde joined Alexandre Lacassagne (Chapter 35) in editing the *Archives d'anthropologie criminelle*, the French counterpart to Lombroso's journal of criminal anthropology.

Tarde's *Penal Philosophy*, the book from which this extract derives, is an effort to explain crime in sociological terms. It begins with a long and witty refutation of Italian criminal anthropology (not reproduced here), after which Tarde puts forth his own theory – that criminal behavior, like other behavior, is caused by *imitation*, the tendency to copy the actions of others. In earlier historical periods, the tendency was for people in the lower social strata to imitate the habits (including the bad habits) of nobility and masters. More recently, imitation has begun more of a lateral spread, from cities to rural areas.

The first edition of *Penal Philosophy* was published in French in 1890, the fourth in 1903. In 1912 the book was translated into English as published as part of the prestigious Modern Criminal Science Series. I worked from the latter, as reprinted in 1968 (Montclair, NJ: Patterson Smith), using pp. 321–3, 326–40, and 416.

GABRIEL TARDE: IMITATION AND CRIME

The fact revealed by statistics that certain seasons or certain climates coincide with a certain recrudescence or a certain decrease of certain crimes no more proves the reality of the *physical causes* of crime than does the fact revealed by anthropology of a greater recurrence of ambidextrous, left-handed, or prognathous persons among malefactors prove the existence of a *criminal type* in the biological acceptation of that word. But this negative conclusion cannot satisfy us; and the physical or physiological explanation of crime having been set aside, we have now to show along what lines the laws of crime are to be sought. We shall find them in a special application of the general laws which appear to us to govern social science.

Preponderance of social causes. The tendency towards imitation

Before anything else, we ought summarily to define and analyze the powerful, generally unconscious, always partly mysterious, action by means of which we account for all the phenomena of society, namely imitation. In order to judge of its inherent power, we must first of all observe its manifestations among idiots. In them the imitative inclination is no stronger than in ourselves, but it acts without encountering the obstacle which is met with in our ideas, our moral habits, and our wishes. Now, a case is cited of an idiot who "after having taken part in the slaughtering of a pig took a knife and attacked a man." Others carry out the imitative tendency in setting fire to buildings.

All the important acts of social life are carried out under the domination of example. One procreates or one does not procreate, because of imitation; the statistics of the birth rate have shown us this. One kills or one does not kill, because of imitation; would we today conceive of the idea of fighting a duel or of declaring war, if we did not know that these things had always been done in the country which we inhabit? One kills oneself or one does not kill oneself, because of imitation; it is a recognized fact that suicide is an imitative phenomenon to the very highest degree. . . .

After this how can we doubt but that one steals or does not steal, one assassinates or does not assassinate, because of imitation? But it is especially in the great tumultuous assemblages of our cities that this characteristic force of the social world ought to be studied. The great scenes of our revolutions cause it to break out, just as great storms are a manifestation of the presence of the electricity in the atmosphere, while it remains unperceived though none the less a reality in the intervals between them. A *mob* is a strange phenomenon. It is a gathering of heterogeneous elements, unknown to one another; but as soon as a spark of passion, having flashed out from one of these elements, electrifies this confused mass, there takes place a sort of sudden organization, a spontaneous generation. This incoherence becomes cohesion, this noise becomes a voice, and these thousands of men crowded together soon form but a single animal, a wild beast without a name, which marches to its goal with an irresistible finality. The majority of these men had assembled out of pure curiosity, but the fever of some of them soon reached the minds of all, and in all of them there arose a delirium. The very man who had come running to oppose the murder of an innocent person is one of the first to be seized with the homicidal contagion, and moreover, it does not occur to him to be astonished at this. . . .

After these few words as to the force and the forms of imitation, we must set forth its general laws, which must be applied to crime as well as to every other aspect of societies. But the limits of this work will only allow us a brief indication of the subject. We already know that the example of any man, almost like the attraction of a body, radiates around himself, but with an intensity which becomes weaker as the distance of the men touched by his ray increases. "Distance" should not here be understood merely in the geometrical sense, but especially in the psychological sense of the word; the increase in the relations established by correspondence or by printing, of the intellectual communications of all kinds between fellow-citizens scattered over a vast territory, has the effect of diminishing in this sense the distance between them. Thus it may happen, let us repeat, that the honest example of an entire surrounding but distant society may be neutralized in the heart of a young vagabond by the influence of a few companions. . . .

It is especially in fostering the spread of example that a social hierarchy is useful; an aristocracy is a fountain reservoir necessary for the fall of imitation in successive cascades, successively enlarged. . . .

Strange as it may seem, there are serious reasons for maintaining that the vices and the crimes of today, which are to be found in the lowest orders of the people, descended to them from above. In every nascent or renascent society when the producing of wine becomes difficult or limited, drunkenness is a royal luxury and a privilege of the aristocracy. It is quite certain that the kings of Homer's time got drunk far more often than did their subjects. . . .

The smoking habit, at present so widespread in every sort of surroundings, perhaps already more widespread among the people than among the socially elect, where they have begun to combat this passion, was propagated in the same manner. James I of England, Roscher tells us, put a very heavy tax upon tobacco in 1604, "because," says the law, "the lower classes, incited by the example of the upper classes, impair their health, taint the air, and corrupt the soil." The irreligiousness of the masses, which today here and there contrasts with the relative religiousness of the last survivors of the old aristocracy, is just as much due to this same cause. Vagabondage, under its thousand and one existing forms, is an essentially plebeian offense; but by going back into the past, it would not be very difficult to connect our vagabonds, our street singers, with the noble pilgrims and the noble minstrels of the Middle Ages.

Poaching, another hotbed of crime, which in the past, together with smuggling, has played a part which may be compared with that played by vagabondage at the present time, is still more directly connected with the life of the lords. . . .

Poisoning is now a crime of the illiterate; as late as the seventeenth century it was the crime of the upper classes, as is proven by the epidemic of poisonings which flourished at the court of Louis XIV. . . .

Must not murder by bravos, by "bravi," so much used in Germany and Italy in the Middle Ages, have been the transition phase which homicide passed through in descending from the highest stratum of society to the lowest? The fact remains that the power to kill, from which was derived the right to kill, has been, in every primitive society, the distinguishing indication of the upper classes. . . .

Arson, the crime of the lower classes today, was one of the prerogatives of the feudal lords. "Did we not hear the Margrave of Brandenburg boasting one day of having, during his lifetime, burned one hundred and seventy villages?" Counterfeiting today takes refuge in a few caverns in the mountains, in a few underground places in towns; we know that for a long time it was a royal monopoly. Now governments limit themselves to sometimes putting false rumors in circulation. Finally theft, so degrading in our day, has had a brilliant past. Montaigne tells us, without being very indignant about it, that many young gentlemen of his acquaintance, to whom their fathers did not give enough money, got funds by stealing. . . .

What has just been said does not imply that there was a time, even during the most barbarous period, when murder, theft, rape, and arson were a monopoly belonging exclusively to the higher ranks of the nation; but it does mean that when a man of the lower ranks was found to be a murderer, a thief, a "struprator [rapist – N.R.]," an incendiary, he stood out by reason of the terror which he inspired, ennobled himself to a certain extent, and broke into government circles. . . .

While crime formerly spread, like every industrial product, like every good or bad idea, from the nobility to the people, and while the nobility, in those remote times, drew to itself the audacious and criminal elements of the people, today we can see crime spreading from the great cities to the country, from the capitals to the provinces, and these capitals and great cities having an irresistible attraction for the outcasts and scoundrels of the country, or the provinces, who hasten to them to become civilized after their own manner, a new kind of ennobling. For the time being this latter fact is a fortunate one for the provinces, which are being purified by means of this emigration and passing through an era of comparative security. Never, perhaps, in rural regions has there been less fear of assassination and even of robbery with violence than at the present time. But unfortunately the attraction of the great cities for criminals is closely connected with the influence exercised by them over the remainder of the nation, with the fascinating power their example has in all matters. As a consequence it is to be feared that the benefits derived from this betterment of conditions in the provinces is but temporary. The capitals send to the provinces not only their political and literary likes and dislikes, their style of wit or folly, the cut of their clothes, the shape of their hats and their accent, but they also send their crimes and their misdemeanors.

Indecent assault upon children is an essentially urban crime, as is demonstrated by its chart; in its spread it is seen to form a dark spot around the great cities. Each variety of murder or theft invented by evil genius is born or takes root in Paris, Marseilles, Lyons, etc., before becoming widespread throughout France. The series of corpses cut to pieces began in 1876 with the Billoir case and was for a long time confined to Paris, Toulouse, and Marseilles; but it was carried on in the Departments of Nièvre, Loir-et-Cher, and Eure-et-Loir. The feminine idea of throwing vitriol in the face of a lover is entirely Parisian; it was the widow Gras who, in 1875, had the honor of inventing this, or rather of re-inventing it. But I know of villages where this seed has borne fruit, and the peasant women themselves now try their hand at the handling of vitriol. . . .

With regard to thefts the same thing applies. There is not a single means of swindling employed at village fairs which did not first see the light of day upon a sidewalk of Paris. . . .

To sum up this entire chapter, we have every right, it seems to me, to conclude that criminality without any doubt, like every other branch of social activity, implies physiological and even physical conditions, but that, like industry especially, it is to be accounted for better than in any other way, by the general laws of imitation, in its local color as in its special force at each period of time, in its geographical distribution as in its historical trans-formations, in the varying proportion of its various motives or the unstable hierarchy of its varying degrees as in the succession of its changing methods. . . . It has been said that our body is a small quantity of condensed air, living in the air. Can it not be said that our soul is a small quantity of society incarnate, living in society? Born from society, it lives by means of society. . . .

Chapter 58

Edward Alsworth Ross: The system of social control, 1901

At the end of the nineteenth century, Edward Alsworth Ross became one of America's best-known sociologists through publication of a series of articles on the phenomenon he labeled *social control*.[1] Ross (1866–1951) concerned himself with not criminology per se, but rather social control – factors that maintain social order. From this perspective, crime control is an aspect of social order that can be deliberated, manipulated, and organized to increase or relax the mechanisms of order maintenance, according to current needs. In his book *Social Control*, from which this extract comes, law is one form of social control among many others (including sympathy, religion, and the sense of justice). Formal systems of social control are best operated by experts who work largely behind the scenes for the good of the social whole. Here we see Ross sharing his Progressive contemporaries' faith in experts who can run society according to scientific principles.

Ross's analysis makes crime itself almost disappear from consideration. Crime becomes a given, a lower-class phenomenon (there are holdovers in Ross's writing from criminal anthropology and scientific racism), something for Progressive experts to deal with professionally. Society becomes an abstract, complex social phenomenon for experts to mold and model for the good of the whole. This view, if chilly, offered a more sociologically sophisticated approach to crime than could be found in, for instance, contemporaneous debates on prison reform. While Ross viewed social control positively, his approach enabled some later theorists to conceptualize the criminal justice system as a possibly malign system of social control, one that functions (say) to maintain a black underclass.

Working from a 1920 reprint of the 1901 original, I have reproduced two short passages (pp. vii–viii and 395) that indicate how Ross used the term *social control* (although he never defined it precisely). Then I reproduce all of chapter 30, "The system of social control" (pp. 411–16).

EDWARD ALSWORTH ROSS: THE SYSTEM OF SOCIAL CONTROL

Preface

The foundation of this book was laid in a series of articles under the title "Social Control," contributed to the *American Journal of Sociology* between March, 1896, and May, 1898. . . .

All these studies fall within one narrow tract in the province of Sociology. Social Psychology, which term I apply to the branch of knowledge that deals with the psychic interplay between man and his environing society, falls into two sub-divisions. One of these, Social Ascendency, deals with the domination of society over the individual; the other, Individual Ascendency, – embracing such topics as invention, leadership, the rôle of great men, – deals with the domination of the individual over society. Social Ascendency is further divided into Social Influence, – mob mind, fashion, convention, custom, public opinion, and the like, – and Social Control. The former is occupied with the social domination which is without intention or purpose; the latter is concerned with that domination which is intended and which fulfils a function in the life of society. This work, therefore, deals with only one subdivision in the field of Social Psychology.

In this book I seek to determine how far the order we see all about us is due to influences that reach men and women from without, that is, *social* influences. . . .

In a really competitive society the hopelessly poor and wretched are, to a large extent, the weak and incompetent who have accumulated at the lower end of the social scale, because they or their parents have failed to meet the tests of the competitive system. In a society cleft by parasitism, on the other hand, the poor are poor because they are held under the harrow, and not because they are less capable and energetic than the classes that prey upon them.

Now a class of beaten people, a proletariat from which the industrially fittest have escaped or are escaping, has neither the will nor the strength to strain against the social system with the vigor of a resentful proletariat held down and exploited by means of artificial social arrangements. However sharply it may differentiate, however rude the clash of conflicting interests, a competitive society will still require no such elaborate apparatus of control as a parasitic society, with perhaps no greater contrasts of economic condition, will find it necessary to maintain. Moreover, its control will not exhibit the traits of class control, but will show the sincerity, spontaneity, and elasticity that mark the control that is truly social.

The vicissitudes of social control

Never do we find the social pressure uniform through a long period. There are times when society holds the individual as in a vise, and times when he wriggles almost from under the social knee. There are epochs when the corporate will is ascendant, and epochs when the individual is more and more. In other words, social control fluctuates between strong and weak, between more and less. . . .

The most likely and obvious cause of such vicissitudes is *change in social need*. The function of control is to preserve that indispensable condition of common life, social order. When this order becomes harder to maintain, there is a demand for more and better control. When this order becomes easier to maintain, the ever present demand for individual freedom and for toleration makes itself felt. The supply of social control is evoked, as it were, by the demand for it, and is adjusted to that demand.

The changes that rack the social frame and so lead to a tightening of all the nuts and rivets in it are nearly all connected with economic conditions. The multiplication of numbers or the decline of prosperity may make the struggle for existence more wolfish and harder to keep within bounds. New methods of production which sharpen economic contrasts may relax the natural bonds among men and so throw more strain on the artificial bonds. A static condition of industry may allow differences in wealth to be aggravated by accumulation through a number of generations. A bad institution, – a defective system of land tenure or inheritance or taxation, – working worse and worse as time goes on, may require stronger props to support it. Alien ethnic elements introduced among a people, one in blood and culture and hence fitted to get along smoothly, may lead to race or class tension. Social mis-selections which hinder the survival of the best breeds of men may in the course of centuries weaken character and necessitate the application of a moral truss. . . .

The system of social control

In respect to their fundamental character, it is possible to divide most of the supports of order into two groups. Such instruments of control as public opinion, suggestion, personal ideal, social religion, art, and social valuation draw much of their strength from the primal moral feelings. They take their shape from sentiment rather than utility. They control men in many things which have little to do with the welfare of society regarded as a corporation. They are aimed to realize not merely a social order but what one might term a *moral* order. These we may call *ethical*.

On the other hand, law, belief, ceremony, education, and illusion need not spring from ethical feelings at all. They are frequently the means deliberately *chosen* in order to reach certain ends. They are likely to come under the control of the organized few, and be used, whether for the corporate benefit or for class benefit, as the tools of policy. They may be termed *political*, using the word "political" in its original sense of "pertaining to policy."

Now, the prominence of the one group or the other in the regulative scheme depends upon the constitution of the society. The *political* instruments operating through prejudice or fear will be preferred: –

1   In proportion as the population elements to be held together are antipathetic and jarring.
2   In proportion to the subordination of the individual will and welfare by the scheme of control.
3   In proportion as the social constitution stereotypes differences of status.
4   In proportion as the differences in economic condition and opportunity it consecrates are great and cumulative.
5   In proportion as the parasitic relation is maintained between races, classes, or sexes.

In confirmation of these statements, we have but to recall that the chief influences which history recognizes as stiffening State, Church, Hierarchy, Tradition, are conquest, caste, slavery, serfdom, gross inequalities of wealth, military discipline, paternal regimentation, and race antipathies within the bosom of the group. The disappearance of any one of these conditions permits a mellowing and liberalizing of social control.

On the other hand the *ethical* instruments, being more mild, enlightening, and suasive, will be preferred: –

1   In proportion as the population is homogeneous in race.
2   In proportion as its culture is uniform and diffused.
3   In proportion as the social contacts between the elements in the population are many and amicable.
4   In proportion as the total burden of requirement laid upon the individual is light.
5   In proportion as the social constitution does not consecrate distinctions of status or the parasitic relation, but conforms to common elementary notions of justice.

In confirmation of these propositions, we have but to remember that the mild, democratic régime is now recognized as presupposing a homogeneous and enlightened population, free social intercourse, minimum interference with the individual, sanctity of the person, and equality before the law. When any of these conditions fail, the democratic forms soon become farcical.

Again, the instruments of control may be distinguished in respect to the functions that devolve upon them. There is a tendency to assign to each form of control that work for which it is best fitted. Law represses that undesirable conduct which is at once important and capable of clear definition. Central positive qualities – courage or veracity in man, chastity in woman – are taken in charge by the sense of honor or self-respect. The supernatural sanction is ordinarily reserved for those acts and abstinences requiring the utmost backing. Religion mounts guard over the ancient, unvarying fundamentals of group life, but takes little note of the temporary adjustments required from time to time. The taking of life or property, adultery, unfilial conduct, and false swearing encounter its full force; but not adulteration, stock gambling, or corporation frauds. In its code, as well as in its ritual and creed, religion betrays its archaic character.

In morals as well as in microscopes there is provided a major and a minor adjusting apparatus. In adaptability public opinion stands at one end of a series of which religion constitutes the other extreme. Connected with this there is a gradation in the nature of the sanction. Public opinion bans many things not unlawful, law may require much more than self-respect, and self-respect may be wounded by that which is not regarded as sinful. But the universality of the sanction widens as the scope of prohibition narrows. In the first case the offender encounters the public here and now, in the second the crystallized disapproval of society, in the third the opinion of generations of men who have conspired to frame a standard or ideal, and in the last case the frown of the Ruler of the Universe.

The champions of each detail of regulation strive, therefore, to get all these successive sanctions behind their pet commandments. The opponents of drinking, dancing, divorce, usury, horse racing, duelling, speculation, or prize-fighting strive to make these practices first blameworthy, then unlawful, then shameful, and finally sinful. But this massing of sanctions very naturally stirs up resistance. The attempt to get God against a new vice, such as liquor selling, always encounters fierce opposition from those who find themselves suddenly deprived of the odor of sanctity. New moral tests, like new party tests or new denominational tests, endanger ground already won, and so imperil the sanctions for the cardinal virtues. It is not well, therefore, to associate loss of honor with white lies or the Divine Displeasure with card playing. Sympathy, religious sentiment, self respect, sense of duty, fear, regard for public opinion, enlightened self-interest, – each of these motives has its due place and task and no one motive should be overworked.

Again, the agencies in the system of control differ in their vitality. All are not equally available throughout the life of a society.

Changes in knowledge, in the level of civilization, and in the nature of social requirements cause a method of control to wax or wane from age to age. We might compare the social order to a viaduct across some wooded ravine, which rests partly on timbers that slowly rot away, and partly on living, growing tree-trunks. Or, we might liken it to a bridge resting on piers, built some of stone which crumbles in time, and some of stone which hardens with exposure to the air. No doubt etiquette and ceremony have done their best work. The seer of visions and dreamer of dreams has had his day. The hero will never again be the pivot of order. The reign of custom with its vague terrors is about over. The assizes of Osiris, Rhadamanthus, Jehovah, or Allah, with their books of record, inquisitions, and judgments, will hardly lord it over the imagination in the days to come. The reputed dispensations of Providence will less and less affect conduct. A feigned blood kinship is of no avail for binding men into the national groups of to-day. So public action in the form of mob, ban, or boycott is justly regarded as a relic of barbarism.

But there are other instruments that are coming into wider usefulness. Instruction as to the consequences of actions, with a view to enlisting an enlightened self-interest in support of all the conduct it is competent to sanction will meet with universal approval in an age of public education; and the passiveness of the average mind will make it safe to weave into such moral instruction certain convenient illusions and fallacies which it is nobody's interest to denounce. Suggestion, that little-understood instrument, will, no doubt, be found increasingly helpful in establishing moral imperatives in the young. But it will render its greatest service in aiding us to shape in the youth those feelings of admiration or loathing that determine the ruling ideals of character, and in influencing those imputations of worth which enable society to impose upon the individual its own valuations of life's activities and experiences. This work society will facilitate by cutting with cameo-like clearness the types of character it chooses to commend, and by settling ever more firmly in tradition and convention the values it seeks to impose. It is social art, however, which promises the most. I would place it next to religion in power to transform the brute into the angel. Art is one of the few moral instruments which, instead of being blunted by the vast changes in opinion, have gained edge and sweep by these very changes. So far as the eye can pierce the future, there is nothing to break it or dull it. The sympathies it fosters do not, it is true, establish norms and duties; but they lift that plane of general sentiment out of which imperatives and obligations arise. If there is any one in this age who does the work of the Amoses and Isaiahs of old, it is an Ibsen, a Tolstoi, or a Victor Hugo.

Note

1   The first article in this series, titled simply "Social control," was published in the March 1896 issue of the *American Journal of Sociology* 1(5) (March 1896): 513–35. It was followed in May 1896 by "Social control II: Law and public opinion," with the series running through "Social control XX: The vissicitudes of social control" (January 1901). The book based on this series, *Social Control: A survey of the foundations of order*, was published in 1901 (New York: MacMillan).

Chapter 59

Émile Durkheim: Crime as a normal and useful phenomenon, 1895

Émile Durkheim (1858–1917), was one of the founders of sociology as a distinct field of study and also a contributor to the founding of anthropology and political science. *The Rules of Sociological Method* (as his own title *Les Règles de la méthode sociologique* is usually translated) was one of his most important works; it raises fundamental issues in the methods and philosophy of science.

In some ways, Durkheim's personal story paralleled that of Lombroso. Both were Jews, both chose a secular path, and both were instrumental in the founding of a social science. However, while Lombroso pathologized the criminal, Durkheim – with a brave leap of sociological imagination – declared crime to be a normal phenomenon, one necessary to the health of a social group.

I translated this passage from Émile Durkheim, *Les Règles de la méthode sociologique* (orig. published in 1895, repr. Paris: Presses Universitaires de France, 1960), pp. 65–70.

ÉMILE DURKHEIM: CRIME AS A NORMAL AND USEFUL PHENOMENON

If there is any phenomenon that seems unarguably pathological, it is crime. All criminologists agree on this point. Although they explain this pathology in different ways, they are unanimous in recognizing it. Nonetheless, the issue requires less hasty treatment.

Let us apply the preceding rules [of scrutiny and analysis]. Crime is found not only in the majority of societies of such and such a group but in all societies of all types. There is no place where criminality does not exist. It changes form, and the acts which are thus defined are not everywhere the same; but everywhere and always, there have been men who act in such a way as to bring punishment down upon themselves. If, as societies evolved from inferior to superior, the ratio of criminality (the relationship between annual crime statistics and the population) tended to fall, one might be able to believe that crime, while still a normal phenomenon, was becoming less normal. But we have no reason to believe that such a regression is taking place. Instead, the facts seem to demonstrate a movement in the opposite direction.

Since the beginning of the [nineteenth] century, statistics have enabled us to trace the direction of criminality; and everywhere, it has increased. In France, the growth has been nearly 300 percent. Crime presents undeniable signs of normality, since it appears so tightly tied to the conditions of collective life. To make of crime a social sickness would be to argue that, far from being accidental, it derives from society's innermost being; and that argument would wipe out all distinction between physiology and pathology. Doubtless, crime itself has abnormal forms; that happens, for example, when the rates shoot up. Unquestionably, such an excess is pathological in nature. What is normal is simply that there is criminality, so long as it stays regular in its levels, which can perhaps be calculated according to the preceding rules.

Thus we have arrived at an apparently paradoxical conclusion. I do not want to be misunderstood. To classify crime among the phenomena of normal sociology is not only to say that it is an inevitable, if regrettable, phenomenon, owing to the incorrigible viciousness of men; it is to affirm that it is a factor in public health, an integral part of all healthy societies. This conclusion is, at first, so surprising that for a long time it disconcerted even me. Nevertheless, once one overcomes the initial surprise, it is not difficult to discover reasons that explain this normality and, at the same time, confirm it.

In the first place, crime is normal because a society lacking it would be completely impossible.

Crime, as I have shown elsewhere, consists of an act that offends certain energetic and particularly clear collective feelings. In order for actions considered criminal to cease in a particular society, the feelings that they affront would have to be lodged in every individual conscience, without exception and with the degree of force necessary to suppress contrary feelings. Even if this condition could be effectively realized, crime would not disappear; it would only change form. For the very cause that would thus dry up the sources of criminality would immediately open up new ones.

In order for those collective feelings that are protected by a people's right to punish to penetrate, at a certain moment in history, people's previously closed consciences and reign where they had not reigned before, they must acquire a new and superior intensity. The community as a whole must experience them more sharply, for it is the only source of the power that enables it to control refractory individuals. In order for murderers to disappear, the horror of spilling blood must become more acute in the social strata from which murderers are recruited; but for that to happen, it must become more acute throughout society. Formerly, even the absence of crime contributed directly to this outcome, for a feeling seems much more respectable when everyone shares it. But no one noticed that these strong states of communal conscience could be strengthened only if weaker states, previously considered merely moral lapses, were not reinforced at the same time; for the weaker were only attenuated forms of the stronger.

Theft and simple unscrupulousness damage the same altruistic feeling: respect for the property of others. However, that feeling is offended more weakly by one of those acts than by the other; and because most consciences lack sufficient intensity to actively resent the smaller of these two offenses, it is tolerated. This is why one blames simple unscrupulousness while punishing theft. But if this same feeling grows so strong that it silences in all consciences the inclination to steal, they become more responsive to harms that, previously, affected them only lightly. Reacting against them with more strength, the collective conscience elevates what were formerly simple moral faults to the level of crimes. For example, contracts that are foolish or foolishly executed, and which used to result only in public blame or in civil damages, become crimes.

Imagine a society of saints, an exemplary and perfect cloister. Crimes that we recognize would be unknown; but faults that appear defensible to ordinary people would there be just as scandalous as ordinary crimes are to ordinary consciences. If this society were armed with the power to judge and punish, it would make these acts criminal and punish them as such. For the same reason, the totally honest man judges his weakest moral feelings with a severity that the mob reserves for acts that are truly criminal. In earlier times, violence against the person was more frequent than it is today because respect for the individual was weaker. As respect grew, those crimes became more rare; but also, acts that damaged such respect became part of the penal code, where they were not included earlier.

To exhaust all possible hypotheses, one has to ask why such unanimity does not exist for all the collective feelings, without exception – why even the weakest of them does not take hold with sufficient energy to prevent all dissent. Society's moral conscience can be found everywhere and with sufficient strength to prevent offensive acts, purely moral faults as well as crimes. But a universal and absolute uniformity is utterly impossible; for the immediate physical circumstances in which each of us is placed, our heredity and our social influences, vary from one individual to the next and, it follows, make for various consciences. It is not possible that we should all resemble one another in this way, for each one of us has his own organism, and organisms occupy different points in space. That is why, even among inferior peoples in whom individuality is little developed, it is nonetheless not absolutely lacking. Since it is not possible to have a society where individuals do not diverge more or less from the collective type, it is inevitable that among the divergences, some will seem criminal. For that which makes them crimes has nothing to do with their intrinsic importance, but rather with that which the communal conscience lends them. If the communal conscience is strong enough and has sufficient authority to suppress these divergences, it will also be more responsive and more exacting toward small deviations, reacting against them with an energy which formerly it did not deploy for even large infractions. It will deem them grave – in other words, it will define them criminal.

Crime is thus necessary. It is bound up with the fundamental conditions of social life but, at the same time, it is useful; for the conditions with which it is interdependent are themselves indispensable to the normal evolution of ethics and of law.

Chapter 60

Enrico Ferri: The data of criminal statistics, continued, 1884

An earlier extract (Chapter 53) illustrated Enrico Ferri's thinking on the use and meaning of crime statistics. The passages of this extract set forth the theory of crime and punishment that Ferri built on the basis of those statistics.

Ferri begins by countering charges that his Positivist school denies free will. All crimes are the outcome of free will, he explains, but free will "has no scientific value" and so cannot form the basis of "a scientific explanation of crime." Instead, he and his school view crime as the product of three factors: organic or physical (those on which Lombroso concentrated); "psychical" (mental and psychological); and social, including the physical environment of the social group. How these three combine to produce crime in varying combinations is the subject matter of criminology.

In the first passage reproduced here, Ferri is on the defensive, working hard to show that positivists do indeed take the social into account, while refusing to attribute crime to social factors alone. Then he turns to a topic about which the Positivist School felt particularly strongly: the inefficacy of harsh punishments. While Quetelet exaggerated the stability of crime rates, there is certainly sufficient stability to demonstrate the unresponsiveness of criminality to deterrent measures. Instead of harsh punishments, Ferri recommends *penal substitutes*, responses tailored to the needs of offenders and the social organism, directing them "into non-criminal channels, leaving free scope for energy and the satisfaction of individual needs." Penal substitutes will not eliminate crime, but at least they will provide a better social defense than repression does.

Indeed, Ferri maintains in the final passage selected here, penal substitutes can work in harmony with "the universal law of evolution," helping society to progress beyond primitive responses to crime. With his final metaphor of the channeling effects of punishment on crime, Ferri expresses the positivists' longing for crime control policies that will be guided by science and aimed at producing a better society.

These passages come from the chapter on "The data of criminal statistics" in Ferri's *Criminal Sociology* (New York: D. Appleton and Company, 1898 [originally 1884]), pp. 54–63, 112–14, and 141–2.

ENRICO FERRI: THE DATA OF CRIMINAL STATISTICS, CONTINUED

No crime, whoever commits it, and in whatever circumstances, can be explained except as the outcome of individual free-will, or as the natural effect of natural causes. Since the former of these explanations has no scientific value, it is impossible to give a scientific explanation of a crime (or indeed of any other action of man or brute) unless it is considered as the product of a particular organic and psychical constitution, acting in a particular physical and social environment.

Therefore it is far from being exact to assert that the positive criminal school reduces crime to a purely and exclusively anthropological phenomenon. As a matter of fact, this school has always from the beginning maintained that crime is the effect of anthropological, physical, and social conditions, which evolve it by their simultaneous and inseparable operation. And if inquiries into biological conditions have been more abundant and more conspicuous by their novelty, this in no way contradicts the fundamental conclusion of criminal sociology.

That being stated, we have still to examine the relative value of these three classes of conditions in the natural evolution of crime.

It seems to me that this question is generally stated inaccurately, and also that it cannot be answered absolutely, and in a word.

It is generally stated inaccurately; because they who think, for instance, that crime is nothing else than a purely and exclusively social phenomenon in the evolution of which the organic and psychical anomalies of the criminal have had no part, ignore more or less consciously the universal correlation of natural forces, and forget that, in regard to any phenomenon whatsoever, it is impossible to set an absolute limit to the network of its causes, immediate and remote, direct and indirect.

To put this question in an arbitrary sense would be like asking if a mammal is the product of its lungs, or its heart, or its stomach, or of vegetable constituents, or of the atmosphere; whereas each of these conditions, internal and external, is necessary to the life of the animal.

In fact, if crime were the exclusive product of the social environment, how could one explain the familiar fact that in the same social environment, and in identical circumstances of poverty, abandonment, lack of education, sixty per cent. do not commit crimes, and, of the other forty, five prefer suicide, five go mad, five simply become beggars or tramps not dangerous to society, whilst the remaining twenty-five actually commit crimes? And amongst the latter, whilst some go no further than theft without violence, why do others commit theft with violence, and even kill their victim outright, before he offers resistance, or threatens them, or calls for help, and this with no other object than gain?

The secondary differences of social condition, which may be observed even amongst the members of a single family, rotting in one of the slums of our great towns, or amongst those who are surrounded by the temptations of money or power, or the like, are clearly not enough in themselves to explain the vast differences in the actions which grow out of them, varying from honesty under the greatest discouragement to suicide and murder.

The question, therefore, must be asked in a relative sense altogether, and we must inquire which of the three kinds of natural causes of crime has a greater or less influence in determining each particular crime at any given moment in the individual and social life.

No clear answer of general application can be given to this question, for the relative influence of the anthropological, physical [probably a misprint for "psychical" – N.R.], and social conditions varies with the psychological and social characteristics of each offence against the law.

For instance, if we consider the three great classes of crimes against the person, against property, and against personal purity, it is evident that each class of determining causes, but especially the biological and social conditions, have a distinctly different influence in evolving homicide, theft, or indecent assaults. And so it is in every category of crimes.

The undeniable influence of social conditions, and still more of economic conditions, in leading up to the commission of theft, is far inferior in the genesis of homicides and indecent assaults. And similarly, in each category of crimes, the influence of the determining conditions varies greatly according to the special forms of crime.

Certain casual homicides are plainly the result of social conditions (gambling, drink, public opinion, &c.) in a much higher degree than homicides which for the most part spring from brutality, from the moral insensibility of individuals, or from their psycho-pathological conditions, corresponding to abnormal organic conditions.

In like manner, certain indecent assaults, incests, &c., are largely the outcome of social environment, which, condemning a number of persons to live in hovels without air or light, with a promiscuity of sex between parents and children such as obtains amongst the brutes, effaces or deadens all normal sense of modesty. On the other hand, there are cases of rape and the like which are mostly due to the biological condition of the individual, either in manifest forms of sexual disease or, less manifest though none the less actual, of biological anomaly. . . .

Meanwhile, a last objection has been raised against the conclusions which I have maintained for many years past.

It has been said that, even if we admit that for certain crimes and criminals the greatest influence must be recognised as due to the physical and psychical conditions of the individual, extending from slightly manifested anomalies of an anthropological character to the most accentuated pathological condition, this does not exclude the possibility of a crime being due to social conditions. In fact, it is said the anomalies of the individual are in their turn only an effect of a debasing social environment, which condemns its victims to organic and psychical degeneration.

This objection is sound enough if it be taken in a relative sense, but groundless if it be insisted on absolutely.

It must be considered, in the first place, that the distinctions of cause and effect are only relative, for every effect has its cause, and *vice versâ;* so that if wretchedness, material and moral, is a cause of degeneration, degeneration itself, like biological anomaly, is a cause of wretchedness. And in this sense the question would be simply metaphysical, like the famous Byzantine discussions as to whether there was originally an egg before a hen or a hen before an egg.

And, in fact, when it was said, in regard to criminal geography, that the extent and quality of crime in such and such a province, instead of being the effect of biological conditions (race, &c.) and physical conditions (climate, soil, &c.), were but the effect of social and economic conditions (of rural and industrial pursuits, and the like), I was able to make a very simple reply. For, apart even from statistical proofs, if the social conditions of such and such a province, which have an unquestionable influence, are really the absolute and exclusive cause of crime, we may still ask whether these social conditions of the province are not themselves the effect of the ethnical qualities of energy, intelligence, and so forth, in its inhabitants, and of the more or less favourable conditions of the climate and the soil. . . .

The practical conclusion, therefore, of these general observations on the natural genesis of crime is this: Every crime is the result of individual physical and social conditions; and, since these conditions have a more or less dominant influence for various forms of crime, the most certain and profitable mode of defence which society can employ against criminality is of a twofold character, and both modes ought to be employed and brought into action simultaneously − in the first place, the amelioration of the social conditions, as a natural preventive of crime, in the nature of a substitute for punishment; and, secondly, measures of perpetual or temporary elimination of criminals, according as the influence of biological conditions in the evolution of crime is all but absolute, or more or less great, and more or less curable.

As a matter of fact, when we follow the periodic variations of crime, with its measured growth and decrease, we cannot fail to conclude that these constant and constantly occurring variations depend upon a corresponding variation of anthropological and physical factors. For, whilst criminal statistics are far from showing the regularity which Quetelet claimed with much exaggeration, the proportional figures in regard to the bearings of age, sex, calling, &c., upon criminality exhibit very insignificant variations from year to year. And as for the physical factors, if marked variations are explicable at some given period, it is nevertheless evident that neither climate, nor the nature of the soil, nor atmospheric conditions, nor the seasons, nor the temperature of different years could have undergone in the last half-century such constant and repeated variations as to correspond to those waves of criminality which we shall presently exhibit in almost every nation of Europe.

Thus it is to the social factors that we must chiefly attribute the periodic variations of criminality. For even the variations which can be detected in certain anthropological factors, like the influences of age and sex upon crime, and the more or less marked outbreak of anti-social and pathological tendencies, depend in their turn upon social factors, such as the protection accorded to abandoned infants, the participation of women in non-domestic, commercial and industrial life, preventive and repressive measures, and the like. And again, since the social factors have special import in occasional crime, and crime by acquired habit, and since these are the most numerous sections of crime as a whole, it is clear that the periodic movement of crime must be attributed in the main to the social factors. So true is this, that, as we shall presently see, the gravest crimes, especially against persons, precisely because they mostly indicate congenital criminality, follow a more steady and regular movement than these slighter but far more frequent offences against property, public order, and persons, of a more occasional character, and that, as microbes of the world of crime, they are the more direct outcome of social environment.

It is therefore another point in favour of the experimental school that it has insisted on this sociological aspect of the problem of criminality, by showing legislators, outside the limits of their punitive remedies, as easy as they are illusory, how they might, as far as circumstances will permit, apply a genuine social remedy to crime. . . .

In the economic sphere, it has been observed that when a staple product fails, recourse is had to less esteemed substitutes, in order to supply the natural wants of mankind. So in the criminal sphere, as we are convinced by experience that punishments are almost devoid of deterrent effect, we must have recourse to the best available substitutes for the purpose of social defence.

These methods of indirect defence I have called *penal substitutes*. But whereas the food substitutes are as a rule only secondary products, brought into temporary use, penal substitutes should become the main instruments of the function of social defence, for which punishments will come to be secondary means, albeit permanent. For in this connection we must not forget the law of criminal saturation, which in every social environment makes a minimum of crime inevitable, on account of the natural factors inseparable from individual and social imperfection. Punishments in one form or another will always be, for this minimum, the ultimate though not very profitable remedy against outbreaks of criminal activity.

These penal substitutes, when they have once been established in the conscience and methods of legislators, through the teaching of criminal sociology, will be the recognised form of treatment for the social factors of crime. And they will also be more possible and practical than that universal social metamorphosis, direct and uncompromising, insisted on by generous but impatient reformers, who scorn these substitutes as palliatives because humanitarian enthusiasm causes them to forget that social organisms, like animal organisms, can be only partially and gradually transformed.

The idea of these penal substitutes amounts, in short, to this. The legislator, observing the origins, conditions, and effects of individual and collective activity, comes to recognise their psychological and sociological laws, whereby he will be able to obtain a mastery over many of the factors of crime, and especially over the social factors, and thus secure an indirect but more certain influence over the development of crime. That is to say, in all legislative, political, economic, administrative, and penal arrangements, from the greatest institutions to the smallest details, the social organism will be so adjusted that human activity, instead of being continually and unprofitably menaced with repression, will be insensibly directed into non-criminal channels, leaving free scope for energy and the satisfaction of individual needs, under conditions least exposed to violent disturbance or occasions of law-breaking.

It is just this fundamental idea of penal substitutes which shows how necessary it is that the sociologist and legislator should have such a preparation in biology and psychology as Mr. Spencer justly insisted on in his "Introduction to Social Science." And it is the fundamental idea rather than the substitutes themselves that we should bear in mind if we would realise their theoretical and practical value as part of a system of criminal sociology.

As for the efficacy of any particular penal substitute, I readily admit, in some sense at least, the partial criticisms which have been passed upon them. Apart from such as simply say that they do not believe in the use of alternatives to punishment, and such as confine themselves to the futile question whether this theory belongs to criminal science or to police administration, a majority of criminal sociologists have now definitely accepted the doctrine of penal substitutes. This theory is accepted, not as an absolute panacea of crime, but, as I have always stated it, in the sense of a combination of measures analogous to penal repression; in place of trusting solely to repression for the defence of society against crime. . . .

We have thus studied the data of criminal statistics in their theoretical and practical relations with criminal sociology, and come to the conclusion that, since crime is a natural phenomenon, determined by factors of three kinds, it answers on that account to a law of criminal saturation, whereby the physical and social environment, aided by individual tendencies, hereditary or acquired, and by occasional impulses, necessarily determine the extent of crime in every age and country, both in quantity and quality. That is to say, the criminality of a nation is influenced in the natural sphere by the bio-psychical conditions of individuals and their physical environment, and, in the social sphere, by economic, political, administrative and civil conditions of laws, far more than by the penal code.

Nevertheless the execution of punishment, though it is the less important part of the function of social defence, which should be carried out in harmony with the other functions of society, is always the last and inevitable auxiliary.

And this entirely agrees with the universal law of evolution, in virtue of which, amidst the variation of animal and social organisms, antecedent forms are not wholly eliminated, but continue as the basis of the forms which succeed them. So that if the future evolution of the social administration of defence against crime is to consist in the development of the primitive forms of direct physical coercion into the higher forms of indirect psychical discipline of human activity, this will not imply that the primitive forms must entirely disappear, especially for the gravest crimes, which, in the biological and psychological conditions of those who commit them, take us back to the primitive epochs and forms of individual and social violence.

I end with a modification of an old comparison which has been much abused. Crime has been compared to an impetuous torrent which ought to be enclosed between the dykes of punishment, lest civilised society should be submerged. I do not deny that punishments are the dykes of crime, but I assert that they are dykes of no great strength or utility. All nations know by sad and chronic experience that their dykes cannot save them from inundations; and so our statistics teach us that punishments have but an infinitesimal power against the force of criminality, when its germs are fully developed.

But as we can best protect ourselves against inundations by obeying the laws of hydrostatics and hydrodynamics, by timbering the banks near the source of the stream, and by due rectilineation or excavation along its course and near its mouth, so, in order to defend ourselves against crimes, it is best to observe the laws of psychology and sociology, and to avail ourselves of social substitutes, which are far more efficacious than whole arsenals of repressive measures.

Chapter 61

W. E. B. DuBois: The causes of crime and poverty, 1899

An earlier extract (Chapter 26) excerpted passages on the underclass from W. E. B. DuBois's pioneering study *The Philadelphia Negro*. This extract deals with the causes of crime and poverty, phenomena that DuBois refused to decouple.

DuBois identifies three causes of Negro crime. The first is slavery and emancipation, a process of "sudden social revolution" that strained the people's personal and social resources. The second is immigration: the movement north of "raw recruits" who must be assimilated into the population. Third is color prejudice, "the widespread feeling all over the land, in Philadelphia as well as in Boston and New Orleans, that the Negro is something less than an American."

This extract comes from W. E. B. DuBois, *The Philadelphia Negro* (Philadelphia: University of Pennsylvania Press, 1899), pp. 282–4.

W. E. B. DUBOIS: THE CAUSES OF CRIME AND POVERTY

A study of statistics seems to show that the crime and pauperism of the Negroes exceeds that of the whites; that in the many nevertheless, it follows in its rise and fall the fluctuations shown in the records of the whites, *i.e.*, if crime increases among the whites it increases among Negroes, and *vise versa*, with this peculiarity, that among the Negroes the change is always exaggerated – the increase greater, the decrease more marked in nearly all cases. This is what we would naturally expect: we have here the record of a low social class, and as the condition of a lower class is by its very definition worse than that of a higher, so the situation of the Negroes is worse as respects crime and poverty than that of the mass of whites. Moreover, any change in social conditions is bound to affect the poor and unfortunate more than the rich and prosperous. We have in all probability an example of this in the increase of crime since 1890; we have had a period of financial stress and industrial depression; the ones who have felt this most are the poor, the unskilled laborers, the inefficient and unfortunate, and those with small social and economic advantages: the Negroes are in this class, and the result has been an increase in Negro crime and pauperism; there has also been an increase in the crime of the whites, though less rapid by reason of their richer and more fortunate upper classes.

So far, then, we have no phenomena which are new or exceptional, or which present more than the ordinary social problems of crime and poverty – although these, to be sure, are difficult enough. Beyond these, however, there are problems which can rightly be called Negro problems: they arise from the peculiar history and condition of the American Negro. The first peculiarity is, of course, the slavery and emancipation of the Negroes. That their emancipation has raised them economically and morally is proven by the increase of wealth and co-operation, and the decrease of poverty and crime between the period before the war and the period since; nevertheless, this was manifestly no simple process: the first effect of emancipation was that of any sudden social revolution: a strain upon the strength and resources of the Negro, moral, economic and physical, which drove many to the wall. For this reason the rise of the Negro in this city is a series of rushes and backslidings rather than a continuous growth. The second great peculiarity of the situation of the Negroes is the fact of immigration; the great numbers of raw recruits who have from time to time precipitated themselves upon the Negroes of the city and shared their small industrial opportunities, have made reputations which, whether good or bad, all their race must share; and finally whether they failed or succeeded in the strong competition, they themselves must soon prepare to face a new immigration.

Here then we have two great causes for the present condition of the Negro: Slavery and emancipation with their attendant phenomena of ignorance, lack of discipline, and moral weakness; immigration with its increased competition and moral influence. To this must be added a third as great – possibly greater in influence than the other two, namely the environment in which a Negro finds himself – the world of custom and thought in which he must live and work, the physical surrounding of house and home and ward, the moral encouragements and discouragements which he encounters. We dimly seek to define this social environment partially when we talk of color prejudice – but this is but a vague characterization; what we want to study is not a vague thought or feeling but its concrete manifestations. We know pretty well what the surroundings are of a young white lad, or a foreign immigrant who comes to this great city to join in its organic life. We know what influences and limitations surround him, to what he may attain, what his companionships are, what his encouragements are, what his drawbacks.

This we must know in regard to the Negro if we would study his social condition. His strange social environment must have immense effect on his thought and life, his work and crime, his wealth and pauperism. That this environment differs and differs broadly from the environment of his fellows, we all know, but we do not know just how it differs. The real foundation of the difference is the widespread feeling all over the land, in Philadelphia as well as in Boston and New Orleans, that the Negro is something less than an American and ought not to be much more than what he is. Argue as we may for or against this idea, we must as students recognize its presence and its vast effects.

Bibliography

d'Agostino, Peter, "Craniums, criminals, and the 'cursed race': Italian anthropology in American racial thought, 1861–1924," *Comparative Studies in Society and History* 44 (2) (2002): 310–43.

Anderson, Elijah, "Introduction to the 1996 edition" of W. E. B. DuBois, *The Philadelphia Negro* (Philadelphia: University of Pennsylvania Press, 1996).

(Arthur) *The Life, and Dying Speech of Arthur, a Negro Man; Who was Executed at Worcester, October 20, 1768. For a Rape committed on the Body of one Deborah Metcalfe*, available online at http://docsouth.unc.edu/neh/arthur/arthur.html (accessed 3 February 2009).

Beccaria, Cesare, *On Crimes and Punishments* (Philadelphia: R. Bell, 1778).

Becker, Peter, "The criminologists' gaze at the underworld: Toward an archeology of criminological writings," Ch. 5 (pp. 105–33) in Peter Becker and Richard F. Wetzell, eds., *Criminals and their Scientists: The history of criminology in international perspective* (Cambridge: Cambridge University Press, 2006).

Becker, Peter and Richard F. Wetzell, eds., *Criminals and their Scientists: The history of criminology in international perspective* (Cambridge: Cambridge University Press, 2006).

Beirne, Piers, "Heredity versus environment: a reconsideration of Charles Goring's *The English Convict* (1913)," *British Journal of Criminology* 28 (3) (1988): 315–39.

Beirne, Piers, *Inventing Criminology: Essays on the rise of "Homo Criminalis"* (Albany: State University of New York Press, 1993).

Beirne, Piers, ed., *The Origins and Growth of Criminology: Essays on intellectual history, 1760–1945* (Aldershot: Dartmouth, 1994).

Benedikt, Moriz, *Anatomical Studies upon Brains of Criminals*, translated from the German by E. P. Fowler, M.D. (orig. 1881; repr. New York: Da Capo Press, 1981).

Bertillon, Alphonse, "The Bertillon system of identification," *The Forum* 11(3) (1891): 330–41.

Bertillon, Alphonse, *Signaletic Instruction* (Chicago: The Werner Company, 1896).

Boies, Henry M., *Prisoners and Paupers* (New York: G. P. Putnam's Sons, 1893).

Bondio, Mariacarla Gadebusch, "From the 'atavistic' to the 'inferior' criminal type: The impact of the Lombrosian theory of the born criminal on German psychiatry," Ch. 8 in Peter Becker and Richard F. Wetzell, eds., *Criminals and their Scientists: The history of criminology in international perspective* (Cambridge: Cambridge University Press, 2006).

Brace, C. Loring, "The roots of the race concept in American physical anthropology," Ch. 1 (pp. 11–29) in Frank Spencer, ed., *A History of American Physical Anthropology 1930–1980* (New York: Academic Press, 1982).

Capen, Nahum, "Biography of the author," pp. 7–173 in Johann Gaspar Spurzheim's *Phrenology, in Connexion with the Study of Physiognomy* (Boston: Marsh, Capen & Lyon, 1834).

Carpenter, Mary, "On the importance of statistics to the Reformatory Movement, with returns from female reformatories, and remarks on them," *Journal of the Statistical Society of London* 20 (1) (1857): 33–40.

Cole, Simon A., *Suspect Identities: A history of fingerprinting and criminal identification* (Cambridge: Harvard University Press, 2001).

Crapsey, Edward, *The Nether Side of New York* (New York: Sheldon & Company, 1872).

Darwin, Charles, *Descent of Man* (London: J. Murray, 1871).

Davie, Neil, *Tracing the Criminal: The rise of scientific criminology in Britain, 1860–1918* (Oxford: Bardwell Press, 2005).

Despine, Prosper, *Psychologie naturelle: Étude sur les facultés intellectuelles et morales* (Paris: F. Savy, 1868).

DuBois, W. E. B., *The Philadelphia Negro* (Philadelphia: University of Pennsylvania Press, 1899).

Dugdale, Richard L., *"The Jukes": A study in crime, pauperism, disease, and heredity; also further studies of criminals* (New York: G. P. Putnam's Sons, 1877).

Durkheim, Émile, *Les Règles de la méthode sociologique* (orig. 1895; repr. Paris: Presses Universitaires de France, 1960).

Ellis, Havelock, *The Criminal* (London: Walter Scott; and New York: Charles Scribner's Sons, 1890).

Engels, Friedrich, *The Condition of the Working Class in England* (orig. 1845; first English ed., 1887; repr. David McLellan, ed., Oxford: Oxford University Press, 1993).

Farnham, Eliza W., "Notes and illustrations" to Marmaduke B. Sampson and Eliza W. Farnham, *Rationale of Crime and Its Appropriate Treatment* (New York: D. Appleton and Company, 1846).

Ferri, Enrico, *Criminal Sociology* (Orig. 1884; New York: D. Appleton and Company, 1898).

Fletcher, Joseph, "Moral and educational statistics of England and Wales," *Journal of the Statistical Society of London* 12 (2) (1849): 151–76.

Foucault, Michel, *Discipline and Punish: The birth of the prison* (New York: Pantheon, 1977).

Frigessi, Delia, *Cesare Lombroso* (Turin: Einaudi Editore, 2003).

Fry, Elizabeth and Joseph John Gurney, *Report Addressed to the Marquess Wellesley, Lord Lieutenant of Ireland* (orig. 1827; 3d ed., Norwich: Josiah Fletcher, 1847).

Galton, Francis, *Inquiries into Human Faculty and its Development* (London: Macmillan and Co., 1883).

Galton, Francis, *Finger Prints* (London: MacMillan, 1892).

Garland, David, "British criminology before 1935," *British Journal of Criminology* 28 (2) (1985): 1–17.

Garland, David, "Of crimes and criminals: The development of criminology in Britain," Ch. 1 (pp. 17–68) in Mike Maguire, Rod Morgan, and Robert Reiner, eds., *The Oxford Handbook of Criminology* (Oxford: The Clarendon Press, 1994).

Gibson, Mary, "Biology or environment? Race and southern 'deviancy' in the writings of Italian criminologists," pp. 99–115 in Jane Schneider, ed., *Italy's "Southern Question": Orientalism in one country* (New York: Berg, 1998).

Gibson, Mary, *Born to Crime: Cesare Lombroso and the origins of biological criminology* (Westport, CT: Praeger, 2002).

Gibson, Mary, "Cesare Lombroso and Italian criminology: Theory and politics," Ch. 6 in Peter Becker and Richard F. Wetzell, eds., *Criminals and their Scientists: The history of criminology in international perspective* (Cambridge: Cambridge University Press, 2006).

Gilbert, James B., "Anthropometrics in the U.S. Bureau of Education: The case of Arthur MacDonald's 'laboratory,'" *History of Education Quarterly* 17 (2) (Summer, 1977): 169–95.

Gould, Stephen Jay, *The Mismeasure of Man* (New York: W. W. Norton, 1981).

Guerry, A. M., *Essai sur la statistique morale de la France* (Paris: Chez Crochard, 1833).

Hecht, Jennifer Michael, *The End of the Soul: Scientific modernity, atheism, and anthropology in France* (New York: Columbia University Press, 2003).

Henderson, Charles Richmond, *An Introduction to the Study of the Dependent, Defective and Delinquent Classes* (Boston: D.C. Heath, 1893).

Horn, David G., *The Criminal Body: Lombroso and the anatomy of deviance* (New York: Routledge, 2003).

Kaluszynski, Martine, "The International Congresses of Criminal Anthropology: Shaping the French and international criminological movement, 1886–1914," Ch. 13 in Peter Becker and Richard F. Wetzell, eds., *Criminals and their Scientists: The history of criminology in international perspective* (Cambridge: Cambridge University Press, 2006).

Krafft-Ebing, Richard von, *Psychopathia Sexualis* (Philadelphia and London: The F. A. David Co., 1892).

Lacassagne, Alexandre, "Speech of the President," *Archives de l'Anthropologie Criminelle*, v. IX (1894): 404–10.

Laub, John H., *Criminology in the Making: An oral history* (Boston: Northeastern University Press, 1983).

Laub, John H., "The life course of criminology in the United States," *Criminology* 42 (1) (2004): 1–26.

Lavater, Johann Kaspar, *Essays on Physiognomy* (London: printed for G. G. J. and J. Robinson, 1789).

Leps, Marie-Christine, *Apprehending the Criminal: The production of deviance in nineteenth-century discourse* (Durham, NC: Duke University Press, 1992).

Lieber, Francis, "Preface and introduction of the translator," pp. v–xxxv in Gustave de Beaumont and Alexis de Tocqueville, *On the Penitentiary System in the United States and its Application in France* (orig. Philadelphia: Carey, Lea & Blanchard, 1833; repr. New York: Augustus M. Kelley, 1970).

Lombroso, Cesare, *L'uomo delinquente studiato in rapporto alla antropologia, alla medicina legale ed alle discipline carcerarie* (Milan: Hoepli, 1876).

Lombroso, Cesare, *The Female Offender* (New York: D. Appleton & Company, 1895).

Lombroso, Cesare, *Crime: Its causes and remedies* (orig. 1911; repr. Montclair, NJ: Patterson Smith, 1968).

Lombroso, Cesare, *Criminal Man*, translated and with a new introduction by Mary Gibson and Nicole Hahn Rafter (Durham, NC: Duke University Press, 2006).

Lombroso, Cesare and Guglielmo Ferrero, *La donna delinquente, la prostituta e la donna normale* (Torino: Roux, 1893).

Lombroso, Cesare and Guglielmo Ferrero, *Criminal Woman, the Prostitute, and the Normal Woman*, translated and with a new introduction by Nicole Hahn Rafter and Mary Gibson (Durham, NC: Duke University Press, 2004).

Lombroso-Ferrero, Gina, *Criminal Man According to the Classification of Cesare Lombroso* (orig. 1911; repr. Montclair, NJ: Patterson, Smith, 1968).

Lowell, Josephine Shaw, "One means of preventing pauperism," National Conference of Charities and Correction, *Proceedings for 1879*, pp. 189–200.

MacDonald, Arthur, *Criminology* (New York: Funk & Wagnalls, 1893).

McKim, W. Duncan, *Heredity and Human Progress* (New York: G. P. Putnam's Sons, 1900).

Mannheim, Hermann, ed., *Pioneers in Criminology* (2d ed. enlrg., Montclair, NJ: Patterson Smith, 1972).

Manouvrier, Léonce, "Deuxième question: Existe-t-il des caractères anatomiques propres aux criminels?" *Actes du deuxième congrès international d'anthropologie criminelle, biologie et sociologie*, Paris, 1889 (Lyon: Storck, 1890), pp. 28–35.

Maudsley, Henry, *Responsibility in Mental Disease* (orig. 1874; New York: D. Appleton, 1898).

Mayhew, Henry and John Binny, *The Criminal Prisons of London* (London: Griffin, Bohn, and Company, 1862).

Morel, Bénédict-August, *Traité des dégénérescences physiques, intellectuelles et morales de l'espèce humaine* (Paris: J. B. Baillière, 1857).

Mucchielli, Laurent, "Criminology, hygienism, and eugenics in France, 1870–1914: The medical debates on the elimination of 'incorrigible' criminals," Ch. 9 in Peter Becker and Richard F. Wetzell, eds., *Criminals and their Scientists: The history of criminology in international perspective* (Cambridge: Cambridge University Press, 2006).

Nordau, Max, *Degeneration* (New York: D. Appleton, 1895).

Nye, Robert A., "Heredity or milieu: The foundations of modern European criminological theory," *Isis* 47 (238) (1976): 335–55.

Pancaldi, Guiliano, *Darwin in Italy: Science across cultural frontiers* (Bloomington: Indiana University Press, 1991).

Philippe Pinel, *A Treatise on Insanity* (Sheffield, England: printed by W. Todd, 1806).

Pick, Daniel, *Faces of Degeneration: A European disorder, c. 1848–c. 1919* (Cambridge: Cambridge University Press, 1989).

Prichard, James Cowles, *Treatise on Insanity* (London: Sherwood, Gilbert, and Piper, 1835).

Quetelet, Adolphe, *Sur l'homme et le développement de ses facultés*, vol. 2 (Paris: Bachlier, 1835).

Rafter, Nicole Hahn, *Partial Justice: Women, Prisons, and Social Control* (2d ed., New Brunswick, NJ: Transaction Publishers, 1990).

Rafter, Nicole Hahn, "Claims-making and socio-cultural context in the first U.S. eugenics campaign," *Social Problems* 39 (1992): 17–34.

Rafter, Nicole Hahn, "Criminal anthropology in the United States," *Criminology* 30 (4) (1992): 525–45.

Rafter, Nicole Hahn, *Creating Born Criminals* (Urbana: University of Illinois Press, 1997).

Rafter, Nicole, "The murderous Dutch fiddler: Criminology, history, and the problem of phrenology," *Theoretical Criminology* 9 (1) (2005): 65–96.

Rafter, Nicole, *The Criminal Brain* (New York: New York University Press, 2008).

Regener, Susanne, "Criminological museums and the visualization of evil," *Crime, History, and Societies* 7 (1) (2003): 43–56.

Rock, Paul E., ed., *History of Criminology* (Aldershot, England: Dartmouth Publishing Co., 1994).

Ross, Edward Alsworth, "Social control," *American Journal of Sociology* 1 (5) (March 1896): 513–35.

Ross, Edward Alsworth, "Social control II: Law and public opinion," *American Journal of Sociology* 1 (6) (1896): 753–70.

Ross, Edward Alsworth, "Social control XX: The vissicitudes of social control," *American Journal of Sociology* 6 (4) (1901): 550–62.

Ross, Edward Alsworth, *Social Control: A survey of the foundations of order* (New York: MacMillan, 1901).

Runes, Dagobert D., ed., *The Selected Writings of Benjamin Rush* (New York: Philosophical Library, 1947).

Rush, Benjamin, "An inquiry into the influence of physical causes upon the moral faculty," orig. 1786; pp. 93–124 in Benjamin Rush, *Medical Inquiries and Observations*, vol. 1 (4th ed., Philadelphia: M. Corey 1815).

Salvatore, Ricardo D., "Positivist criminology and state formation in modern Argentina, 1890–1940," Ch. 11 in Peter Becker and Richard F. Wetzell, eds., *Criminals and their Scientists: The history of criminology in international perspective* (Cambridge: Cambridge University Press, 2006).

Sampson, Marmaduke B. and Eliza W. Farnham, *Rationale of Crime and Its Appropriate Treatment* (New York: D. Appleton and Co., 1846).

Shepard, Edward Morse, "The work of a social teacher: Being a memorial of Richard L. Dugdale," *Economic Tracts* XII (1884): 1–14.

Slotkin, Richard, "Narratives of Negro crime in New England, 1675–1800," *American Quarterly* 25 (1) (March 1973): 3–31.

Spurzheim, Johann Gaspar, *A View of the Elementary Principles of Education* (orig. 1821; London: Treuttel, Wurtz, and Richter, 1828).

Spurzheim, Johann Gaspar, *Phrenology, in Connexion with the Study of Physiognomy* (Boston: Marsh, Capen & Lyon, 1834).

Tarde, Gabriel, *La Criminalité comparée* (Paris: Ballière et Félix Alcan, 1890).

Tarde, Gabriel, *Penal Philosophy* (orig. 1890; first English transl. 1912; repr. Montclair, NJ: Patterson Smith, 1968).

Tarnowsky, Pauline, *Étude anthropométrique sur les prostituées et les voleuses* (Paris: Bureax du Progrès and E. Lecrosnier et Babé, 1889).

Tarnowsky, Pauline, *Les Femmes homicides* (Paris: Félix Alcan, 1908).

Thomson, J. Bruce, "The hereditary nature of crime," *The Journal of Mental Science* 15 (72) (1870): 487–98.

Thomson, J. Bruce, "Psychology of criminals," *Journal of Mental Science* 16 (1870): 321–50.

Tuke, Daniel Hack, "Case of moral insanity or congenital moral defect, with commentary," *Journal of Mental Science* 31 (October 1885): 360–6.

Wetzell, Richard F., *Inventing the Criminal: A history of German criminology 1800–1945* (Chapel Hill: University of North Carolina Press, 2000).

Wines, Frederick Howard, "Introductory remarks" to *Report on the Defective, Dependent, and Delinquent Classes of the Population of the United States, as Returned at the Tenth Census (June 1, 1880)* (Washington: Government Printing Office, 1888).

Wines, Frederick Howard, *Punishment and Reformation* (New York: Thomas Y. Crowell & Company, 1895).

Index